More Than a Promise

The Everlasting Covenant as Presented Throughout History

By Hubert F. Sturges, MD

TEACH Services, Inc.
P U B L I S H I N G
www.TEACHServices.com ● (800) 367-1844

Copyright © 2014 TEACH Services, Inc.
ISBN-13: 978-1-4796-0142-4 (Paperback)
ISBN-13: 978-1-4796-0143-1 (ePub)
ISBN-13: 978-1-4796-0144-8 (Mobi)
Library of Congress Control Number: 2013944451

Published by

TEACH Services, Inc.
PUBLISHING
www.TEACHServices.com ● (800) 367-1844

Table of Contents

Section 3: The Everlasting Covenant and The Last Days

Introduction

God loves to communicate with His creation. In Eden Adam and Eve enjoyed face-to-face communication with their Creator. After the fall and the introduction of sin, God communicated with His people directly and through prophets, priests, and kings. Above all, God desires His people to trust Him and have faith in His promises, which are packaged in the everlasting covenant He has committed to fulfill.

The everlasting covenant is a broad subject with many ramifications. It is the framework for Christian theology and the basis for the interaction between God and humanity. In order to understand theology in general, we need to understand the covenant. By studying the covenant, one learns how things started, why things on this earth are as they are, and the eventual answers to many problems in life.

I have been studying the everlasting covenant since 2004. Anyone who has looked into the covenant subject will quickly find that there are many views on the subject. This is true even within the Seventh-day Adventist Church. As I studied, if I came across a passage of Scripture that did not match the viewpoints I had heard or read, I spent much time in prayer as I examined Scripture. The answers did not always come easily. Many evenings, the problem still unsolved, I would retire late at night. Often, during the night or early in the morning, the answer would come as I prayed.

This was the pattern by which a number of problems were solved. I believe God has a message in the covenant that we need today. And I thank Him for the hand I see in the writing of this book. I recognize that there may be mistakes, and for these I take full responsibility, but within the pages of this book I humbly present the study that has occupied my heart and mind for so many years.

It is my intent to present the truth about the covenant of God while at the same time making it interesting and easy to understand. More than 90 percent of this study is taken from the pages of the King James Version Bible. I received much help from an electronic Bible study program, WORDsearch Bible, which provided fast and accurate concordance and extensive cross-referencing services.

I appreciate what scholars have written on this topic, but I have chosen to rely on the King James Version Bible and make this a personal study to avoid the confusion of opinions among other students and scholars. However, I would recommend the following books for more study: *In Granite or Ingrained* by Skip MacCarty, pastor, Pioneer Memorial Church, Berrien Springs, Michigan; and *Calvary at Sinai* by Paul Penno, pastor, Seventh-day Adventist Church, Hayward, California. Also, I have conversed extensively with Pastor MacCarty; John Goley, longtime friend and retired pastor; and Randy Mills, pastor of my home church. I have read a number of other books, and have referred to a number of Web sites within the footnotes of each chapter.

I would like to recognize my wife, the most beautiful creature God has ever made. She has been very patient with me, has provided me with a tranquil home where angels love to dwell, and has fed me three times a day with food that is the best in the world and that tastes good too! This work would not have been possible without her support.

I would also like to thank Timothy Hullquist, Kalie Kelch, and Bill Newman of TEACH Services who have been very helpful in the editing, layout, and final corrections needed of this work; Lynn Del Newbold for her wisdom and discerning eye in removing excess repetition and adding additional text to expound on certain points; and Pastor Kevin Morgan who spent more than three months editing this work, correcting mistakes, putting references in their proper form, and making suggestions to clarify the message of this book.

This book is a presentation of the covenant of God from before Creation, through the history of humankind, and concluding in the new earth. There is much to learn and digest in regards to this topic, but by studying the covenant in these sections, it will make it so much easier to understand.

Are my conclusions always true? Is my view the last word on the covenant? I sincerely hope that this is not the case. I believe that my work may have its greatest benefit if it stimulates people to deeper Bible study. When you read, pray for the guidance of the Holy Spirit, and open your understanding to the message He has for you. It is my hope that you will be blessed in your study of the covenant, even as I have.

Chapter 1
The Everlasting Covenant

Now the God of peace, that brought again from the dead our Lord Jesus, that great shepherd of the sheep, through the blood of the everlasting covenant, Make you perfect in every good work to do his will, working in you that which is wellpleasing in his sight, through Jesus Christ; to whom be glory for ever and ever. Amen.
Hebrews 13:20, 21

The focus of the everlasting covenant of God is the life and sacrificial death of Jesus.[1] It is through the cross that God has blessed us and given us hope for restoration and eternal life with Jesus. The holy Son of God is the "lamb slain from the foundation of the world" (Rev. 13:8). Because of His great sacrifice, the hosts of heaven grant Him seven-fold praise, crying, "Worthy is the Lamb that was slain to receive power, and riches, and wisdom, and strength, and honour, and glory, and blessing" (Rev. 5:12).

The Story of Jesus Christ

In the eternity before the creation of this world, God made the *everlasting covenant.*[2] When God created humans in His image, He gave them free will, accepting the risk that they would use that will wrongly. In His foreknowledge, God knew what they would choose to do. However, God loved His creation and highly valued the freedom of choice He gave humankind.

> For God so loved the world, that he gave his only begotten Son, that whosoever believeth in him should not perish, but have everlasting life. (John 3:16)

God made the plan of salvation to save and restore humankind and to support His creation. The Father gave His only begotten Son to live a sinless life as a human being and to die to pay the penalty for sin (John 3:16; 10:17, 18). The Holy Spirit brings to the human family the knowledge and power of grace. Grace is the focus of the everlasting covenant of God, and it is the basis for all the covenant interactions of God with the family of man: "This grace was given us in Christ Jesus before the beginning of time" (2 Tim. 1:9, NIV).

The story of Jesus Christ, "the Lamb slain from the foundation of the world" (Rev. 13:8), is the golden thread that runs throughout Scripture.[3] Was Jesus actually slain before the Creation? No, He was not. Yet, God laid the plan at that time as a mystery hidden through the ages.[4] Why would God keep hidden the mystery of Christ and the plan of salvation? It seems that, in spiritual things, human beings cannot grasp all truth at once. Moreover, they must have a willing mind in order to understand the things of God (1 Cor. 2:7–14; John 16:12). Now when the time was right, God desired that His human children understand the mystery of Christ.

> For he chose us in him before the creation of the world to be holy and blameless in his sight. In love he predestined us to be adopted as his sons through Jesus Christ, in accordance with his pleasure and will. (Eph. 1:4, 5, NIV)

> In hope of eternal life, which God, that cannot lie, promised before the world began. (Titus 1:2)

The Godhead: the Divine Agents in the Everlasting Covenant

"For in him dwelleth all the fulness of the Godhead bodily" (Col. 2:9). Who and what is this "Godhead"? From the beginning of the Old Testament, we find God described in the plural term *Elohim*. (*El* is singular.) Genesis chapter one uses this plural form for God thirty-two times! Here, the Creator says: "Let *us* make man in *our* image" (Gen. 1:26, emphasis supplied). Who is the "us"?

The first person of the Godhead is God the Father. He is a Spirit who desires that His creatures worship Him "in spirit and in truth" (John 4:24).

The second person of the Godhead is Jesus Christ. He is the Creator, Jehovah and the lawgiver of the Old Testament, humankind's Redeemer, and the "Friend of sinners." Of the members of the Godhead, it is Jesus whom we know best. It is He who came to this earth, lived a sinless life, and died that humankind might be redeemed.

The Holy Spirit is the active agent in applying grace to change lives. In Genesis 1, it was the Spirit who "moved upon the face of the waters" (Gen. 1:2). It is the Holy Spirit who also moves upon human beings, giving them power to do the will of God, and who makes plain what God has said in His Word (John 16:13).

The Father, Son, and Holy Spirit worked together to establish the plan of salvation.[5] The Bible uses the plural form of God (*Elohim*) in the Old Testament but does not explain it, nor is the concept of three persons in one God made clear. Since idolatry was prevalent in the Old Testament, had the triune nature of God been clearly declared, it likely would have led the people to think they were worshipping three gods.

> What then does it mean that God exists as the Trinity? It is a basic principle of biblical faith that there is only one God. "Hear, O Israel! The Lord our God the Lord is one! (Deut. 6:4).[6]

The Jews call this verse the "*Shema*" because of its first word in Hebrew, which, according to *Strong's Concordance* means to "hear intelligently, attentively, and with consent and obedience." The word for "God" is the plural "Elohim"; "the Lord our *Elohim* is one!" "The unity of the Godhead cannot be questioned. God does not consist of parts. He is one. Scripture reveals that there are, in that one divine essence, three eternal distinctions. Those distinctions" are "best described as Persons, known as the Father, the Son, and the Holy Spirit. All three have identical attributes; therefore, they are one—not merely one in mind and purpose," but one in essence (Deut. 6:4).[7] As human beings, we can understand God only through what He has revealed. Beyond what God has revealed, we must say with Job, "Canst thou by searching find out God?" (Job 11:7).

The Covenant of God, the Response of a Man

Within the council of the Godhead, the Father, Son, and Holy Spirit developed the plan of salvation. Jesus, the second person of the Godhead, volunteered to come to earth as a human being, live a sinless life, and take on Himself the sins of humankind. He would submit to death on the cross to pay the penalty for the sin of every person. Sin is so offensive to God that the Father's face would be hidden from the Son as He hung on the cross. Jesus, as a man, could not see beyond the grave.

Satan challenged the government of God and the principle of freedom, which God gave to humanity. He claimed that the earth and everyone who walked upon it was his to do with as he pleased. If Jesus failed, humanity would be lost, and sin would become a blot on the universe of God.

It was a difficult decision, even within the Godhead. It became more difficult when Adam sinned and the covenant became a reality. It was a crisis in Gethsemane when Jesus as a man, alone, weighed the final decision. Fortunately, Jesus' faith and resolve to do His Father's will saved the human race, enabling anyone to choose to accept the gift of salvation.

Abraham's call to sacrifice Isaac on Mount Moriah shows that an "only begotten Son" would be the true sacrifice (Gen. 22). When Abraham experienced an "horror of great darkness" (Gen. 15:12), it was a foretaste of Jesus' experience on Calvary. The Passover ceremony on the eve of the Exodus emphasized that people are saved through the blood of the Lamb (Exod. 12:13, 23).

The term "my covenant" pointed to a covenant already in existence. It was made in heaven by God,[8] and presented to Abraham (Gen. 17). At Sinai, God gave Israel the Abrahamic covenant, and the people responded with promises of dedication.[9] Their intentions were good, yet the people bypassed God's grace, refused to come into His presence, and, within forty-six days, violated the covenant they had made with God.

When God gave His covenant to the people, the faith response was required to complete the covenant. The faith response is a human response, a commitment that must be renewed daily and for each generation.

Only One Way Humanity Could be Saved

Could God not simply forgive sin and let the sinner start over? To forgive and forget would trivialize the gravity of sin. Sin is a serious matter. Even a small sin, like eating from the tree of the knowledge of good and evil, manifested rebellion and a distrust of God. Sin separates from God, and, in that separation, there is death (Gen. 2:16, 17; Rom. 6:23). Christ came to this world to suffer that death for humankind.[10] God cannot accept sin, for it brings disorder and unhappiness into His government.

Could God not start over with a new creation? If God should destroy all sinners and simply start over with a new creation, it would not be an act of love. God loved the world, even this world. Because of His love, we have God's assurance that He will not abandon His creation. By love and persuasion, He will reveal His character. He permits sin to run its course to prove to all that in the very nature of sin is death, and all will see ever more clearly the mercy and justice of God.[11]

God is holy; sin cannot exist in His presence (Hab. 1:13). God commands His people to be holy, even as He is holy (1 Peter 1:16). It is Christ who cleanses sinners from all sin, makes them a new creature, and gives them spiritual new birth.[12] "The gift of God is eternal life" (Rom. 6:23). "But God commendeth his love toward us, in that, while we were yet sinners, Christ died for us" (Rom. 5:8).

Jesus Lived Out the Father's Will

Scripture speaks of Jesus' coming to do the pre-determined will of the Father (Isa. 53:3; Heb. 10:7, 9). Though He was equal with the Father through eternity, Jesus willingly became His servant, even taking the form of humanity, accepting poverty, humiliation, and death (Phil. 2:5–8). When Jesus said "And truly the Son of man goeth, as it was determined" (Luke 22:22), He referred to the covenant with the Father. He referred to the covenant again, when He said, "For I came down from heaven, not to do mine own will, but the will of him that sent me: and this is the Father's will which hath sent me, that of all which he hath given me I should lose nothing, but should raise it up again at the last day" (John 6:38, 39).

Through His sacrifice Jesus made a claim upon the Father, that those who believe in Him, "them also I must bring" (John 10:16). In His high priestly prayer, Jesus pled, "Father, I will that they also whom thou hast given me, be with me, where I am" (John 17:24). Christ was claiming something that was due Him in return for the work He had done. Jesus' statement, "I have finished the work which thou gavest me to do" (John 17:4), reveals an arrangement with the Father for which Jesus was putting in His claim and for which He was Himself the surety. He could make His claim only because a promise had already been made. This is one reason why, immediately afterward, Jesus addressed God as "righteous Father" (John 17:25), acknowledging the Father's faithfulness to the heavenly agreement.

Jesus is the Creator, the Redeemer of the human race, and the new head of the human race for all eternity. Because of His sacrifice on the cross, He has bought back the human race. Jesus made His sacrifice, knowing the joy that the redemption of humankind would bring. Paul wrote: "... for the joy that was set before Him [Jesus] endured the cross, despising the shame, and is set down at the right hand of the throne of God" (Heb. 12:2). He willingly endured the suffering, knowing "the glories to follow" (1 Peter 1:11, NASB). The prophet Isaiah wrote: "As a result of the anguish of His soul, He will see it and be satisfied; by His knowledge the Righteous One, My Servant, will justify the many, as He will bear their iniquities" (Isa. 53:11, NASB).

Jesus Is the Champion of the Covenant

The Bible calls the agreement He made before the foundation of the world, the everlasting covenant.[13] The Father gave His Son, and the Son willingly came to live as a human being and pay the penalty for the sins of humankind by dying as our sacrifice.[14]

The everlasting covenant focuses on Jesus, using a number of covenant titles. The Father speaks of the Son: "I, the Lord, have called thee in righteousness, and will hold thine hand, and will keep thee, and give thee for a covenant of the people, for a light of the Gentiles" (Isa. 42:6). All blessings Christ gives to the human family come through the cross (Rom. 8:32).[15]

Christ is the "messenger of the covenant" (Mal. 3:1) because He came to earth to make known its contents and proclaim its glad tidings. Christ is "the surety of a better covenant" (Heb. 7:22), which means that He legally represents humanity and thereby acts in our name and for our benefit. Christ paid the debt of His bankrupt people, settling all their liabilities.

Christ is the mediator of the new covenant (Heb. 9:15; 12:24) by His effective sacrifice on the cross. He is the High Priest in heaven, and, by His intercession, God brings His children into relationship with Himself, giving grace, power, and freedom from sin (2 Cor. 5:18; 12:9; 1 John 2:1).

Living as a human being on earth, Jesus looked to the Father as "my God," giving expression to the covenant made within the Godhead. Christ took the role of a creature, a servant, depending on the Father for guidance, power, and fellowship. Through the prophetic word of David, the Savior declared, "I have leaned on you since the day I was born; you have been my God since my mother gave me birth" (Ps. 22:10, NCV). From the cross He called out, "my God." On the resurrection morning, He told the disciples He would ascend to "my God" (John 20:17). Once in heaven, having become the glorified Redeemer, He spoke of "my God" four times in a single verse (Rev. 3:12).

His God is our God, the God who has made a commitment to humanity in the everlasting covenant through Jesus.

Endnotes

1. The term "everlasting covenant" is used in this book as a description of God's plan from eternity for the redeeming of the fallen human race (e.g. Heb. 13:20; Gen. 17:7, 13, 19; 1 Chron. 16:17; Ps. 105:10; Isa. 24:1). The bow in the cloud reminded God of His "everlasting covenant" with "every living creature of all flesh that is upon the earth" (Gen. 9:16). Providing the ingredients for the shewbread was an "everlasting covenant" for Israel (Lev. 24:8). God's daily provisions are an "everlasting covenant" (2 Sam. 23:5). "Everlasting covenant" also describes binding contracts between God and His people (Isa. 55:3; 61:8; Jer. 32:40; Ezek. 16:60; 37:26). From the above, it is apparent that God's everlasting covenant was given to save and to preserve human life, all creation, and to support creation on a daily basis.

2. The plan of salvation was made before Creation. "Blessed be the God and Father of our Lord Jesus Christ, who hath blessed us with all spiritual blessings in heavenly places in Christ: according as he hath chosen us in him before the foundation of the world, that we should be holy and without blame before him in love" (Eph. 1:3, 4; see also Micah 5:2, which says His "goings forth" are "from everlasting"; John 17:24, which says that the Father loved the Son "before the foundation of the world"; and 1 Peter 1:19, 20, which says that Jesus' role as the sacrificial "lamb" was "foreordained before the foundation of the world"). The Father and Son are pledged to fulfill the terms of the everlasting covenant. "God so loved the world, that He gave His

only begotten Son, that whosoever believeth in Him should not perish, but have everlasting life" (John 3:16). Christ's death on the cross has made it possible for God to receive and pardon every repentant soul. It was the fulfillment of the covenant made between Him and His Father before the foundation of the world was laid.

"The salvation of the human race has ever been the object of the councils of heaven. The covenant of mercy was made before the foundation of the world. It has existed from all eternity, and is called the everlasting covenant. So surely as there never was a time when God was not, so surely there never was a moment when it was not the delight of the eternal mind to manifest His grace to humanity" (Ellen G. White, *The Signs of the Times*, June 12, 1901).

3. Jesus is "the Lamb slain from the foundation of the world" (Rev. 13:8; 1 Peter 1:19, 20; Rev. 5:6–9; 12–14). Jesus knew, delighted in, and fulfilled the "will of the Father" (John 5:30; cf. Ps. 40:7, 8; Matt. 26:39, 42; Luke 22:22; John 4:34; 5:19; 6:38; 8:16, 28, 42; 14:10; 17:4; 18:11). Jesus is the center and focus of the everlasting covenant, a plan formulated before the creation to redeem humankind if he should sin (2 Tim. 1:8, 9; Titus 1:2; 1 Peter 1:20). The term "from the foundation of the world" refers to what God did in eternity past (Matt. 13:35; 25:34; Luke 11:50; Heb. 4:3; 9:26; Rev. 13:8; 17:8; cf. "since the world began," Rom. 16:25; and "from the beginning," Prov. 8:23).

4. The mystery kept secret since before the creation of the world is now revealed in Jesus Christ, who dwells in human hearts by faith (Col. 1:26–28; Rom. 16:25, 26; and Eph. 3:9–11, 17–19).

5. "Two central passages bring the three members of the Godhead together in providing for man's eternal salvation"— Heb. 9:14 and 1 Peter 1:1, 2 (Michael Houdman, "What is the Godhead?" available at: http://www.gotquestions.org/ Godhead.html, accessed 8/27/12). The Bible also relates the Father, Son, and Holy Ghost in Isaiah 11:2; 48:16; Matthew 3:16, 17; 28:19, 20; 1 Corinthians 12:3, 4; 2 Corinthians 13:14; and Ephesians 2:18. *Godhead* is a term used in Acts 17:29; Romans 1:20; and Colossians 2:9.

6. "What is the Godhead?" http://www.gotquestions.org/Godhead.html (accessed 1/16/13). The author quoted Deuteronomy 6:4 from the NIV.

7. "What is the Godhead?" http://www.gotquestions.org/Godhead.html (accessed 1/16/13). For more on the Father, Son, and Holy Spirit, see Fernando Canale, "Doctrine of God," *Handbook of Seventh-day Adventist Theology* (Hagerstown, MD: Review and Herald Publishing Association, 2000), pp. 140–151.

8. The term "My covenant" occurs fifty-one times in the Bible and is associated with words such as "establish," "remember," "make," "keep," "take hold," "give," "break," "transgress," and "this is." The possessive "My" shows that this covenant uniquely belongs to God. It is equivalent to the terms "the everlasting covenant" and "the new covenant."

9. God remembered His pre-arranged covenant (Exod. 2:24; 6:5; Lev. 26:45; Ps. 105:8).

10. Christ died for the sins of the human family; we are ransomed, redeemed, and bought back by His cross (Rev. 13:8; Col. 1:26–28; Isa. 53:11; Matt. 20:28; Rom. 3:24; 5:9, 18; 1 Cor. 6:19, 20; Heb. 9:28; 12:2; 1 Peter 2:24; 3:18; Rev. 5:9).

11. Sin must run its course to establish the mercy and justice of God before the inhabitants of the universe—fallen and unfallen (1 Cor. 4:9; Eph. 3:10; 1 Peter 1:12).

12. Jesus gives spiritual new birth (John 3:3; 1 John 5:11; 2 Cor. 5:17). God's people are cleansed that they need not sin (1 John 1:7–9; 2:1, 5, 6; 3:3, 5–9, 24; 5:18).

13. "Christ was not alone in making His great sacrifice. It was the fulfillment of the covenant made between Him and His Father before the foundation of the world was laid. With clasped hands they had entered into the solemn pledge that Christ would become the surety for the human race if they were overcome by Satan's sophistry" (Ellen G. White, *Youth's Instructor*, June 14, 1900, p. 186).

14. The Father gave His Son (John 3:16), and Christ "gave himself" for us (Gal. 1:4; 2:20; Eph. 5:25; 1 Tim. 2:6; Titus 2:14) and "offered himself" to God (Heb. 9:14).

15. There is life in the Son (John 6:35, 40, 47, 54, 63; 8:51; 11:25, 26; 14:1–3, 6; 17:11).

Chapter 2
What Makes a Covenant?

For when God made promise to Abraham, because he could swear by no
greater, he sware by himself, Saying, Surely blessing I will
bless thee, and multiplying I will multiply thee.
Hebrews 6:13, 14

God's words contain power. Whatever God promises is as certain as already accomplished. In God's plan to redeem humankind, He made redemption more than a promise; He made it a covenant. God made a commitment to save His creation, including humankind. Even more, He committed Himself to meet the challenge, having established the government of God on love, freedom, and creativity for the whole universe forever. God will reveal that He is a God of mercy and justice.

The Law of God Is Holy, Just, and Good

The whole of God's universe is under the laws of nature, which provide for order and beauty in all created things.[1] God created human beings in His image and wrote the moral law in their hearts. God placed within human beings the desire to be like God to the limits of human capability. Love and harmony guided all their actions.

When God created intelligent beings with free will, they needed a moral law to guide their interactions with God and with other created beings. A loving God values free will in angelic and human beings; He desires that His creatures give their love freely by their own choice rather than by compulsion or instinct. Free will makes life attractive and offers pleasant surprises. It opens the door to new beauty in music and art. Freedom, however, can only exist within the boundaries of the law.

When Satan rebelled against God, he challenged the concept of a moral law, claiming that angels and human beings were so wise that they did not need a law. Satan raised questions about God's character, asserting that God is arbitrary, selfish, and unwilling to accept for Himself the conditions under which He expected humans to live. Without law, he said, angels and human beings could be free! Free! Free! (or so he claimed).

When Satan objected to a moral law, why did God not deal with him immediately? The very nature of God's government, based on free choice, requires that angels and human beings see the nature of sin and contrast the methods of Satan with the plans and purposes of God (1 Cor. 4:9). They must see that God is merciful and just (Ps. 85:10; Rev. 15:3). They must also see that, in God, there is love, freedom, life and joy, while, in sin, there is nothing but death (Rom. 6:23).[2]

Was There a Covenant Before Sin?

It is not clear whether sinless beings—the uncounted millions of angels in heaven or the beings on other planets (Rev. 5:11; 14:4; Job 1:6)—knew of an objective law. In their happy and holy state, they willingly patterned their lives after their heavenly Father (John 13:15; 1 Peter 2:21; Matt. 5:45, 48). God's actions were an example for them; the law was and is a transcript of His character.[3]

Why then is a law needed at all? As soon as God created the second angel with intelligence and free will, He had to lay down rules for the behavior of intelligent beings. It is only within the boundaries of law that freedom can exist. Without law, there is anarchy, oppression, and tyranny. The results of Satan's attack on the law of God are all too evident in the world today.

In Eden, God gave Adam and Eve instructions and responsibilities. Since there were just two people, the whole earth was theirs to enjoy. Imagine how big it must have seemed to them! They were to demonstrate their loyalty and obedience to God by not eating of a certain tree in the garden (Gen. 2:16, 17).

As sinless human beings, the law of God was their covenant.[4] God wrote this law on the hearts of every human being when He created the first humans in His image. In Eden, they did not focus on law but rather on how best to praise and honor their Creator, thereby reaching far beyond the law and surpassing its minimum requirements. Sinless beings lived only to do God's will; they kept the law of God by their very nature.

Today, if people keep the minimum requirements of the civil law, they will stay out of jail. This is what many choose to do with God's law; they keep the bare minimum—that which is written in stone. The problem is that, when people keep a law that is written only on stone, obedience is mechanical and without love. God wants to write His law in our hearts so that we can keep His law from a heart filled with love for Him and our fellow human beings. When Jesus came to earth, He introduced the kingdom of grace. In the Sermon on the Mount, He emphasized keeping the law from the motives and attitudes of the heart.

The everlasting covenant, with its promise of grace and redemption, became effective only after sin but remained a mystery until Christ came.[5]

Various Covenantal Agreements

One can use different terms to describe an agreement between parties. These vary in commitment. *Intent* to do something is often unspoken and is subject to the whims of the individual. A *promise* must be kept to meet another's expectations. When a person makes a promise and breaks it, it lessens the credibility of the person who promised. A *vow* is a more serious commitment than a promise and must be fulfilled to avoid a specified consequence.

A *covenant* includes the concepts of *intent, promise,* and *vow.* A covenant is formal and includes commitment, stipulations, and consequences. In ancient times, signatories often sealed a covenant by blood, either that of both parties, of one party, or by animals representing the parties. A covenant may be one-sided or binding on both sides. By contrast, a modern contract incurs only monetary loss.

Scripture uses the term "everlasting covenant" to describe the covenant made in the council of the Godhead before the foundation of the world. Scripture also uses the term for the covenant that God made with Abraham (Gen. 17), showing that the covenant has two aspects. That God called it "My covenant" shows that He considers it to be uniquely His own, especially because the term bears close relation to two other terms, which establish its independence from humans: the everlasting covenant and the new covenant. That Abraham had to accept it by faith shows that humans have a role to play in accepting the covenant. That the covenant was confirmed by Jesus' sacrifice on Calvary, we understand. It was anticipated by faith in the Old Testament, and became a fact remembered by faith in the New.

What is little known is that the covenant was made real in the Old Testament by the oath of God (Gen. 22:16-18; Ps. 105:9; Luke 1:73; Heb. 6, 13, 14). God cannot lie, because when He speaks, His word becomes reality in itself. By His word heaven and earth were created (Ps. 33:6, 9). And by His word and His oath, the covenant became real in the Old Testament, it became more than a promise!

The Faith Response

Careful reading will show that God expected a faith response from humans every time He gave them His covenant. He assumed this response from Adam and Eve when, fresh out of Eden, they sinned. Noah responded in faith by preaching and building the ark over the course of 120 years. Abraham responded in faith, believing that God would do all that He promised.

However, this response was missing when the people at Sinai made their own promises instead of receiving the covenant in faith.[6] Obedience has always been important, and it is important today. It was God's will that people have faith in the prophesied Redeemer to take hold of grace for power to do God's will. The issue of faith was and is always critical.

After Israel broke their covenant of human promises, Moses interceded with God four times until God took them back into His covenant. God said, "Behold, I make a covenant: …" (Exod. 34:10).

Whenever God makes a covenant, it is serious business. He had already made a covenant with Abraham. The real and effective ratification was yet to come when Jesus gave Himself in sacrifice on the cross. What covenant then did God make with Israel in Exodus 34:10? He had already given Israel what He referred to as "My covenant" in Exodus 19:5.

One must distinguish God's unique "My covenant" from other covenants He has made with humans. In Exodus 34:10, God is not speaking of His "My covenant," which humanity cannot change or break but can only accept by faith. It is the faith response that makes it a covenant between God and the human family. On that occasion, they showed their faith by liberally contributing gold, silver, and other materials, and their meticulous handwork to make the sanctuary.

The Covenant of God Is More Than a Promise

God made much, much more than a promise; He made an everlasting covenant, which is a formal commitment *to* humanity. The Creator of this earth covenanted to live on this sinful planet as a human being and die that we might live! The *plan of salvation* and the *everlasting gospel* are terms that express the same idea as the everlasting covenant. When we understand the covenant, it brings into sharp focus the gospel and the plan of salvation.

God's commitment to the covenant assures us of the permanence of His intent. Jesus Christ confirmed the everlasting covenant at Calvary. The cross makes clear the meaning of all doctrines and makes possible the promises and blessings of God.

God always knows "the end from the beginning" (Isa. 46:10). This makes His answers to problems always the best. The Godhead, in council before the creation of the world, made God's everlasting covenant. Human beings cannot break this covenant, for they had no part in making it. We can only trust and have confidence in God's solemn promise (Heb. 6:13–16).

The concept of the covenant is ancient, and it takes a number of forms. Since ancient times, covenants between men and nations were common. Some scholars look to the covenant of God with Adam after sin for the origin of the covenant. Others look to the classic ancient covenant of the Hittite Suzerainty Treaty, the components of which are listed below.

- First came a preamble, introducing the parties involved and describing the gifts they were to exchange.
- Then there was a prologue, discussing the ability of each party to perform expected conditions.
- At this point, there was often a blood ceremony.
- Then came the stipulations, delineating the actions that were expected of either one or both parties for the duration of the treaty. These were followed by blessings if the stipulations of the treaty were upheld and curses if they were not.
- Lastly, the parties shared a sacrificial meal to symbolize their joint participation in the treaty.

Scripture does not always use the terms "covenant" or "testament" in every presentation of the covenant. Often it identifies the covenant by using the names of Abraham, Isaac, and Jacob or by repeating the promise of land. Since a covenant with God is either long lasting or permanent, Scripture often does not repeat all the same details. The promise of a Redeemer, of pardon for sins, of salvation, and of restoration are permanent aspects of God's covenant. When God "makes" a covenant with humankind, it often includes promises specific to a local situation or the promise of land. Many of God's promises in Scripture are not covenants. These He gave in response to particular needs. The focus on Jesus' sinless life and sacrifice on the cross identifies the everlasting covenant. The specific covenant promise is, "I will be to them a God, and they shall be to me a people" (Heb. 8:10).[7]

Endnotes

1.   The creation is kept under the laws of God (Gen. 1; John 1:1–3; Ps. 8:3, 136:7–9; Isa. 40:26).
2.   Regarding Satan's role in the origin of sin, see Ellen G. White, "Why Was Sin Permitted?" *Patriarchs and Prophets* (Nampa, ID: Pacific Press Publishing Association, 2005), pp. 35–43.

3.	"The law of God is as sacred as God Himself. It is a revelation of His will, a transcript of His character, the expression of divine love and wisdom" (*Patriarchs and Prophets*, p. 52).

4.	When God created Adam and Eve, He gave them instructions on how to live (Gen. 1:26–2:24). This will be expanded in our next chapter, "Adam and Eve in Eden."

5.	The plan of salvation was a mystery hidden from the foundation of the world (Rom. 16:25–26; 1 Cor. 2:6–9; Eph. 3:9–11, 17–19; Col. 1:26–28).

6.	That the missing ingredient was faith is seen in Paul's statement in Hebrews 4: "For unto us was the gospel preached, as well as unto them: but the word preached did not profit them, not being mixed with faith in them that heard it" (Heb. 4:2).

7.	Various forms of "I will be to them a God, and they shall be to me a people" are repeated throughout Scripture (Gen. 17:7, 8; Exod. 6:7; 33:14–17; Lev. 26:12; Deut. 29:13; Jer. 11:4; 24:7; 30:22; 31:1, 33; 32:38; Ezek. 11:20; 14:11; 34:30; 36:28; 37:23, 26, 27; 39:22; Hosea 2:23; Zech. 8:8; 13:9; 2 Cor. 6:16; Heb. 8:10; and Rev. 21:3, 7).

Chapter 3
Adam and Eve in Eden

---

*And God saw every thing that he had made, and, behold, it was very good. And
the evening and the morning were the sixth day. … Thus the heavens and the
earth were finished, and all the host of them.*
Genesis 1:31; 2:1

God created this world in six twenty-four-hour days, a world with features and beauty that may
have been previously unknown. As the crowning act of His creation, God created "man in His own
image … male and female created He them" (Gen. 1:27). Humans are material creatures, created
in the image of God. God equipped them with intelligence, free will, and awareness of themselves
and God. Built into this creation was the desire for fellowship with God. Their intelligence was a
function of their material brain, an organ of seemingly unbounded capacity to learn and store new
information. God knew that humans would sin and that His Son would live on this earth as a human
and redeem humankind through His death. God gave Adam and Eve superior intellect, which all
humans—including the only begotten Son of God—would need to recognize and resist evil. When
Jesus came into this world, He said: "Sacrifice and offering thou wouldest not, but a body hast thou
prepared me" (Heb. 10:5).

Creation of Adam

Creation week on this earth was a time of intense interest and excitement for all intelligent beings
in the universe. Having witnessed the beauty of the suns and stars, they watched as beauty appeared in
mountains, rivers, and seas, followed by stately trees, colorful flowers, and lush waving grass. Next they
saw living creatures consisting of physical matter appear—creatures that could show affection and learn
new things. Finally, they watched as God created a being of superior intelligence, made of physical
substance like the animals but in God's very image.

> All heaven took a deep and joyful interest in the creation of the world and of man.
> Human beings were a new and distinct order. They were made "in the image of God,"
> and it was the Creator's design that they should populate the earth. They were to live
> in close communion with heaven, receiving power from the Source of all power.[1]

God's creative acts in making the world are unlike anything humans have ever experienced. Yet,
God constrained His creative work into the six days of the creation week, as the Bible uses the words,

"and the evening and the morning," to mark each day. This expression shows that each day was a twenty-four-hour day, as we mark time today.

We cannot explain the creation. No findings of science can tell us how God created this earth. Evolution is an attempt to explain how the earth created itself through eons of time without a Designer. Yet, this requires more faith than accepting what the Bible says: "In the beginning God created the heaven and the earth" (Gen. 1:1). God does not reckon time as we do, but when He created this earth, He did it in just six twenty-four-hour days.

We take the creation of the earth by faith—a faith that originates from the beauty, design, and order that makes life possible. We know little of *how* God worked in creation; yet, the Psalmist tells us: "By the word of the Lord were the heavens made; and all the host of them by the breath of his mouth. For he spake, and it was done; he commanded, and it stood fast" (Ps. 33:6, 9).

On the sixth day, God created Adam.[2] Earlier that same day, He had created all the land animals. The Bible gives more written space to the creation of man than to that of all other animal life. Even then, the record is short, though it holds a depth of meaning. God did not create this earth and then leave it to run on its own. Not only was all the creation under God's guiding laws, but God personally formed each step in the creation and continued to guide and uphold the creation thereafter.[3]

> And God said, Let us make man in our image, after our likeness: and let them have dominion over the fish of the sea, and over the fowl of the air, and over the cattle, and over all the earth, and over every creeping thing that creepeth upon the earth. (Gen. 1:26)

> And the Lord God formed man of the dust of the ground, and breathed into his nostrils the breath of life; and man became a living soul. (Gen. 2:7)

That "the Lord God formed man of the dust of the ground" means that he was made a *physical* being and not a spirit. The account of how Adam began to live is simple: God "breathed into his nostrils the breath of life" and Adam "became a living soul."

Only God Can Make a Cell

Creating is an activity that only God can do (Ps. 96:5). Men have walked on the moon and are now exploring Mars, but we cannot fully explain how these celestial bodies move in their orbits without colliding with other bodies. In the heavens beyond are the sun, stars, and other heavenly bodies, about which we are just beginning to learn.

On this earth, we see order, beauty, and a system that was established to make life possible for all animal and vegetable life, as well as for humankind.[4] God is the creator of the greatness of the starry heavens, the beauty of this earth, and the order of every microscopic cell (Ps. 19:1–6).

The cells of all living things are complex structures that scientists only partially understand.

Humans cannot make a cell, much less a living one. A number of necessary parts make up each cell. The cell membrane holds the cell together yet permits certain substances and particles to pass into the cell or to pass out of it. The cell could not live or function without this ability.

Inside the cell is a semi-liquid cytoplasm in which the organelles are suspended and carry on their functions. This cytoplasm contains food substances, vitamins, hormones, and proteins. Every cell has a nucleus containing DNA, which is a complex molecule containing the digital instructions for all parts and functions of the body. Even more astounding is the RNA, which is capable of reproducing the DNA as well as other proteins.

The mitochondria are the energy stores; the lysosomes are collections of chemicals, which could be damaging were it not for the cell membranes that hold them in place. Cells can feed themselves, repair damage to themselves and to the tissues, and carry out their various functions. Nerve cells carry messages; muscle cells contract and move the body; retinal cells can see; cochlear cells can hear. The cell contains many other structures and functions. This makes each cell more detailed and sophisticated than even the most complicated machine made by human beings.

The Human Brain

Even more detailed than the cells of the body is the human brain. We can take the brain apart, examine it with CAT scans, PET scans, MRIs, and the electron microscope, thereby identifying its parts and learning something of its functions. There is much that humans have not yet learned. Human beings are aware of their surroundings and receive knowledge through their special senses. The brain thinks, plans, and stores memories. The nerves carry impulses from the brain and spinal cord to govern the movements and functions of the body. It is principally the uniqueness of the human brain that affirms that God created humankind in His image.

God put into the human brain the ability to be self-aware, to be aware of the world, and to be aware of God. To be made in the image of God means to have God's law written on the heart. This includes having love for God and for our fellow human beings. Because of their love for God, simply seeing what God did was an unspoken command for Adam and Eve to do likewise, to the limits of their capabilities.

When God created the human race, He knew that the time would come when His only begotten Son would come to this earth to live a sinless life as a human being. God put into the human brain all the capabilities His Son would need to resist sin. Human beings still possess those capabilities today!

The brain has often been compared to a computer. In some ways, the comparison is valid; in other ways, the brain functions differently. The brain is an electro-chemical organ. This makes it slower than a computer, allowing the brain to gather value, attitude, and emotion to make wiser decisions. The capability of the brain, as well as the storage capacity for memory, is immense—more than any computer.

God Gave Humanity Free Will

Being created in the image of God, human beings possess free will: the ability to choose. Free will provides the ability to choose whom he will serve, God or self. Choosing to serve God gives one access to the power and purpose of God, which enable success in life. Serving God brings freedom, power to do, and life itself.

Why would humans choose anything else? The answer comes from Eden. Satan deceived Eve into believing that yielding to selfish desires would bring her a heightened degree of happiness; instead, it brought slavery, sorrow, weakness, and death. Rather than trusting God to save Eve, Adam joined her in sin.

The Bible repeatedly shows that, to serve God, humans need to exercise choice. The Bible also reveals the effects of choosing not to serve God (Isa. 59:2). From these revelations, we recognize that humans have free will to choose their destiny, either to serve God willingly or to rebel.[5] At the same time, Paul uses the word "predestinate" (Rom. 8:28, 30). Does this suggest that free will is of no effect? While God does predestine all to be saved (1 Tim. 2:4; Eph. 1:11) and while the will of God is effective in the lives of human beings, it is only by the consent of human beings that the Holy Spirit changes lives (Isa. 59:2; Rom. 8:13–15).

> God placed man under law, as an indispensable condition of his very existence. He was a subject of the divine government, and there can be no government without law. God might have created man without the power to transgress His law; He might have withheld the hand of Adam from touching the forbidden fruit; but in that case man would have been, not a free moral agent, but a mere automaton. Without freedom of choice, his obedience would not have been voluntary, but forced.[6]

The Power of God Sustains the Creation

Did God create this earth to run on its own power and direction? No, God created this earth as an expression of His love, and He continues to support and guide His creation so that all creatures can enjoy the happiness and beauty He designed from the beginning. Such knowledge evokes praise and love for the Creator in the human heart. Creation could not have come into existence and cannot now continue without God. Hear this beautifully expressed in the following words:

> The seed has in itself a germinating principle, a principle that God himself has implanted; yet if left to itself the seed would have no power to spring up. Man has his part to act in promoting the growth of the grain....
>
> There is life in the seed, there is power in the soil; but unless an infinite power is exercised day and night, the seed will yield no returns....
>
> Without the life of God, nature would die. His creative works are dependent on Him. He bestows life-giving properties on all that nature produces. We are to regard the trees laden with fruit as the gift of God, just as much as though He placed the fruit in our hands....

In the production of earth's harvests, God is working a miracle every day. Through natural agencies the same work is accomplished that was wrought in the feeding of the multitude. Men prepare the soil and sow the seed, but it is the life from God that causes the seed to germinate.

God's handiwork in nature is not God Himself in nature. The things of nature are an expression of God's character; by them we may understand His love, His power, and His glory; but we are not to regard nature as God.[7]

Endnotes

1. Ellen G. White, "Purpose of Man's Creation," *Advent Review and Sabbath Herald*, February 11, 1902.

2. The work of creation was finished on the sixth day (Gen. 1:31; 2:1). God did not stop work on the seventh day of creation and rest for the balance of history but simply rested from the work of creating, before going on to other work. Jesus told the Pharisees: "My Father worketh hitherto, and I work" (John 5:17). He acknowledged the sustaining work of the Father: "But the Father that dwelleth in me, he doeth the works" (John 14:10; see also Isa. 40:26; Acts 17:28; 1 Cor. 12:6).

    Facts about the seventh-day Sabbath:

    a. The Sabbath was made holy by God as a day of rest and a memorial of creation for the benefit of man (Gen. 2:1–3; Mark 2:27, 28).

    b. It is the seal of obedience within the law and a memorial to creation (Exod. 16:28, 29; 20:8–11; 31:17).

    c. It is the sign of sanctification, indicating that God has changed our lives (Exod. 31:13; Ezek. 20:12, 20).

    d. Its rest is for the full day of twenty-four hours, not just for a short two hours of worship (Lev. 23:32)!

    e. It was part of what God expected of Gentiles who "joined themselves to the Lord." They were to keep the Sabbath as God invited the people of the earth to make the Jerusalem temple "an house of prayer for all people" (Isa. 56:6, 7).

    f. It is a seal that marks God's people in the end time (Rev. 7:1–4; 12:17; 14:1–5, 12).

3. *Deism* is the "belief that understands God as distant, in that God created the universe but then left it to run its course on its own, following certain 'laws of nature' that God had built into the universe" (Stanley J. Grenz, David Guretzki, and Cherith Fee Nordling, *Pocket Dictionary of Theological Terms* [Downers Grove, IL: InterVarsity Press, 1999], p. 36).

    Paul, in his sermon on Mars Hill in Athens, connected the term "the unknown God" with the true Creator God of heaven and earth, who not only gives form, life, and ability, but also sustains His creatures on a daily basis. "God that made the world and all things therein, … seeing he giveth to all life, and breath, and all things; … And hath made of one blood all nations of men for to dwell on all the face of the earth, … for in him we live, and move, and have our being" (Acts 17:24–28).

4. Were it not for God's "fine tuning" of the universe, life could not exist. See Guillermo Gonzalez and Jay Richards, *The Privileged Planet: How Our Place in the Cosmos is Designed for Discovery* (Washington, DC: Regnery Publishing, Inc., 2004), 464 pp.

5. God gave humans free will to choose Him or to rebel (Deut. 4:29; Joshua 24:15; Isa. 1:19, 20; 55:6, 7; 65:12; Ezek. 18:24; 33:11; Amos 5:4; Matt. 7:7; John 3:16; Acts 3:19; Rom. 6:11–13; Rev. 3:18, 20). The conditional element in these statements ("if," "let," "choose," and God's imploring them) requires that humans have a voluntary choice in whether or not to serve God.

6. Ellen G. White, *Patriarchs and Prophets* (Nampa, ID: Pacific Press Publishing Association, 2005), p. 49.

7. Ellen G. White, *Medical Ministry* (Nampa, ID: Pacific Press Publishing Association, 1963), pp. 7, 8, 11.

Chapter 4
Temptation and Fall of Man

And there was war in heaven: Michael and his angels fought against the dragon;
and the dragon fought and his angels, and prevailed not;
neither was their place found any more in heaven.
Revelation 12:7

It was not a war with tanks and guns. Christ is pictured as riding a white horse with a sharp sword coming out of His mouth (Rev. 19:15). The sharp sword is the Word of God (Heb. 4:12; Eph. 6:17). By speaking the truth, Jesus rules the "nations with a rod of iron" (Rev. 12:5). Satan and his evil angels "prevailed not; neither was their place found any more in heaven" (Rev. 12:8); they were cast out of heaven to this earth.

Satan could tempt Adam and Eve only by causing them to eat of one designated tree: "the tree of the knowledge of good and evil" (Gen. 2:17).[1] It was a serious limitation for Satan and an easy test for Adam and Eve. This test would demonstrate whether they were willing to accept God's will in all things. If they should stay away from the tree and not eat of it, they would live forever. If they should submit to Satan and eat of the tree, they would die.

Temptation is something that we face every day. It may be imperceptible at first, but, through the senses and our normal desires, at times we may face temptation that leaves little or no time for a reasoned response. Is it possible to stand guard and not be taken unaware? Yes, it is! However, it requires that a person resist sinful thoughts that can lead into sin. We must avoid seeing or being in the presence of evil. We must store the mind each day with messages from the Bible and pray for the Holy Spirit to guard the avenues of the soul: what we think, see, say, and do.

Warning: Rebel on the Loose

When Lucifer the leading angel in heaven rebelled, he became *Satan*, the "Adversary." There was war in heaven and God cast Satan, with his evil angels, to earth. Jesus told His disciples, "I beheld Satan as lightning fall from heaven" (Luke 10:18). Mercifully, God limited Satan's ability to tempt Adam and Eve to just one place: a tree in the middle of the garden. God warned that they must not eat fruit from that tree:

> And the Lord God commanded the man, saying, Of every tree of the garden thou mayest freely eat: But of the tree of the knowledge of good and evil, thou shalt not eat of it: for in the day that thou eatest thereof thou shalt surely die. (Gen. 2:16, 17)

This warning indicated that God told the newly created pair much more about sin and the devil than what is recorded in Scripture. "Surely the Sovereign Lord does nothing without revealing his plan to his servants the prophets" (Amos 3:7, NIV).

Adam and Eve could eat of every tree in the garden except one. God gave this test to determine whether they were willing to obey Him in all things. It was not wrong to eat fruit from a tree. God restricted them from eating of one special tree to determine if Adam and Eve were willing to lay aside their own reasoning and accept His will, to recognize a mind and an authority higher than their own. If they chose to eat of that tree, thereby choosing not to serve God, they would disconnect from the One who gives life, and they would die. God informed Adam and Eve of the consequences of disobedience and gave them the power of choice and the ability to resist the devil and obey God's clear command.

The Garden Tragedy

One day, as Eve was exploring the garden by herself, she came upon the forbidden tree. The fruit was ripe and beautiful, shimmering in the sunlight. Just then she remembered what God had said. As she quickly turned to find Adam, a beautiful, musical voice caught her attention. She looked back, but all that she saw was a serpent—a very beautiful serpent—in the tree.

"Hello, Eve. My but you are beautiful! Can you and I talk?"

"Who are you?" Eve responded, surprised to be addressed by such a creature. "I have never before heard a serpent talk. How did this happen?"

The serpent noisily bit off a piece of fruit. "I knew nothing about talking until I ate this fruit. Tell me, did God really say you are not to eat from every tree of the garden?"

"No," said Eve, "God told us that we could eat from every tree in the garden except this one. He said we must not eat from it or even touch it, or we will die."

Turning from the fruit, the serpent slyly cocked his head. "Well, the truth is, God knows that, when you eat of this tree, your eyes will be opened, and you will be able to choose your own way. You will be like God, knowing both good and evil."

Deception is often imperceptible. Without realizing it, Eve was falling under the spell of the devil's deceptive sale's pitch. Hearing the serpent talk was enticing. Without Eve's awareness, the serpent in-volved her in something she had never done: she had never questioned God. Apparently Adam was not with her at the time, for he is never mentioned or addressed until after she ate of the fruit. Alone and naive, she was attempting to reason with an intelligence far superior to her own. It was the intelligence of Satan himself, who was using the serpent as a medium.[2] The Bible says:

> Now the serpent was more subtle than any beast of the field which the Lord God had
> made. And he said unto the woman, Yea, hath God said, Ye shall not eat of every tree
> of the garden? And the woman said unto the serpent, We may eat of the fruit of the
> trees of the garden: But of the fruit of the tree which is in the midst of the garden,
> God hath said, Ye shall not eat of it, neither shall ye touch it, lest ye die. And the

serpent said unto the woman, Ye shall not surely die: For God doth know that in the
day ye eat thereof, then your eyes shall be opened, and ye shall be as gods, knowing
good and evil. And when the woman saw that the tree was good for food, and that
it was pleasant to the eyes, and a tree to be desired to make one wise, she took of the
fruit thereof, and did eat, and gave also unto her husband with her; and he did eat.
(Gen. 3:1–6)

Satan, through the serpent, offered strange and wonderful things to pique Eve's curiosity. However,
curiosity can be dangerous. Eve mistook the curse for a blessing. Her experience with Satan, the master
of hypnosis, is a warning that humans must never put themselves in the path of temptation, even if it
appears to offer exceptional benefits.

The devil can offer us nothing of benefit except that which God, the Creator of all science and of
all the arts throughout all history has already created. God is the source of all wisdom, and He bids us
choose the gift of His true wisdom over the counterfeit knowledge Satan has to offer.

Satan identified Eve's weaknesses: worldly ambition, pride, curiosity about forbidden things, and
willingness to question what God had said. She did not know that the "advantages" in distrusting God
are self-serving pride, disappointment, disease, and death. Only in serving God do people gain real
benefit.

Eve should have immediately left when she found herself nearing temptation and, certainly, when
she heard the serpent questioning what God had said. Instead, she allowed his temptations to blind her
to the one option that could save her: to turn immediately to God and flee temptation! To linger in the
presence of temptation and sin is to invite disaster. Yet, God has a promise:

There hath no temptation taken you but such as is common to man: but God is faithful, who will not suffer you to be tempted above that ye are able; but will with the
temptation also make a way to escape, that ye may be able to bear it. (1 Cor. 10:13)

Eve received at least three warnings to help her avoid danger, but she continued to linger. Eventually,
she took the fruit and ate it, yielding to the temptations of appetite, beauty, and wisdom.

The Fall of Man

When Eve accepted the fruit from the serpent and ate it, she immediately felt a change. Imagining
new vitalizing power, she picked more fruit and took it to share with Adam. As she approached her
mate, she was enthusiastic about the fruit's beauty, taste, and promise of greater wisdom. In alarm,
Adam averted his eyes. Eve was without her beautiful robe of fluorescent light and was naked![3] As she
explained what she had done, Adam listened through tears with a sinking heart. Eve must die, but how
could he give her up? Deciding that he would rather die than live without her, he quickly took the fruit
and ate.

As the robe of light faded from Adam's form, Eve realized for the first time what had happened to her. The enthusiasm of the moment quickly turned to dread. In sorrow, the two watched the long rays of the afternoon sun give way to the shadows of evening. Soon it was time for their visit with God. They quickly looked for a way to cover for their loss.

> And the eyes of them both were opened, and they knew that they were naked; and they sewed fig leaves together, and made themselves aprons. And they heard the voice of the Lord God walking in the garden in the cool of the day: and Adam and his wife hid themselves from the presence of the Lord God amongst the trees of the garden.
>
> And the Lord God called unto Adam, and said unto him, Where art thou?
>
> And he said, I heard thy voice in the garden, and I was afraid, because I was naked; and I hid myself. And he said, Who told thee that thou wast naked? Hast thou eaten of the tree, whereof I commanded thee that thou shouldest not eat? And the man said, The woman whom thou gavest to be with me, she gave me of the tree, and I did eat. And the Lord God said unto the woman, What is this that thou hast done? And the woman said, The serpent beguiled me, and I did eat. (Gen. 3:7–13)

Why should this world be thrown into chaos and confusion, disease and death from two people eating fruit? What are the issues? God's holiness and glory cannot allow sin to exist. In the malignant, destructive nature of even minor sins, there is an element of pride, unbelief, and rebellion. When small sins enter the soul, they only grow and lead to deeper sin. A Christian must not see, listen to, taste, feel, or harbor feelings for sin in any guise.

When people sin, they choose to obey another master. When Satan fell, he planned to cause humans to sin, make them his slaves, and become ruler of this world. However, he could not take control of this earth until both Adam and Eve had fallen.

Steps to Sin

God had warned Adam and Eve to stay together. Eve was to be a "helpmeet" to Adam and he to her (Gen. 2:20). When Eve wandered away from Adam, she was more vulnerable to deception. When she found herself at the forbidden tree, she lingered. When she heard the serpent talking, it was a cause of alarm, but she did not quickly leave. When the serpent raised doubts about God's instructions, she listened. And when the serpent offered her wisdom from eating the fruit, she believed his lie. This took her across the line into sin as she took the next fatal step, ate the fruit, and became the devil's emissary.

While Eve became an agent of Satan to cause Adam to sin, Adam ultimately held the greater responsibility. He made a conscious choice to sin while fully aware of the consequences. Satan could not entice and deceive Adam as he had Eve. Also, while Adam loved Eve with all his heart, did not God love her more? Would not God have had a better way of solving the problem of Eve's sin than that which

Adam could devise?

By choosing their own way instead of God's, Adam and Eve separated from their Creator. They experienced the results of trying to find their own solutions to their problems, depending on themselves rather than seeking God for wisdom. They would continue down a path that was the beginning of old covenant legalism.

The fall of our first parents in following their own way affected everything on the earth. Animals became wild, and the land became less productive. Weeds, thorns, and thistles began to grow, and the weather became unpredictable. Man had to work harder to make a living, and women gave birth in pain. Human beings became selfish by nature, adversely affecting their worship of God.

Yet, through His everlasting love and mercy, God had a plan. He provided the mysterious born-again experience and gave Adam and Eve the covenant of grace.

Endnotes

1. God did not wait until Eve was created to warn Adam about the tree. The warning is in Genesis 2:16, 17, while Eve was created in verse 22.
2. The book of Revelation identifies the devil as "that ancient serpent" (Rev. 12:9).
3. Before they sinned, Adam and Eve did not wear fabric or skins. They "were both naked ... and were not ashamed" (Gen. 2:25). Immediately after they sinned, "the eyes of them both were opened, and they knew that they were naked" (Gen. 3:7). Something had changed. Once naked and innocent, now they were naked and ashamed. There is no record of their having clothes or of their taking them off, though some describe Adam and Eve as wearing "robes of light" in the Garden of Eden. For example, the Jewish *Midrash Rabba on Genesis* describes Adam and Eve wearing "garments of light." Ellen White described Adam and Eve before they sinned: "The sinless pair wore no artificial garments; they were clothed with a covering of light and glory, such as the angels wear. So long as they lived in obedience to God, this robe of light continued to enshroud them" (*Patriarchs and Prophets*, p. 45). Indeed, angelic beings in the Bible are described as wearing white raiment (Matt. 28:3; Mark 16:5; John 20:12; Acts 1:10). (Do sinless beings always "shine"?) So what happened to that which clothed Adam and Eve's nakedness? It turns out that there is a feature of human skin that provides a basis for their having had "garments of light."

    Fluorescence and Phosphorescence are found in human skin. Dermatologists have found that there are cells in human skin that are capable of fluorescence and phosphorescence. "Cells with autofluorescent granules are common in the dermal connective tissue of human skin. The cytoplasmic granules appear to be of lipo-pigment nature. The cells show phagocytic properties and it can therefore not be excluded that the cytoplasmic granular structures are ingested material. There are certain similarities between the observed dermal auto fluorescent cells (DAF-cells) and chromatophores (melanophages) of the dermis" (Gunnar D. Bloom and E. Martin Ritzén, "Autofluorescent granules in cells of human dermis," *Zeitschrif für Zellforschung und Mikrospokische Anatomie* [Stockholm, Sweden, January 31, 1964], vol. 61, is. 6, pp. 841–854, available at: http://www.springerlink.com/content/q567n05868276n2r, accessed 1/10/13).

    Human skin contains cells called fluorophores (which include aromatic amino acids such as tryptophan and tyrosine, collagen and elastin, nicotinamide adenine dinucleotide, porphyrins, and flavins) that give the epidermis the capacity to fluoresce or to reflect light, usually in the presence of certain wavelengths of ultraviolet light. Skin cells also show the capacity to phosphoresce or produce light. This process is a measure of a person's general health or responsiveness to certain types of treatment. The effect can be increased or decreased by the use of certain chemicals and drugs (Robert Gillies, George Zonios, R. Rox Anderson, and Nikiforos Kollias, "Fluorescence Excitation Spectroscopy Provides Information About Human Skin *In Vivo*," *Journal of Investigative Dermatology* [2000], vol. 115, pp. 704–707;

doi:10.1046/j.1523-1747.2000.00091.x, available at: http://www.nature.com/jid/journal/v115/n4/pdf/5600851a.pdf, accessed 1/10/13).

The skin color of the face is hard to reproduce, as photographers and artists well know. When people are happy and their face is beaming, there may be something more to it than just a happy smile! When Moses came down from Mount Sinai with the second set of tables of stone, the skin of his face shone so brightly that he had to cover it with a vail (Exod. 34:29, 35)! Human skin apparently has the capacity both to intensely reflect and produce light, though the activating energy to shine brightly may be lacking. While the discovery of the skin's ability to fluoresce and phosphoresce does not prove that Adam and Eve's "garments of light" were the glowing of their skin, such clothing is compatible with the concept.

Chapter 5

God's Covenant with Adam

And they heard the voice of the LORD God walking in the garden in the cool of the day: and Adam and his wife hid themselves from the presence of the LORD God amongst the trees of the garden. —Genesis 3:8

The covenant is a formal commitment that God made to support and redeem His creation. God's presence with His people is a central element of that covenant (Matt. 28:20). Adam and Eve were not to eat of the "tree of the knowledge of good and evil" (Gen. 2:17). When they did, they separated themselves from God, passed under the control of Satan, and were condemned to die. This is the same desperate situation of every human being on this earth. Without God's remedy, we are all condemned to die. Yet, through God's covenant of peace and the sacrifice of Jesus on the cross, God gives us eternal life.

God Responds with the Covenant

Before sin, Adam and Eve had God's approval and perfect, trusting fellowship with Him. After sin, they stood under the condemnation of the law and were deserving of death (Rom. 5:18, 21). God had warned them, "… in the day that thou eatest thereof thou shalt surely die" (Gen. 2:17). Obviously, Adam and Eve did not die that day, and the human race continued. Before the sun set that day, the Lord came and gave them the covenant in a pronouncement directed at Satan, represented by the serpent: "And I will put enmity between thee and the woman, and between thy seed and her seed; it shall bruise thy head, and thou shalt bruise his heel" (Gen. 3:15). The "seed of the woman"—the Messiah—would be stricken for them. God gave them probation and another chance to choose whom they would serve—whether Christ or Satan.

In the phrase, "I will put enmity between thee and the woman," God took the initiative and actively "put" enmity against evil in the hearts of humankind. God gave Adam and Eve the everlasting covenant and wrote the law in their hearts (Jer. 31:31–34). He gave them a conscience, a means of resistance to evil and sin.

Christ is the seed of the woman, who would "bruise" the serpent's "head." By this God meant that Christ would destroy unrepentant sinners and sin. This could occur only through His suffering, the serpent's bruising of "his heel," which He would ultimately survive.

God graciously brought the guilty pair back under the everlasting covenant, with the new provision of forgiveness for sin. God the Father, Son, and Holy Spirit had decreed the everlasting covenant in a special council before the creation of this world. Jesus became the Lamb long before He died on the cross (Rev. 13:8). He would Himself meet the demands of the law and take the sin of humankind upon Himself, offering His life a redeeming sacrifice. Through His sacrifice He would buy back the human race (1 Cor. 6:20) and place humanity where the grace of God could again work in their lives.[1]

God immediately clothed Adam and Eve in skins (Gen. 3:21), removing the inadequate and uncomfortable fig leaves that had covered their shame. This symbolized that the "covering" for their sin would come only through the shedding of blood (Heb. 9:22). This was a prototype of the sacrificial system, pointing forward to the Messiah who would make the true sacrifice for humankind's sin.

What Is the Sinful Nature?

Sin caused humans to have a sinful nature. Our first parents mistrusted God, thereby breaking the bond of fellowship. Self now became the center and the focus of the human personality rather than God.

> When man transgressed the divine law, his nature became evil, and he was in harmony, not at variance, with Satan. There exists naturally no enmity between sinful man and the originator of sin. Both became evil through apostasy.... Had not God specially interposed, Satan and man would have entered into an alliance against Heaven; and instead of cherishing enmity against Satan, the whole human family would have been united in opposition to God. (Ellen G. White, *The Great Controversy*, p. 505)[2]

A lawyer asked Jesus one day: "Master, which is the great commandment in the law?" Jesus said to him, "Thou shalt love the Lord thy God with all thy heart, and with all thy soul, and with all thy mind. This is the first and great commandment. And the second is like unto it thou shalt love thy neighbour as thyself. On these two commandments hang all the law and the prophets" (Matt. 22:36–40).

These two commandments were articulated in the wilderness of Sinai (Deut. 6:5; Lev. 19:18). The Ten Commandments expand upon these two great commandments and have been the law of love and liberty from the start (James 1:25).[3] If people do not love God, they will display unbelief and pride. If they do not love others, they will be selfish. The underlying motives of disbelief, pride, and selfishness are the core of the sinful nature.

Jesus emphasized in the Sermon on the Mount that obedience to the law consists in more than just outward actions. It must arise from the motives of the heart. This is the reason that humans can break the law even while seeming to keep it. Only by grace can the motives of the heart be changed.

The Fruit of Eating the Fruit

As we see from Eve's experience, Satan does not directly ask humans to worship him. Instead, he deceives sinners into serving themselves. The Bible describes the sinful self as "deceitful above all things, and desperately wicked: who can know it" (Jer. 17:9)? When Adam and Eve chose to turn from the Lord God, they chose "another god" and gave dominion of the earth to Satan. Nonetheless, God retains His position as Creator and owner of the earth, and Satan is restrained and cannot utterly destroy the planet. Paul wrote: "Don't you know that when you offer yourselves to someone to obey him as slaves, you are slaves to the one whom you obey—whether you are slaves to sin, which leads to death, or to obedience, which leads to righteousness?" (Rom. 6:16, NIV).

What did Satan mean when he said through the serpent, "… and ye shall be as gods, knowing good and evil" (Gen. 3:5)? Adam and Eve in Eden knew only what was right. Their experience in evil did broaden their choices. They could now choose their own way, but what a tragedy that was! Truly, "it is not in man that walketh to direct his steps" (Jer. 10:23).

In following their own way, they would now seek their own pleasure, work for their own support, gather to themselves material necessities and, more, seek for their own power and their own meaning in life. In self-seeking, humankind would fail, separate from God, and die. "And the Lord God said, Behold, the man is become as one of us, to know good and evil" (Gen. 3:22).

God interposed to change all this. The Father and Son covenanted for Jesus to die in man's place to pay the penalty for sin. God put humans on probation and continued their life so that they could learn of His mercy and self-sacrificing love and then His joy, gentleness, patience, purity, and peace. In knowing Him, men and women could again become like Him and respond to Him in kind. God would again become Creator, Saviour, and friend. Sin would cease to be an option.

The "wisdom" they gained from eating the fruit quickly turned into a curse. It caused Adam to blame Eve, Eve to blame the serpent, and both to blame God. The fruits of disobedience were immediately apparent: condemnation, guilt, blame, loss of fellowship, and fear to meet God. Adam and Eve lost their love and their joy.

> The test given our first parents was the lightest conceivable. It was so light that there could be no possible excuse for transgression.…
>
> After Adam's fall God could have let Adam and Eve die, and started again with a new pair. But that would be to confess failure. Would it not be better, to give Adam and Eve another opportunity? Perhaps they had learned their lesson, and would not disobey again. God could simply forgive them, and give them another trial. But that involved other considerations. If given another probation, and if they again should fail, would not still another trial have to be given them, and another and another, without end? And if that were done would they ever learn the lesson that death lurks in the least deviation from God's will?
>
> Unless they learned this, safety could never be attained in this world or in the universe. God could indeed forgive, but the matter was not so simple as that. Man had sinned, and it was necessary that he learn what the wages of sin are, and that God does not arbitrarily decree death because of transgression, but that death is wrapped up in the sin itself.[4]

God Desires a Relationship of Faith

Adam and Eve in their sinless pristine state lived in perfect surroundings. God and the holy angels visited them regularly. This was their life. They thought about God, spoke of Him, made the Garden of Eden beautiful for Him. All their creativity in song, art, word, and action was to bring praise to His name. God had created Adam and Eve in His image! They had a love for God that we, as sinners, only dimly appreciate. Sin did not even enter their thinking.

God never intended that humans know and experience sin. When sinners receive the new birth (John 3:3–21), they become a new creature (2 Cor. 5:17) and all things become new. As they realize what Christ has done, the Holy Spirit changes the motives. They now love God and want to live for Him. Jesus hides the sinful nature under the robe of His righteousness.

If people exercise faith and give consent to the work of grace, they receive power to obey the law and become more like Christ. The memory of sin fades. This is what God wants for every person.

There are still steps to take, and there are besetting sins to overcome: the habits of the past and the tendencies of the sinful nature. Why does not God take all these away too? Remember, God gave humans free will as a sacred gift. He never overrides one's power to choose. Trials, temptations, and testing reveal weak points. Sinners must now recognize their sin, confess it, and ask for the grace of God to overcome sinful tendencies. Such prayer God is always glad to answer with a "yes"!

Is this process ever complete? Are all sins ever overcome? We have the promise that when Jesus comes again, the sinful nature will be removed: "The dead shall be raised incorruptible, and we shall be changed. For this corruptible must put on incorruption, and this mortal must put on immortality" (1 Cor. 15:52, 53). Jesus Christ stands for us in the judgment. Until then, our "perfection" on this earth is always in Jesus Christ and His perfection.

> For whatsoever is born of God overcometh the world: and this is the victory that overcometh the world, even our faith. (1 John 5:4)

> But without faith it is impossible to please him: for he that cometh to God must believe that he is, and that he is a rewarder of them that diligently seek him. (Heb. 11:6)

God's plan has always been that He have a close association with the human family. This beautiful relationship began in Eden. The efficacy of the grace of God is to restore the image of God in humankind, to show "Christ in you, the hope of glory" (Col. 1:27). This is the goal for the Christian today. We are sinners. We need the objective standard of the law to show what is right and what God is like. More than this, we need to know Jesus Christ. By faith, the relationship with Christ can be close and personal. Our thoughts, words, and actions may be patterned after what Christ says and does. Jesus must be everything to us. Is the law set aside? Of course not! (Rom. 3:31) However, people in close connection with Jesus do not focus on law; they see Jesus as "My Lord and my God" (John 20:28), as "the way, the truth, and the life" (John 14:6).

How is this attained? It is by loving God as did Adam and Eve before sin; it is by obeying God as did Noah and Abraham; it is by seeking God's presence as did Moses; it is by rejoicing in God's favor as did David; it is by trusting God as did Job; and it is by praying as did Jesus Christ. We will find Him as we study God's Word (Luke 24:27; John 5:39, 46).

Cain and Abel's Sacrifices

While living near the gate to Eden, God instructed Adam and Eve to make animal sacrifices as an illustration of the sacrifice Jesus must make to take the penalty for their sin. Abel honored God by offering a lamb as he had been instructed. Cain, hoping to make a more valuable sacrifice, offered fruit. God did not recognize his bloodless sacrifice. Cain's offering was not by faith (Heb. 11:4).

This experience humiliated Cain. As the older brother, he expected to be the leader in all things. Cain misunderstood the meaning of the sacrifice. He rebelled against God by going his own way and disobeying a direct command. He tried to gain the favor of God by his "valuable" sacrifice. He expected that God would be pleased with his generosity. The problem was that only a blood offering could illustrate Jesus' dying in the sinner's place, paying the penalty for sin that it might be pardoned. In giving fruit, Cain refused to recognize that he was a sinner (Heb. 9:22).

The sacrifice of the lamb showed the heart of the gospel. The shed blood of Jesus Christ at Calvary mediates grace to the family of man, and only through grace is the law written in the heart. This is the focus of the new covenant.

The bloodless offering of Cain was an attempt to do God's will through human effort. It was a valuable offering, but, without the shedding of blood, it could not point to the coming Redeemer. The offering of Cain did not show forgiving grace or exercise enmity against sin or reflect the law in the heart. It was the essence of the old covenant.

The everlasting covenant is not something that one *does* to be saved. The old covenant is the attempt to do the work of God by human efforts. Accepting reconciliation and salvation through the grace of Jesus Christ is the *new* covenant—it is the everlasting covenant. This truth every Christian must clearly understand. Grace changes the life and restores in us the image of God.

Endnotes

1. After Adam and Eve sinned, they were at the mercy of Satan, having chosen another master (Rom. 6:16). Left to themselves, they would unite with Satan in rebellion against God. However, they did not have full knowledge of the character of God nor of His grace. God gave them probation to learn and to repent.
2. For a further discussion of the human sinful nature, see Ellen G. White, "Enmity Between Man and Satan," *The Great Controversy* (Mountain View, CA: Pacific Press Publishing Association, 1911), pp. 505–510.
3. Those who love God and their fellow human beings do not find God's commandments burdensome (1 John 5:3).
4. M. L. Andreasen, *The Book of Hebrews* (Washington, DC: Review and Herald Publishing Association, 1948), p. 285.

Chapter 6
Authority of the Prince

Christ created this earth (John 1:1–3; Col. 1:16; Heb. 1:2). He is the Owner and Prince of this earth. Satan cannot take this from Him. By tempting Adam and Eve to fall, he could only take the dominion that Adam had and position himself to have a greater opportunity to tempt humans.

Through His anticipated sacrifice, Christ received all power and authority over Satan. He exercised this power to give grace to humankind, and, by their consent, to change the lives of humans. Christ gives this power to His people through the Holy Spirit in answer to prayer and with the choice and willing consent of each person.

Christ is the "Prince of Peace," the "Prince of the covenant," and the "Prince of Princes."[1] He is the true "Prince." Satan falsely claims the title through his usurpation of the dominion of Adam. However, Satan has no relation with God and is the enemy of humankind. His claim is false.

War in Heaven

Pride led to open rebellion and war in heaven. Revelation describes this war. "And there was war in heaven: Michael [Christ] and his angels fought against the dragon; and the dragon fought and his angels, and prevailed not; neither was their place found any more in heaven. and the great dragon was cast out, that old serpent, called the Devil, and Satan, which deceiveth the whole world: he was cast out into the earth, and his angels were cast out with him" (Rev. 12:7–9).

God cast Satan onto this earth where Adam and Eve lived in the perfection of their garden home. He allowed Satan only one place in which to tempt Adam and Eve. It was only at the "tree of knowledge of good and evil."

Adam, One-Time Prince of This World

In disobeying the direct command of God and obeying Satan, Adam had chosen another master and forfeited his dominion of the earth to Satan. In giving Adam and Eve free will, even God would not overrule their choice. In anticipation of Jesus' sacrifice, God put enmity between human beings and Satan, giving them a conscience and a new probation that they might choose again to serve Him.

The beauty and order of Eden changed after Adam and Eve sinned and forfeited their dominion. God cursed the earth, and Adam had to work hard for a living. Animals became wild. Women bore children in the pains of labor. God banished Adam and Eve from Eden. Satan even challenged the position of God, planning to usurp the rulership of this world, take over Adam's dominion, and reduce all humankind to slaves.

> For thou hast said in thine heart, I will ascend into heaven, I will exalt my throne above the stars of God: I will sit also upon the mount of the congregation, in the sides of the north. (Isa. 14:13; cf. verses 12–20)

> Know ye not, that to whom ye yield yourselves servants to obey, his servants ye are to whom ye obey; whether of sin unto death, or of obedience unto righteousness? (Rom. 6:16)

After Adam and Eve sinned, Satan claimed the title of "prince of this world."[2] While he had no right to the title, Satan strongly maintained his claim and insisted that God had no right to intervene (Job 1:8–11).[3]

Satan soon demonstrated hatred, murder, and no end of other sins. He had neither the support of God above nor the support of humans below. From first to last, he is a usurper of the position he now claims. He planned to destroy everything of beauty, order, peace, and love in the creation of God.

God So Loved the World

One must distinguish between what God *can* do and what He has *chosen* to do. God chose to delegate free will and responsibility to created beings. He had an already extensive creation with innumerable affectionate creatures whose love and loyalty were intuitive. However, this was not enough. God desired a love given freely by choice. Creatures with free choice must be persuaded by love, not automated or intimidated by threat. Even Adam's choice to disobey must be respected!

Through deception, Satan broke the tie between God and Adam and claimed Adam and all his descendants as his own. However, Jesus came and paid the price for their sins. Through His great sacrifice, Jesus redeemed sinful humanity and opened an endless supply of grace. His redeemed creation He would continue to rule, and He would continue His blessings for the human family.

> Shall the prey be taken from the mighty, or the lawful captive delivered? But thus saith the Lord, Even the captives of the mighty shall be taken away, and the prey of the terrible shall be delivered: for I will contend with him that contendeth with thee, and I will save thy children. And I will feed them that oppress thee with their own flesh; and they shall be drunken with their own blood, as with sweet wine: and all flesh shall know that I the Lord am thy Saviour and thy Redeemer, the mighty One of Jacob. (Isa. 49:24–26)[4]

Once humans sinned, God did not stand idly by. "Behold, he that keepeth Israel shall neither slumber nor sleep" (Ps. 121:5). The plan of salvation, which was presented to Adam and Eve the day they sinned, provided a way of escape: the covenant of grace. "And I will put enmity between thee and the woman, and between thy seed and her seed; it shall bruise thy head, and thou shalt bruise his heel" (Gen. 3:15; cf. Rom. 16:20).

This is the promise and the hope of the covenant. Mankind was not to be helpless before Satan. The law of God, written on their hearts, provided an inborn sense of right and wrong. Included in the everlasting covenant is God's mandate for people to follow their conscience to do what is right. Here are the two parts of the promise:

- "It [the seed of the woman] shall bruise thy [Satan's] head": the "seed of the woman," the Sin Bearer, would destroy sin and Satan.
- "And thou [Satan] shalt bruise his [the Sin Bearer's] heel": sin would be destroyed but only through the suffering of the Sin Bearer.

Authority of the Prince

Humans do not always consider the necessary authority of God in the events of their lives. Through His anticipated sacrifice, Christ bought all of humanity and placed it in a position of favor with God (1 Cor. 6:20). God's gift of grace, with the consent of our free will, will restore in us the image of God. With this in mind, several things become clear:

1. Blessings come only through the authority of Christ and His sacrifice on the cross.
2. In Old Testament times, blessings, answers to prayer, and even God's interventions were given in anticipation of the cross of Christ. In New Testament times, these blessings are given by faith in what Jesus has already done at Calvary.
3. The presence of even one righteous person refutes Satan's claim on this world (Job 1:6–8).
4. When God's people sin and excuse their faults, Satan taunts Christ and the holy angels that Jesus died in vain.[5]

Endnotes

1. Christ is "the Prince of Peace" (Isa. 9:6). He is also "the prince of the host" (Dan. 8:11); "the Prince of princes" (Dan. 8:25); "the Messiah the Prince" (Dan. 9:25); "Michael, one of the chief princes" (Dan. 10:13); "Michael your Prince" (Dan. 10:21); "prince of the covenant" (Dan. 11:22); "the great prince" (Dan. 12:1); "a Prince and a Saviour" (Acts 5:31); and "the prince of the kings of the earth" (Rev. 1:5).
2. Satan is called "the prince of the power of the air" (Eph. 2:2) and "the prince of this world." "Now is the judgment of this world: now shall the prince of this world be cast out" (John 12:31; see also John 14:30 and 16:11). Satan can claim this position only by default, or by the willing decision by people of the world.
3. The presence of even one righteous person is a challenge to Satan's accusations. "And the Lord said unto Satan, Hast thou considered my servant Job, that there is none like him in the earth, a perfect and an upright man, one that feareth God, and escheweth evil? Then Satan answered the Lord, and said, Doth Job fear God for nought? Hast not thou made an hedge about him, and about his house, and about all that he hath on every side? thou hast blessed the work of his hands,

and his substance is increased in the land. But put forth thine hand now, and touch all that he hath, and he will curse thee to thy face" (Job 1:8–11).

4.   For more on Satan's role in the conflict, see Job 1:6–8; John 12:31; 14:30; 2 Corinthians 4:4; and Ephesians 2:2.

5.   It is a special problem when God's people sin (Heb. 6:4–6). "If those who hide and excuse their faults could see how Satan exults over them, how he taunts Christ and holy angels with their course, they would make haste to confess their sins and to put them away. Through defects in the character, Satan works to gain control of the whole mind, and he knows that if these defects are cherished, he will succeed. Therefore he is constantly seeking to deceive the followers of Christ with his fatal sophistry that it is impossible for them to overcome. But Jesus pleads in their behalf His wounded hands, His bruised body; and He declares to all who would follow Him: 'My grace is sufficient for thee.' 2 Corinthians 12:9. 'Take My yoke upon you, and learn of Me; for I am meek and lowly in heart: and ye shall find rest unto your souls. For My yoke is easy, and My burden is light.' Matthew 11:29, 30. Let none, then, regard their defects as incurable. God will give faith and grace to overcome them" (Ellen G. White, *The Great Controversy* [Mountain View, CA: Pacific Press Publishing Association, 1911], p. 489).

Chapter 7
God's Covenant with Noah

And God saw that the wickedness of man was great in the earth, and that
every imagination of the thoughts of his heart was only evil continually. And it
repented the Lord that he had made man on the earth, and it grieved him at his
heart. And the Lord said, I will destroy man whom I have created from the face
of the earth; both man, and beast, and the creeping thing, and the fowls
of the air; for it repenteth me that I have made them.
Genesis 6:5–7

Many people today cannot believe that judgment is coming. While we should not be obsessed about the judgment, it is essential that we be prepared for it. Judgment has been poured out in the past. Take, for example, the worldwide flood of Noah, the destruction of Sodom and Gomorrah, the captivity of Israel and Judah, and the destruction of Pompey and Herculaneum. Other cataclysmic events have seemed to have a natural cause, but behind the scenes may be the hand of God. Prophets have spoken of an end-time judgment for centuries. After a long delay, people tend to forget that these long foretold events eventually happen. Not knowing when this judgment will occur, we need to commit ourselves to God now, on a daily basis.

Conditions Leading Up to the Flood

God drove Adam and Eve from Eden after they sinned. As the human race expanded, people soon forgot God. Eden was still present, but barring the way were "Cherubims, and a flaming sword which turned every way, to keep the way of the tree of life" (Gen. 3:24). With this daily reminder, how could people forget that there is a Creator God and that only by sin is the Creator separated from His children? God cursed the earth after sin entered the world (Gen. 3:17–19), but the curse as yet rested lightly. There was still incredible beauty everywhere. Living was easy. Wealth was well nigh universal. Vigorous and living over 900 years, humans had time for art, for science, and for wickedness of every imaginable kind, that is, until God saw that it had to stop (Gen. 6:5–7).[1]

As God looked over the earth, He saw "that the wickedness of man was great in the earth, and that every imagination of the thoughts of his heart was only evil continually" (Gen. 6:5). In contrast with the rest of the people, God found Noah "a just man and perfect in his generations" (Gen. 6:9). Noah wasted no time in building the ark "... according to all that God commanded him" (Gen. 6:22). God made a covenant with him to save him and his family (Gen. 6:18), even as the flood destroyed all else. His family had faith that Noah communicated the message of God.

God patiently gave the people of earth time to repent. Noah preached for 120 years (2 Peter 2:5; Gen. 5:32; 7:6) to people who had never seen a flood and had never seen it rain (Gen. 2:5, 6). What Noah said was unscientific, unexpected, and unbelievable. Hundreds listened to Noah preach. Thousands knew of the ark. It was a monument to all, but only Noah and his family chose salvation. In the ark God also saved a sampling of all the animals.

Though the ark could not have been large enough to save everyone who lived on earth, the people had Noah's patient example of building an ark for 120 years. There was plenty of time for people to make arks for themselves!

Evil thoughts and decadent lifestyles gradually came into the world. Thus, the cumulative condition of society was not alarming. One hundred twenty years is a long time! Yet, if sacred history teaches us anything, it is that events long foretold will eventually happen. The time to make preparations is always the present![2]

Covenant with Noah

The covenant with Noah was unique, but, of course, so was the Flood event itself. It was without equal. Nonetheless, the wording of the covenant puts it in line with other covenants in the Bible. To build an ark of such proportions with hand tools was a monumental task, but finally the ark was complete. Then God announced: "With thee will I establish my covenant; and thou shalt come into the ark, thou, and thy sons, and thy wife, and thy sons' wives with thee" (Gen. 6:18).

God's statement was a formal announcement. Calling it "My covenant" makes this covenant God's unique possession. The Bible repeats this term in Genesis 9:9, 11, and 15. In verse 16, the term "everlasting covenant" is equivalent to "My covenant."

Aside from the stupendous events of building the ark and the flood itself, we see God covenanting to maintain and support the human race throughout human history. God gave promises and instructions in His covenant to Noah (Gen. 6–9).

- God saved the family of Noah (Gen. 6:18), using the word "covenant" for the first time.
- He instructed them to be fruitful and increase in number and fill the earth (Gen. 9:1, 7).
- He changed their diet to allow them to eat the flesh of animals. However, they were not to eat or drink the animals' blood (Gen. 9:3, 4).[3]
- He prohibited murder: "Whoso sheddeth man's blood, by man shall his blood be shed" (Gen. 9:6).
- He promised not to destroy the human race again by a flood (Gen. 9:8–11).
- He gave the rainbow as the "sign" (or "token," KJV) of the covenant (Gen. 9:12–17).
- Noah offered a sacrifice of animals on an altar (Gen. 8:20).

Changes After the Flood

After the waters subsided, God renewed the covenant He made with Noah before the flood (Gen. 6:17, 18), giving, as a token of His covenant with the human family, the rainbow, which is depicted as surrounding His throne in heaven (Ezek. 1:28; Rev. 4:3). He gave it as an everlasting assurance that He would never again send a universal flood upon the earth.

> And I will remember my covenant, which is between me and you and every living creature of all flesh; and the waters shall no more become a flood to destroy all flesh. And the bow shall be in the cloud; and I will look upon it, that I may remember the everlasting covenant between God and every living creature of all flesh that is upon the earth. And God said unto Noah, This is the token of the covenant, which I have established between me and all flesh that is upon the earth. (Gen. 9:15–17)

Seedtime and harvest, cold and heat, summer and winter, day and night would conform to normal cycles. Life would be secure. Large and unmanageable animals would be restrained by their fear of humans (Gen. 9:2). God liberalized the diet, giving permission to eat green herbs and flesh, and He covenanted to never again curse the ground because of humankind's sin or to destroy all living creatures as He did in the flood (Gen. 8:21, 22).

The Commands Given to Noah

Some people believe that God only intended the commandments that He gave to Noah for the whole of humanity and not the Ten Commandments, which they believe He gave only to the Hebrews. God's explicit commands to Noah included:

1. The command to be fruitful, multiply, and fill the earth (Gen. 9:1)
2. Permission to eat flesh food (Gen. 9:3)
3. Prohibition against eating blood (Gen. 9:4)
4. Prohibition against murder (Gen. 9:6)

These four commands are clearly outlined in Genesis 9. In the thinking of some, there were six additional commands given to Noah, including proscriptions against idolatry, blasphemy, sexual misconduct, theft, eating the limb of a live animal, and the positive command to set up courts of justice. The list varies according to the source. To arrive at this additional list of commands, Genesis 1–6 must be included, and some of these commands are merely implied.

As good as the additional commands are, it is highly unlikely that the principles of the Ten Commandments were unknown before Sinai or that God only intended the Noatic commands "for everyone in the world" while the Ten Commandments were just for the Jews. The commands given Noah have only limited scope and are of a different character from the principles of the Ten Commandments given at Sinai.[4]

Endnotes

1. There comes a time in the affairs of men and nations that evil reaches such a level that God brings judgment. The Bible uses the metaphor of "the cup" to symbolize either God's limit for wickedness or the maximum blessing a person can enjoy (Ps. 11:6; 75:8; Isa. 51:17, 22; Jer. 25:15, 17, 28; Ezek. 23:31–33; Rev. 14:10; 16:19; 18:6). The cup may be full of suffering (Matt. 20:22, 23; 26:39, 42; Mark 10:39; 14:36; John 18:11) or of false doctrine (Rev. 17:4). The righteous may receive a cup that is full or overflowing (Ps. 16:5; 23:5; 116:13) with blessing (1 Cor. 10:16) or with consolation (Jer. 16:7).

2. The time to accept God is *now* (Acts 17:30; 22:16; Rom. 13:11; 2 Cor. 6:2; Heb. 3:7, 13, 15; 4:7).

3. Some take the statement, "Every moving thing that liveth shall be meat for you; even as the green herb have I given you all things," (Gen. 9:3), as permission to eat unclean animals, however, had Noah and his family eaten any one of the pairs of unclean animals coming out of the ark, it would have defeated the very purpose that God brought them to the ark—"to keep them alive" (Gen. 6:19).

4. The record of the patriarchal age gives evidence that the ten precepts listed in the Ten Commandments, though not codified, were understood. Even in insisting that the Ten Commandments were not given to the patriarchs, D. M. Canright wrote: "That the main principles and requirements of this code were taught to the fathers in some way no one can doubt" (Dudley M. Canright, *Seventh Day Adventism Renounced* [New York: Fleming H. Revell, 1889], 14 ed., p. 320).

    1.) "Thou shalt have no other gods before me." Abram was made to know the one true God, and he abandoned the gods of Ur of the Chaldees (Gen. 12:1; 13:4). Melchizedek blessed the name of the "most high God" and Abram acknowledged "the most high God" as "the possessor of heaven and earth" (Gen. 14:20, 22). False gods were not mentioned until Abraham's grandson Jacob was confronted about the "gods" of his father-in-law, and he buried the "strange gods" carried by his family under the oak of Shechem (Gen. 31:32; 35:4).

    2.) "Thou shalt not make unto thee any graven images …" We recognize that the patriarchs knew that there is only one God to be worshipped by Jacob's command to "put away the strange gods that are among you" (Gen. 35:2–4).

    3.) "Thou shalt not take the name of the Lord thy God in vain." Abraham required his servant to fulfill his pledge to find Isaac a wife, as he swore "by the LORD God of heaven" (Gen. 24:2, 3).

    4.) "Remember the Sabbath day to keep it holy …" Evidence for the existence of the Sabbath from the creation include: (a) the Lord God's predication of the holiness and blessedness of the Sabbath upon His resting and blessing the Sabbath at creation, as is described in the Genesis account. (b) The natural sense of the parallel wording between Genesis 2:3 and Exodus 20:11 is that the Sabbath was considered holy and blessed from the creation on. (c) It is not reasonable to postulate that God alone rested while Adam worked on the seventh day. That Adam observed the Sabbath is acknowledged by Martin Luther (Martin Luther, George V. Schick (trans.), Jaroslav Pelikan (ed.), *Luther's Works*, vol. 1, "Lectures on Genesis," Chapters 1–5, [Saint Louis: Concordia Publishing House, 1958], pp. 79, 80). (d) That God was *assuming* the holiness of the Sabbath in Exodus 16 rather than *declaring* it holy on that occasion is evidence that the holiness of the Sabbath originated before Sinai (Exod. 16:23). (e) Another evidence that the patriarchs were aware of the creation account and the significance of the seventh day, indirect though it may be, is the prominence in Genesis of both the number seven and the seven-day unit of time. The two most frequent groupings of days in Genesis are *three* and *seven*; they are both used six times. The grouping of seven-day periods in the account of Noah is noteworthy (Gen. 7:4, 10; 8:10, 12). (f) Also, the story of Jacob and Rachel uses the term "week" metaphorically for a period of seven years, implying that the people of this era were aware of the seven-day weekly cycle, which ends with the seventh-day Sabbath, or at least had been aware of it.

    5.) "Honor thy father and thy mother." Evidence of patriarchal awareness of honoring parents is found in the disrespect of Ham and the respect of Shem and Japheth for their father, Noah (Gen. 9:22–27).

    6.) "Thou shalt not kill." Awareness of the moral command against murder is in the sad story of a brother who killed a brother (Gen. 4:8–13) and in the treachery of brothers plotting the death of a brother (Gen. 50:17).

    7.) "Thou shalt not commit adultery." Joseph recognized that "lying with" his master's wife would be committing a "great wickedness and sin against God" (Gen. 39:7–9).

8.)   "Thou shalt not steal." Jacob's sons recognized stealing to be wrong (Gen. 44:8).

9.)   "Thou shalt not bear false witness." God exposed Cain's lie to cover up the death of his brother (Gen. 4:9). Jacob's lie about being Esau ended in alienation from brother and separation from his mother (Gen. 27:24, 42, 43).

10.) "Thou shalt not covet." Eve's coveting of the prohibited fruit, caused the fall of the human race (Gen. 3:6). Abram magnanimously forwent taking spoils so others would know that his blessings are from God and not from mercenary actions (Gen. 14:23).

Chapter 8

Abraham, Chosen for Covenant

Now the Lord had said unto Abram, Get thee out of thy country, and from thy
kindred, and from thy father's house, unto a land that I will shew thee: and I will
make of thee a great nation, and I will bless thee, and make
thy name great; and thou shalt be a blessing.
Genesis 12:1, 2

With God's command to leave his home and relatives and go to a land that God would show him, Abram promptly obeyed and set out with his nephew Lot for the land of Canaan.

In time, God would change Abram's name to *Abraham*, which means the "father of many nations" (Gen. 17:5). God specially chose him to receive His covenant. Abram was not perfect, and, consequently, God led him through a series of tests in some ways more severe than He would give nearly any other human. By grace, Abram learned faith and became a towering figure in the purpose of God. "And Abram took Sarai his wife, and Lot his brother's son, and all their substance that they had gathered, and the souls that they had gotten in Haran; and they went forth to go into the land of Canaan; and into the land of Canaan they came" (Gen. 12:5).

The Call of Abram

When Adam and Eve sinned in Eden, God announced the plan of salvation based on the everlasting covenant He gave them. Through the prophesied Redeemer and the cross of Calvary, God bought back the human race and gave them a new probation, placing within them a conscience, an enmity against evil. This was the covenant of redemption, which became effective for the entire human race.

God next gave the covenant of redemption to Noah and his descendants. It was a covenant to preserve the human race and life on the planet. After the worldwide flood, the human race again turned away from God; and sin, apostasy, and idolatry were everywhere. God found, in Abram, a man who, like Noah, would respond to His special calling.

> Get thee out of thy country, and from thy kindred, and from thy father's house, unto
> a land that I will show thee. And I will make of thee a great nation, and I will bless
> thee, and make thy name great; and thou shalt be a blessing: And I will bless them
> that bless thee, and curse him that curseth thee: and in thee shall all families of the
> earth be blessed. (Gen. 12:1–3)

In this statement, God used the pronoun "I" five times:

- "Unto a land that *I* will shew thee …
- "*I* will make of thee a great nation …
- "*I* will bless thee, and make thy name great …
- "*I* will bless them that bless thee, and curse him that curseth thee …
- "In thee shall [*I* bless] all families of the earth."

In the repeated use of "I," God showed His personal interest in Abram and what He would do for him. This was the everlasting covenant and the essence of the new covenant. God also promised Abram His presence as Abram continued to obey God's voice (Gen. 26:3–5).

In Abram, God would raise up a people to preserve His name among the nations of earth and prepare for the coming of the Messiah. For this purpose, God gave him promises as a foretaste of His covenant. Abram packed up his caravan and set out for Canaan. "They went forth to go into the land of Canaan; and into the land of Canaan they came" (Gen. 12:5).

Abram was seventy-five years old when he started his trip. He had one wife, the beautiful Sarai, but they had no children. How would God make of him a strong nation? How would all the families of the earth be blessed through one who had no son? (Gen. 12:3; 28:14; Gal. 3:16). Abram exercised faith in God in obeying His command to leave Haran and go "unto a land that I will shew thee" (Gen. 12:1). He believed that God would fulfill His covenant.

Promise of Protection; His Own Son to be Heir

When famine came to Canaan, Abram went to Egypt. After Abram's return from Egypt, God again spoke to him, promising that Abram would have descendants "as the dust of the earth" and that God would give him the land on which he dwelt (Gen. 13:15–17).

Four kings from the east made war on five local kings (Sodom, Gomorrah, Admah, Zeboim, Bela) in Canaan and held them in servitude for twelve years. The Canaanites rebelled but failed to gain independence. The kings from the east returned and sacked Sodom, confiscated their goods, and took prisoners, including Lot and his family.

Love of pleasure and wickedness characterized Sodom and the other "cities of the plain" (Gen. 13:12). The wealth of these cities had attracted the invasion of the four kings of the east. Behind the scenes was God's hand, giving Sodom and the other cities of the plain a warning about their need to repent of their wickedness.

The capturing of Lot and his family roused Abram to action. Though a peaceful man, he mustered an army of 318 trained servants and joined with his friends Aner, Eschol, and Mamre, and pursued the Babylonians. They routed the Babylonian army by strategy and surprise in a night attack, rescued all the prisoners, and recovered the confiscated goods. They chased the Babylonians all the way to Damascus and beat them so severely that the Babylonians did not attempt another such attack against Israel for 1,000 years.

God did not plan for Abram to become a man of war. There was no need for Abram to trust in arms, for God would be his shield (Gen. 15:1). Concerned that he still had no son, Abram suggested that perhaps Eliezer could be his heir to fulfill God's purpose (Gen. 15:2, 3). God responded by insisting that Abram's heir would be his natural child, and his descendants would be as numerous as the stars (Gen. 15:4, 5). Abram believed God and his faith was counted to him as righteousness (Gen. 15:6).

A Covenant Ceremony

When God added the promise of land, Abram's faith wavered (Gen. 15:7). He asked God, "Whereby shall I know that I shall inherit it?" (Gen. 15:8).

God initiated a covenant ceremony with Abram, according to the custom of the people. At sundown, Abram fell into a deep sleep, "and, lo, an horror of great darkness fell upon him" (Gen. 15:12). The Bible does not explain the significance of these words. Several Bible verses tell us that God is light and the source of light (1 John 1:5; Rev. 22:5). Other verses associate sin and evil with darkness and the absence of God. With this as a background, the expression "an horror of great darkness" suggests that Abram looked into an eternity of darkness without life and without God. Such a great darkness Jesus looked into when He cried out on the cross, "My God, My God, why hast Thou forsaken Me?" (Matt. 27:46).

God then revealed to Abram that he and his descendants would be in Egypt 400 more years. It had been thirty years since Terah left Ur with Abram (Gen. 11:31). Adding another 400 years to their deliverance from Egypt would be a total of 430 years (Exod. 12:41).[1] At the time of fulfillment there had arisen a king who "knew not Joseph" (Exod. 1:8). Fearing that Israel would side with the Hyksos, who had just been driven out, the Egyptian Pharaoh began to afflict them and enslave them. God delivered Israel after the fourth generation of their enslavement—on the very day that the 430 years ended (Exod. 12:41).

To complete the covenant ceremony, God, as "a smoking furnace and a burning lamp … passed between" the pieces, totally consuming them (Gen. 15:17). In keeping with recognized custom, God pledged Himself to fulfill His covenant with Abram, though it would be 400 years before his descendants would possess the land. The long delay disappointed Abram, but God needed for him to show patience as He was giving more time for the Amorites to repent (Gen. 15:16).

Jesus would ratify the everlasting covenant of God on the cross. (Daniel 9 said that He would "confirm" it.) What then was this ceremony? God directed this ratification ceremony after promising land to Abram. Abram asked: "Lord God, whereby shall I know that I shall inherit it?" (Gen. 15:7). As a kindness to Abram, God again emphasized the promise of land (Gen. 15:18).

Did God twice ratify the everlasting covenant He gave Abram? God reassured Abram by a covenant procedure in Genesis 15 that he would receive the land. This was a singular covenant, which God gave only to reassure Abram that his descendants would, in truth, receive the land. It contains no mention of the everlasting covenant, which Jesus would ratify by His sacrifice on the cross.

The Covenants of God with Abram

Before the creation, the three persons of the Godhead formed the everlasting covenant of God.[2] The Father gave the Son, who came to earth as a man and died on the cross, and the Holy Spirit mediated grace to change the lives of sinners. Some instances of the covenant use other terms: the new covenant refers to the covenant's ratification at Calvary after the ratification of other covenants. The covenant God called "My covenant" was His unique possession. Yet, He made the covenant *for* humankind. The covenant of grace, also called the covenant of redemption, describes the main purpose and action of this covenant, which was to bring salvation to earth. These terms all refer to God's everlasting covenant.

Thirteen years later, God again appeared to Abram to tell him to "walk before me and be thou perfect" (Gen. 17:1). This may have been as a warning to Abram that he might not act again in mistrust as he did in attempting to gain an heir through Hagar.[3] God is patient; this time He presented the covenant to Abram in greater detail (Gen. 17:1–8; 19–21).

God again promised that Abram would have a multitude of descendants. Abram believed Him and fell on his face in reverent awe, believing that God would do as He said. God changed Abram's name to *Abraham*, meaning "father of a great multitude." He would also be the father of nations and kings.[4] The covenant again included the land where he lived and the covenant promise of His being their God: "And I will give unto thee, and to thy seed after thee, the land wherein thou art a stranger, all the land of Canaan, for an everlasting possession; and I will be their God" (Gen. 17:8).[5]

The addition of circumcision as a token of the covenant may have been because of Abram's mistake with Hagar. One should note that circumcision was not the covenant itself but was only the token of the covenant. (There will be more on this in our next chapter.)

God also changed the name of Sarai to Sarah. God promised that Sarah, at ninety years of age, would have a son. Abraham silently laughed and offered, "O that Ishmael might live before thee!" (Gen. 17:18). God responded that Sarah would bear a son within the year and the son's name was to be Isaac. The name means "laughter," which is an appropriate name since Abraham and Sarah's laughter of unbelief would turn into laughter of joy at the birth of their miracle child (Gen. 17:17; 18:12; 21:6). Isaac, and Isaac alone, would be the covenant son.

God presented the covenant to Abram with incredible promises right from the first. In the first four presentations, God gave promises; in the last three, He made a covenant. The covenant specified *land* in six of these seven presentations. God gave the covenant on each occasion, associated with significant events in Abram's life. Here is a summary of the seven presentations:

1. Genesis 12:1–3. God called Abram to leave his kindred and go to "a land that I will shew thee:"
2. Genesis 12:7. When Abram arrived at Shechem, the Lord promised him the land of Canaan. Abram built an altar.
3. Genesis 13:14–17. Abram and Lot separated. God promised Abram land and many descendants. Abram settled at Mamre and built an altar.
4. Genesis 15:1–6. After the battle with the four kings, God came to Abram in a vision, saying: "I am thy shield." It was not the will of God for Abram to be a man of war. God promised Abram protection, a naturally born son, and that his own descendants would be as numerous as the stars of heaven. Abram "believed in the Lord, and he counted it to him for righteousness."

5. Genesis 15:7–18. After God promised him land, Abram asked, "Whereby shall I know that I shall inherit it?" God directed a unique covenant ceremony to ratify the promise of land. It would be another 400 years before the land would be theirs.

6. Genesis 17:1–19. God presented the covenant in greatest detail at this time. He repeated all the previous promises. He changed Abram and Sarai's names to Abraham and Sarah. God repeated the term "My covenant" eight times and the term "everlasting covenant" three times. He gave circumcision as the "token of the covenant" (Gen. 17:11).

7. Genesis 22:16–18. "By myself have I sworn," the Lord declared. God gave the covenant to Abraham the last time after Abraham obeyed God in going up the mountain to sacrifice Isaac. All nations were to be blessed through the seed of Abraham. Abraham understood this promise to include not just a multitude of descendants but the Messiah (Gal. 3:16).

Endnotes

1. "In the fourth generation, they shall come hither again" (Gen. 15:16). The language in these verses is difficult. The Egyptians did not enslave Israel while they were in Canaan or during the first part of their sojourn in Egypt. Their enslavement did not happen until the Egyptians drove out the Hyksos kings and Egypt regained its sovereignty.

2. The triunity of God was explained in chapter 1, "The Everlasting Covenant."

3. Hagar's story is found in Genesis 16. It seemed to Abram that God needed help to fulfill the covenant. Abram arranged to have a child by their maid Hagar. With her pregnancy, Hagar tried to usurp the place and authority of Sarai, causing trouble between Sarai and Hagar. When Ishmael was a teenager, he "mocked Isaac," and Abraham banished him and his mother from the camp. God is forgiving and merciful, and He gave Ishmael a covenant (Gen. 21:13, 17–21).

4. The descendants (or "seed") of Abraham would receive the covenant throughout history.
    *   Isaac (Gen. 26:2–5, 24)
    *   Jacob, with his dream of the ladder (Gen. 28:13–15), after he wrestled with God (Gen. 32:26–29), when he received the name Israel (Gen. 35:10–12), and when he was promised that he would return from Egypt to the promised land and become a great nation (Gen. 46:2–4)
    *   Abraham, Isaac, and Jacob (Lev. 26:42; 1 Chron. 16:14–18; Ps. 105:8–11, "the covenant which he made with Abraham, and of the oath unto Isaac; and hath confirmed the same to Jacob for a law, and to Israel for an everlasting covenant")
    *   Moses (Exod. 3:5, 14–17, "The Lord is the God of your fathers, the God of Abraham, of Isaac, and of Jacob")
    *   The children of Israel (Exod. 4:29–31, "the Lord who looked upon their affliction"; Exod. 6:2–8, the same one who "appeared unto Abraham, unto Isaac, and unto Jacob"; Exod. 19:4–6, "keep my covenant" and you will "be a peculiar treasure unto me above all people … a kingdom of priests, and an holy nation")
    *   Those who belong to Christ (1 Peter 2:9, 10, "ye are a chosen generation, a royal priesthood, an holy nation, a peculiar people … which in time past were not a people, but are now the people of God"; Gal. 3:29, "And if ye be Christ's, then are ye Abraham's seed, and heirs according to the promise.")

5. Minus the land, this promise was echoed in the language of the new covenant in Jeremiah 31:33 and Hebrews 8:10.

Chapter 9

Circumcision:
Token of the Covenant

This is my covenant, which ye shall keep, between me and you and thy seed after thee; Every man child among you shall be circumcised. And ye shall circumcise the flesh of your foreskin; and it shall be a token of the covenant betwixt me and you.

Genesis 17:10, 11

Circumcision has always been a significant ritual for the Israelite nation. It was, possibly, the most notable token of membership among the chosen people. The significance of circumcision has always been a matter of discussion. One aspect of its significance was to keep the nation pure that there might be a people through whom the Messiah could come. After the Messiah came and provided the true sacrifice for sin, circumcision was no longer meaningful.

Another aspect of its significance is that God wanted them to see circumcision as a symbol of entire obedience and holiness in the life. God has always been disappointed when people depended on circumcision alone as a qualification for belonging to Him.[1]

Children of Abraham

Abraham and his descendants had a strong self-identity as God's chosen covenant people.[2] God chose Abraham to receive the covenant, a legacy to his descendants throughout time, reinforced by the detailed system of laws given at Sinai. The Sabbath became a sign of the close relationship between God and His people, tangibly demonstrating their belief in His being a loving and approachable God who desires their fellowship (Exod. 31:13; Ezek. 20:12, 20). Yet, circumcision was to be the physical token of the covenant, identifying Abraham's descendants as followers of the living God.

It was in giving the covenant that God changed Abram's name to Abraham (Gen. 17:5), meaning "to be populous, the father of a multitude." In this same setting, God provided the token of circumcision. When Abraham understood the will of God, his obedience was prompt. On the same day that God explained the meaning of circumcision, Abraham circumcised every male in his household (Gen. 17:23).

In Jewish tradition, circumcision is the primary symbol of male membership within the Jewish people and the sign of entry into the covenant made with Abraham. The Jews performed the rite of circumcision (*brit milah*) on the eighth day. Creation took place in six days; the seventh day was the Sabbath; our first parents began their work together on the eighth day. The Hebrew child also received his name on the eighth day. When God rejected the nation of Israel as His chosen people, circumcision no longer had value, and it would have no religious significance for the Christian church.[3]

Is circumcision itself a "covenant?" There is no punctuation in the original manuscripts, hiding the division in thought in Genesis 17:10. The first part of the verse, "This is my covenant, which ye shall keep, between me and you, and thy seed after thee" (Gen. 17:10), is a summary of the covenant previously described (Gen. 17:2–9). The second part of the verse, "Every man child among you shall be circumcised," introduces how circumcision was to be practiced (Gen. 17:11–14). Verse 11 clarifies the relation between circumcision and the covenant, declaring that God gave circumcision as "a token of the covenant," not as a covenant in itself.

In Acts 7:8, we find, in several translations, the problematic phrase "the covenant of circumcision." However, the Amplified version clarifies that circumcision is the "seal" of the covenant, and the New Century Version calls it the "sign" of the covenant.[4] In other words, "the covenant of circumcision" means the covenant *that includes* circumcision as its sign. In no passage does the Bible specifically say that circumcision is the covenant itself. Moreover, the rite of circumcision lost its significance at the cross.[5]

The commonwealth of Israel required non-Jews to be circumcised to become members of the community and receive the benefits of the covenant.[6] At the time of the Passover in Egypt, non-Jews could partake of the Passover only if circumcised and, in effect, became Jews. "He that is born in thy house, and he that is bought with thy money, must needs be circumcised: and my covenant shall be in your flesh for an everlasting covenant" (Gen. 17:13).

The Jews also spoke of circumcision in a figurative sense. The Philistines were called "the uncircumcised" (Judges 14:3). This was literally true, but the term came to be practically equivalent to the word "heathen" or "Gentile." Jeremiah referred to Israel as being "uncircumcised in the heart" (Jer. 9:26), and "their ear is uncircumcised" (Jer. 6:10). To have uncircumcised ears and heart is to be unwilling to heed divine instructions.

To Preserve the Family

God gave the everlasting covenant to Abraham with the promise and prophecy, "in thy seed shall all the nations of the earth be blessed" (Gen. 22:18). The promise is fulfilled in Christ, through whom Abraham's descendants would teach all peoples holiness and faith in the true and living God (Gal. 3:14, 16). In response to these promises, Abraham "believed in the Lord; and he counted it to him for righteousness" (Gen. 15:6; Rom. 4:3). Because of his faith, Abraham commanded his household after him, walked as if in the presence of God, and accepted circumcision as a sign of the covenant (Gen. 17:23 27; 18:19).[7]

Considering that circumcision was a rite symbolizing the dedication to God of man's reproductive and family life to preserve Abraham's heredity in preparation for the coming Messiah, one can see why this rite would come to an end once the Messiah had come. This is exactly what happened (Acts 15:1, 5, 19–21; Rom. 2:21–29; 1 Cor. 7:19). The council at Jerusalem upheld the law but ruled that Gentiles who come to God are not required to keep any part of the law of Moses except for four things: "abstain from meats offered to idols, and from blood, and from things strangled, and from fornication" (Acts 15:29).[8]

Circumcision was also a symbol of purity. Once a person had chosen his mate with care, no one was to come between a man and his wife or break the circle of their home. Their heredity was to be closely guarded. They were to follow the laws of healthful living. Homes were to be happy, a foretaste of heaven. Children were to learn a useful trade and to value work. The education and the example of the home life were to be preserved from generation to generation. To be circumcised meant to dedicate one's lifestyle to God, to prepare a people to receive the Messiah.

Covenant Complete

Just before He died while hanging upon the cross of Calvary, Jesus cried with a loud voice, "It is finished" (John 19:30). He had paid the price for humankind's redemption. Without retaliation, He had met the demands of the broken law. He had taken the worst that Satan could give Him. He could say, "The prince of this world cometh, and hath nothing in me" (John 14:30). The battle was now over, and Jesus Christ was the victor![9] "And, behold, the veil of the Temple was rent in twain from the top to the bottom; and the earth did quake, and the rocks rent" (Matt. 27:51).

Jesus fulfilled the moral law by living a sinless life and becoming an example to all His followers. He fulfilled the ceremonial law by His willing sacrifice on the cross.[10] Jesus' victory on the cross provides grace for every Christian to live a victorious life. The "hour" for people to worship God "in spirit and in truth" had come (John 4:23, 24). The Temple in Jerusalem would be destroyed, and the ceremonies, rituals, and sacrifices no longer had significance. Among these was circumcision, though it continued to be an issue in the New Testament church (see Acts 15).

Circumcision was never to be a physical sign only. Dedication of the heart and mind were of even greater importance, even from the first. Moses had said, "And the Lord thy God will *circumcise* thine *heart*, and the heart of thy seed, to love the Lord thy God with all thine heart, and with all thy soul, that thou mayest live" (Deut. 30:6, emphasis supplied).[11]

Endnotes

1.   God has always wanted circumcision to be more than "skin deep," as the following examples demonstrate. "*Circumcise* therefore the foreskin of your *heart*, and be no more stiffnecked" (Deut. 10:16, emphasis supplied). "And the Lord thy God will *circumcise* thine *heart*, and the heart of thy seed, to love the Lord thy God with all thine heart, and with all thy soul, that thou mayest live" (Deut. 30:6, emphasis supplied). "*Circumcise* yourselves to the Lord, and take away the foreskins of your *heart*, ye men of Judah and inhabitants of Jerusalem: lest my fury come forth like fire, and burn that none can quench it, because of the evil of your doings" (Jer. 4:4, emphasis supplied). "But he is a Jew, which is one inwardly; and *circumcision* is that of the *heart*, in the spirit, and not in the letter; whose praise is not of men, but of God" (Rom. 2:29, emphasis supplied).

2.   Through Abraham, Israel was the "chosen people of God." In the language of the covenant given to Abraham, God declared that He would "be a God unto thee [Abraham], and to thy seed after thee" (Gen. 17:7). Long before this, Adam and Eve had a close relationship with God. God took a personal interest in Adam's creation and acted openly in a number of

the events of his life (Gen. 2). When sin increased in the world, Noah stood out as "a just man and perfect in his generations" (Gen. 6:9). These verses emphasize that God has always had a "chosen people" and that Israel would become that people (Deut. 7:6; 14:2; 1 Chron. 16:12, 13; Ps. 33:12; 89:3, 4; 105:6; 135:4; Eph. 1:4, 5; 1 Peter 2:9; Rev. 17:14).

3. Circumcision was a token of the covenant, *not* the covenant itself. The Bible uses "everlasting covenant" sixteen times but never in reference to circumcision. In Genesis 17:11, God declared circumcision to be a "token" of the everlasting covenant. As some have said, circumcision is a *sign* of the everlasting covenant, *not* the everlasting sign of the covenant!

4. Similarly, the rainbow was said to be the "token" of God's covenant with humanity following the flood (Gen. 9:12, 13, 17). The Hebrew word for "token" is also translated "sign." The Sabbath is called the sign of sanctification of the relationship between God and His people (Exod. 31:13, 17; Ezek. 20:12, 20).

5. Baptism became the sign of the church (Col. 2:11, 12; cf. Gen. 17:11; Titus 3:5; 1 Peter 3:21).

6. Non-Jews were accepted and allowed to participate in Israel's festivals (and could marry into their families) if their males were circumcised (Gen. 17:10–13, 23; 34:14–17; Exod. 12:43–48). For more on circumcision, see Ronald L. Eisenberg, *The JPS Guide to Jewish Traditions* (Philadelphia: The Jewish Publication Society, 2004), pp. 7–13; and Francis D. Nichol, ed., *Seventh-day Adventist Bible Commentary* (Washington, D.C., Review and Herald Publishing Association, 1953), vol. 1, pp. 322, 323.

7. Dr. Ralph F. Wilson has written an excellent article that covers important aspects of circumcision at http://www.jesuswalk.com/abraham/6_circumcision.htm, accessed 7/20/12. One must understand that circumcision was not the sum total of the covenant but was rather the "sign" or "token" of the covenant (Gen. 17:11), an important part of the covenant, nevertheless.

8. Gentiles were called "strangers" in Leviticus. The four requirements for Gentiles in Acts 15:20, 29; 21:25 parallel the four requirements for "strangers" in Leviticus 17:10, 12, 15, 18:26; 19:3, 4.

9. The victory that overcomes the world is faith in our Lord, Jesus Christ (1 Cor. 15:57; 1 John 5:4, 5; Rev. 12:11).

10. Whenever I use the term "ceremonial law," I am referring to the ceremonial requirements of the law aside from the moral code of the Decalogue, as recorded in the "book of the law of Moses," sometimes called "the law of Moses" or merely "the law" (Josh. 8:31; 23:6; 2 Kings 23:25; 2 Chron. 30:16; Dan. 9:13; Luke 2:22; Heb. 7:5).

The term "ceremonial law" has been commonly used by writers of different backgrounds in describing the ceremonial requirements of the law. Search on "ceremonial law" in Google Books and you will find older and more recent uses of the term. See, for example: William Barclay, *The Gospel of Matthew* (2001); Albert Barnes, *Notes, Explanatory and Practical on the Gospels* (1836), vol. 1; Rudolph Bultmann, *Theology of the New Testament* (1951); F. F. Bruce, *The Epistle to the Hebrews* (1990); John Calvin, *Institutes of the Christian Religion* (2008); Adam Clarke, *The Holy Bible Containing the Old and New Testaments* (1823); John Edmund Cox, *Protestantism Contrasted with Romanism by the Teaching of Each* (1852), vol. 1; Jonathan Dickinson, *Familiar Letters to a Gentleman* (1835); M. G. Easton, *Illustrated Bible Dictionary* (2006); Jonathan Edwards, *The Works of Jonathan Edwards, A.M.* (1840); John Flavel, *Whole Works of the Rev. Mr. John Flavel* (1799); Norman Geisler, *Christian Ethics: Contemporary Issues and Options* (1989); John Gill, *A Collection of Sermons and Tracts* (1773); Matthew Henry, *The Comprehensive Commentary on the Holy Bible* (1839); Charles Hodge, *Systematic Theology* (n.d.), vol. 2; Walter C. Kaiser, *The Promise-Plan of God: A Biblical Theology of the Old and New Testaments* (2009); James L. Kugel, *Early Biblical Interpretation* (1986); John Lightfoot, *The Works of the Reverend and Learned John Lightfoot* (1684); Martin Luther, *Commentary on Galatians, Luther* (2002); John MacArthur, *The MacArthur Bible Commentary* (2005); John Milton, *A Treatise on Christian Doctrine* (1825); A. W. Pink, *Studies in the Scriptures* (2001), vol. 9; Matthew Poole, *Annotations upon the Holy Bible* (1700); Thomas Ridgley, *A Body of Divinity* (1815); Charles Ryrie, Basic Theology (1999); Thomas Scott, *The Holy Bible, with Explanatory Notes* (1822); John Wesley, *Sermons on Several Occasions* (1825); and Henry A. Virkler, *Hermeneutics: Principles and Processes of Biblical Interpretation* (2007); etc.

Though the term does not appear in the biblical text, Moses did divide the law into various categories. First were the Ten Commandments (literally "the ten words"), also called the "testimony," which were inscribed in stone and deposited in the ark. Then there were also the *statutes, judgments,* and *laws* (Lev. 26:15; Deut. 5:31; 6:1; 7:11; 8:11; 11:1; 26:17; 30:16), which Moses wrote in a book (Lev. 26:45, 46). Nehemiah acknowledged these categories in describing what God gave on

Sinai: "Thou camest down also upon mount Sinai, and spakest with them from heaven, and gavest them right *judgments*, and true *laws*, good *statutes* and *commandments*" (Neh. 9:13, emphasis supplied).

11. Other references on circumcision of the heart (and ear) include Leviticus 26:41; Deuteronomy 10:16; 30:6; Jeremiah 4:4; 6:10 (ear); 9:26; Ezekiel 44:7, 9; Acts 7:51; Romans 2:28, 29. References on the inapplicability of circumcision for Gentiles include Acts 15:5–29; Galatians 2:3–5 (Titus, a Gentile, was not circumcised); Acts 16:1–3 (Timothy, whose mother was a Jewess, was circumcised, Luke says, "because of the Jews"); Galatians 5:6; 6:15; and 1 Corinthians 7:19.

Chapter 10

The Testing of Abraham's Faith

And He said, Take now thy son, thine only son Isaac, whom thou lovest, and get
thee into the land of Moriah; and offer him there for a burnt offering
upon one of the mountains which I will tell thee of.
Genesis 22:2

In Genesis 17, God gave the covenant with more detail than before. He also changed the names of Abram and Sarai to Abraham and Sarah and gave circumcision as a token of the covenant. God promised Abraham that Sarah would give birth to the covenant son. Abraham had accepted the idea that Sarah would never have a son, and he replied to God: "O that Ishmael might live before thee!" (Gen. 17:18). In response, God affirmed that the covenant son would be born of Sarah, though Ishmael would also be blessed.

A Promised Miracle Child

A short time after that conversation, as Abraham sat in the door of his tent, he saw three travelers coming down the dusty road (Gen. 18). Hospitality was his habit, so he ran to meet them, insisting that they stop for refreshment. As they ate and talked together, they asked, "Where is your wife Sarah?"

He might have thought, *How did these strangers know my wife's name?* Yet, he indicated no surprise, simply saying, "There, in the tent."

The One who spoke continued, "Sarah your wife will have a son."

When Sarah laughed, He added, "Is anything too hard for the Lord? I will return to you at the appointed time next year and Sarah will have a son" (Gen. 18:9–14, NIV). It was clear now who these visitors were and that the promised child would come through Sarah. They pointedly referred to "Sarah thy wife" twice but to Hagar not once.

Abraham, Friend of God, Intercedes on Behalf of Sodom

The men rose, and as they started down the road, One spoke to the others: "Shall I hide from Abraham that thing which I do? Seeing that Abraham shall surely become a great and mighty nation, and all the nations of the earth shall be blessed in him? For I know him, that he will command his children and his household after him, and they shall keep the way of the Lord, to do justice and judgment; that the Lord may bring upon Abraham that which he hath spoken of him" (Gen. 18:17, 19).

He continued, "The cry of Sodom and Gomorrah is great.... I will go down now and see" (Gen. 18:20, 21).

The Speaker meant for Abraham to overhear Him. Abraham quickly grasped the intent of their visit and took heart in the information given him. Sodom was going to be destroyed, but maybe Lot could be saved! Abraham stepped "before the Lord" (Gen. 18:22) as the other two travelers continued down the road toward their destination.

What followed was an intense negotiation in which Abraham tested the judgment and mercy of God. Abraham asked, "Wilt thou also destroy the righteous with the wicked?" (Gen. 18:13). Pleased with the intercession of Abraham, the Lord told him that He would save the city if there were fifty righteous. As negotiations continued, the Lord cut the number down to forty, then down to thirty, and, finally agreed that if only ten righteous were present, He would not destroy the city for their sake (Gen. 18:22–32; cf. Isa. 43:3, 4). The longsuffering of God comforted Abraham. *Surely, Lot has at least ten servants who would qualify!* he thought. Why, not long before, Abraham himself mustered a small army of 318 from his staff of servants!

Abraham had done what he could for Lot. He had, with fear in his heart, interceded directly with God as far as he dared. Sadly, Lot had been impotent in his witness in Sodom. Ten righteous people could not be found (Gen. 19).

Abraham had become the "friend of God," not because God was partial to Abraham, but because Abraham was partial to God.[1] Abraham loved God and had made Him first in his life. God was able to speak freely with him because Abraham had faith to believe incredible things of God.

What is the significance of the story of Sodom in the overall history of the covenant of God? It is that God will go to extraordinary lengths to save souls. He had warned the people of judgment when the four kings of the east invaded the cities of the plain some years before; He would have saved a whole wicked city if He could find ten righteous persons there (Gen. 18). God is extremely patient; Israel had to wait over 400 years because "the iniquity of the Amorites" was "not yet full" (Gen. 15:16).

God had shown that He is merciful. Yet, He is also just, for there is a point beyond which He will not permit evil to flourish without passing judgment. Sodom had passed that point. God had to destroy Sodom and limit wickedness in the earth. Likewise, in the end time, God will destroy evil on this earth and restore the planet to Edenic purity and beauty.

The Test of Faith

When Abraham was 120 years old and Isaac about twenty, God commanded Abraham to take Isaac and offer him for a burnt offering in the land of Moriah. Only Abraham received this command (Gen. 22:1, 2). Neither Isaac nor the two servants, who went with them, knew what God had said. "Early in the morning," Abraham, the two servants, Isaac, and the donkeys carrying their supplies set out on their journey (Gen. 22:3).

Isaac and the servants did not think their object strange, for Abraham regularly offered burnt offerings to God. As they approached the mountain, Isaac asked, "Where is the lamb for the burnt offering?" Abraham replied, "My son, God will provide himself a lamb for a burnt offering" (Gen. 22:7, 8). Isaac did not notice the tears in his father's eyes as Abraham turned his face away.

Abraham and Isaac went alone to the top of the mountain. Isaac learned that he was to be the sacrifice. At twenty years of age, Isaac could have easily resisted his elderly father. However, Isaac had learned that his father had a close relationship with God. Trusting God and his father, he willingly helped his father in the difficult task, allowing himself to be bound and put on the altar.

As Abraham raised the knife to take the life of his son, just then, an Angel called from heaven, "Lay not thine hand upon the lad, neither do thou any thing unto him: for now, I know that thou fearest God …" (Gen. 22:12). A noise behind the patriarch caught his attention. A ram was caught in a nearby thicket. God had indeed provided the sacrifice.

Abraham had learned to recognize the voice of God and to trust Him without question. He did not know how God would fulfill His promises *before* He gave him Isaac, and He did not know how God would make him a father of a great nation if he sacrificed his only son. Yet, he had learned to trust God.

This sacrifice was a dramatized parable to instruct another "only begotten Son." Many years later, a twelve-year-old only begotten Son would visit the Temple and observe the sacrifices and learn their meanings. He would remember that Abraham was willing to sacrifice his only son. Through that story, the boy Jesus would learn more of His Father's will for His own life.

When God Tests

God severely tested Job, as He did for Abraham. In the story of Job, we see that God allows tests and trials only by His permission. "Then Satan answered the Lord, and said, Doth Job fear God for nought?… And the Lord said unto Satan, Behold, all that he hath is in thy power; only upon himself put not forth thine hand. So Satan went forth from the presence of the Lord" (Job 1:9, 12).

We also recognize that God limits the tests and temptations according to one's capacity. Paul wrote: "There hath no temptation taken you but such as is common to man: but God is faithful, who will not suffer you to be tempted above that ye are able; but will with the temptation also make a way to escape, that ye may be able to bear it" (1 Cor. 10:13).

Abraham knew that God would fulfill His covenant. He had faith to believe that if he sacrificed Isaac, God would raise him up from the dead to make His covenant promise possible. "By faith Abraham, when he was tried, offered up Isaac: and he that had received the promises offered up his only begotten son, of whom it was said, That in Isaac shall thy seed be called: Accounting that God was able to raise him up, even from the dead; from whence also he received him in a figure" (Heb. 11:17–19).

Isaac, Quiet Man of Peace

In Genesis 17, God gave Abraham the covenant in greater detail. He promised that Abraham would be the "father of many nations" (Gen. 17:4, 5). He also emphasized that the covenant was for "thy seed after thee" (Gen. 17:7–10). For emphasis, He repeated the first quoted phrase four times and the second quoted phrase, six.

We do not associate Isaac with any great events. We might even think that he was a rather passive link between Abraham and Jacob. On the other hand, heroes stand out in times of crisis when they might not even be noticed in times of peace. With this in mind, what can we find out about Isaac?

God appeared to Isaac and presented the covenant to him on two occasions. The first was when he went to Gerar to live among the Philistines. God promised Isaac all the land that He had promised to Abraham. He repeated the promise about having descendants as the stars of heaven, and He added, "in thy seed shall all the nations of the earth be blessed." (Gen. 26:2–4).

Later, Isaac moved to Beersheba and God again appeared to him, saying: "I am the God of Abraham thy father: fear not, for I am with thee, and will bless thee, and multiply thy seed for my servant Abraham's sake" (Gen. 26:23–24).

The godly example of his father, Abraham, strongly influenced Isaac. When God had commanded Abraham: "Take now thy son, thine only son Isaac, whom thou lovest, and [go unto] the land of Moriah; and offer him there for a burnt offering" (Gen. 22:2), Isaac was then a young man capable of having ideas of his own. However, Abraham had taught Isaac to obey the voice of the Lord, and Isaac recognized that God had again guided his father in what to do. Even though it meant his becoming a burnt offering, Isaac willingly cooperated with his aged father, allowing Abraham to bind him as the sacrifice. Yet, as we know, God interrupted the sacrifice and provided a ram to be used instead.

In later years, Isaac loved peace and moved several times rather than fight over wells for watering. God gave Isaac the Abrahamic covenant to pass on to his descendants.

Jacob, Tenacious Man of Action

Isaac's son Jacob was a man, who, with considerable difficulty, overcame his personality defects and the wrong choices of his younger years. He deceived Isaac into giving him the birthright blessing (Gen. 27:6–29) and fled to avoid his brother's wrath (Gen. 28:11). As he slept by the path with a stone for a pillow, God came to him in a dream, giving him the covenant of Abraham (Gen. 28:12–15; cf. John 1:51).

After twenty years, Jacob began his return trip to Canaan. He sent his family, servants, and animals ahead while he stayed to pray by the brook Jabbock. There he was accosted by what he thought was a man and wrestled all night for his life. As dawn was breaking, the one he had been wrestling "touched the hollow of his thigh" and put it out of joint (Gen. 32:25). Jacob then realized that it was not a man at all, but an angel with whom he had been wrestling. He held onto the angel, saying: "I will not let thee go, except thou bless me" (Gen. 32:24–30; see Gen. 35:10–12 for the blessing). With the blessing, Jacob was given a new name, Israel, which became the name of his nation thereafter.[2]

The covenant given to Abraham was to extend to all his descendants. Isaac and Jacob were the first of these. God gave His covenant directly to Isaac and to Jacob. There would be many other presentations of the covenant during the history of Israel and of the Church in the New Testament (Gal. 3:29).

Endnotes

1. Abraham is described as "the friend of God" (Gen. 18:1–8; 2 Chron. 20:7; Isa. 41:8; James 2:23).

2. The Hebrew word *Yisra'el* is translated "Israel" in the KJV 2489 times and as "Israelites" sixteen times. It means, "he will rule as God." It is the symbolical name of Jacob and of his posterity (Strong's no. 3478, James H. Strong, *A Concise Dictionary of the Words in the Hebrew Bible; with Their Renderings in the Authorized English Version* [New York, Cincinnati: The Methodist Book Concern, 1890]).

Chapter 11
Moses, Prepared to Lead

Come now therefore, and I will send thee unto Pharaoh, that thou mayest
bring forth my people the children of Israel out of Egypt.
Exodus 3:10

For His chosen people in the slavery of Egypt, God planned ahead. In His foreknowledge, His plans for them were perfect. In the eternity before the creation, He made a perfect plan of salvation that human beings might be saved should they sin. Yet plans are dependent upon human response, while the purpose of God is sure and will always be fulfilled. God chose Abraham and, through a series of events, led him into an understanding of God's covenant.

When Israel was in Egypt, enslaved and oppressed, God chose and trained Moses to lead them out of Egypt to the Promised Land. Moses' life was dramatic from the time of his birth. Egyptian law required that all male infants be cast into the Nile and drowned. Meeting the letter of the law, Jochebed, Moses' mother, made a basket of reeds, waterproofed it with pitch, and put baby Moses into it, and set the basket afloat on the river Nile. Pharaoh's daughter, coming to bathe, found the baby and arranged to adopt him, offering his natural mother pay to nurse and care for him.

When Moses was twelve years old, Pharaoh's daughter took him to the palace and gave him an education appropriate for his class. Egyptian officials expected that Moses, a potential Pharaoh, would join the priestly caste. This he did not do. Rather, he chose to support the cause of the enslaved and oppressed Hebrews. One day, in mistaken pursuit of this cause, he killed an Egyptian taskmaster who was beating a Hebrew slave. When word of Moses' act became known, he fled for his life to the land of Midian (Exod. 2:15).

There, Moses met a family of girls herding sheep. When Midianite boys drove the girls away from the watering trough, Moses single-handedly sent the boys running in all directions, and the girls got home early that day and told their father what had happened. Now, any father with seven daughters is always on the lookout for a good husband. So, Jethro sent the girls back to invite their Egyptian defender home for supper.

Four-Hundred-Thirty-Year Sojourn

God had told Abram in a vision that his descendants would live in a foreign land for 400 years from the time of the vision. They would be afflicted and enslaved, but, "in the fourth generation," they would be delivered and return to Canaan, laden with gifts from the people of that foreign nation (Gen. 15:13–16).

Egypt controlled and administered Canaan during this time and considered Canaan a part of its territory. Throughout Abraham and Isaac's and most of Jacob's lifetime, Abraham and his descendants lived in Canaan. Jacob and his family went to live in Egypt proper about 1660 BC. Their sojourn of four hundred and thirty years began when Terah, Abraham's father, left Ur for Haran (Gal. 3:17; Gen. 11:31).

> Now the sojourning of the children of Israel, who dwelt in Egypt, was four hundred and thirty years. And it came to pass at the end of the four hundred and thirty years, even the selfsame day it came to pass, that all the hosts of the Lord went out from the land of Egypt. (Exod. 12:40–41)

Afflicted in Egypt

Jacob and his household moved to Egypt about 1660 BC (Gen. 37–50), marking the beginning of the second half of the prophesied 430 years (Exod. 12:40, 41). At the time, the Hyksos kings ruled Egypt (1730–1580 BC) and were friendly to the Hebrews. The Hebrews prospered in the land until the Hyksos were driven out in 1525 BC. Thutmose I was the first of a dynasty of Pharaohs who "knew not Joseph" (Exod. 1:8). The Egyptians enslaved Israel for eighty years until the "fourth generation" (Gen. 15:16), which ended with the exodus in 1445 BC.[1]

The following table shows the chronology of the exodus. Dates are all in years BC ("Before Christ") and are approximate. Each king is counted as reigning from his accession year to the accession year of the next king.

Kings of Egypt[2]	Dates BC	Biblical Events
Hyksos kings reign in Egypt	1730–1580	
	1660	Jacob moves to Egypt
Sekenenre begins revolt (inconclusive)		
Kamose drives Hyksos to eastern Delta		
Ahmose expels Hyksos from Egypt		
Thutmose I	1525	"Asiatic" slaves in Egypt
	1525	Moses born
	1513	Moses to palace at age 12
Thutmose II has a short reign	1508	
Hatshepsut, daughter of Thutmose I	1504	Moses' adopted mother
Thutmose III, co-regent with Hatshepsut	1485	Moses flees to Sinai
Thutmose III also has Asiatic slaves	1482	Pharaoh when Moses fled
Amenhotep II, pharaoh of the exodus	1450	

Kings of Egypt[2]	Dates BC	Biblical Events
	1445	Moses returned to Egypt
		Crown prince disappeared
		The exodus began
Thutmose IV, a younger son	1425	
Amenhotep III	1412	
	1405	Israel occupies Canaan
Amenhotep IV	1387–1366	

Years of Preparation

Moses was born in about 1525 BC. His own mother cared for him the first twelve years of his life. His adoptive mother, the princess, took him into the royal palace about 1513 BC (Exod. 2:1–10). He never forgot his early training or the faith instilled in him by his faithful mother.

> By faith Moses, when he was come to years, refused to be called the son of Pharaoh's daughter; choosing rather to suffer affliction with the people of God, than to enjoy the pleasures of sin for a season. (Heb. 11:24, 25)

In the palace, he received the best of the world's education and became mighty in word and deed. He would have been twenty-one years old when his foster mother became queen of Egypt. While he did remember what his mother taught him, his later education also influenced his thinking. It was natural for Moses to think of using force to solve problems, though it was not God's way.

Moses also had a tendency to take into his own hands the work that God had promised to do. He showed his impulsive nature when he killed the Egyptian. This was about 1485 BC, when he was forty years old (Exod. 2:11–15). God did not intend to deliver His people by warfare but through the manifestation of His own mighty power that His people might look to Him alone. Moses fled into the desert to spend forty long years herding sheep. He learned to be humble, and he unlearned much of what he had learned in the schools of Egypt.

During this time, he lived with Jethro, a descendant of Abraham through Keturah (Gen. 25:2). Quite likely Jethro knew the stories and legends of the creation and the flood. How fascinating it would be to hear the long conversations around the campfire between Moses and Jethro! Moses, trained in the highest science of his day, listened humbly as Jethro described God's interactions with the human family.

Hesitant to Lead

After forty years (about 1445 BC), God came to Moses in a burning bush that did not burn up (Exod. 3:2). God called Moses to return to Egypt to deliver His people—a difficult task. He was to go into the presence of Pharaoh, the most powerful king on earth and ask—no, demand—that Israel be allowed to leave.

Moses hesitated. God made extravagant promises of what He would do through Moses. Still Moses all but refused to go. Finally, "the anger of the Lord was kindled against Moses," and God promised to send Aaron to go with him (Exod. 4:14). During his forty years herding sheep, Moses had learned humility, but he also became weak in faith.

When God calls someone to service, He gives the person the needed abilities to succeed (Exod. 3:10; 4:1–5). It was the Lord God who would give Moses and Aaron the words to say (Exod. 4:10–12). It was the Lord God who also brought the plagues on Egypt so that Pharaoh would let the people go.

The Covenant in Egypt

Speaking from the burning bush, God identified Himself to Moses in relation to the covenant given to Abraham and repeated to Isaac and Jacob (Exod. 3:6, 8). He staked His character ("name") and reputation ("memorial") on fulfilling this covenant with Israel. "The Lord God of your fathers, the God of Abraham, the God of Isaac, and the God of Jacob, hath sent me unto you: this is my name for ever, and this is my memorial unto all generations" (Exod. 3:15).

Aaron came to see Moses, and together they returned to Egypt and repeated God's words to the elders of Israel. The elders knew from prophecy that the time for their deliverance was soon to arrive, but they also knew that the people had rejected Moses' leadership forty years earlier. Cooler heads prevailed as they realized that they would never be delivered if they rejected the means for their deliverance! Now Moses had reappeared as out of nowhere, and the people responded in faith and gratitude. "The people believed: and when they heard that the Lord had visited the children of Israel, and that he had looked upon their affliction, then they bowed their heads and worshipped" (Exod. 4:31).

Moses and Aaron entered Pharaoh's court with the message from the Lord, "Let my people go." Pharaoh immediately replied in determined rebellion against God: "Who is the Lord, that I should obey his voice to let Israel go? I know not the Lord, neither will I let Israel go" (Exod. 5:2). Because of this response, Egypt has come to symbolize atheism, hatred of God, and open rebellion against Him.

In staunch obstinacy, Pharaoh commanded that straw not be provided as before, yet the people were to make the same number of bricks. The people became discouraged. They had expected an easy deliverance. They had not yet learned faith, but God is merciful, and He renewed the covenant of Abraham, Isaac, and Jacob. He promised, "… I will take you to me for a people, and I will be to you a God" (Exod. 6:7). To Moses, God said:

> I am Jehovah: and I appeared unto Abraham, unto Isaac, and unto Jacob, as God Almighty; … I have heard the groaning of the children of Israel, whom the Egyptians keep in bondage; and I have remembered my covenant.… I am Jehovah, and I will bring you out from under the burdens of the Egyptians, and I will rid you out of their bondage, and I will redeem you with an outstretched arm, and with great judgments: and I will take you to me for a people, and I will be to you a God; … And I will bring

you in unto the land which I sware to give to Abraham, to Isaac, and to Jacob; and I
will give it you for a heritage: I am Jehovah. (Exod. 6:2, 3, 5–8, ASV)

Moses presented these words to the people, but their discouragement was much harder to dislodge
than their previous elation. "They hearkened not unto Moses for anguish of spirit, and for cruel bondage" (Exod. 2:9).

The elders initially showed faith and trust in God, while the people were weak, stressed and discouraged as they returned to work.

Tested Leadership

Before recounting the story of the exodus, as we shall do in the next chapter of this book, let us run
ahead and consider Moses' character as revealed in the wilderness with the people.

During the march through the desert, the people constantly complained. The ignorance and in-
fidelity of the people severely tested Moses' patience. In most cases, he immediately pled with God,
often interceding for the people. Yet, when he saw the rebellious, heathen festival at Sinai, his patience broke, and he threw down the tables of stone, written with the finger of God. This was the Ten
Commandments, the covenant of what God would do for the people through grace.[3]

The table may have broken and the people may have gone back on their pledge, but the everlasting
covenant can never be broken. God required Moses to make his own tables of stone for a replacement.
God once again wrote the words of the covenant. "My covenant will I not break, nor alter the thing that
is gone out of my lips" (Ps. 89:34). "Brethren, I speak after the manner of men; though it be but a man's
covenant, yet if it be confirmed, no man disannulleth, or addeth thereto" (Gal. 3:15).

For the second time, God revealed Moses' defect to him, in the hope that he would learn in time.
In loving concern, God tests His children over and over until they gain the victory over the fault in their
character or they choose to hold onto sin and lose their soul.

Moses' impatience showed itself again near the end of their forty years' wandering in the desert.
The people were again without water. Again, they chided with Moses for bringing them into the desert
from the gardens of Egypt, forgetting their sore bondage. Moses and Aaron fell on their faces before
the Lord. When God spoke, He told them to gather the people and speak to the rock (Num. 20:7–11).

Moses was under considerable stress. God had given him instructions, but his anger proved his
undoing. Instead of speaking to the rock as God had commanded, Moses called the people rebels and,
in anger, struck the rock with his rod. He had again taken into his own hands the work that God purposed to do. The rock, which produced water for the people, represented Christ (1 Cor. 10:4). For their
sins, Christ would be "smitten." Yet, Moses was to strike it but once, as Jesus was offered but once as
sacrifice forever (Isa. 53:4; Heb. 9:28). Thereafter, a sinner could come into His presence by prayer and
find forgiveness. To strike the rock a second time destroyed the symbolism.

This was an impetuous sin, and it was grievous because Moses was a leader. As a lesson to the people, God denied Moses and Aaron entrance into the land of Canaan. Humanly speaking, one cannot

blame Moses and Aaron for what they did. However, there is no excuse for sin—not even fatigue, frustration, or stress. Moses and Aaron openly disobeyed God's command. It was a public sin, and the reprimand must be public. Moses and Aaron would not be allowed to enter the land of Canaan. Aaron was first to see these consequences as he "went up into Mount Hor, in the sight of all the congregation" (Num. 20:27) and there died. His son Eleazar took his place. Later, Moses went up into Mount Nebo and laid down his life (Deut. 34:1–6).

The people must see that, even if Moses and Aaron confessed their sin and repented and God forgave them, they must bear the consequences of their sin. God had uniquely prepared Moses to deliver Israel and lead them to the Promised Land. This was possible because Moses chose to do the will of God.[4] Nonetheless, while Moses was one of the greatest men to ever live, he was still human. Now he must die on the edge of the Promised Land as a result of the loss of his temper. However, God would not allow His beloved servant to remain in the grave, but took him up to be in His presence (Jude 9; Matt. 17:3).[5]

Endnotes

1. "The date is based on a statement synchronizing the 480th year from the Exodus with the 4th year of Solomon, in which the foundation of the Temple was laid in the month of Zif (1 Kings 6:1). This year was, according to the chronology accepted for this commentary, 967/66 b.c., that is, the Jewish regnal year beginning in the fall of 967 and ending in the fall of 966 ... Thus the laying of the foundation in the month of Zif (approximately our May) would have occurred in the spring of 966 b.c. Then Zif in the 1st year, in which the Israelites left Egypt, was 479 years earlier than 966, which is 1445 b.c. This can be computed easily by the equation:

    If Zif in the 480th yr. = 966 b.c.

    then, going back 479 yrs. (479),

    Zif in the 1st yr. = 1445 b.c."

    (Francis D. Nichol, *The Seventh-day Adventist Bible Commentary* [Washington, DC: Review and Herald Publishing Association, 1978; 2002], vol. 1, p. 191).

2. *The Seventh-day Adventist Bible Commentary*, vol. 1, pp. 492, 502, 493, 189.

3. This was the Ten Commandments, the covenant encompassing what God would do for the people through grace. On Sinai, God offered the people the Abrahamic covenant. In this covenant, He promised to make of the people a "peculiar treasure ... a kingdom of priests, and an holy nation." The details of the Old Covenant of Sinai are found in Exodus 19–31. The ten-commandment law was "the testimony" and was kept inside the ark. The harmony of the universe depends on this law. It is a reflection of the character of God. When Adam sinned, he broke the law of God. If there had been no law, there would have been no sin (Rom. 4:15; 1 John 3:4). The wages of sin is death (Gen. 2:16–17; Rom. 6:23), but, in the council of the Godhead, Jesus agreed to pay the price for the broken law of God so that human beings might again have the opportunity to choose to serve God and have eternal life. As part of the covenant of God, the Ten Commandments provide the pattern for human's being an "holy nation" once again.

4. While it is true that Moses made a choice, it was only by the grace of God that he could hold onto that choice and live for God. "By faith Moses, when he was come to years, refused to be called the son of Pharaoh's daughter; choosing rather to suffer affliction with the people of God, than to enjoy the pleasures of sin for a season; esteeming the reproach of Christ greater riches than the treasures in Egypt: for he had respect unto the recompense of the reward" (Heb. 11:24–26). "... without faith it is impossible to please him: for he that cometh to God must believe that he is, and that he is a rewarder of them that diligently seek him" (Heb. 11:6). God's people depend on the new covenant, the covenant by which God

puts enmity against evil in the hearts of the woman and her seed (Gen. 3:15). From these texts, we see that Moses had a faith relationship with God. His God-fearing mother taught him from early childhood to depend on God. Moses made mistakes, but he never lost his faith.

5. Jude 9 says that Michael contended for Moses' body; Matthew 17:3 and Luke 9:30 say that Moses was alive, talking with Jesus.

Chapter 12
"Let My People Go!"

And the Lord said unto Moses, Rise up early in the morning, and stand before
Pharaoh, and say unto him, Thus saith the Lord God of the Hebrews,
Let my people go, that they may serve me.
Exodus 9:13

In the covenant with Abraham, Isaac, and Jacob, God promised them the land in which they then lived. It was a land that was fertile, productive, and located at the crossroads of the world. Israel was to be the place where the world would learn about the Messiah and about the salvation given through His sacrifice on the cross.

To accomplish this purpose, Israel must first be delivered from Egyptian slavery. God called Moses and Aaron to confront Pharaoh and lead the people out of Egypt. It was an unequal contest: Egypt, the greatest kingdom in the world, against Israel, an enslaved race. However, Israel had an advantage—the sovereign God was on their side!

Pharaoh demonstrated the classic spirit of rebellion against God. As a result, God allowed the plagues to fall on Egypt. Even though Pharaoh could not modify the plagues, or lessen the damage they caused, he refused to let the people go.

God's Power Over the False Gods of Egypt

The plagues called down upon the Egyptians showed the ineffectiveness of their gods (Exod. 12:12). Many individual Egyptians recognized this and joined the Jews, becoming "the mixed multitude" that followed the Israelites in the exodus (Num. 11:4). The plagues, in their order, were:

Nile turned to blood	Exodus 7:17, 18
Frogs	Exodus 8:2–4
Lice	Exodus 8:16, 17
Flies	Exodus 8:21
Murrain, animals die	Exodus 9:3
Boils	Exodus 9:9, 10
Hail	Exodus 9:18, 19
Locusts	Exodus 10:4–6
Darkness	Exodus 10:21, 22
All firstborn die	Exodus 11:4, 5

As one plague after another took its toll on Egypt, it became clear to the Egyptians what was happening. When Moses and Aaron threatened Pharaoh with a plague of locusts, the servants begged Pharaoh to let the people go (Exod. 10:4–7). They said, "How long shall this man be a snare unto us? let the men go, that they may serve the Lord their God: knowest thou not yet that Egypt is destroyed?" (Exod. 10:7). Pharaoh consented to let only the men go. Not accepting this partial answer, Moses stretched out his rod, and God covered the land of Egypt with locusts, which ate every green thing. Pharaoh begged for forgiveness and relief from the locusts. A strong west wind came and blew them into the Red Sea. Then, following his habitual pattern, Pharaoh hardened his heart again.

The most significant of the plagues was the tenth and last. After each of the previous plagues, Pharaoh had initially relented then hardened his heart and refused to let the people go. Pharaoh's persistent rebellion ended his probation, and now God worked mightily to accomplish His purpose. With the tenth and final plague, the crown prince was slain. Pharaoh finally let the people go. Yet, even then, when Israel left Egypt, Pharaoh changed his mind and pursued Israel with his armies. Under the mighty hand of the Lord, the pursuing army drowned in the Red Sea.

The Passover

The tenth plague began after the celebration of the first Passover feast. On that incredible night, the firstborn died in every house that was not marked by the blood of the lamb. Even among the cattle, there was death (Exod. 11, 12). The firstborn in houses marked with the blood of a lamb were protected. The Egyptians knew about the threatened plague; they could have been protected had they circumcised their men and united with God's people.

God had specified the procedures for the Passover: On the tenth day of the month, they were to provide a lamb of the first year, without blemish, and keep it as part of the household until the fourteenth day of the month. In the evening of the fourteenth, they were to kill the lamb and use hyssop to strike the blood on the doorposts and the lintel of the door.

They were then to roast the lamb with fire and eat it with unleavened bread and bitter herbs. The meal was to be eaten in haste with everyone dressed for travel and with shoes on their feet and a staff in their hand (Exod. 12:11). After this, they were to continue eating unleavened bread for the following seven days (Exod. 12:15).

This became a regular festival every year for Israel, the most meaningful of their yearly feasts.[1] The lamb represented Jesus Christ and His blood, which was shed for the remission of sins. The lamb's four days with the family represented the almost four years that Jesus would minister among the people.[2] The unleavened bread represented the Bread of Life in which there is not the least impurity or sin. The festival was to be a constant reminder of the gospel of salvation, the focus of the covenant.

Jethro's Visit

After the exodus was well on its way, Moses had a visitor. It was his father-in-law Jethro. What a pleasant surprise!

"Jethro! O my father, Jethro! Are you here?"

"Yes, my son, I am here. And I have brought Zipporah and your two sons with me."

"Oh, my father Jethro, you do not know how glad I am to see you."

Immediately, Moses was taken back to his youth. He ran, bowed low, and threw his arms around the father of his wife. In the days to follow, Moses and Jethro were constant companions, talking, talking, and talking some more. So much had happened since they were last together. As Jethro sat with Moses during the day, people in unending lines came to him with their problems. Jethro noticed Moses' tired eyes, the deep lines of fatigue in his face, and the sagging of his shoulders. Finally, he had to speak:

"Moses, you are doing too much! You sit all day long listening to these people."

"Yes, father. This is a nation of slaves. I am trying to teach them God's laws and ways."

"But, Moses, you are killing yourself. You cannot do it all by yourself."

Jethro then conceded that Moses had done a good job in organizing the camp and the march. Yet, he needed to organize a government as well. There were able men in the camp. These must be chosen and made to be rulers over thousands, hundreds, fifties, and tens. They would judge the ordinary problems of life. Only the tough matters would then be brought to Moses.

Moses listened. The plan was eminently logical. Moses put it immediately into practice, with good results. Standing to one side, Miriam and Aaron talked quietly to one another, "Haven't we been telling Moses to do that for weeks? Now Jethro shows up and Moses listens to him and does what we were saying right away. Go figure!" (See Num. 12.)

Arrival at Sinai

Israel came now to rest at Sinai. Here they would have time to listen to God and become familiar with His will and covenant. While the civil law helped them to organize a society and the ceremonial law provided a framework for their worship, the moral law showed them the character of God, an ideal that they, personally, might reach through grace.

The "gods" that were everywhere in Egypt were anything but holy. Close association with people, who were immersed in wanton pleasure of all kinds, made the Israelites become very much like them. God purposed to demonstrate to them His majesty and holiness. They needed to understand the sinfulness of sin and their own inability to rise above their sinful nature. The people needed to know the life-changing power of God. They needed grace.

The history of the creation and the flood were now stories that had lost their impact. The miracles of the plagues in Egypt and even of the deliverance through the Red Sea meant for them that Jehovah merely had more power than the gods of the Egyptians. The people needed to know that there is only one God, the God of love, and they needed to appreciate His character.

The people learned about the judgments of God as they observed the effects of the plagues on the Egyptians. They learned about His mercy in the provisions of the Passover and about His power as they crossed the Red Sea on dry land. Every day they experienced His guidance from the pillar of cloud by day, and the pillar of fire by night. They ate manna from heaven, drank water from the rock, and were secured from raiding bandits after they defeated the Amalekites. The new plans for organization gave them a sense of pride about who they were.

Now it was the right moment for God to declare His covenant to the nation and for each person to make a commitment to Yahweh, the one true God.

Endnotes

1. Passover and unleavened bread were to be a "sign" and a "memorial" for Israel throughout their generations (Exod. 12:14; 13:9, 16).

2. Jesus' ministry was actually three and a half years, according to the harmony of the Gospels' account and according to the half "week" of Daniel 9:26, 27, marked by His being cut off and Israel's sacrifices coming to an end. The three and a half years would have been four years by inclusive reckoning because they counted *parts* of a day or a year as an additional day or year.

Chapter 13
The Sinai Covenant

Ye have seen what I did unto the Egyptians, and how I bare you on eagles' wings,
and brought you unto myself. Now therefore, if ye will obey my voice indeed, and
keep my covenant, then ye shall be a peculiar treasure unto me above all people:
for all the earth is mine: And ye shall be unto me a kingdom of priests, and an holy
nation. These are the words which thou shalt speak unto the children of Israel.
Exod. 19:4–6

God intended that the Abrahamic covenant should continue throughout Israel's history (Gen. 17:7). God renewed the Abrahamic covenant with Isaac and Jacob. He also renewed it with Moses at the burning bush at Sinai and with the elders of Israel through Moses and Aaron. Now back at Sinai, the people promised to obey God's voice and keep His covenant (Exod. 19:8).[1] These were excellent promises; yet, they were faulty in that they focused on law and the people's *doing* rather than on the grace that God offered them. The people reacted out of fear rather than faith when God came to them on the mount. Within forty-six days of the ceremony of ratification, they broke the covenant.

The Covenant Presented

Israel's presence before Sinai was evidence that God was fulfilling His covenant with Abraham. Now a nation, Israel was as figuratively numerous as the stars of the heavens. They were on their way to Canaan with promises from God that they would succeed and settle in the land. The covenant of Abraham, Isaac, and Jacob must now be given to the nation of Israel. The law of God must be written so all could understand and remember it. God called Moses into the mount and presented the covenant.

God knew, after they had been exposed for 215 years to the wanton idolatry of Egypt, that they had forgotten the covenant of Abraham and were not much different from the Egyptians. Slavery left the people dejected and ignorant. In saying, "Now, therefore," God reminded the people how He had delivered them from Egypt. He was saying that, by the same power that He used to free them, He would make of them His covenant people.

By His power and grace, God would write the law in their hearts and minds. Yet, they must consent to the work of grace, obey the law as He spoke it, and keep His covenant. They must respond as did Abraham; by faith "he believed in the Lord; and he counted it to him for righteousness" (Gen. 15:6). They were not to depend on mechanical obedience. God gave humans the gift of free will, which He will not override. Only when we believe and commit ourselves to God can He act for our benefit.

He gave them glorious promises on condition that they obey His voice (Exod. 19:5). God spoke the ten commandment law in the hearing of the people to instruct them regarding what obedience entailed. God wrote the Commandments on stone so that they would not forget. They were to "keep my covenant" (Exod. 19:5), He said. It was a covenant that had previously been given to Abraham and his descendants (Gen. 17:7): Isaac, Jacob, the children of Israel, and, through Jesus, the church (Gal. 3:29).[2]

> There is hope for us only as we come under the Abrahamic covenant, which is the covenant of grace by faith in Christ Jesus. The gospel preached to Abraham, through which he had hope, was the same gospel that is preached to us today, through which we have hope. Abraham looked unto Jesus, who is also the Author and the Finisher of our faith [Heb. 12:2].[3]

This covenant was the ten commandment law. It was a law that was "holy, and just, and good" (Rom. 7:12)—very different from the harsh demands of the taskmasters in Egypt.[4] The Sinai covenant was unique in that it emphasized obedience, yet it also promised grace to make obedience possible. Through His law, God would make of them "a peculiar treasure … a kingdom of priests, and an holy nation" (Exod. 19:6).

Was the Sinai Covenant Given Just to the Jews?

The promises given to Israel as a nation were an extension of those given to the patriarchs (Exod. 19:6; cf. Gen. 22:18). These promises are also applied to the church today (1 Peter 2:9), indicating that the covenant itself was not temporary, nor "old," neither was it about to "pass away." For the first time, in this covenant at Sinai, God asked a response of obedience. With Adam, Eve, Noah, and Abraham, He was already confident that they would obey.

Compare these two verses:

- "I will establish my covenant between me and thee and thy seed after thee in their generations for an everlasting covenant, to be a God unto thee, and to thy seed after thee" (Gen. 17:7).
- "If ye be Christ's, then are ye Abraham's seed, and heirs according to the promise" (Gal. 3:29).

Christians need to realize the debt we owe to Abraham and to the Jews. The covenant given Abraham was to continue to all "his seed." The phrase, "if ye be Christ's," makes all true Christians a part of that seed.

Perceptions

The people at Sinai knew about the covenant given to Abraham, the father of their nation and race. They could also understand that God had again given them the covenant. The promise of the land of Canaan was part of their heritage from Abraham. They knew and loved the God who had delivered them from Egypt, yet they knew very little about Him. They also knew about the gods of Egypt, and it was reasonable for them to imagine that the Lord God of Israel was like them. The heathen gods were selfish and demanding. Sacrifices were necessary to appease them. The gods were whimsical, threatening one moment while kind and helpful the next.

God saw that the people had much to learn and to unlearn. They had become too accustomed to the idolatry of Egypt and had largely forgotten the Redeemer who was promised in the sacrifices. They had seen the plagues on the Egyptians, experienced delivery through the Red Sea, been provided manna to eat and water to drink, and had stood under the pillar of cloud by day and the pillar of fire by night. They had good reason to trust God.

When God presented the covenant, He asked for a response, "*If* ye will obey my voice indeed, and keep my covenant ..." (Exod. 19:5, emphasis supplied). The people promised, "All that the Lord hath said we will do," and they repeated this promise twice more when they ratified the covenant. Their promises have come to be called the *historical* old covenant or the covenant of works. There is a sharp distinction between the covenant presented by God (Exod. 19:4–6) and the promises made by the people (Exod. 19:8; 24:3–11). The covenant they made through their promises was temporary, and their promises were broken within forty-six days.[5]

Two Classes of People

There have always been two classes of people on this earth: the people of the world and the people of God. This has been true all through history. Today there is the thinking, believing remnant, and there is the unthinking, unbelieving multitude.[6] Two classes can even be found in the church. We can see the contrast between true understanding and commitment to the covenant among the remnant and the thoughtless disregard of the covenant among the majority.

Among the majority of the Jews, the sacrifices and sanctuary services became the people's focus. They forgot the Redeemer to whom the symbols pointed. The sanctuary services and the sacrifices became a form of idolatry when they were seen as a means of salvation. It was a short step from this to frank image worship, which was a continual problem in Israel.[7]

The righteous remnant was sometimes a small remnant. Noah and his family are an example of this. So were Abraham and his encampment, the 7,000 of Israel in the time of Elijah who had not bowed the knee to Baal, those who waited *in expectation* for Jesus to come the first time, the early Christians who faced persecution, and the church in the wilderness during the Dark Ages. At present, the remnant are those who pray and read the Bible for themselves, following the Bible's teachings.[8]

It was a remnant who waited *in expectation* for Jesus to come and who understood the meaning of the covenant, the judgment, and the atonement. It is a remnant again who will sacrifice the world in preparation for Jesus' return.

A Parallel Track

It was the believing remnant who kept alive the hope of a Redeemer who would bring them forgiveness and everlasting life. At this same time, the unbelieving multitude developed an idolatrous view of the sacrifices and sanctuary services. They held a corrupted view of the Temple service as being redemptive in itself. It was this second view that was predominant when Jesus came to earth and that led to His rejection and eventual crucifixion.

Jesus' life was a testimony about who He was. His teaching, healing, and raising the dead were signs that He was "the Christ, the Son of the living God" (Matt. 16:16). The majority of the leaders and people refused to believe that Jesus was "Immanuel, God with us." They refused to believe even with the very direct testimony of the guards at the tomb when Jesus arose from the dead. Yet, God is patient. He gave Israel another three and a half years to observe the teaching and healings accompanying the work of the early church. The probation of Israel as a nation would come to a climactic end in Stephen's testimony and his stoning by the Sanhedrin. What more could God do to reach His people?[9]

Endnotes

1.   The people's response is recorded in Exodus 19:8; 24:3, 7, as part of the ratification ceremony of the *historical* old covenant. This covenant is both the first covenant and the old covenant because it was ratified before Jesus ratified the new covenant at Calvary.

2.   The Abrahamic covenant is identified by the promises given to Abraham. God promised Abraham that he would have as many descendants as the sand of the seashore or as the stars in the heavens. This is referring to the people of the world who would be brought to God through his descendants. God promised:
   - The land of Canaan was to be their home, an everlasting possession.
   - Abraham's descendants would be a blessing to all families (Gen. 12:3) and to all the nations of the earth (Gen. 22:18). They were to be a strong influence for righteousness in the earth, especially through the "one seed," which is Christ (Gal. 3:16).
   - Abraham's continued blessing would be on condition of obedience, for which God commended him. He said that Abraham commanded his household after him (Gen. 18:19) and that he kept God's laws, statutes, and ordinances (Gen. 26:5). Abraham's greatest test of faith and obedience came when God commanded him to sacrifice Isaac on Mount Moriah (Gen. 22:1, 2).
   - The Abrahamic covenant was to extend to Abraham's seed. When God spoke to Moses from the burning bush, He remembered His covenant, which He had given "unto Abraham, unto Isaac, and unto Jacob" (Exod. 6:3), and Moses repeated to the elders of Israel what God had said when He spoke with him (Exod. 6:8, 9).

3.   Ellen G. White, *The Youth's Instructor*, September 22, 1892.

4.   That the Ten Commandments are the covenant is substantiated in Exodus 31:18; 34:28; Deuteronomy 9:9, 11, 15; and Hebrews 9:4.

5.   I discuss the details of this event in the next two chapters, and Paul's exposition on Jesus' heavenly ministry, in chapter 37, "Christ Our High Priest."

6.   There are always two classes of people: the righteous remnant and the unbelieving careless multitude. It is the righteous remnant who kept the covenant, looked for a Redeemer through the sacrifices, and expected Jesus when He came.

7.   The unbelieving careless multitude went through the forms of religion, but forgot the Redeemer whom the symbols prefigured; then they rejected Jesus when He came and crucified Him in the end. The leaders in Judah fell into this group, making the rejection of Jesus a national tragedy. They compounded their error by the persecution of the church and the stoning of Stephen.

8.   The concept of the righteous remnant and examples of the same are found in Genesis 4:25, 26; 6:8–10; 12:1–3; 1 Kings 19:18; 2 Kings 19:31; Ezra 3:8; 9:8; Isaiah 1:9; 10:20–22; 11:11, 16; 37:32; Joel 2:32; Amos 5:15; Zephaniah 2:7, 9; 3:13; Haggai 1:12, 14; Romans 9:27; 11:4, 5; and Revelation 12:17.

9.   See chapter 35, "The Vision of Stephen."

Chapter 14
The Ten Commandments

And he declared unto you his covenant, which he commanded you to perform,
even ten commandments; and he wrote them upon two tables of stone.
Deuteronomy 4:13

God has called the Ten Commandments the covenant. It has long been the basis for the government of intelligent beings throughout the universe. For sinless beings, it was the only form of the covenant that they needed. Even then, sinless beings did not focus on the law but rather on the God whom they loved. In their close association, the attitudes and actions of God were an example and a command for His children in heaven and earth to do the same.

God designed the Ten Commandments as a reflection of His character. He made angels and human beings in His image, with God's law written in their hearts. Freedom of His creatures required the boundaries of law to assure harmonious interaction between His earthly and heavenly children. Human beings have recognized the justice and mercy of this law and have used the Ten Commandments as a basis for national laws in each country.

Sin and Its Consequences

After Adam and Eve sinned, the new reality of sin entered the world. As sin, disease, and oppression became common, humans quickly learned the results of breaking the law. Ever since Eden, they have recognized sin. There are gaps in the written history of the patriarchs, which were probably filled in by oral tradition. Every sin or crime identified in the Ten Commandment law was recognized as a sin long before Sinai.

The very nature of human beings had deteriorated so that many were obsessed continually with sin and wickedness (Gen. 6:5). Different forms of sin became increasingly common, including murder, theft, polygamy, covetousness, war, oppression, and idolatry. Sin had reached a threshold, beyond which God would not allow humans to go. The "cup" of the human race was "full" and judgment was due.

The presence of sin also implied a knowledge of God's law. It is the law that defines what sin is (Rom. 3:20; 5:13). The Bible does not say anything about Sabbath breaking in the patriarchal age, yet Israel knew about it before Sinai (Exod. 16:22–30).

Sinai

Now that God was dealing with a nation rather than just a family, they needed a written law. By His mighty power, God delivered Israel from Egypt. God sustained the people by water from a rock and by manna that fell each morning. The presence of God was constantly before them in a pillar of cloud by day and a pillar of fire by night.

Moses talked "face to face" with God. Messages from God also came from the Urim and Thummim carried by the high priest. The prophets of God gave additional guidance. The priests and Levites taught the people the laws of God.

In addition to all these blessings, the people were designated the "chosen people of God." A more humble evaluation is that they were barely a step away from being the slaves that made bricks for Pharaoh. God knew the people. They were stiff-necked and stubborn.[1] While they kept alive their identity as children of Abraham and their hopes in the covenant, they had also been exposed to the idolatry and wanton pleasures of the Egyptians for generations. They had much to learn and much to unlearn!

Avoiding Legalism Does Not Mean Discarding the Law

Is keeping the law legalism? People are quite willing to forget arguments of "legalism" when it comes to their neighbors. They want neighbors who keep the Ten Commandments! If legalism is unacceptable, it must be something different from just keeping the Ten Commandments, which all agree are essentially correct. A clear definition of legalism is when people spurn grace and keep the commandments as a method to earn salvation.

The Ten Commandments, which God wrote on stone with His own finger, God called "the covenant" and Moses put inside the ark.[2] There was also a "book of the law," or "book of the covenant," which included the civil and ceremonial laws. The civil law was an expansion of the Ten Commandments, and the ceremonial law was a "shadow" that pointed forward to the promised Redeemer (Heb. 8:5; 10:1). Moses kept this book at the side of the ark (Deut. 31:26).

Why was the law necessary? Martin Luther gave three uses for the law:

To restrain or curb external evil, which was the civil use[3]

To show one's sin, as in a mirror[4]

To show us God's character as a guide to holy living through grace.[5]

How God's Character and the Law of God Compare

God's Character	The Law of God
righteous (Ps. 119:137; 1 John 3:7)	righteous (Deut. 4:8; Ps. 119:172)
perfect, just, true, pure, right (Deut. 32:4)	true and good (Neh. 9:13)
perfect (Ps. 18:30; Matt. 5:48)	perfect and sure (Ps. 19:7)
merciful, gracious, longsuffering, good, true, forgiving, and just (Exod. 34:6, 7)	pure, (Ps. 19:8)
pure, peaceable, gentle, approachable, merciful, impartial, and righteous (James 3:17, 18)	broad, gives wisdom and understanding, protects from evil (Ps. 119:95–100)
holy (Lev. 11:44, 45; 19:2; 20:26; 1 Peter 1:16)	holy, just, and good (Rom. 7:12; 2 Peter 2:21)

God's Character	The Law of God
perfect, peace, love (2 Cor. 13:11)	the law of liberty (James 1:25)
love (1 John 4:7, 8)	good (1 Tim. 1:8)

It is natural for human beings to be legalistic. Sinful human beings are selfish and will often do things that are beneficial for others simply to achieve their own goals. Shall we then discard the law and break it whenever we feel like it in order to avoid legalism? We know instinctively that this is wrong. The law must be kept, though keeping the law does not save a person.

Obedient From the Heart

Obedience is a word that has a breadth of meaning, yet it leaves out much that is important. A Christian should focus on the positive aspects of the law. God created human beings "in the image of God" (Gen. 1:27). To be in the image of God is to have His law and character written on our heart as we become "partakers of the divine nature" (2 Peter 1:3–8).

Through grace, the Ten Commandments make God first in an individual's life. Nothing is to come between the individual and God. The individual will be pure in speech and will avoid hypocrisy, and the family will be pure, to the blessing of children and parents alike. By God's grace, the individual will treat his or her neighbor with kindness and love, avoiding hatred, lust, theft, and lying.

Christians must take hold of the power of grace through faith. They must consent—even decide—to obey, knowing that only by grace can their decision be firm. Through their love for God, they will desire to be like Him in character; and, through love to their neighbor, they will recognize their own debt to God. What they see in the attitudes and actions of God will be to them an example and a command to do likewise.

Can the Law be Kept?

What happened to Adam and Eve at their fall from grace? Their lives moved from being God-centered to being self-centered. All sin and sorrow came from self-centeredness. A person can do even admirable things for selfish reasons. Keeping the law for selfish reasons leaves a person's life unchanged, still under the control of sin and rebellion.

> "Teacher, which is the greatest commandment in the Law?" Jesus replied: "'Love the Lord your God with all your heart and with all your soul and with all your mind.' This is the first and greatest commandment. And the second is like it: 'Love your neighbor as yourself.'" All the Law and the Prophets hang on these two commandments." (Matt. 22:36–40, NIV)

Jesus summarized the Ten Commandments as love for God and love for our fellow human beings. If people lack love for others, they are selfish. If people lack love for God, they are proud and lack faith, refusing to follow the will of God. Pride, unbelief, and selfishness are the basic characteristics of the sinful nature and can be overcome only by the grace of God.

Knowledge of God and His law has merit only as it leads a person to Christ. Belief alone is not enough. "Thou believest that there is one God; thou doest well: the devils also believe, and tremble" (James 2:19).

At the moment of temptation, believers must consent to let Christ live in them. Is it easy? No, it is not! The battle with self is the hardest battle human beings ever have to fight. It is always easy to *do* something; it is often difficult to *submit* to Christ as Lord of our life.

By habitually turning to Christ with the temptations of daily life, Christians will "wear ruts" in the road so that, when great temptation comes, they can find their way in the dark. In the faith experience, Christ becomes real. We must think about Christ, talk about Him, focus our life on Him, and leave no room for sin.

The Saviour's Sabbath

In the middle of the ten-commandment law is the command to keep holy the seventh day as the Sabbath. In this command, the seventh day is to be kept holy because God made it holy.[6] God gave the "Sabbath of the Lord thy God" as a memorial to the creation. God is the Creator, and His domain encompasses all of "heaven and earth." The Sabbath command is God's "signature" in the middle of His law. It is also the "sign" of sanctification (Exod. 31:13; Ezek. 20:12, 20), and it is, therefore, a vital sign of the covenant that will make of His people "an holy nation."

> Remember the sabbath day, to keep it holy. Six days shalt thou labour, and do all thy work: But the seventh day is the sabbath of the Lord thy God: in it thou shalt not do any work, thou, nor thy son, nor thy daughter, thy manservant, nor thy maidservant, nor thy cattle, nor thy stranger that is within thy gates: For in six days the Lord made heaven and earth, the sea, and all that in them is, and rested the seventh day: where-fore the Lord blessed the sabbath day, and hallowed it. (Exod. 20:8–11)

Why does it need to be the *seventh* day? Would not another day be acceptable to worship God? What is wrong with keeping holy another day, or even keeping holy every day? As a measure of time, the seventh day is no different from the other days of the week. The day is holy because God made it so. He gave the Sabbath as a sign of human relationship with Him. Would humans accept God's will or would they choose to go their own way? It was an easy test and it was easy to understand. To break the Sabbath was wrong because it was forbidden, not because it was evil by nature. The Sabbath demonstrates whether people accept God as Creator and Lord and place God's will above their own reasoning. From reverent obedience to this command, obedience to the other nine naturally flows.

> Speak thou also unto the children of Israel, saying, Verily my sabbaths ye shall keep:

for it is a sign between me and you throughout your generations; that ye may know that I am the Lord that doth sanctify you. It is a sign between me and the children of Israel for ever: for in six days the Lord made heaven and earth, and on the seventh day he rested, and was refreshed. (Exod. 31:13, 17)

Moreover also I gave them my sabbaths, to be a sign between me and them, that they might know that I am the Lord that sanctify them. And hallow my sabbaths; and they shall be a sign between me and you, that ye may know that I am the Lord your God. (Ezek. 20:12, 20)

Another question follows: Why should the Sabbath commandment be kept any differently than the other nine commandments? Christians are insistent about the other nine. Did God not mean what He said about keeping the seventh day as the Sabbath? If Sabbath-keepers are legalistic or idolatrous because they keep the seventh-day Sabbath, what about those who keep the other nine? Are they not just as "legalistic and idolatrous?" These concepts need to be thought and prayed through. A person needs to ask the Holy Spirit for guidance. When Jesus said, "If ye love Me, keep my commandments" (John 14:15), He meant that keeping the commandments brings us closer to Him and, as we are closer to Him, we will want to do what pleases Him.

Is it essential then that we be accurate in our service to Christ? Are a person's sincerity and love for Christ not more important than "details?" Falsehood and error never bring honor to God, however innocent they may seem. Truth has consequences. Truth affects our relationship with God. A correct understanding of truth has often been an issue that divides those who seek to serve God from those who follow another master.

There is only one God, only one Holy Spirit, and only one truth. Our understandings may differ, but, by reading the Bible under the guidance of the Holy Spirit, we will learn the truth. "But the hour cometh, and now is, when the true worshippers shall worship the Father in spirit and in truth: for the Father seeketh such to worship him" (John 4:23). "Jesus saith unto him, I am the way, the truth, and the life: no man cometh unto the Father, but by me" (John 14:6).

Jesus kept the Sabbath. "As his custom was, he went into the synagogue on the Sabbath day" (Luke 4:16). He was more liberal than the Jews in Sabbath keeping. His teaching and practice did not follow the multitude of ordinances that the Jews had added to the law. Jesus stated that He was "Lord also of the Sabbath" (Mark 2:28). Like His women followers, Jesus rested in the grave over the hours of the Sabbath after the crucifixion (Luke 23:56). Looking forward forty years to the destruction of Jerusalem in Matthew 24, Jesus told the disciples that they were to pray that their flight be not in the winter or on the Sabbath day.

The last book of the Bible is "the Revelation of Jesus Christ" (Rev. 1:1). The four angels in Revelation 7 hold the four winds of trouble until God's people receive the seal. What is the seal? God gave the Sabbath as the "sign" of sanctification (Exod. 31:13; Ezek. 20:12, 20). The Holy Spirit seals (verb) God's people (Eph. 4:30), showing those who are His. Paul wrote: "Nevertheless the foundation of God standeth sure, having this seal, The Lord knoweth them that are his. And, Let every one that nameth the name of Christ depart from iniquity" (2 Tim. 2:19). The seal of relationship with God is being known of God and keeping the "righteousness of the law" (Rom. 2:26; 8:4). The seal (noun) of the law is the Sabbath of the fourth commandment, His signature in the midst of His law. In this way, the Holy Spirit prepares a special people to see Jesus when He comes again!

Endnotes

1. God described His people as a "stiffnecked people" (Exod. 32:9; 33:3, 5; 34:9; Deut. 9:6, 13; 10:16; 2 Chron. 30:8; Acts 7:51).

2. Moses put the two tablets inside the ark (Exod. 25:16, 21; 40:20; Deut. 10:2, 5) with the manna and Aaron's rod. "And I will write on the tables the words that were in the first tables which thou brakest, and thou shalt put them in the ark" (Deut. 10:2). Later, God instructed Moses to include a pot of manna and Aaron's rod that budded, "which had the golden censer, and the ark of the covenant overlaid round about with gold, wherein was the golden pot that had manna, and Aaron's rod that budded, and the tables of the covenant" (Heb. 9:4). "And Moses said unto Aaron, Take a pot, and put an omer full of manna therein, and lay it up before the Lord, to be kept for your generations. As the Lord commanded Moses, so Aaron laid it up before the testimony, to be kept" (Exod. 16:33, 34). "And the Lord said unto Moses, Bring Aaron's rod again before the testimony, to be kept for a token against the rebels; and thou shalt quite take away their murmurings from me, that they die not" (Num. 17:10). During the time of Solomon, there was "… nothing in the ark save the two tables of stone, which Moses put there at Horeb, when the Lord made a covenant" (1 Kings 8:9; cf. 2 Chron. 5:10).

3. "What I have stated earlier so often about both uses of the Law, the political or Gentile use and the theological use, indicates clearly that the Law was not laid down for the righteous but, as Paul teaches elsewhere (1 Tim. 1:9), for the unrighteous" (Martin Luther, *Luther's Works* [Saint Louis: Concordia Publishing House, 1999], vol. 26, comment on Gal. 3:23.)

4. "This is a more majestic and excellent teaching than is the Law, whose purpose is only to tell us what we are to do. The Gospel does not, however, dispose of the Law. For the Law is also the voice of God, and it is fitting for all to be subject to it. Yet even though the Law remains, the Gospel teaches something higher" (*Luther's Works*, vol. 12, comment on Psalm 2:7). "The other use of the Law is the theological or spiritual one, which serves to increase transgressions" (*Luther's Works*, vol. 26, comment on Gal. 3:19).

5. Luther never used the phrase "the third use of the law," but a recent work on Luther by Edward A. Engelbrecht, entitled *Friends of the Law: Luther's Use of the Law for the Christian Life* (St. Louis, MO: Concordia Publishing House, 2011), claims, "Luther maintained a third use of the law, even if he did not always use that specific phrase" (http://beggarsall-reformation.blogspot.com/2011/09/luther-maintained-third-use-of-law-even.html). Luther wrote: "It is proper that the Law and God's Commandments provide me with the correct directives for life; they supply me with abundant information about righteousness and eternal life" (*Luther's Works*, vol. 22, comment John 1:17).

6. It was at God's command that the seventh day was sanctified and blessed at Creation. Whether God ever gave a command to the Jews or not, the day became holy and blessed by God's command. Those who accept Genesis 2:1–3 as an actual account of the end of the creation account, recognize that the Sabbath was then blessed and sanctified by the Creator.

Chapter 15
The Historical Old Covenant

And he took the book of the covenant, and read in the audience of the people:
and they said, All that the Lord hath said will we do, and be obedient.
Exodus 24:7

Every believer needs to understand the difference between the old covenant and the new covenant. This can be complicated because the old covenant was presented in many forms and people use different terms to describe it. I have chosen to use the term *"historical* old covenant" to describe the covenant Israel made and ratified with God at Sinai. Within a another forty-six days Israel had already broken this covenant. The term "old covenant" does not occur in the Bible, except for "old testament" (2 Cor. 3:14) and "first testament" (Heb. 9:15). Yet, any attempt to gain pardon for sins, approval of God, or eternal life by human effort is the old covenant method!

The new covenant described in Jeremiah 31:31–34 is different from the covenant the children of Israel broke (Jer. 31:32). In the new covenant, God, by His initiative, puts the law in the human heart.

Hebrews 8 to 10 describes a covenant that was *first, faulty, decayed, old,* and *ready to vanish away.* It is *first* because it was the first covenant officially ratified between Israel and God. Jesus Christ ratified the second (or new) covenant on the cross (*Patriarchs and Prophets*, p. 370). The first was *faulty* because it was based on weak and presumptuous human promises, bypassing grace.[1] It is *decayed* because the law was corrupted by rabbinical additions and by the Jewish focus upon the performance of sacrifices and sanctuary services as the fulfillment of the "covenant" and the means of salvation. It was growing *old* and was *ready to vanish away* because its legitimate ceremonial aspects were no longer needed once Jesus died upon the cross and the Temple ceased to be (Heb. 8:13). Jesus is the Redeemer to whom the symbols in the ceremonial law pointed. In Jesus' time the ceremonial law had become a corrupted attempt by humans to gain salvation through their own efforts.

The Covenant at Sinai

The covenant of God, or "My covenant," was made in the eternity before the creation of the world in the council of the three persons of the Godhead. God made this covenant for humans, yet humans cannot break or modify it. God offered this covenant to Abraham, and Abraham "believed in the Lord; and [the Lord] counted it to him for righteousness" (Gen. 15:6). The Abrahamic covenant had two parts, the "My covenant" of God plus the faith response of Abraham.

God gave the covenant to Abraham in a series of seven presentations, with the greatest detail in Genesis 17. In His statement to Abraham, "I will establish my covenant between me and thee and thy seed after thee in their generations for an everlasting covenant" (Gen. 17:7), God intended this covenant to be effective throughout the history of Israel and the church. God gave the covenant also to Isaac, to Jacob, to Moses at the burning bush, and to the elders of Israel in Egypt.

Shortly after Israel arrived at Sinai, Moses went up into the mountain and communed with God. God presented to the people "My covenant," a covenant previously established: the covenant of Abraham (Exod. 19:4–6). God presented promises to Israel as a nation that were more glorious than the promises given to Abraham, Isaac, and Jacob. The covenant given at Sinai included the preamble of grace to give them strength to obey the ten-commandment law.[2]

The People's Promise

God asked for a response to "obey my voice indeed, and keep my covenant" (Exod. 19:5). "And Moses came and called for the elders of the people, and laid before their faces all these words which the Lord commanded him" (Exod. 19:7).

The people answered with enthusiasm, "All that the Lord hath spoken we will do. And Moses returned the words of the people unto the Lord" (Exod. 19:8). If God wanted them to "obey my voice and keep my covenant," that is what they would do. What else could they do for the God who delivered them from the Egyptians, took them through the Red Sea, and supplied them with water and food? They would *do* whatever He desired of them.

> And the Lord heard the voice of your words, when ye spake unto me; and the Lord said unto me, I have heard the voice of the words of this people, which they have spoken unto thee: they have well said all that they have spoken. O that there were such an heart in them, that they would fear me, and keep all my commandments always, that it might be well with them, and with their children for ever. (Deut. 5:28, 29)

Their words were commendable. It pleased God to have His people make a commitment to Him, but faith was lacking in their response. The people failed to understand the majesty and holiness of God and their own weakness. God accepted their words, but how could weak humanity add anything to the covenant of God (Deut. 5:28, 29)? While Abraham fell on his face in reverence before God, the elders of Israel confidently planned to do their part, as though they could be equal partners in a covenant with God![3]

God purposed to teach them lessons they needed to make a success. They must see His majesty, His holiness, and the power of His grace to be able to fulfill their promises. They must know that He is not just another god like the gods of Egypt. They must know that He is the one God, the Creator of heaven and earth. They needed to recognize that only God could make up for their weakness.

God Appears to the People

God gave Moses instructions for the people to wash their clothes and sanctify themselves for two days. On the third day, they were to come to the mount but not to go beyond the bounds set by Moses. If the people had put away all sin and worldly thoughts from their minds, leaving a deep hunger to know God, they would rejoice to see God when He came. They would be like Moses at the burning bush and remove their shoes, for the place where they stood was holy ground.

God came onto the mount with fire and smoke, a trumpet blast, thunder and lightning, and an earthquake. It was a demonstration of power and majesty never seen from the gods of the heathen (Exod. 19:16, 18, 19). God came to instill awe and holy fear at His presence. The people were to experience the power of God as Creator and Lord. God Himself stood behind His covenant and would fulfill its terms.

The demonstration came to a halt, and there was silence as, from the mountain, God spoke the ten-commandment law, also referred to as "the covenant." He spoke the law before the ratification ceremony so people would know what their promises entailed. The law was the pattern on which God would make of them "an holy nation."[4] They failed to understand the preamble of grace by which God would fulfill the promises of the Ten Commandments in their lives: "I am the Lord thy God, which have brought thee out of the land of Egypt" (Exod. 20:2). Instead, they endeavored to keep the law in their own power.

When people come into the presence of the living God in reverence and awe, it is a life-changing experience.[5] If they believed in a God who is "merciful and gracious, longsuffering, and abundant in goodness and truth" (Exod. 34:6), like Abraham, they would have fallen on their faces as God spoke to them (Gen. 17:3). Instead, the presence of God terrified them, and "they removed, and stood afar off" (Exod. 20:18). They asked Moses not to let God speak to them again, but rather that God speak through Moses to them.

In spite of what God had done for them, the people still had the heathen concept that God is vengeful and judgmental, seeking only to punish. God has always desired that His people come close to Him, but fear of God will not be totally resolved until shortly before Jesus comes again! At that time, He will have a people who have consented to the work of grace in their lives and who look for His coming with joy. Jesus' coming will terrify the wicked (Rev. 6:15, 16), as His presence terrified the Israelites. However, of the righteous, "It shall be said in that day, Lo, this is our God; we have waited for him, and he will save us: this is the Lord; we have waited for him, we will be glad and rejoice in his salvation" (Isa. 25:9).

The Response of Faith

Faith is the response of the human heart to the love of God. It is trust, belief, and an emotional commitment to God as to a friend. In faith, one takes hold of grace, which is the supernatural power of God to change the sinner's heart. The Holy Spirit, speaking through God's Word, initiates faith in the human heart (Rom. 10:17). God always respects the gift of free will that He gave to the human family. He awaits the response of faith to the covenant, which is to consent for God to work His will in the believer's life by His grace (Heb. 11:6). How does one come to Christ unless he takes these steps? One must do as Abraham did when he fell on his face in awe and believed all that God said He would do (Gen. 15:6). Belief is a form of decision because people live out everything they truly believe!

This is the new covenant relationship that God desires. "Ye have seen what I did unto the Egyptians, and how I bare you on eagles' wings, and brought you unto myself. Now therefore …" (Exod. 19:4).

The prayer that God always hears is the cry for help. In the Temple of Israel one day, a publican standing afar off "smote upon his breast, saying, God be merciful to me a sinner" (Luke 18:13). In this brief view, we find a man who recognized his need, recognized his inability to help himself, and fell upon the mercy and strength of God for the help he needed.

In answering that prayer, God possesses all that He requires, and He will give all the help that one needs. In gratitude, we can take no pride in what we have done, and we will thank God for what He has done. God looked in vain for the elders of Israel to recognize their need and show faith in Him as they responded to the covenant (Exod. 19:8).

In making these promises, the people forgot the power of God shown in their deliverance from Egypt; they indicated that they would obey God and keep His Commandments and covenant, but they did not have faith in His grace. They did not believe God, as did Abraham, but rather relied upon their own ability to obey. Their separate ratification ceremony lacked the faith response and further separated the covenant of human promises from the covenant presented by God (see Exod. 19:4–6). Only Jesus' sacrifice on the cross can ratify the everlasting covenant.

The Historical Old Covenant Ratified

Moses went into the mount where God gave him instructions regarding the civil law (Exod. 21–23). He also received a modified Abrahamic covenant consistent with their human promises.

> Behold, I send an Angel before thee, to keep thee in the way, and to bring thee into the place which I have prepared. Beware of him, and obey his voice, provoke him not; for he will not pardon your transgressions: for my name is in him. But if thou shalt indeed obey his voice, and do all that I speak; then I will be an enemy unto thine enemies, and an adversary unto thine adversaries. For mine Angel shall go before thee, and bring thee in unto the Amorites, and the Hittites, and the Perizzites, and the Canaanites, the Hivites, and the Jebusites: and I will cut them off. (Exod. 23:20–23)

The "Angel" or "Messenger" (Heb. mal'ak) was Jesus Christ, "for my name is in him" (Exod. 23:20, 21; cf. Mal. 3:1). God respected their promise to obey. Yet, in making their human promise, they failed to accept the grace that God promised. Other translations of this verse indicate that the sins that He will not pardon were rebellion, bitterness, and repeated conscious sins, which lead to the loss of the covenant (Heb. 6:4–6).

The people did not recognize the majesty and holiness of God and the comprehensive requirements of the holy ten-commandment law. They failed to recognize their own weakness and proceeded with ratification (Exod. 19:8), repeating their promises twice again, "All that the Lord hath said will we do, and be obedient" (Exod. 24:3, 7; Joshua 1:16). They forgot the grace that liberated them from slavery (Exod. 19:4).

Moses wrote these instructions in the "book of the covenant" (Exod. 24:7), which he read before the people. This book was an expansion of the Ten Commandments. It contained laws to govern civil affairs and details regarding the sanctuary, the priesthood, and the sacrifices.[6]

How did they ratify the covenant with God? They conducted a formal covenant ceremony in the presence of certain young men. As Moses repeated to them the words of the Lord, they responded with, "All the words which the Lord hath said will we do" (Exod. 24:3). They made animal sacrifices and Moses sprinkled blood on the altar, on the people, and on the book (Exod. 24:6–8; Heb. 9:19–21). The *historical* old covenant was in effect! Aaron, Nadab, Abihu, and the seventy elders of Israel ate a covenant meal in the presence of God.

The covenant was faulty, but it was not because God offered a faulty covenant. God offered the same covenant He gave Abraham and the same covenant Peter referenced in 1 Peter 2:9 for the Christian church. The old covenant was faulty because the promises of the people did not include the faith response. They broke their covenant by worshiping the golden calf (Exod. 32).

The Experiential Old Covenant Perpetuates Problems

The old covenant reappeared in Jewish history, with dependence on law keeping and on the rituals themselves as the means of salvation. The people made these rituals the sum and substance of their religion, obeying God's command by rote with no heart-felt obedience or change in their life. They even forgot the Redeemer to whom the sacrifices pointed and failed to recognize the Redeemer when He came.

This corrupted perception of the covenant constituted the *experiential* old covenant. Periodically men have made covenants with God. A covenant of dedication, which is a commitment to God, is admirable. The six righteous kings of Judah made covenants of this sort. As long as they kept their focus on the everlasting covenant of God and accepted His grace, their intent was admirable. When the covenant was without faith and dependent on human promises, it could not succeed. The corrupted perception of the covenant was the predominant belief when Jesus came, causing Jesus' rejection and condemnation by the nation's religious leadership.

By the time of Christ, the sanctuary services and ritual had become a religion of externals. The people did the rituals and kept the letter of the law to earn salvation. There was no love, faith, or grace. The people did not accept the power of grace to change their lives. Jesus' sermon on the mount showed that God desired a religion from the heart. The sacrifices were of no use unless there was an accompanying change in the life. The sacrifices served only as an object lesson to show how the blood of Christ purchased their salvation.

Endnotes

1. The Scriptures say: "For finding fault *with them*" and "unto us was the gospel preached, as well as unto them: but the word preached *did not profit them, not being mixed with faith* in them that heard it" (Heb. 8:8; 4:2, emphasis supplied).

2. Grace is often defined as the unmerited favor of God, but it is also the supernatural power of God to change the life, as we find in Hebrews 4:16. Grace was to change the motives of human beings from pride and selfishness to love—love for God and love for our fellow humans—and to enable sinners to keep the law of God, which is why God's laws in the heart are the first stipulation of the new covenant (Heb. 8:10). That He also writes his laws in the mind would indicate a conscious awareness of what God expects.

3. The people's promise was a covenant of dedication. Men praise God when they choose to serve him. The six righteous kings of Judah each renewed this covenant with God, usually after a revival from idolatry. The problem with the people at Sinai was their lack of understanding of the holiness of God and of their own weakness. They thought they could do it in their own strength and did not understand the implications of God's sustaining grace (Exod. 19:4; 33:12–17). They lacked the faith response and had yet to understand faith and grace.

4. "The covenant that God made with his people at Sinai is to be our refuge and defense.... And all the people answered together, and said, All that the Lord hath spoken we will do.... This covenant is of just as much force today as it was when the Lord made it with ancient Israel" (Ellen G. White, *The Southern Watchman*, March 1, 1904). See also *The Seventh-day Adventist Commentary*, vol. 1, pp. 592–598).

    The covenant was the Ten Commandments written by God on two tablets of stone, which was also called "the testimony." One must also recognize and understand the preamble of grace before both the covenant promises and the law (Exodus 19 4; 20:2). Exodus 32:15 calls the tablets "the two tables of the testimony." Deuteronomy 9:9, 11, 15 identifies them as "the tables of the covenant." Exodus 34:28 describes Moses' reception of the covenant. "And he was there with the Lord forty days and forty nights; he did neither eat bread, nor drink water. And he wrote upon the tables the words of the covenant, the ten commandments." Deuteronomy 9:11 says, "... The Lord gave me the two tables of stone, even the tables of the covenant."

5. God's presence changed lives (Gen. 32:24–30; Exod. 3:4–10; Joshua 5:13–15; 1 Kings 3:5–15; Isa. 6:1–13; Jer. 1:4–10; and Acts 9:3–6, 15–20).

6. The expansion of the ten "words" of the covenant can be seen in Leviticus: "But I will for their sakes remember the covenant of their ancestors, whom I brought forth out of the land of Egypt in the sight of the heathen, that I might be their God: I am the Lord. These are the *statutes* and *judgments* and *laws*, which the Lord made between him and the children of Israel in mount Sinai *by the hand of Moses*" (Lev. 26:45, 46, emphasis supplied). It can also be seen in Nehemiah: "Thou camest down also upon mount Sinai, and spakest with them from heaven, and gavest them right *judgments*, and true *laws*, good *statutes* and *commandments*" (Neh. 9:13, emphasis supplied). The judgments were casuistic (or case) law, describing the penalty for violations of the statutes.

Chapter 16

Ratified, Broken, and Renewed

And the Lord said unto Moses, Go, get thee down; for thy people, which thou
broughtest out of the land of Egypt, have corrupted themselves.
Exodus 32:7

The promises of the people, without the response of faith, made up the *historical* old covenant. Forty-six days after ratification, the people took part in a rebellious, heathen festival at the base of Sinai. They broke the law of God and the covenant they had just ratified. A large part of the people took part in this festival, though most repented in shame when Moses came down from the mount. Moses called the tribe of Levi, who did not take part in the festival, to execute judgment on those who persisted in rebellion. Three thousand fell that day. The next day a plague broke out among the people.

Without the favor of God or an effective covenant, the whole enterprise of going to the Promised Land was in doubt.

What God Intended

The everlasting covenant, is a term used for the covenant of redemption, a covenant of what God would do to restore humans to His image. It is renamed the *new* covenant in Jeremiah because Israel failed to understand it when it was given to them at Sinai. It is in this sense that God gave the new covenant to Adam and Eve and to Abraham. In each case, it was received by faith. The covenant given to Adam and Eve was for the whole human race. The covenant with Abraham was to go to his seed after him. This included Isaac and Jacob. It also included Moses at the burning bush, the elders of Israel when Moses and Aaron returned to Egypt, and Israel at Sinai. The covenant given by God at Sinai was the Abrahamic covenant, with promises that were to extend throughout Jewish, and later, church history.

The Abrahamic covenant, the foundation of the new covenant, was ratified or confirmed by the sacrifice of Jesus on the cross. Then Jesus became the mediator of the new covenant, which He continued for the Christian church. On Mount Sinai, God demonstrated His majesty, holiness, power, and grace by which He fulfills the promises of the covenant.

At Sinai the people needed to fall on their faces and believe that God would do what He said. Instead, they repeated their human promises. The covenant of human promises was "another covenant" ratified by the blood of animals.[1]

Ratified and Then Broken

After the ratification ceremony, God called Moses and Joshua to meet with Him in the mountain. While waiting on the Lord for six days, they had time to confess all sin in their lives. On the seventh day, God called Moses into the cloud. There he stayed for forty days, during which time he neither ate nor drank. God gave Moses the ten-commandment law, which God wrote on stone with His own finger. He also gave Moses instructions for the priesthood and for building the sanctuary (Exod. 24:12–31:18). Abruptly, God announced that the people had corrupted themselves.

After forty-six days, the people in the camp imagined that something had happened to Moses. They approached Aaron and insisted that he make them a golden calf to represent the only god they knew (Exod. 32:1–6).[2] Before long, there was a rebellious heathen festival at the base of the mountain. Thinking they would be returning to Egypt, the people chose the security of slavery over the freedom and hope of going to the Promised Land (Exod. 14:11, 12; 17:3; 32:23; Num. 14:4). It seemed the easy way. They forgot all that God had done for them.

As Moses and Joshua came near the camp, they realized what was going on. In anger, Moses threw the tables of stone onto the rocks and broke them to pieces, just as the people had broken their covenant of human promises. The covenant the people ratified lasted just forty-six days. It was faulty only because the people failed to accept God's gift of grace by faith.

Ever since the sacrifice of Cain, human beings have tried to earn their salvation (Gen. 4:3, 5). Animal sacrifices and ceremonies in themselves could not forgive sin. Only in looking forward to Jesus' true sacrifice on the cross were animal sacrifices effectual (Heb. 9:13–15).

Some people now, as well as in the days of Jesus, believe the ceremonial law was a part of the old covenant. However, in the old covenant, the people promised obedience but did not ask for God's grace (Exod. 16:6; 19:8; 24:3, 7; Deut. 5:27). The ceremonial law illustrated grace and provided pardon through animal sacrifices, which pointed forward to the promised Redeemer. It was an illustration of the Abrahamic or new covenant. From beginning to end, the ceremonial law was an instrument of grace! The provisions of the new covenant continue today through the priesthood of Christ in the heavenly sanctuary.

Intercession by Moses

The heathen festival at Sinai was a calamity. Because of the people's rebellion, Moses melted down the golden calf and caused the people to drink it. The Levites slew 3,000 rebellious Israelites, including all the ringleaders of the rebellion. God plagued the people. He would have abandoned the whole enterprise except for the intercession of Moses.

Moses, with desperate faith, interceded with God for another forty-six days to restore the covenant. Initially, God offered to destroy Israel and make of Moses a powerful nation. Though accepting his role as a messenger of God to the people (Exod. 32:10–14), Moses realized that he could be nothing more. God then directed that an angel go with them to the Promised Land. Moses insisted that God personally go with them on their journey and lead them. He talked with God "face to face" but did not see His person. As he got to know God better, he finally asked, "I beseech thee, show me thy glory" (Exod. 33:18).

God granted his request. He put Moses in a cleft in the rock, covered him with His hand, and passed by, allowing Moses to see His back as He moved into the distance (Exod. 33:22, 23). As He passed, He proclaimed His name and His attributes:

> And the Lord passed by before him, and proclaimed, The Lord, The Lord God, merciful and gracious, longsuffering, and abundant in goodness and truth, keeping mercy for thousands, forgiving iniquity and transgression and sin, and that will by no means clear the guilty; visiting the iniquity of the fathers upon the children, and upon the children's children, unto the third and to the fourth generation. (Exod. 34:6, 7)

> Then the Lord said: "I am making a covenant with you. Before all your people I will do wonders never before done in any nation in all the world. The people you live among will see how awesome is the work that I, the Lord, will do for you." (Exod. 34:10, NIV)

God heard Moses' intercessions and promised His presence as Israel journeyed to the Promised Land (Exod. 33:14). The reason God answered Moses' prayer is useful to us in our prayers. "The Lord said unto Moses, I will do this thing also that thou hast spoken: for thou hast found grace in my sight, and I know thee by name" (Exod. 33:17).

The Covenant Renewed

More than anything else, Moses desired the presence of God as the people traveled to the Promised Land. As God passed by, Moses saw that the glory of God is neither His power, His majesty, nor His consuming fire. His glory is in His character, and this He proclaimed as He passed by Moses. His character includes "keeping mercy for thousands, forgiving iniquity and transgression and sin" (Exod. 34:7). Moses took this blessing from God as a reason to ask one more thing—the thing he desired most for the children of Israel.

> And he said, If now I have found grace in thy sight, O Lord, let my Lord, I pray thee, go among us; for it is a stiffnecked people; and pardon our iniquity and our sin, and take us for thine inheritance. And he said, Behold, I make a covenant: before all thy people I will do marvels, such as have not been done in all the earth, nor in any nation: and all the people among which thou art shall see the work of the LORD: for it is a terrible thing that I will do with thee. Observe thou that which I command thee this day: behold, I drive out before thee the Amorite, and the Canaanite, and the Hittite, and the Perizzite, and the Hivite, and the Jebusite. (Exod. 34:9–11)

Moses was permitted to enter the very presence of God (Exod. 33:21–23). It was an experience the people had refused on Mount Sinai. God did not renew the "old" covenant of human promises. He did much better; He brought the people back into the Abrahamic covenant. He would go with them and give them the Promised Land. He would do "marvels" among His people, taking them as His "peculiar treasure" and making them into a "kingdom of priests and an holy nation," which would be an example to the heathen nations around them. He pardoned sins through the blood of the sacrificial lamb. The Messiah would come through the seed of Abraham. Jesus Christ confirmed this covenant at Calvary.

The people joyfully responded with sacrifices. They brought so much gold and other valuable materials to build the sanctuary that they had to be stopped. If people today would respond in a similar fashion, just think what the churches could do in carrying the gospel!

They then built the sanctuary, following detailed instructions from God. The ceremonial law was to become their pattern for worship and an illustration of the covenant. The sacrifices pointed forward to the Messiah who would pardon sin through His death on the cross.

Endnotes

1.   "Another compact—called in Scripture the 'old' covenant—was formed between God and Israel at Sinai, and was then ratified by the blood of a sacrifice...." (Ellen G. White, *Patriarchs and Prophets* [Nampa, ID: Pacific Press Publishing Association, 2005], p. 371).

     Why was another covenant formed at Sinai (Exod. 24:3–8) if the "everlasting covenant"—God's "My Covenant" (Gen. 17:7, 9, 10, 13, 19, 21)—was already in effect?

     "In their bondage the people had to a great extent lost the knowledge of God and of the principles of the Abrahamic covenant. In delivering them from Egypt, God sought to reveal to them His power and His mercy, that they might be led to love and trust Him...." (Ellen G. White, *Patriarchs and Prophets* [Nampa, ID: Pacific Press Publishing Association, 2005], p. 371).

2.   It is possible that the golden calf was an image of the goddess Hathor, "Hathor is an ancient Egyptian goddess who personified the principles of love, beauty, music, dance, motherhood and joy...." Hathor was "worshipped in Canaan in the eleventh century BC, which at that time was ruled by Egypt.... The Sinai Tablets show that the Hebrew workers in the mines of Sinai about 1500 BC worshipped Hathor, whom they identified with the goddess Astarte" ("Hathor," article at http://www.crystalinks.com/hathor.html, accessed 3/23/13).

Chapter 17
Atonement Through Sacrifice

And he shall lay his hand upon the head of the sin offering, and slay the sin offering in the place of the burnt offering. And the priest shall take of the blood thereof with his finger, and put it upon the horns of the altar of burnt offering, and shall pour out all the blood thereof at the bottom of the altar.... and the priest shall make an atonement for him, and it shall be forgiven him.
Leviticus 4:29–31

The central focus of the everlasting covenant was the restoration of the creation of God to Edenic perfection. God devised a plan before the creation of the world that Jesus, the second person of the Godhead, would come to this earth and live a sinless life as a human being. He would then take the sins of the world and die as a sacrifice to pay the penalty for sin that people might live.[1] God gave the ceremonial law as an illustration of the covenant to teach the people the meaning of His law. The sacrifices were a vital part of the ceremonial law as pointing forward to the coming of the Messiah and what He would do for humankind.

The term "everlasting covenant" also refers to the plan of salvation and the everlasting gospel. The great controversy between Christ and Satan will soon end, and God will destroy sin and Satan and restore the perfection of Eden. Christ's victory on the cross established His love, mercy, justice, and law as the eternal basis of His government. Free will and creativity remain as gifts to us. Praise and love to God will pour forth from every avenue in creation.

How Did Sacrifices Begin?

After Adam and Eve sinned, they were under the condemnation of death. Jesus, the Creator, Lawgiver, Redeemer, and second person of the Godhead covenanted to take the penalty of sin and die for humankind. In the Garden of Eden, immediately after Adam sinned, God made coats of skins for Adam and Eve. Only by the death of an animal could they be covered (Gen. 3:21). This action was highly symbolic of the sacrificial system that God instituted.

The first formal sacrifice recorded in Scripture is that of Cain and Abel. God accepted Abel's sacrifice of a lamb. This reinforced the significance of the shedding of blood, for "without shedding of blood is no remission" (Heb. 9:22). The sacrificed lamb was a symbol of the Messiah whose death on the cross made it possible for sins to be forgiven.

"By faith Abel offered unto God a more excellent sacrifice than Cain, by which he obtained witness that he was righteous, God testifying of his gifts: and by it he being dead yet speaketh" (Heb. 11:4).

God did not accept Cain's sacrifice, for Cain's offering was not of faith. He had rejected God's instruction and chosen to do things his own way. His sacrifice of choice fruit might have "cost" more than a lamb, but it could not represent the Redeemer-Substitute's dying for the sinner. All it could represent was an attempt to earn salvation by his own works. By not bringing a lamb, Cain, in effect, rejected the sacrifice of Christ on the cross and showed rebellion, which in a short time ripened into the murder of his brother Abel.

Sacrifices by the Patriarchs

During the patriarchal age, the sacrifices were usually burnt offerings. After the flood, Noah offered sacrifices from among the surviving clean beasts (Gen. 8:20). This pleased God, and He gave Noah the covenant of regular seasons and promised never to send a worldwide flood again. Though the record of sacrifices is sparse and intermittent during the patriarchal age, the patriarchs probably offered sacrifices more frequently than the record shows.

Ten generations later we have the record of Abraham, the "friend of God" (James 2:23), who built a series of altars for the worship of God. God gave Abraham the everlasting covenant in more detail than to any other person. God promised "an everlasting covenant … to be a God unto thee, and thy seed after thee" (Gen. 17:7).[2]

When Abraham was ready for the supreme test, God asked him to sacrifice his only son, Isaac, on Mount Moriah (Gen. 22:2, 8, 12, 13). Abraham could feel the agony the Father felt when He sacrificed His only begotten Son at Calvary—so can everyone who reads this story. It was a dramatized parable of Jesus' sacrifice on the cross. God stopped the sacrifice of Isaac and provided a ram, which was caught in a thicket, for the sacrifice. This showed that God Himself would provide the true sacrifice.

The Last Night in Egypt

The Passover, instituted in Egypt on the eve of the exodus, made clear the meaning of sacrifice. On this last night in Egypt, they were to kill a lamb for a sacrifice and sprinkle the blood on the posts and lintel of the door. God saved the lives of the firstborn only through the blood of the sacrificial lamb, pointing forward to Jesus Christ. In houses that were not marked with the blood of the lamb, the firstborn died.

> For I will pass through the land of Egypt this night, and will smite all the firstborn in the land of Egypt, both man and beast; and against all the gods of Egypt, I will execute judgment: I am the Lord. And the blood shall be to you for a token upon the houses where ye are: and when I see the blood, I will pass over you, and the plague shall not be upon you to destroy you, when I smite the land of Egypt. (Exod. 12:12, 13)

When sinners offered a sacrifice, they looked for pardon and salvation through the blood of the lamb, representing the promised Redeemer who would make the true sacrifice on Calvary. This became a "sweet savour" to God when accompanied by a life changed by grace.[3]

The Ceremonial Law

God gave the ceremonial law in detail at Sinai. He ordained sacrifices for thanksgiving, for dedication and first fruits, for peace offerings, for sins and trespasses, and for the continual daily burnt offerings (Lev. 1–7). Only domesticated clean animals without blemish were acceptable. Sinners chose the type of animal depending on their status and on what they could afford. The law also provided offerings to cleanse the priests of sin, offerings for purification, and offerings for the Day of Atonement.

The ceremonial law was the most detailed part of the law, yet the term "ceremonial law" is not in the Bible. The ceremonial law consisted largely of the sacrifices and sanctuary services. It also included rituals, festivals, laws of sanitation, guidelines for clean meats and for holiness. These parts were often quite different in application and purpose. Some were temporary, ending at Calvary; some continued in the heavenly sanctuary; and some are eternal.[4]

Atonement through Sacrifice

The sinner brought an animal and killed it in the court at the door of the tabernacle. When the sinner was either the whole congregation or a priest, the officiating priest took the blood into the tabernacle and sprinkled it toward the veil; when the sinner was an individual, the priest placed the blood on the horns of the altar to "make an atonement for him, and it shall be forgiven him" (Lev. 4:31). The blood of an animal cannot really pardon sins (Heb. 8 and 9); the sacrifice pointed forward to the true sacrifice of the Lamb of God. By faith in the promised Redeemer, the blood of the lamb provided pardon and atonement.

When Jesus died on the cross, He made a complete atonement for the sins of humankind. One should view the heavenly priesthood of Christ as an integral part of His sacrifice. His mediation in the heavenly sanctuary is meaningless without His shed blood from Calvary, and His shed blood from Calvary is of no avail without His mediation in the heavenly sanctuary.

Atonement through the mediation of Christ in the heavenly sanctuary is a necessary complement of His death on the cross. These two phases of Christ's ministry are illustrated in the atonement in Leviticus 4.

1. The sinner brought the animal to the door of the tabernacle, placed his hand on its head, and slew it.
2. The priest took the blood into the tabernacle to make atonement and to pardon the sinner.

Israelite Priesthood

Godly patriarchs and firstborn sons functioned initially as priests in faithful homes. Job offered priestly sacrifices for his family (Job 1:5). Melchizedek represented a priestly remnant from the line of Noah, parallel to the line in which we find Abraham. Abraham built altars and offered sacrifices, influencing his household of more than 1,000 persons and his neighbors and friends.[5] The ceremonial law at Sinai established the first organized and well-defined priesthood.

God chose the tribe of Levi, Jacob's third son, to teach the people His will. Those of the Levitical family of Aaron were to be priests (Exod. 28:1; 32:26). Other Levites had duties related to the sanctuary and, later, to the Temple. Priests were organized to carry the sins of the people through the blood of the sacrifice into the sanctuary. Hebrews 8 to 10 says the sacrifices were symbolic "shadows" of heavenly things to come and effective only in anticipation of Jesus' sacrifice at Calvary. There is no language in the Bible to indicate that the sacrifices were the covenant or even a part of the covenant. Only Jesus' death on the cross could make effectual all the sacrifices offered during Israel's history (Heb. 9:15).

At His ascension, Jesus "sat down on the right hand of the Majesty on high" (Heb. 1:3). This points to the position of a king. Yet, Jesus also functioned as High Priest in heaven, first, in the Holy Place, and, after 1844, in the Most Holy Place. This is consistent with Jesus' position as priest-king after the order of Melchizedek.

The true antitypical Day of Atonement began in 1844 (Dan. 8:14) with Jesus' ministry in the Most Holy Place of the temple in heaven. This is the ministry in which Jesus blots out the forgiven sins of God's people from the Book of Life (Lev. 16; 23:24–32; Ps. 51:9; Phil. 4:3; Rev. 20:12, 15; 21:27). The priestly ministry of Jesus in the heavenly sanctuary completes the atonement for God's people—even God forgets their sins (Jer. 31:34).

At the close of probation, Jesus will have completed His mediation for sin, and all those who are alive at that time will have accepted Christ as Saviour or will have finally rejected Him to their eternal loss.[6]

The Sacrifices and Sanctuary Services

After sin entered the world, the sacrifices were initiated as an illustration of the substitutionary death of Jesus Christ. The sacrificed animal symbolically took the place of the sinner. Its death represented the prophesied Redeemer who would die for every person's sins. The sinner in reality receives the atonement through the sacrifice of Jesus Christ on the cross (Heb. 9:15).

The blood of the lamb was a symbol of the shed blood of Christ. Sacrifices were effective only as people, by faith, consented to the work of grace in changing their lives. After Jesus' died, "sacrifice and oblation" on earth ceased to have significance (Dan. 9:27).

At Sinai and during the rest of Old Testament history there was considerable discussion of the covenant. The terms we use today were unknown then. The people depended on the promises and the description of the covenant given to them. Nor were they aware of the council within the Godhead in which God formed the everlasting covenant. These mysteries would be explained in the life, death, and resurrection of Jesus Christ.

Corruption of the Ceremonial Law

Later, as Israel fell into apostasy, the people forgot the Messiah to whom the sacrifices pointed. Instead, they began to think that the sacrifices were what saved them. It was a form of idolatry. While Israel did not renew the *historical* old covenant, an old covenant mindset returned. Sinful humans often seem willing to do required works "to be saved," as long as those works do not interfere with their sinful way of life.[7]

The Jewish people also looked for salvation to their descent from Abraham and to their meticulous observance of the law of Moses, including the moral and ceremonial laws. As time went on, the Jews developed an extensive legal system of ordinances, which they added to the law of God. Their beliefs tended to trivialize sin, and they thought little of repentance to absolve guilt. Also, sacrifices took a lesser role, and there was little or no belief in a Messiah who would substitute for them before the judgment seat of God.

Endnotes

1. That Jesus would be our sacrificial lamb was a plan made before the creation of the world (John 1:29, 36; Eph. 1:4; 1 Peter 1:19, 20; Rev. 5:6–13; 7:17; 13:8).

2. Abraham built altars to worship God (Gen. 12:7, 8; 13:4, 18). God gave him His "My Covenant," showing that it belonged uniquely to God (Gen. 17:2, 4, 7, 9, 10, 13, 14, 19, 21). This covenant was to extend to all his "seed," which included the Jews and all who are in Christ (Gen. 17:1–10; Gal. 3:29).

3. Sacrifices are useless without a change in the life. In a number of places, the Bible speaks of the pleasure that God and the holy angels experience over the conversion of a sinner to God. In the sacrifices, this is expressed in the phrase, "an offering made by fire, of a sweet savour unto the Lord" (Lev. 1:9, 13, 17; 2:2, 9).

    Burnt flesh, fat, and hair are not something pleasant to smell. However, as the symbol of a dedicated life, they are sweet to God. The expression "sweet savour(s)" is used forty-four times in the Bible (Gen. 8:21; Exod. 29:18, 25, 41; Lev. 1:9, 13, 17; 2:2, 9, 12; 3:5, 16; 4:31; 6:15, 21; 8:21, 28; 17:6; 23:13; 23:18; Num. 15:3, 7, 10, 13, 24; 18:17; 28:2, 6, 8, 13, 24, 27; 29:2, 6, 8, 13, 36; Ezra 6:10, "sweet savours"; Ezek. 6:13; 16:19; 20:28, "sweet savour" to idols is offensive; 20:41; 2 Cor. 2:15, the offering of our lives is "a sweet savour of Christ").

4. One part of the ceremonial law that is eternal is Jesus bearing His humanity and carrying the scars of His suffering on earth, for eternity (resurrection is in the flesh, Job 19:26; Jesus carries the wounds in His hands, Zech. 13:6; light comes out of His hand, Hab. 3:4; we conform to His image, Rom. 8:29; we are to bear His heavenly image, 1 Cor. 15:49; we are changed into the glorious image of Christ, 2 Cor. 3:18; our vile body will be made like His glorious one, Phil. 3:21; we will be like Him, 1 John 3:2).

5. "Abraham's household comprised more than a thousand souls. Those who were led by his teachings to worship the one God, found a home in his encampment; and here, as in a school, they received such instruction as would prepare them to be representatives of the true faith. Thus, a great responsibility rested upon him. He was training heads of families, and his methods of government would be carried out in the households over which they should preside.

    "In early times, the father was the ruler and priest of his own family, and he exercised authority over his children, even after they had families of their own…. Abraham sought by every means in his power to guard the inmates of his encampment against mingling with the heathen and witnessing their idolatrous practices, for he knew that familiarity with evil would insensibly corrupt the principles…." (Ellen G. White, *Patriarchs and Prophets* [Nampa, ID: Pacific Press Publishing Association, 2005], p. 141).

6. The redeemed who now have access to God through Christ (Heb. 4:15, 16) will have access to Him in the New Earth (Rev. 21:3, 7, 22; 22:4).

7. The purpose of the ceremonial law was corrupted. The covenant God gave to Abraham (Gen. 17) was the covenant of redemption and grace. This covenant came entirely from God and by His initiative. In this covenant is the promise of descendants, which was a miracle considering Abraham and Sarah's ages—ninety-nine and eighty-nine. God promised Abraham land at a time when he possessed none. He also gave him the blessing, "in thy seed shall all the nations of the earth be blessed" (Gen. 22:18). This was a promise that signified that the Messiah would come through Abraham's line (Gal. 3:14, 16, 29).

    God presented the Abrahamic covenant to Israel at Sinai and renewed it after Moses' intercession for the nation. He first gave the new covenant to Adam and Eve and to Noah and his family (Gen. 3:15; 6:18; 8:21; 9:1–17). The promises and blessings of these early covenants extend to the entire human family. God saves men through His covenant.

For 215 years, Israel lived in the midst of a heathen, idolatrous society. It was inevitable that they would take on some of their ideas. Even so, there was always a "remnant" who maintained true faith and resisted heathen culture. With this background, it is understandable, yet inexcusable, that people would fall back into old ways of thinking. The thrilling experiences of Sinai and their new, impressive forms of worship began to fade in time as they looked on those forms as the sum and substance of their religion. They attributed power and efficacy to performance of the sacrifices and ceremonies themselves, and they looked less and less to the Redeemer to whom they pointed. It was this mindset that brought on the *experiential* old covenant' that grew into dominance at the time of Jesus and which led to His being rejected.

Chapter 18
Sacrifices in the Ceremonial Law

For the law having a shadow of good things to come, and not the very image
of the things, can never with those sacrifices which they offered year by year
continually make the comers thereunto perfect.
Hebrews 10:1

The sacrifices, sanctuary services, priesthood, and other aspects of the "ceremonial law" are intricately associated with the covenant of God. In working out this relationship, one must recognize the different parts of the "ceremonial law." Some parts of this law were fulfilled and had no more meaning after Calvary. Other parts continued as the priestly ministration of Jesus in the heavenly sanctuary. Still others are practical matters of continued value for us today.

Some people have looked on the ceremonial law as the old covenant. Hebrews 9 and 10 may appear to support this view. However, there is no correlation between the true sacrifice and priesthood of Jesus Christ and the human priesthood of the Old Testament and the corrupted Jewish perceptions of the ritual sacrifices, which were thought to appease God.

The Functions of Mosaic Law

The types and functions of law in Old Testament Israel requires careful evaluation. Is it one law, three laws, or more? God gave the moral law, the Ten Commandments, to define sin. These commandments were brief and comprehensive. They provided the boundaries necessary for true liberty to exist and were a description of how to show love to God and to our neighbors. The moral law is by nature eternal.

The civil law was an extension of the Ten Commandments with applications for the nation of Israel. They did not add anything that was new to the Ten Commandments. After Israel's defeat in AD 70, the civil law had no more function.

The ceremonial law was a system of rituals, ceremonies, and sacrifices to illustrate the covenant and the people's relationship with God. The ceremonial law is more detailed than either the moral or civil law, and, to a large degree, interacted with them.

What Is the Ceremonial Law?

The sacrifices and sanctuary services are the heart of that which we call the ceremonial law. Animal sacrifice came into practice shortly after sin. An animal took the place of the sinner and, in dying, represented the prophesied Redeemer who would die for the sins of humanity. It was an example of the substitutionary death of Jesus Christ paying the penalty for our sins.

During the patriarchal age, all sacrifices were burnt offerings. The patriarch or firstborn son carried out the priestly function. These offered sacrifices on an altar near their home. However, there was no scheduled time for the sacrifices. Most sacrifices were to atone for sin. Other sacrifices were for offerings of thanksgiving or offerings for other purposes (Gen. 8:20, 21).

At Sinai, Israel had become a nation, and God gave them laws, statutes, ordinances, and judgments in a codified and written form (2 Kings 17:37). The ceremonial law was the most detailed part of the law. The ceremonial law consisted of:

1. The system of sacrifices to provide forgiveness for sin, devotion to God, and thanksgiving for God's providence. A sinner would take the appropriate animal to the door of the tabernacle, lay his hand on its head to transfer his sin and then slay the animal. If the sinner was the congregation or a priest, the priest took the blood, sprinkled it before the vail; otherwise, he put some of the animal's blood on the horns of the altar and poured out the rest at the bottom of the altar (Lev. 4:27–30). Transgression of the law separated the sinner from God, and required death of the sinner (Gen. 2:16, 17; Rom. 6:23).The animal's death was symbolic of the death of the Redeemer, who took the place of the sinner. At Calvary, sacrifice and oblation ceased as the "shadow" had now given birth in the true and real sacrifice of Jesus on the cross.

2. The human priesthood of the sanctuary and the Temple symbolized the priesthood of Jesus Christ. The perfection and beauty of the priestly robes symbolized Jesus' sinless life, and the "robe of righteousness" He provides to His people. Human priests also had a healing ministry as did Jesus. They taught the people, and received messages from God as did Jesus in the divine insights of His teaching. The Urim and Thummim on the ephod of the priests pointed forward to Jesus' prophetic ministry. In this Jesus continued the ceremonial law as the true High Priest for the human family. Through His blood, mediated in the heavenly sanctuary, God gave humankind pardon and atonement.[1]

3. The sanctuary that Moses constructed, provided a place for God to dwell among His people. God's continued presence among His people was the most important issue in the covenant. From the mercy seat God communed with His people.

4. Circumcision is a token of the covenant and of a man's belonging to the covenant people. It showed dedication to pure living in preparation for the coming Messiah. After Jesus had come, the rite was no longer needed for either Jews or Gentiles.

5. God established rituals for holiness, clean meats, and healing. Repeatedly He commanded the people to make a difference between what is holy and what is common, what is clean and what is unclean. Some of these rituals make common sense and are still useful today. God's purpose has always been that Christians be holy as He is holy.[2]

These ceremonies shaped Israel's form of worship. With constant repetition, the ceremonies became the focus of worship in the minds of many, and they forgot the Redeemer to whom the ceremonies pointed.[3]

The sacrificial system was closely related to the covenant, for it illustrated Jesus' taking our punishment for the broken law of God. There is never any assertion that it was the covenant or even a part of the covenant. In the extensive literature describing the ceremonies and the sacrifices, neither God nor Moses employed covenant language.

Yet, along with His resurrection and His ministry in heaven, Jesus' sacrifice on the cross is the heart of the everlasting (or *new*) covenant. As a form of worship, animal sacrifice was temporary, coming to an end when the true sacrificial lamb, Jesus Christ, died on the cross (Dan. 9:27; Col. 2:17; Heb. 8:5; 10:1). At Calvary, Jesus fulfilled the ceremonial law. He also became our true High Priest and mediated His blood in the heavenly sanctuary to give pardon and atonement to the human family.

1. Animal sacrifices were no longer needed after Jesus made the true and effective sacrifice on the cross.
2. Circumcision came to an end, having fulfilled its purpose.
3. Jesus took over the priestly mediation in the heavenly sanctuary as our heavenly High Priest, carrying on the "continual" (or "daily") services at first, and later officiating in the true Day of Atonement service, which has to do with judgment.
4. The spring festivals of Passover, firstfruits, and Pentecost were fulfilled during Christ's first advent (1 Cor. 5:7; 15:23; Acts 2:1). The fall festival of the Day of Atonement is an ongoing service for the latter time, carried out in the most holy place of the heavenly sanctuary.
5. Festivals of thanksgiving and memorials are still relevant, though the names and timing may be different.

The Ceremonial Law and the Covenant

Hebrews 8–10 speaks extensively of what is *first, faulty, old, decayed*, and *ready* to *vanish away*. These chapters describe the animal sacrifices and the human priesthood as being ineffective, temporary, and now fulfilled with the true and effective sacrifice of Jesus and His mediation in the heavenly sanctuary.

The Old Testament never speaks of an old covenant. We understand the concept of an old covenant by understanding the new covenant (Jer. 31:31), which, by implication, contrasts with an old one (see Heb. 8:13). In the New Testament, Hebrews 8 to 10 provides a study of what is old, faulty, and ineffective.

The issue in Israel at that time was their corrupted view of the covenant and the ceremonial law. As the months and years passed, the people increasingly looked upon the sacrifices and sanctuary services as their means of salvation. In doing these things, they forgot the Redeemer to whom they pointed, the one who would die that their sins might be pardoned. Through the sacrifices and meticulous observance of the law of Moses and their being from Abraham's line, the people looked for salvation and eternal life.

Were these sacrifices a part of the covenant of God? It is true that they were related to the covenant, for they were a provision for the forgiveness of sin. Yet, they were temporary. They came to an end at Calvary. They functioned solely as an illustration of the covenant and could not forgive or cleanse our sins (Hebrews 8–10) except in anticipation of Jesus' true sacrifice (Heb. 9:15). In addition, the Bible tells us that God was not pleased with sacrifices unless they were accompanied by lives that were changed by grace.[4]

What God Intended for Israel

God gave the ceremonial law as an illustration of the covenant. Through the ceremonial law, grace was mediated, and sins were forgiven—by faith in the Redeemer to come. In the *historical* old covenant, the people took upon themselves the work of obedience of the law. They promised, "All that the Lord hath said, we will do." What they failed to realize was that human obedience can only be superficial and mechanical. Only by grace can a person obey God from the changed heart. In forty-six days, this covenant was broken, abrogated, and never officially renewed. Though there is evidence that the people looked on the covenant ratified at Sinai (Ex. 24:3-8) as still being in force (Jer. 31:32).

There was no way that the ceremonial law could be any part of the old covenant, *historical* or *expe riential*. The descriptions in Hebrews 8–10 are of the corrupted view of the ceremonial law, which had become, for the people, an *experiential* old covenant.

The new covenant describes what God will do by putting the law into human hearts. Adam and Eve's being created in the image of God included the law of God as an integral part of their being. After sin, God said, "I will put enmity between thee [Satan] and the woman [mankind]" (Gen. 3:15). This was the new covenant of redemption, and it pardoned people's sin through Jesus' sacrifice on Calvary.

Through His close friendship with Abraham, God put what is described as the new covenant into Abraham's heart (Genesis 26:5). Abraham was the "friend of God" (James 2:23; 2 Chron. 20:7; Isa. 41:8); and, through this close association, Abraham partook "of the divine nature" (2 Peter 1:4). When God gave Abraham the covenant in detail, He told him that he was to be the "father of many nations" and that the covenant was to reach "to thy seed after thee.[5] It was the covenant for God's people throughout history.

God used the term "My covenant" eight times in the covenant given to Abraham, pointing to a covenant uniquely belonging to God.[6] It was the covenant given by God at Sinai (Exod. 19:4-6). It was renewed after Moses' intercessions (Exod. 34:9-11, 27, 28) and was to be the covenant for God's people. As God said, it was given "to thy seed after thee" (Gen. 17:7).

The promise of the gospel was given to Abraham (Gal. 3:14-16, 29). It was the new covenant, which provided pardon for sins and was illustrated by the sacrifices of the ceremonial law. After Jesus died on the cross, the sacrificial system was fulfilled and no longer needed.

Endnotes

1.   Jesus is the mediator of the new covenant (Matt. 26:26–28; Mark 14:28; Luke 22:20; 1 Cor. 11:24–26; Heb. 9:15; 12:24; the word for "covenant," *diathēke*, is also translated "testament.") The new covenant was first named and described in Jer. 31:31–34. This is the covenant of grace in which sinners depend upon God to change their life and to provide pardon and salvation. Careful reading will show that God gave this covenant to Adam and Eve and to Abraham. God's people are

saved throughout history under the Abrahamic covenant. The new covenant was confirmed at Calvary but was first given to Adam and Eve. The old covenant could not forgive sins through the promises of the people. Sacrifices for sin illustrated the pardon given through Christ in the new covenant!

2. There were laws regarding diet, cleanliness, health, and sanitation. In Eden, Adam and Eve were given a diet consisting of fruit, grains, and nuts. The health of humans diminished after the fall, but they retained much of their early strength and vigor. Is there anyone today who can make a wooden ship 450 or 320 feet long, using simple tools (Gen. 6:14–16)? (The length depends on whether Moses used the 18-inch or 20.6-inch Egyptian standard.) Human beings lived over 900 years and enjoyed health, strength, and mental powers that we can only envy today. After the flood, there was a radical change when men were allowed to eat flesh food. From that time on the health of men deteriorated and the length of life decreased until it was soon reduced to the "three score and ten" (Ps. 90:10) that we see today.

    At Sinai, God gave laws governing cleanliness, health, and sanitation. These were laws to make a "holy nation" of Israel and a beautiful land of Canaan. God loves order and beauty. While these laws were given with the ceremonial laws, they were common sense laws that would benefit humankind for all time and eternity. They were not a part of the covenant but were a "help" to make the people healthy and "an holy nation" (Lev. 11:43–47). The distinction predates Sinai; the concept of what constituted a "clean" animal was known at the time of the flood (Gen. 7:2).

3. Because God gave the ceremonial law, the people reverently followed its rituals at first. As time went on, Jewish religious leaders added hundreds of human ordinances to the law. The services became corrupted with heathen practices. Sometimes the services were neglected entirely as the people went into idolatry. At other times, sacrifices were offered carelessly with blemished animals. Eventually, the very meaning and purpose of the sacrifices were lost as the people looked on these activities as the means of salvation. Because of the corruption of the services many people did not recognize or accept the Messiah and eventually called for Him to be crucified.

4. Sacrifices, without a change in the life and obedience, are not pleasing to God. God calls them an abomination (1 Sam. 15:22; Isa. 1:18; Amos 5:21).

5. The covenant given to Abraham was to extend to all his "seed"—the Jews—and to all who are in Christ—the Christian church (Gen. 17:1–10; Gal. 3:29).

6. God gave Abraham His "My Covenant," a covenant belonging uniquely to Him (Gen. 17:2, 4, 7, 9, 10, 13, 14, 19, 21).

Chapter 19

Covenant on the Banks of the Jordan

Now all the people that came out were circumcised: but all the people that were
born in the wilderness by the way as they came forth out of Egypt,
them they had not circumcised.

Joshua 5:5

Israel had wandered forty years in the desert. All the adults over age twenty, who came out of Egypt, died in the desert. It was now a new generation with "new worlds to conquer." For forty years, Moses had taught the people the law of the living God. They had learned to depend on God for food, water, and guidance.

On the bank of the Jordan, they could see the Promised Land. The covenant promises given to Abraham were about to be fulfilled. The nations across the Jordan were larger and stronger than Israel was, but God, as Israel's leader, assured their success. God saw that they needed to reaffirm and commit themselves again to the covenant.

They had much to learn and seemingly insurmountable challenges to overcome before they could settle down in the Promised Land. As they rested on the banks of the Jordan, Moses had some last words for the people.

The Covenant at the Jordan

Israel was again approaching Canaan, but this time through Gilead and Bashan. By the power of God, they dispossessed the Amorites and took their lands. Now camped on the east side of Jordan, opposite Jericho, Moses gathered all Israel. There he reminded the people of their covenant with God, with blessings and curses dependent on their obedience or disobedience.

> The Lord our God made a covenant with us in Horeb. The Lord made not this covenant with our fathers, but with us, even us, who are all of us here alive this day. The Lord talked with you face to face in the mount out of the midst of the fire. (Deut. 5:2–4)

The covenant God offered at Horeb contained new promises for the nation. God said, "Ye shall be a peculiar treasure unto me … a kingdom of priests, and an holy nation" (Exod. 19:5, 6). These words were what God called "My covenant" (Exod. 19:5; Gen. 17:2, 4, 7, 9, 10, 13, 14, 19, 21), pointing to the everlasting covenant of God, established with Abraham. God personally came to the Mt. Sinai in fire and smoke, with a trumpet loud and long and an earthquake. Silence enshrouded the people as God spoke the words of the covenant, the Ten Commandments, in the people's hearing.

Moses went into the cloud and communed with God, receiving more details of what God wanted for His people (Exod. 20:21–23:33). The people bypassed the grace of the Abrahamic covenant (Ex. 19:4) and ratified their covenant of human promises with God through animal sacrifices, and the people promised, "All that the Lord hath said will we do, and be obedient"(Exod. 24:3–11). This was the *historical* old covenant. Moses went into the mount again and received the tables of the testimony, written with the finger of God.

"The Lord made not this covenant with our fathers" (Deut. 5:3), Moses said. This was because of the new features, which included new promises, a conditional statement asking for a response from the people, and the ten-commandment law that had been both spoken and written. The everlasting covenant given to Abraham, Isaac, and Jacob did not have these features, yet it formed the basis for the Sinai covenant. Abraham "obeyed my voice and kept my charge, my commandments, my statutes, and my laws" (Gen. 26:5). Those who receive God's "My covenant" will obey Him out of love.

Talking With God Face to Face

The people could visualize the covenant promise fulfilled as they looked across the Jordan. The descendants of Abraham were now the nation of Israel. They were to take the land and, once settled, were to be a blessing to many people through their example, through God's teachings, and through the Messiah to come.

Moses talked with God "face to face" at Sinai (Exod. 33:11). "Face to face" is a common idiom for close communion. The above verse speaks of the people of Israel talking with God "face to face" through their representative Moses. God was still close to Israel, and the "face to face" communion was present in the sanctuary services, the Urim and Thummim, and the priests and prophets.

Moses did not see God's person, so later Moses asked God to show him His glory (Exod. 33:18). God proclaimed His character; "merciful and gracious, long suffering, and abundant in goodness and truth," then He restored the Abrahamic covenant in place of the "old covenant" (Exod. 34:9–11). which was broken by their sin at Sinai. Would they now accept the covenant of God? Would they learn the Commandments of God "and keep and do them" (Deut. 5:1)? The covenant made at Horeb is of *no* benefit unless each generation makes the covenant its own.

Moses said that God made this covenant with all "who are here alive this day." The covenant that God made with Adam and Eve, with Abraham, Isaac, and Jacob, and that He renewed at Sinai is built upon the everlasting covenant. All the people standing before Him that day received the covenant through their fathers. Symbolically each one was present in his father, who was there to hear it given. Every person must now make his commitment to the covenant, and respond in faith.. No one can ride on the coattails of an ancestor. God has no grandchildren.

Ahead of the people was the invasion of Canaan and their settlement on the land. There would be challenges, and there would be temptations. They needed a clear concept of God's purpose in giving them the land and of the responsibilities they would bear as the chosen people of God. Most important-ly, they needed to remember how God had delivered them from bondage in Egypt.

Moses' Last Messages

Moses, who had lead them in the exodus for forty years, gave the closing addresses of his life. He spoke of God making the covenant with each one of them present that day. Joshua became the embod-iment of the message and was granted the spirit of Moses. Moses' influence continued as long as any of that generation lived. It was the legacy of a righteous man and a merciful God. "And Israel served the Lord all the days of Joshua, and all the days of the elders that overlived Joshua, and which had known all the works of the Lord, that he had done for Israel" (Joshua 24:31).

The covenant (Deut. 29:9–16), called by some the Palestinian covenant, was a renewal of the Abrahamic covenant. The rest of Deuteronomy 29 and 30 gives more details.

> Carefully follow the terms of this covenant, so that you may prosper in everything you do. All of you are standing today in the presence of the Lord your God—your leaders and chief men, your elders and officials, and all the other men of Israel, to-gether with your children and your wives, and the aliens living in your camps who chop your wood and carry your water. You are standing here in order to enter into a covenant with the Lord your God, a covenant the Lord is making with you this day and sealing with an oath, to confirm you this day as his people, that he may be your God as he promised you, and as he swore to your fathers, Abraham, Isaac and Jacob. I am making this covenant, with its oath, not only with you who are standing here with us today in the presence of the Lord our God but also with those who are not here today. (Deut. 29:9–15, NIV; cf. Deut. 30:11–15)

Was this covenant different from the covenant made at Sinai? It was a covenant "beside ["in ad-dition to," NIV] the covenant which he made with them in Horeb" (Deut. 29:1). It was a covenant of dedication to the previous covenant.[1] People cannot depend on a covenant made with their fathers. They must express their own commitment to God.

Covenant language is the theme of the whole book. Covenant promises seemed absolute, yet ; they are conditional. Obedience brings blessings (Deut. 7:1–26; 8:1–10; 11:10–15; 28:1–14); apostasy brings curses (Deut. 28:15–68; and 29:18–29).

The Covenant after Moses' Time

Israel had reached a high point in their spiritual life at the time the nation occupied Canaan. This was because of the new emphasis on the covenant and their relation to God and to the influence of

Moses and Joshua.

Soon after their settlement in Canaan, Israel went into cycles of apostasy, oppression, repentance and deliverance—over and over again. Repeated apostasy broke the everlasting covenant over and over again, but each repentance restored the covenant, at least temporarily. Moses made the first of these renewals just before Israel crossed the Jordan into Canaan (see Deuteronomy 29:12–15). Each renewal reflected the original covenant as it was summarized by Moses in Deuteronomy 5:2, 3.

Most of these renewals were manmade but pointed to the everlasting covenant and the ten-commandment law. The renewals were a rededication to God following revivals. With time, the apostasy deepened until there was "no remedy," and Babylon took Israel into captivity (2 Chron. 36:16; Isa. 3:7, NIV; Jer. 30:13, NIV).

Rededication

If the covenant of God is an everlasting covenant, why are the promises different with each presentation? God planned the everlasting covenant before the foundation of the world. His covenant focused on the substitutionary death of Jesus and His sinless life as a human being, illustrating the mercy and love of God. These aspects of the covenant are permanent and cannot be changed by any human being.

God also purposed to change the lives of human beings on this earth, to destroy sin and Satan, and to restore what Adam lost in Eden. This is the covenant presented to the human family by God, and it is from this covenant that all blessings flow from the throne of mercy.

Humans must accept the covenant to receive its blessings and responsibilities. There must be a faith commitment to God and consent for the work of grace in the life. It is this response on the part of humanity that makes the covenant complete and effective. This human aspect must be renewed on a regular basis with rededication and renewed commitments to keep the covenant fresh and effective in the life.

Human experience is constantly varying—from childhood to youth, from youth to adulthood, from child-raising to the prime of life to old age. Yet, these are not the only variables. There are also the challenges of work, of making a living, of maintaining our homes, of changes in society. You can add many others. We need to present ourselves and our plans to God on a daily basis. We need constant reminding of what living the Christian life is and how we need to do it.

We also need a reminder of creation every week. We need to remember redemption and our dependence upon God for everything. To help us do this, God gave us the Sabbath. It is all too easy to forget the ultimate purpose of God in our lives. From time to time, we must make a new commitment to serve Him. The covenant must be renewed with every generation and person (Deut. 5:3, 4).

Jesus in His life on earth met all these problems as a human being. The victory He gained is for our children and us.

Endnotes

1.   Deuteronomy 30 foreshadows elements of the new covenant in Jeremiah 31. Moses predicted: "And it shall come to pass, when all these things are come upon thee, the blessing and the curse, which I have set before thee, and thou shalt call them to mind among all the nations, whither the Lord thy God hath driven thee, and shalt return unto the Lord thy God, and shalt obey his voice according to all that I command thee this day, thou and thy children, *with all thine heart*, and with all thy soul … And the Lord thy God will circumcise thine heart, and the heart of thy seed, to love the Lord thy God *with all thine heart*, and with all thy soul, that thou mayest live. For this commandment which I command thee this day, it is not hidden from thee, neither is it far off. It is not in heaven, that thou shouldest say, Who shall go up for us to heaven, and bring it unto us, that we may hear it, and do it? Neither is it beyond the sea, that thou shouldest say, Who shall go over the sea for us, and bring it unto us, that we may hear it, and do it? But the word is very nigh unto thee, in thy mouth, and *in thy heart*, that thou mayest do it. See, I have set before thee this day life and good, and death and evil." (Deut. 30:1, 2, 6, 11–15, emphasis supplied).

   Through Jeremiah, God declared: "I will put my law in their inward parts, and write it *in their hearts*; and will be their God, and they shall be my people" (Jer. 31:33, emphasis supplied).

   Many verses in Deuteronomy emphasized heart religion and the internalizing of God's teaching (Deut. 4:6; 5:29; 6:5; 7:6; 10:12, 16; 11:1, 13, 18; 14:2; 26:18; 27:9; 28:9; 29:13; 30:6; see also Ps. 51; Isa. 1:10–20).

Chapter 20
The New Covenant

Behold, the days come, saith the Lord, that I will make a new covenant with the
house of Israel, and with the house of Judah: Not according to the covenant that I
made with their fathers in the day that I took them by the hand to bring
them out of the land of Egypt; which my covenant they brake,
although I was an husband unto them, saith the Lord.
Jeremiah 31:31, 32

Preachers, teachers, and theologians often use the term "new covenant." It represents all that is positive and desirable about the covenant of God. The new covenant represents all that God will do for us and in us to change our lives and make us like Him again. It is the covenant of redemption and grace.

The new covenant is a stark contrast to the old covenant whereby people attempt the impossibility of making themselves righteous by their own efforts. One must study this carefully to know what it means for our daily lives.

God gave the new covenant to Adam and Eve when He put enmity against evil in the human heart. He gave the covenant again to Abraham when He chose Abraham to be the father of many nations and of the chosen people through whom the Messiah would come. The covenant to Abraham was to go to all his seed and to the New Testament church (Gal. 3:29). Jesus confirmed the new covenant on the cross.

The New Covenant Promised

The covenant has not always been well understood. When Judah went into captivity, the people could only conclude that God cast them aside from the covenant. God was watching, and He promised them a new covenant that would be different from their current corrupted view of the covenant. Jeremiah was first to describe the new covenant:

Behold, the days come, saith the Lord, that I will make a new covenant with the house of Israel, and with the house of Judah: Not according to the covenant that I made with their fathers in the day that I took them by the hand to bring them out of the land of Egypt; which my covenant they brake, although I was an husband unto them, saith the Lord: But this shall be the covenant that I will make with the house of Israel; After those days, saith the Lord, I will put my law in their inward parts, and write it in their hearts; and will be their God, and they shall be my people. And they shall teach no more every man his neighbour, and every man his brother, saying, Know the Lord: for they shall all know me, from the least of them unto the greatest of them, saith the Lord: for I will forgive their iniquity, and I will remember their sin no more. (Jer. 31:31–34; cf. Ezek. 36:24–31)

How is the new covenant *new*? "New" is an attractive term because humans like new things.

The new covenant is new in its function. In the new covenant, God takes the initiative, writes the law in our hearts, and emphasizes grace for power to obey the law. We still need obedience, though superficial obedience is not enough. The motives of the heart must be changed. Obedience must originate from love to God and our fellow humans.

God's everlasting covenant cannot be broken or modified by any human. The covenant between God and the human family, in which we dedicate ourselves to the covenant of God, is by nature temporary. It must be renewed on a continual basis. God renewed the covenant in Exodus 34:9–27 (Deuteronomy.5:2–22 and Joshua 5:2–15 are a reiteration of Exod. 34) and in Joshua 24:14–27; the six righteous kings of Judah renewed the covenant when they repented from their idolatry.[1]

Jesus ratified the new covenant after the people's ratification of the old. When God promised Abram land, He went through a covenant ceremony with Abram according to the customs of the people (Gen. 15:8–21). At Sinai, the people performed a ratification ceremony for their covenant of human promises. Their promises were presumptuous and lacked faith, and their covenant lasted just forty-six days. We call it the *historical* old covenant, which is the covenant the fathers broke at Sinai (Jer. 31:32). The covenant Jesus ratified or confirmed on Calvary was the New Covenant, or the covenant of redemption.

God also gave the new covenant for the new nation of Israel. He offered "My covenant" on Sinai, a covenant of grace and of what God would do for Israel. It was the new covenant. This was a continuation of the Abrahamic covenant, with important differences: (a) God asked the people for a response; (b) the promises of God applied to Israel as a nation—"then ye shall be a peculiar treasure unto me above all people; … and ye shall be unto me a kingdom of priests, and an holy nation" (Exod. 19:5, 6); (c) God offered grace as part of the covenant; (d) God spoke the ten-commandment law from Sinai and wrote it in stone by His finger. People knew what was right and wrong, and these commands were not new. However, Israel, as a nation, simply needed an official record.

After Calvary, Christ became our new High Priest in heaven. The human priesthood ended, and the priesthood of Jesus in the heavenly sanctuary began. Old Testament believers looked forward; Christians now look back to the work that Jesus accomplished on the cross. In their presumptuous promises, the people bypassed grace and made the *historical* old covenant. The people broke their covenant in forty-six days by a rebellious, heathen festival at the base of Mount Sinai. After a series of intense intercessions by Moses, God took the people back into the Abrahamic or *new* covenant (Exod. 34:9–27) and took the initiative to do "marvels" for the people.

The New Covenant, Step by Step

"I will put my law in their inward parts, and write it in their hearts" (Jer. 31:33). This law is the ten-commandment moral code, which is also called "the covenant." Moses put the tables of the covenant inside the ark.[2] It showed the principles of holiness that God desires in His people (Exod. 19:4–6). Before the captivity, Israel had failed repeatedly by taking part in the idolatry of the surrounding nations. They had broken the Sabbath, oppressed the poor by violence and extortion, and made military alliances with heathen nations against the explicit command of God (Jer. 2–30).

Grace cannot act in a vacuum. Once the law provides knowledge of sin, sinners must identify and confess their sin, consent to do God's will, and receive the grace of God by faith that changes the heart and makes it possible to keep His law (Rom. 3:31). In Christ, human beings become partakers of the divine nature (2 Peter 1:3–8).

In their recurring apostasy and rejection of the covenant and the Ten Commandments, Israel rejected the means by which God could make of them "a peculiar treasure unto [Him] above all people: … and a kingdom of priests, and an holy nation" (Exod. 19:5, 6). The law was not just a document graven on stone, nor written in a book. It needed to be written on the heart to change the person's life. God has always desired changed lives in His people and worship from the heart.[3] Outward forms and ceremonies by themselves are of little value.

"I … will be their God, and they shall be my people" (Jer. 31:33). This is the covenant promise. The promise of God is that He will be with His people and will lift them to again reflect the divine image. He created humans to offer intelligent love and praise to Him. After Adam and Eve's sin, God offered a plan whereby everything that they lost in Eden would be restored.

Finally, there was to be a time when everyone would "know the Lord" and not need to "teach every man his brother" (Jer. 31:33). After the captivity, and after restoration to their land, God gave Israel 490 years to fulfill their purpose as the chosen people (Dan. 9:24). It was God's purpose that the whole earth be prepared for the first advent of Christ, even as, today, the church prepares the way for His second coming.[4] God had glorious plans for Israel, if only they would seek Him.[5]

"I will make a new covenant" (Jer. 31:31). The Bible translates the Hebrew *hadash* as "new," "fresh," or "renewed." Was this a *renewed* covenant, or a completely *new* covenant? There is reason to believe that it was both. To the righteous believing remnant of Israel, it was a renewal of the Abrahamic covenant that they so much loved and relied on for their faith.

There were so many who remained ignorant of the meaning of the sacrifices, but who depended for salvation on their descent from Abraham and their meticulous observance of the law with its sacrifices and rituals. Judaism had become a burdensome religion of works with no power to save. To such people the new covenant was *new*. It replaced the oppressive religion of works with a covenant of grace, in which the power of God through grace would change their lives and give them assurance of eternal life.[6]

The New Covenant in History

When God told the serpent, "I will put enmity between thee and the woman" (Gen. 3:15), He was revealing new covenant principles. God took the initiative by giving humans a conscience and the desire to act rightly. With Noah after the flood, God promised that there would not be another worldwide flood and that the world would have regular seasons so that human beings could plant and harvest food so they might live. God gave Abraham the covenant in detail. He would make of Abraham a strong nation; He would give him land on which to live; He would make him a blessing to all people through his "seed," which is Christ (Gal. 3:16, 29).

God repeated the Abrahamic covenant to Isaac and Jacob, to Moses at the burning bush, to the elders of Israel when Moses returned to Egypt and after Moses first confronted Pharaoh. This covenant, renewed at Sinai, included promises to Israel through grace (Exod. 19:4–6). Because of grace, the ten *commands* (Exod. 20:2–17) became ten *promises* of what God would do in their lives.

When Would God Give the New Covenant?

Jeremiah gave the prophecy regarding the new covenant (Jer. 31:31–34) about ten years into the captivity. The phrases, "Behold the days come" (verse 31) and "after those days" (verse 33), predict that the *historical* new covenant, the covenant of grace, was to be confirmed in the future. There were three dates to consider.

The first date was at the end of the seventy years captivity. They would be restored to their land and to Jerusalem, and the Temple was to be rebuilt. The covenant would be renewed and a process of true heart religion would be instituted. Every truehearted Jew looked forward to this time.

The second date came 490 years after the restoration from the seventy years captivity. This prophecy gave Judah time to fulfill God's purpose for them (Dan. 9:24). It was God's design that the whole earth should be prepared for the first advent of Christ. At that time, the Messiah would come, confirm the covenant, make *one* efficacious sacrifice for sin, and fulfill the ceremonial law. Jesus Himself would become the glory of the second temple. He would take the throne of David, inaugurate His glorious reign, and sanctify His people. The book of Isaiah contains a number of passages that picture a reign of righteousness on this earth, with many other passages that can only be fulfilled in the new earth.

The third date would have to be in the perfection and beauty of the new earth (Jer. 31:34). With the failure of the Jewish nation to accept their Messiah, we must now look forward to His second coming for the final fulfillment of this prophecy.

Endnotes

1.   The Good Kings of Judah who made a Covenant with God :

David	2 Sam. 7:8-16; 23:3-5; 1 Chron. 17:11-14; 2 Chron. 6:16.
Solomon	1 Kings 9:4-7
Asa	2 Chron. 15:12, 13
Jehoshaphat	2 Chron. 20:18, 20, 21

Jehoida & Joash	2 Kings 11:17; 2 Chron. 23:16, 17
Hezekiah	2 Chron. 29:8, 10
Josiah	2 Kings 23:2; 2 Chron. 34:30-32

2. That the Ten Commandments were the covenant can be seen in the following verses: "And he wrote upon the tables the words of the covenant, the ten commandments" (Exod. 34:28). "… the tables of stone, even the tables of the covenant which the Lord made with you" (Deut. 9:9). "… the Lord gave me the two tables of stone, even the tables of the covenant" (Deut. 9:11). "… and the two tables of the covenant were in my two hands" (Deut. 9:15:).

The two tables of "the testimony" (Exod. 31:18) were kept inside the ark, as we learn in Deuteronomy and Hebrews. "I will write on the tables … and thou shalt put them in the ark" (Deut. 10:2). "I … put the tables in the ark which I had made: and there they be" (Deut. 10:5). "… the ark of the covenant overlaid round about with gold, wherein was the golden pot that had manna, and Aaron's rod that budded, and the tables of the covenant" (Heb. 9:4).

3. God desired heart religion in the Old Testament (Gen. 3:15; Deut. 5:29; 30:6; Ps. 37:31; 40:8; 51:10; Isa. 1:17; 51:7; Ezek. 11:19; 36:26).

4. "It was God's design that the whole earth be prepared for the first advent of Christ, even as today the way is preparing for His second coming.… The seasons of prosperity that followed [the restoration] gave ample evidence of God's willingness to accept and forgive, and yet with fatal shortsightedness they turned again and again from their glorious destiny and selfishly appropriated to themselves that which would have brought healing and spiritual life to countless multitudes.… In their self-righteousness they trusted to their own works, to the sacrifices and ordinances themselves, instead of relying upon the merits of Him to whom all these things pointed. Thus, 'going about to establish their own righteousness' (Romans 10:3), they built themselves up in a self-sufficient formalism" (Ellen G. White, *Prophets and Kings* [Mountain View, CA: Pacific Press Publishing Association, 1917], pp. 703–705, 708–709). See Jer. 32:37–40 and Ezek. 36:24–28 which are passages in which God promised to give people a new heart at the restoration.

5. What was God's plan for Judah? Some 490 years after the restoration, Jesus would come, bring glory to the Temple, and begin His reign of righteousness on this earth (Isa. 2:1–4; 25:8, 9; 33:14–24; 35:1–10; 55:11–13; 60:18–20; 65:17–25; 66:22–24).

6. The context of the new covenant is the restoration of Israel; the prophets' promises of restoration anticipated Israel and Judah's return from captivity (Isa. 10:24–34; 14:1–7; 27:12, 13; 40:2–5; 61:4–10; Jer. 16:14–16; 23:3–8; 25:11; 29:10–14; 30:3–11; 32:7–27, 44; Ezek. 34:11–16; 37:1–28; Amos 9:10–15; Micah 2:12, 13).

It was about ten years into the captivity of Judah in Babylon. They had forgotten the Messiah to whom the sacrifices pointed. They had an almost idolatrous understanding of the sacrifices and ceremonies as somehow pleasing God and assuring their salvation. In this setting, the covenant was new again and it was renewed.

The captivity in Babylon was to last for seventy years. Afterward, the people were to have their own land restored (Jer. 31:1–28). Jeremiah also prophesied about a renewed covenant of grace (Jer. 31:31–34). Between the return from Babylon and the coming of the Messiah, Israel was to have its second and final opportunity as a nation to cooperate with the divine plan (see Jer. 12:14–17; Dan. 9:24).

For more on Israel's failure to carry out God's plan, see Francis D. Nichol, *The Seventh-day Adventist Bible Commentary* (Washington, DC: Review and Herald Publishing Association, 1953), vol. 4, pp. 30–32.

Chapter 21

New Testament Insights

> *He was oppressed, and he was afflicted, yet he opened not his mouth: he is*
> *brought as a lamb to the slaughter, and as a sheep before her*
> *hearers is dumb, so he openeth not his mouth.*
> Isaiah 53:7

Animal sacrifice in the Old Testament foreshadowed Christ's giving Himself on the cross to pay the penalty for the broken law that human beings might be saved. This doctrine was but dimly understood or was even totally forgotten during Old Testament times. The fact that the Messiah would be the divine Son of God was virtually unknown, for the Israelites were monotheists and did not believe in a triune God.[1] Their expectation was that the Messiah would take the throne of David and restore the glory of the Temple. To many, the concept of the Messiah's sacrificial death on the cross was unthinkable, and to the Jews it is unthinkable even today. His death was a mystery that became clear, even to the "remnant," only when He came to earth.

The Old Testament Covenant Misperceived

Old Testament discussions of the covenant always revolve around just one covenant—the Abrahamic covenant, which is the major application of the new covenant. Looking back from a New Testament perspective, we see two covenants: the old covenant ratified and broken at Sinai (Exod. 24:3–11; 32) and the new covenant described by Jeremiah and applied throughout human history (Jer. 31:31–34). The difference in perspective between the two is seen in this verse: "For the law was given by Moses, but grace and truth came by Jesus Christ" (John 1:17).

Grace was taught in the Old Testament through the mighty acts of God in delivering His people, by His constant presence in the sanctuary, and through the sacrifices. These were but an indirect illustration of the glory of the grace of God. In Jesus Christ, the veil was taken away, and faith and grace became clear (2 Cor. 3:7–18).

In the new covenant, we see the initiative of God in writing His law in the hearts of His people. We can find grace and God's law written in the heart in the covenant that was given to Adam and Eve, to Abraham, and to Israel at Sinai. God's intended covenant was ratified by Jesus on the cross, and it is the covenant under which true Christians live today (Gal. 3:29).

God specifically asked for a response from Israel at Sinai. The people responded with presumptuous promises of obedience that were lacking in faith. They bypassed the grace that God offered (Exod. 19:4) and, in effect, made a different covenant—the *historical* old covenant, which was broken in forty-six days, but recurred as the "experiential old covenant" whenever people tried to save themselves rather than to accept God's grace.

Over time, the people lapsed into idolatry and developed corrupted views of the covenant and the ceremonial law. These corrupted views were dominant at the time Jesus Christ lived on earth.

There are two required parts to a covenant with God:

- There is the everlasting covenant of God, to which the divine-human covenant points. In His covenant, God gave the Son, the Son came to die for our sins, and the Holy Spirit makes effective the work of grace in the life of every believer. This is what God calls "My covenant," and the new covenant.
- God expected a response from humans. Humans cannot add anything to the covenant of God, yet they cannot be entirely passive either. They must make a commitment to God and to the covenant; they must make a decision to turn to God for help and give consent to the work of grace in their life. In the case of Abraham, God recognized that Abraham already possessed these qualities, so He said nothing more about how Abraham should respond. In the cases of Israel at Sinai and the repetitions of the covenant by the good kings of Judah, God required a response.
- Depending on the circumstances, God added different supporting promises in presenting His covenant.

Why the Jews Rejected Jesus' Divinity

Jesus claimed to be the divine Son of God. He spoke of His pre-existing life in heaven and His following the pre-arranged will of the Father—the covenant of Redemption made before the creation of this world.[2] The Jews consistently denied that Jesus could be divine, in spite of the evidence of His miraculous birth, His teachings, His healing of the sick, and His casting out of devils. They refused to believe even after He raised Lazarus from the dead. We can point to several things that influenced their understanding of the Messiah:

- an increased understanding of the covenant, not well understood at first
- the rigid monotheism of the Jews, which could not accept a Messiah who was divine
- close contact with idolatry in Canaan, Egypt, and Babylon
- the mixed multitude who accompanied Israel to Canaan
- corruption of the ceremonial law attributing merit for salvation to sacrifices and ritual
- misreading the prophecies to expect a human Messiah to restore the throne of David and their former glory
- the influence of Greek philosophy and lifestyle

The life, death, and resurrection of Jesus Christ fully revealed the mystery of the covenant. The believing remnant accepted this understanding and became the early Christian church. The writings of Paul and the other apostles, inspired by the Holy Spirit, presented the final revelation of the covenant of God.

From the New Testament, we see the gospel focus of the everlasting covenant given to Adam and Eve, effective through history, and ratified by Jesus on the cross. The covenant given to Abraham was effectual for Abraham, for his direct descendants, and for all Israel to the end of time, including the church (Gen. 17:7; Gal. 3:29; 1 Peter 2:9).

The Godhead in the New Testament

Only in the New Testament do we learn about the council of the Godhead, in which, before the creation of this world, the heavenly Three formed the covenant of redemption. Jesus, the Son of the living God, is "the Lamb slain from the foundation of the world" (Rev. 13:8). "God so loved the world that He gave His only begotten Son" (John 3:16), and "while we were yet sinners, Christ died for us" (Rom. 5:8; cf. John 10:17, 18). The nature of the divine Son of God was a mystery in Old Testament times. When Christ came, these things were more fully made known. "And without controversy great is the mystery of godliness: God was manifest in the flesh, justified in the Spirit, seen of angels, preached unto the Gentiles, believed on in the world, received up into glory" (1 Tim. 3:16).

There is good reason that people in Old Testament times did not understand the triunity of God: the Hebrews were then strongly monotheistic. Believing in the coequality of the Son and Holy Spirit with the Father would have caused them to think they were worshipping three Gods.[3] It was only after Jesus came that the triunity of God could be explained and understood.[4]

Faith and False Belief

After Adam and Eve's sin in Eden, they were deeply contrite. Their desire was still to do the will of God. Their relationship with God now became their hope. God gave Noah, a righteous man, the covenant and instructions to build the ark. When Abraham received the covenant, he fell on his face in reverence and awe in what God would do. "He believed in the Lord; and he counted it to him for righteousness" (Gen. 15:6). As we look at these patriarchs, God did not ask them for a response. Their lives were an indication of their deep, living relationship with Him.

In Israel, there were two classes of people: the righteous, believing remnant (Rom. 11:2–5, 7) and the unbelieving, careless multitude.[5] It was the righteous remnant who kept the covenant, looked for a Redeemer through the sacrifices, and expected Jesus when He came. These were the people who began the early Christian church.

Between the Old and New Testaments is a significant change in language. The Old Testament contains much discussion and emphasis on the covenant. The New Testament does not discuss the covenant nearly so much. Instead, the "gospel" largely replaces covenant language, describes the meaning of Jesus' sacrifice on Calvary, and calls for men and women to have faith in God and to accept His grace.

All statements about salvation and eternal life arise out of the covenant. Statements about faith and grace emphasize the purpose of the covenant, which became necessary as the purpose of the church was to prepare a people to meet Christ when He came again.[6]

The unbelieving careless crowd went through the forms of religion, expecting that the performance of sacrifices and temple rituals assured them of salvation. They forgot the Redeemer to whom they pointed, rejected Him when He came, and crucified Him in the end. The leaders in Judah fell into this group, making the rejection of Jesus a national tragedy. The leaders of Israel finally and totally rejected Christ in the stoning of Stephen and the persecution of the church (Acts 7, 8).

Grace, Jesus' Mission

Jesus came to establish the kingdom of grace. It was only after people are saved by grace that they are ready for the benefits of salvation and eternity in the new earth. In Jesus' life, He illustrated the divine attributes of character. He was "merciful and gracious, longsuffering, and abundant in goodness and truth" (Exod. 34:6, 7).

The corruption of the ceremonial law had become so ingrained in the thinking of the people that the disciples themselves did not fully understand Jesus' mission until after His resurrection. As Gentile converts came into the church, there were some Jewish converts to Christianity who believed that Gentile Christians must become Jews in order to be saved!

The church held a council in Jerusalem, where they determined that Gentile Christians needed to "abstain from pollutions of idols, and from fornication, and from things strangled, and from blood" (Acts 15:20) and that no other "ordinances" should be required of them (Acts 16:4).[7] A delegation returned to Antioch with this message (Acts 15:22–31). The Gentiles received it gladly in both places, but history shows that certain Jewish Christians continued to cause trouble. Paul wrote several epistles dealing with this problem.

All needed to have faith in Jesus, the One who gave Himself as the one effective sacrifice on the cross and who continues to minister His sacrifice as High Priest in the heavenly sanctuary (Heb. 9:14, 15, 24–28). However, promotion of the ordinances continued to be a problem. Evidences of this controversy are seen in several ways:

- a return to sacrifice and ritual as a denial of Jesus Christ and the efficacy of the cross of Calvary
- the introduction of false doctrines into the young churches in opposition to the meaning of Jesus' sacrifice on the cross
- an old covenant mindset of legalism, denying the meaning and mission of Jesus' sacrifice on the cross
- Paul's focus on Jesus Christ and Him crucified in responding to the issue in Romans, Galatians, 2 Corinthians 3, Ephesians, and Hebrews

Jesus, Mediator of the New Covenant

The center and focus of the everlasting covenant is the willing sacrifice of Jesus on the cross to pay the penalty for the sins of human beings. This was the new (or "renewed") covenant given to Adam and Eve (Gen. 3:15), Noah, Abraham and his descendants, Israel, David, and Solomon.

Jesus is the mediator of the new covenant, a covenant which flows from the everlasting covenant of God and which Jesus confirmed and made effective on the cross. Jeremiah first wrote of the new covenant (Jer. 31:31–34) with God's promise to put the law within their hearts and minds. It is by this covenant that we humans can now live the life of Christ by grace (Gal. 2:20).

Jesus Christ revealed the covenant in all its glory. New Testament writings centered on Jesus Christ Himself rather than on the covenant. While the covenant of grace and salvation pardoned and cleansed from sin, it will not be until Jesus' second coming that the sinful nature is cleansed and the image of God is fully restored in every human being. Meanwhile, Christ covers the human sinful nature by the robe of His righteousness until He returns to earth.

Jesus did not establish a new covenant at His crucifixion. He confirmed a covenant established in heaven before the creation. It was the same covenant given to Adam and Eve, to Israel, and which will be in effect until He comes again. To *confirm* a covenant does *not* mean to finish one covenant and begin another. It means to strengthen and make effective an already established covenant. Daniel 9:27 says "he shall confirm the covenant with many…." Yet, who are the "many"? Hebrews explains:

> And for this cause he is the mediator of the new testament, that by means of death,
> for the redemption of the transgressions that were under the first testament, they
> which are called might receive the promise of eternal inheritance. (Heb. 9:15)[8]

Ever since Eden, men had offered sacrifices for sin. This included the 1500 years of the history of Israel. Through these sacrifices, the priest took their guilt into the Temple and pardoned their sins. Pardon could be obtained only in anticipation of the cross of Christ on Calvary. Now that Jesus has made the true sacrifice on the cross, He has confirmed pardon for humanity's sins and our "eternal inheritance."

Endnotes

1.   However, the angel made His relation to the Almighty plain when he announced to Mary: "He shall be great, and shall be called the Son of the Highest: and the Lord God shall give unto him the throne of his father David: and he shall reign over the house of Jacob for ever; and of his kingdom there shall be no end" (Luke 1:32, 33; cf. Matt. 1:23, in which "Emmanuel" is translated "God with us"). In addition, the prophecies had indicated that this would be the case: "Therefore the Lord himself shall give you a sign; Behold, a virgin shall conceive, and bear a son, and shall call his name Immanuel" (Isa. 7:14). "For unto us a child is born, unto us a son is given: and the government shall be upon his shoulder: and his name shall be called Wonderful, Counsellor, The mighty God, The everlasting Father, The Prince of Peace" (Isa. 9:6).

2.   The will of the Father was established in the council of the Godhead before creation (Ps. 40:8; 53:10; Matt. 26:39, 42; Mark 14:36; Luke 22:42; John 4:34; 5:30; 6:29, 38; Phil. 2:7, 8; Heb. 5:8; 10:7–9).

3. The Bible identifies the Father, Son, and Holy Ghost (Isa. 11:1, 2; 48:16; Matt. 3:16, 17; 28:19, 20; 1 Cor. 12:3, 4; 2 Cor. 13:14; Eph. 2:18; 1 Tim. 3:16). *Godhead* is a term used in Acts 17:29; Romans 1:20; and Colossians 2:9. There are many passages of Scripture on the Holy Spirit (Luke 4:14; John 14:16, 17, 26, 16:7–13; Acts 1:8; 2:1–4, 38; 4:33; 10:38; 1 Thess. 1:5). Jesus' divinity is also mentioned many times (Isa. 9:6, 7; 53; John 1:1–3; 8:58; 10:30; 14:9; 17:11, 21, 22; Titus 2:13; 1 John 5:20). The Bible uses the plural name for God (Gen. 1:1–12, 14, 16–18, 20–22, 24–29, 31). For a discussion of the Hebrew problems with the triune Godhead, see http://www.gotquestions.org/Godhead.html. For more on the Trinity, see Fernando Canale, "Doctrine of God: The Father, Son, and Holy Spirit," *Handbook of Seventh-day Adventist Theology* (Hagerstown, MD: Review and Herald Publishing Association, 2000) pp. 140–151.

4. Other verses on the mystery from the ages now revealed in Jesus Christ include Romans 16:25, 26; 1 Corinthians 2:6, 7; Ephesians 3:9–11, 17–19; and Colossians 1:26–28.

The Spirit of God in the Old Testament: (59 verses)

Gen. 1:2; 6:3; 41:38	Ps. 51:11; 104:30; 139:7; Pr. 1:23
Ex. 31:3	Isa. 11:2; 32:15; 40:13; 42:1; 44:3; 59:19, 21; 61:1; 63:10, 11
Num. 11:19, 25 26, 29	Ez. 2:2; 3:12, 14, 24; 8:3; 11:1, 24; 36:27; 37:1, 14; 39:29; 43:5
Deut. 34:9; Jdg. 3:10; 6:34; 11:29; 14:6	Dan. 4:8, 9, 18; 5:11, 14
1 Sam. 10:6, 10; 11:6; 6:13; 19:20	Joel 2:29; Mic. 2:7; 3:8
2 Sam. 23:2; 2 Chron. 20:14; 24:29; Job 26:13	Zech, 4:6; 6:8; 7:12

5. Scripture provides many examples of the righteous remnant (Gen. 4:25, 26; "the sons of God," 6:2, 8–10; 12:1–3; 1 Kings 19:18; 2 Kings 19:31; Ezra 3:8; 9:8; Isa. 1:9; 10:20–22; 11:11, 16; 37:32; Joel 2:32; Amos 5:15; Zeph. 2:7, 9; 3:13; Hag. 1:12, 14; Rom. 9:27; 11:4, 5; Rev. 12:17).

6. Faith and grace, the response to the covenant of God, are especially emphasized in the New Testament.

Word	Old Testament	New Testament	Total
Faith	2	229	231
Grace	37	122	159
Obey	77	32	109
Covenant	258	21 (12 in Hebrews)	279

7. The word "decrees" (Greek *dogma*) in Acts 16:4 is translated "ordinances" in Ephesians 2:15 and Colossians 2:14.

8. Notice that "testament" is translated from the Greek word for "covenant": *diathēkē*.

Chapter 22

The Throne of David

And thine house and thy kingdom shall be established for ever before thee:
thy throne shall be established for ever.
2 Samuel 7:16

God gave the covenant to David and Solomon with marvelous promises. David made mistakes but never lost his faith in God. God gave Solomon wisdom, but Solomon was not a righteous king. His many pagan wives led him deep into idolatry. His son, Rehoboam, divided the kingdom and broke the covenant of David.

During the next four hundred years, Judah had six righteous kings, who instituted revival and renewed the covenant with God. However, Judah also had twenty-three wicked kings, who led the people deeper and deeper into idolatry. Finally, God had to allow Judah to go into captivity, and the throne of David became vacant. For the rest of history, there were no more kings on David's throne.

Many believe that the promises for the temporal reign of Judah still apply today and that they are essential to the doctrines and politics of today. There are others who look at history and understand that all the promises of God are contingent on human willingness to obey.

The "Forever" Throne of David

Early in its history Israel was a theocracy ruled directly by God through priests and prophets. While Samuel was high priest, the people demanded a king. The first king, Saul, was a disappointment. Of the next king, David, God said, he is "a man after mine own heart" (Acts 13:22). Yet, David was a man of war and a sinner, though he was quick to turn to God, quick to repent, and quick to praise God. When David was king, it was the golden age for Israel. All subsequent kings of Judah sat on the "throne of David." The family line of David culminated in the Messiah, the "priest-king" after the order of Melchizedek.

David, as king and representing God, made a covenant "in the presence of the Lord" with the elders who came to make him king in Hebron. The following verses describe David's faith in God and are in keeping with God's everlasting covenant with Abraham.[1]

> Even when Saul was king, you were the one who led Israel in battle. The Lord your God said to you, "You will be the shepherd for my people Israel. You will be their leader." So all the [elders] of Israel came to King David at Hebron. He made an agreement [covenant] with them in Hebron in the presence of the Lord. Then they poured oil on David to make him king over Israel. The Lord had promised through Samuel that this would happen. (1 Chron. 11:2, 3, NCV)

God made a covenant with David that He would establish David's throne forever (2 Sam. 7:8–16; 23:3–5; Jer. 33:17, 18). When Solomon came to the throne, God gave him the same promises (1 Chron. 22:10, 17; 28:6–8), which were contingent on obedience. Because of apostasy, Judah went into captivity for seventy years. The throne of David became vacant and remained vacant even after the restoration (1 Chron. 17:11–14; 2 Chron. 6:16). The people looked to the coming Messiah to restore the throne of David and the former glory of Israel. However, Jesus came to establish the kingdom of grace and to prepare a people for eternal life in the new earth. Only in the new earth will Jesus take the throne of David and reign over His kingdom forever.

> And thine [David's] house and thy kingdom shall be established for ever before thee: thy throne shall be established for ever (2 Sam. 7:16).

> And I will settle him [Solomon] in mine house and in my kingdom forever: and his throne shall be established for evermore (1 Chron. 17:14).

> "Now Lord, God of Israel, keep for your servant David my father the promises you made to him when you said, 'You shall never fail to have a man to sit before me on the throne of Israel, if only your sons are careful in all they do to walk before me according to my law, as you have done.' " (2 Chron. 6:16, NIV)

"Forever" does not always mean *eternally*, especially in human situations. In Samuel's case, he went to the sanctuary as a child "lent to the Lord" for as long as he lived (1 Sam. 1:22, 28). In that situation "forever" meant for the length of his lifetime. Other prophecies speak of the Messiah as the shepherd, who will sit on David's throne.[2] These prophecies point to Jesus on the throne of David in the new earth.

Was This a Failed Prophecy?

Does the cessation of the throne of David at the time of the captivity mean that this was a failed prophecy? One must realize that God does not change. A number of the prophecies in the Bible are *conditional*. Fulfillment of such prophecy depends on the response of the people. In Deuteronomy, the blessings of the covenant depended on their obedience.[3] At the same time, curses were pronounced in case of apostasy.[4] Why would one expect Israel to be unconditionally blessed when the conditions of blessing are so plainly revealed?

Under David, the kingdom of Israel expanded to its greatest extent, taking in all the neighboring kingdoms that had been their enemies in the past. From these kingdoms, as well as from kingdoms that remained friendly, David and Solomon amassed gifts of silver, gold, cedar trees, horses, chariots, and spices (1 Kings 10:27; 2 Chron. 1:15).

Solomon was given unparalleled wisdom that impressed all the surrounding nations. His reign promised to be even more magnificent than that of David. It was under Solomon that the Temple was built. However, he "loved many strange women." To satisfy his foreign wives, Solomon built temples and groves for pagan practices, and he, himself, took part in their rituals (1 Kings 11:1–13). God warned him that the kingdom would be divided because of his apostasy (1 Kings 9:4–7). The division began during his reign as local revolts began to undermine the kingdom of David (1 Kings 11:14–35). When Solomon's son, Rehoboam, became king, the kingdom was divided, the ten northern tribes allied with Jeroboam, and Judah and Benjamin remained with Rehoboam.

Because of Israel's unfaithfulness and continued apostasy in the face of repeated warnings from the prophets, God finally had to allow first Israel and then Judah to go into captivity. The Jewish leaders believed that the Messiah would restore the throne of David and that there would always be a king to sit upon it (Jer. 33:17–18). This led to the people's failure to recognize Jesus when He came and to their rejection and crucifixion of Him after His three and a half years of ministry.

Covenant Renewed With Solomon

God gave the covenant to David, and renewed it with Solomon, including the conditions for success. Those conditions must also have applied to the covenant God made with David.

> And if thou wilt walk before me, as David thy father walked, in integrity of heart, and in uprightness, to do according to all that I have commanded thee, and wilt keep my statutes and my judgments: Then I will establish the throne of thy kingdom upon Israel for ever, as I promised to David thy father, saying, There shall not fail thee a man upon the throne of Israel. But if ye shall at all turn from following me, ye or your children, and will not keep my commandments and my statutes which I have set before you, but go and serve other gods, and worship them: Then will I cut off Israel out of the land which I have given them; and this house, which I have hallowed for my name, will I cast out of my sight; and Israel shall be a proverb and a byword among all people. (1 Kings 9:4–7)

> "Now, Lord, God of Israel, keep for your servant David my father the promises you made to him when you said, 'You shall never fail to have a man to sit before me on the throne of Israel, if only your sons are careful in all they do to walk before me according to my law, as you have done.' " (2 Chron. 6:16, NIV)

The Kings of Judah

When Solomon became king, God fulfilled his request for a "wise and understanding heart" (1 Kings 3:12). In addition, Solomon received riches, fame, and national security. The righteous kings that followed Solomon each renewed the covenant.

After Rehoboam and Abijah came Asa, who began as a good king. He put idolatry away and reinstituted worship of the true God. Large numbers of people from the northern kingdom came into Judah, because "God was with him." In his fifteenth year, at a great gathering in Jerusalem, they renewed the covenant with God. "And they entered into a covenant to seek the Lord God of their fathers with all their heart and with all their soul; … and he was found of them: and the Lord gave them rest round about" (2 Chron. 15:12, 15).

Jehoshaphat was an excellent king, but not perfect. When threatened by Moab, Ammon, and Edom, he proclaimed a fast "to seek help of the Lord." God promised Jehoshaphat, "Ye shall not need to fight in this battle: set yourselves, stand ye still, and see the salvation of the Lord with you, O Judah and Jerusalem" (2 Chron. 20:17). Jehoshaphat set singers before the army and stood still and watched while their enemies in sudden fear slaughtered each other.

Jehoshaphat was followed by corrupt rulers: Jehoram and Ahaziah and the wicked queen Athaliah, who killed all the king's sons except for Joash. After six years, Jehoiada organized the Temple guard and staged a coup against Athaliah. "And Jehoiada made a covenant between the Lord and the king and the people, that they should be the Lord's people; between the king also and the people" (2 Kings 11:17). However, this revival lasted only until Jehoiada himself died.

Judah went downhill with Amaziah, Uzziah, Jotham, and Ahaz. Hezekiah followed these kings. He immediately repaired the Temple and reestablished temple worship. "Now, it is in mine heart, to make a covenant with the Lord God of Israel, that his fierce wrath may turn away from us" (2 Chron. 29:10).

Hezekiah restored the worship of the true God. He removed the altars, idols, and the priests of heathenism. He called for all those in Judah and the remnant in the northern kingdom to come to Jerusalem for the Passover, repentance, and cleansing. It had been years since they had attended a Passover. Hezekiah assigned priests and Levites to educate the people in the proper way to conduct the rituals. Hezekiah prayed that the Passover would be a success and would call the people back to the worship of the living God. Idolatry was overthrown, and the sanctuary services were renewed. "And the Lord hearkened to Hezekiah and healed the people" (2 Chron. 30:20).

With the apostate kings Manasseh and Amon, idolatry deepened. Josiah, the last righteous king, in his eighteenth year, repaired the Temple and established temple services. Hilkiah, the high priest, found the book of the law and gave it to Josiah. When the book was read to him, the king rent his clothes. Their apostasy had deepened far more than he thought. He called the people and read it to them.

> And the king [Josiah] stood by a pillar, and made a covenant before the Lord, to walk after the Lord, and to keep his commandments and his testimonies and his statutes with all their heart and all their soul, to perform the words of this covenant that were written in this book. And all the people stood to the covenant. (2 Kings 23:3)

Following Josiah, there came in close succession Jehoahaz, Jehoiakim, Jehoiachin, and Zedekiah. All were wicked, and all refused to listen to the prophets. Judah's time had run out. The everlasting covenant was forgotten, broken, and abandoned by the people and their kings. "But they mocked the messengers of God, and despised his words, and misused his prophets, until the wrath of the Lord arose against his people, till there was no remedy" (2 Chron. 36:16).

Jeremiah desperately tried to influence Zedekiah, the king of Judah, to repent. Jeremiah advised him to cooperate with the king of Babylon. If he would listen to the messages from God and cooperate with the king of Babylon, the throne of David would be preserved. If not, the throne of David would become desolate (Jer. 22:4, 5), and the name of God would be dishonored.

> And many nations shall pass by this city, and they shall say every man to his neighbour, Wherefore hath the Lord done thus unto this great city? Then they shall answer, Because they have forsaken the covenant of the Lord their God, and worshipped other gods, and served them. (Jer. 22:8, 9)

In this history, we see God patiently working with Israel at every opportunity, continually trying to bring the people back to Him and back into the everlasting covenant. When there was no response to the efforts of love and grace, God could do nothing more. The armies of Egypt and Babylon in turn invaded Judah. Nebuchadnezzar took many captives to Babylon, and the captivity had begun.

The phrase, "the throne of David," has come to apply to all the kings that followed in the line of David. This came to an end with the captivity of Judah to Babylon. After the restoration, a series of larger nations governed Judah, and the Davidic line of kings was not restored. Prophecy foretold that the Messiah would take the throne of David. Since Jesus did not do this, the governing bodies of Judah rejected Him.

Here is an intriguing thought: What might Jesus have done if the leaders had accepted Him? Had Jesus taken the throne of David, His government would have been vastly different from what many expected.

Many people today look at the covenant and promises to David as being "unconditional" and still awaiting fulfillment. Such thinking does not take into consideration the *blessings* and the *curses* that were the conditions of fulfillment. There is no doubt but that the purposes of God cannot be frustrated. Even so, the people's response often causes their delay or necessitates that they be fulfilled through another agent. Now we must look to Jesus' second coming when He will "set up a kingdom which shall never be destroyed" and which "shall be given to the people of the saints of the most High" (Dan. 2:44; 7:27).[5]

Endnotes

1. David's covenant with God was "forever" (Ps. 89:3, 4; 31–37; 132:11–18).
2. For the Messiah sitting on the throne of David, see Isaiah 9:7 and Luke 1:31, 32. For the Messiah being the shepherd of God's flock, see Isaiah 40:11; John 10:14–16; and Ezekiel 37:24.
3. Wonderful blessings were in store for Israel if they continued in obedience (Deut. 7:1–26; 8:1–10; 11:10–15; 28:1–14).
4. If they should go into apostasy or idolatry, they would be cursed (Deut. 28:15–68; 29:18–29). God applied the blessings and curses to the throne of David (Jer. 17:24, 25; 22:3–5; 36:30).
5. The final endless messianic fulfillment will occur when Jesus comes again (Isa. 9:6, 7; Luke 1:32, 33; Heb. 1:5–9).

Chapter 23
The Messiah Foretold

Now to Abraham and his seed were the promises made. He saith not, and to
seeds, as of many; but as of one, and to thy seed, which is Christ.
Galatians 3:16

Jesus' sacrifice on the cross and resurrection are the crowning events of history. In the providence of God, more than three hundred prophecies in the Old Testament prepared the world for Jesus' coming. Jesus fulfilled the ten-commandment law by His sinless life. His sacrifice on the cross fulfilled the symbolic sacrifices of the ceremonial law. He came to show that the Father is a God of love and is "merciful and gracious, longsuffering, and abundant in goodness and truth" (Exod. 34:6).

Mark's Gospel opens with John the Baptist, waist-deep in the Jordan in fulfillment of prophecy. Matthew portrays the Baptist's powerful message, "Repent ye: for the kingdom of heaven is at hand" (Matt. 3:2). It rang in the ears of the people as they flocked to hear the voice of the one crying in the wilderness, "prepare ye the way of the Lord" (Mark 1:3). Prophecy had declared it, and now it was time for the promised Messiah to emerge (Dan. 9:24–27).

The Purpose of Prophecy

The Bible is a book of prophecy, and prophecy is reality from God's point of view. The Bible reveals the origin of the human race, our history, and what will take place in the future. It is God's purpose to reveal the truth to His people. "Surely the Lord God will do nothing, but he revealeth his secret unto his servants the prophets" (Amos 3:7).

Prophecy is a message from God revealing things that we would not otherwise learn. Learning must be guided by the written Word of God. In answer to prayer, the Holy Spirit will guide our understanding and application of what we read.

> I have yet many things to say unto you, but ye cannot bear them now. Howbeit when
> he, the Spirit of truth, is come, he will guide you into all truth: for he shall not speak
> of himself; but whatsoever he shall hear, that shall he speak: and he will show you
> things to come. (John 16:12, 13)

Prophesying of the end time, Jesus warned four times, "Take heed that no man deceive you" (Matt. 24:4, 5, 11, 24). Knowing the truth is a strong barrier against deception. Prophecies may not be easily understood at the time they are given. It is much easier to recognize a prophesied event once the prophecy is fulilled, and, when it is, it strengthens our faith.

The Old Testament is the foundation for the New Testament. It is in the Old Testament that we find the prophecies of the coming Messiah! By fulfilling prophecy, the New Testament confirms and explains what Old Testament prophecies mean.

> And now I have told you before it come to pass, that, when it is come to pass, ye might believe. (John 14:29)

> Now all these things happened unto them for ensamples: and they are written for our admonition, upon whom the ends of the world are come. (1 Cor. 10:11)

The Coming Messiah

After Adam and Eve sinned, God spoke to them and gave them hope and a promise. He also gave them a conscience and a desire to do what was right. Jesus Christ, the seed of the woman, would "bruise the serpent's head" and destroy sin and Satan. In the new earth, the sinful nature in humankind would be changed and the image of God restored. The perfection of Eden would be brought back again. These were the promises of the Redeemer to come. God permitted Satan to live during human history, to demonstrate to the universe the evil there is in sin. "And I will put enmity between thee and the woman, and between thy seed and her seed; it shall bruise thy head, and thou shalt bruise his heel" (Gen. 3:15).

God gave the gospel covenant to Noah and to Abraham in detail. Jesus Christ fulfills the promises made to Abraham: "In thee shall all families of the earth be blessed" (Gen. 12:3) and "thy seed shall possess the gate of his enemies; And in thy seed shall all the nations of the earth be blessed" (Gen. 22:17, 18). "Now to Abraham and his seed were the promises made. He saith not, and to seeds, as of many; but as of one, and to thy seed, which is Christ" (Gal. 3:16).

Hidden in the promises and renewals of the covenant throughout the Old Testament is the golden thread of the promised Redeemer to come. There were 300 promises of the Messiah in the Old Testament. Here, are some of them:

What was foretold	Old Testament prophecy	New Testament fulfillment
Born of a virgin	Isa. 7:14	Matt. 1:18, 24, 25
Born in Bethlehem	Micah 5:2	Matt. 2:1
Time of His birth	Dan. 9:24–27	Luke 1:5; 2:1
Time of His baptism	Dan. 9:24–27	Luke 3:1
Son of God	Ps. 2:7	Matt. 3:17
His divinity	Ps. 45:6, 7, 11; Isa. 9:6; 25:9	Matt. 16:16; John 8:51, 58; 10:30
His preexistence	Micah 5:2	Phil. 2:5–8; Col 1:17; John 17:24; Heb. 10:5

What was foretold	Old Testament prophecy	New Testament fulfillment
Anointed by Holy Spirit	Isa. 11:2	Matt. 3:16, 17
Ministry of miracles:	Isa. 35:5, 6	Matt. 9:35
Teaching in parables:	Ps. 78:2	Matt. 13:34
Seed of Abraham	Gen. 22:18	Gal. 3:16
Tribe of Judah	Gen. 49:10	Heb. 7:14
Preceded by Messenger	Isa. 40:3	Matt. 3:1–3

Christians understand these Old Testament prophecies through their New Testament fulfillment. Did the Jews have the same understanding before Messiah came? What were their expectations?

The prophecy of the Messiah's coming from Bethlehem was clear. Isaiah 7:14 speaks of the virgin birth, which they could have understood. However, the Jews did not expect a prophet to come from Nazareth of Galilee. They did not expect Him to die or to be resurrected.

For the Jews to accept the Messiah as divine required them to accept a second person being God. The Jews were and are strongly monotheistic. After centuries of struggle against idolatry and seventy years of captivity because of idolatry, they had learned their lesson all too well. Simply and humanly speaking, it was too much for them to accept this concept.[1] Yet there were many who were in expectation when Messiah came!

Dual Expectations of the Messiah

Some Messianic prophecies depicted a lowly and humble Messiah who would come riding a donkey (Zech. 9:9), live a life of suffering, and die as the sacrifices for sin foretell.[2] Other Messianic prophecies predicted a conquering king who would come in imposing triumph "in the clouds," take the throne of David, and live forever.[3] "This 'dual aspect' of Messiah" led "to the idea that there would be two Messiahs: Messiah ben Joseph and Messiah ben David."[4]

The Jews and even Jesus' own disciples did not fully understand His mission. He came to teach mercy and love as the basis for the law. He came to bring the kingdom of grace. The Jews focused their hopes on a Messiah who would take the throne of David and restore the past glories of Israel. What they did not realize was that the kingdom of glory could not come until the kingdom of grace had changed people's lives.

Christians "believe that Yeshua is both *Mashiach Ben Yosef* (the suffering servant—at His first coming) and *Mashiach Ben David* (the reigning King—at His second coming) [see Isaiah 52:13–53:12 and Psalm 22]. He is also the Anointed Prophet, Priest, and King as foreshadowed by other *m'shichim* in the Tanakh."[5]

A Conquering King

The following are prophecies of the Messiah as the conquering king (*Mashiach Ben David*): With this background, one must be sympathetic of Jewish reactions when Jesus came.

He would be a king.	Jer. 23:5, 6; Ps. 2; 110; Matt. 27:37
He would live forever.	Ps. 102:24–27; 89:4;

He would sit on the throne of David forever.	1 Kings 2:45; Isa. 9:7; Jer. 17:25; Luke 1:32
His kingdom shall be forever.	Dan. 2:44; 4:3, 34; 6:26; 7:14
He was to rule the world.	Ps. 2:6–9; cf. Ps. 72

Maimonides, a.k.a. Moses ben Maimon (AD 1135–1204), the greatest medieval Jewish thinker and Talmudic codifier, gave a viewpoint that was common among Jews about the Messiah:

> If a king will arise from the House of David who is learned in Torah and observant of the *mitzvot* [Torah's commandments, counted by Maimonides as 613 in number] as prescribed by the written law and the oral law, as David his ancestor was, and will compel all of Israel to walk in the way of the Torah and reinforce the breaches; and fight the wars of G-d, we may, with assurance, consider him the Messiah. If he succeeds in the above, builds the temple in its place, and gathers the dispersed of Israel, he is definitely the Messiah. ... If he did not succeed to this degree or he was killed, he surely is not the redeemer promised by the Torah ... (*Mishneh Torah*)[6]

"The concept of the Messiah King, the 'Anointed One' who would one day come to deliver His people from oppression at the beginning of an era of world peace has been the sustaining hope of the Jewish people for generations.... Indeed, he functions as Israel's Savior who would be empowered by God to:

- Restore the kingdom of David (Jer. 23:5; 30:9; Ezek. 34:23)
- Restore the Temple (Isa. 2:2; Micah 4:1; Zech. 6:13; Ezek. 37:26–28)
- Regather the exiles (Isa. 11:12; 43:5, 6; 51:11) ...
- Usher in world peace and the knowledge of the true God (Isa. 2:4; 11:9)....
- Spread Torah knowledge of the God of Israel, which will unite humanity as one. As it says, "God will be King over all the world—on that day; God will be One and His Name will be One" (Zech. 14:9)"[7]

The Tanakh gives "Nathan's oracle to David" (2 Sam. 7:12, 13), presenting "the key passage on which the idea of the Messianic king who would rule in righteousness and attain universal dominion." Solomon cannot have fulfilled this covenant, "therefore the Seed of which the oracle refers is another anointed King who would sit on the throne forever and ever."[8]

> And when thy days be fulfilled, and thou shalt sleep with thy fathers, I will set up thy seed after thee, which shall proceed out of thy bowels, and I will establish his kingdom. He shall build an house for my name, and I will stablish the throne of his kingdom for ever. (2 Sam. 7:12, 13)

From Maimonides' writings, Christians learn that they cannot know the detailed fulfillment for any future prophecy beforehand. One must carefully study the prophecy and be ready to recognize its fulfillment when it comes. When Peter affirmed, "Thou art the Christ, the Son of the living God," Jesus said that Peter, a Jew, could know this only by direct revelation from God!

The Jews in Jesus' time had reasons for their beliefs. However, in their unwonted certainty the Jewish leaders closed the door to further revelation. They failed to recognize the abundant number of signs that Jesus was the Messiah when He came.

The Suffering Lamb of God

Equally prominent are references to a Messiah who would be a sin bearer and would suffer (*Mashiach ben Yosef*):

- Genesis 3:15—"Thou shalt bruise his heel." His suffering was foretold.
- Genesis 22:12, 13—A ram caught in the thicket took the place of Isaac for the sacrifice.
- Exodus 12:12, 13—The firstborn was saved in the Passover by the blood of the lamb.
- Psalm 22:1–18—This psalm accurately portrays Jesus' feeling of abandonment on the cross.
- Isaiah 52:13–53:12; Psalm 18:4–6; 35:11, 12; 69:7, 9—These prophecies describe the suffering, persecution, and false accusing of God's "servant."
- Zechariah 9:9—Jesus was lowly and riding upon an ass, even in His triumphal entry into Jerusalem.
- Mark 8:31—Jesus foretold that the Son of man must suffer, be rejected, be killed, and rise again.

Joseph prefigured the Suffering Messiah (Gen. 37–50) "in the oral traditions of Judaism. *Mashiach ben Yosef*" was "to be a forerunner and harbinger of the final deliverer, *Mashiach ben David*." Christians see Messiah as *ben Yosef,* who suffered in His first coming for the sins of Israel (Isa. 53) as the Messiah. Jewish authorities on this topic say:

> Messiah son of Joseph was slain, as it is written, "They shall look unto me whom they have pierced; and they shall mourn for him as one mourneth for his only son" Zech. xii 10 (Suk. 52a)

> The Talmud explains: "The Messiah—what is his name? Those of the house of Rabbi Yuda the saint say, the sick one, as it is said, 'Surely he had borne our sicknesses'" (Sanhedrin 98b)

> Referring to Zech. 12:10–12, "R. Dosa says: '(They will mourn) over the Messiah who will be slain.'" (B. Suk. 52a; also Y. Suk. 55b)

> But he was wounded … meaning that since the Messiah bears our iniquities which produce the effect of His being bruised, it follows that whosoever will not admit that Messiah thus suffers for our iniquities, must endure and suffer for them himself (Rabbi Elijah de Vidas)[9]

There are many prophecies yet to be fulfilled during the end time of earth's history. We must know what these prophecies say and then observe the signs of the times. Most of all, we must listen to the Holy Spirit to recognize when the fulfillment of these prophecies occurs.

Endnotes

1.   *Elohim* is a plural term for God; the "one God in three Persons" concept occurs in Genesis 1:26; Isaiah 48:16; 1 Cor. 12:4–6; 2 Cor. 13:14; and Eph. 2:18. To some people this implies "three Gods." A Christian believes in *one* God in three Persons. The nature of God is beyond human reasoning. One must accept God's revelation about Himself and not speculate on that which has not been revealed about His nature.

2.   Jesus' suffering and death was foretold in the sacrifice of animals. God accepted Abel's sacrifice as it foretold the death of the Messiah, while Cain's sacrifice did not. The Passover most clearly pointed to the blood of the lamb protecting the firstborn (and, by extension, the entire family) from death (Exod. 12:3–13). Abraham's call to sacrifice Isaac showed that it would be an "only begotten Son" who would be sacrificed for sin (Gen. 22:2; Heb. 11:17). Other key prophecies fulfilled by Christ are Zech. 9:9; Isa. 52:13–53:12, and Ps. 22.

3.   There are prophecies that predict that Messiah will rule the nations, but they do not specify the time. His ruling the nations will be fulfilled at the second coming (Gen. 49:10, RSV; Ps. 22:27, 28; 67:4; 72:9; 89:27–29). That He will rule with a "rod of iron" (Rev. 2:27; 12:5; 19:15) means that He will judge the nations, for Psalm 2:9 speaks of breaking the nations "with a rod of iron." Isaiah prophesied a time of world peace, ruled by the Messiah, which will never end (Isa. 2:4; 9:6, 7; 42:1–4; 55:3–5; Micah 4:2, 3). If the Jews had accepted their Messiah, God would have been able to fulfill His glorious purpose for them (Ezek. 21:25–27; Dan. 2:44; 7:13, 14; Zech. 6:13).

4.   http://www.hebrew4christians.com/Scripture/Shloshah-Asar_Ikkarim/Mashiach/mashiach.html, accessed 2/12/13.

5.   http://www.hebrew4christians.com/Scripture/Shloshah-Asar_Ikkarim/Mashiach/mashiach.html, accessed 2/12/13. The term *m'shichim* means other anointed prophets, priests, and kings.

6.   http://www.hebrew4christians.com/Names_of_G-d/Messiah/messiah.html, accessed 2/12/13.

7.   http://www.hebrew4christians.com/Scripture/Shloshah-Asar_Ikkarim/Mashiach/mashiach.html, accessed 2/12/13.

8.   http://www.hebrew4christians.com/Names_of_G-d/Messiah/messiah.html, accessed 2/12/13. Second Samuel 7 is the oracle given by Nathan the prophet to David in which God promises to provide David with a house, and in which his son (Solomon) would build the temple. Yet, if the son should commit iniquity, God would punish him.

9.   http://www.hebrew4christians.com/Names_of_G-d/Messiah/messiah.html, accessed 2/12/13.

Chapter 24
Anointed

The word which God sent unto the children of Israel, preaching peace by Jesus
Christ: (he is Lord of all:) That word, I say, ye know, which was published
throughout all Judaea, and began from Galilee, after the baptism which John
preached; How God anointed Jesus of Nazareth with the Holy Ghost
and with power: who went about doing good, and healing all that
were oppressed of the devil; for God was with him.

Acts 10:36–38

Old Testament prophecies showed that the Messiah, the Anointed One, would appear at the end of the sixty-ninth week of the seventy week prophecy (Dan. 9:25). Jesus' coming was the fulfillment of the everlasting covenant of God. The people knew about the prophecy of Daniel and knew that the time was near. There was a general expectation of the Messiah's advent.

At the Jordan, Jesus was anointed at His baptism by His Father's voice from heaven—"This is my beloved Son, in whom I am well pleased" (Matt. 3:17; Acts 4:27)—and by the Holy Spirit alighting on Him as a dove (Acts 10:38). John confirmed His anointing by the announcement, "Behold the Lamb of God, which taketh away the sin of the world" (John 1:29) and by the two disciples who began to follow Him. The Father made His mission clear as they communed in the wilderness, and Satan tested that mission through his temptations.

The Fullness of Time

As Jesus worked in the carpenter shop, He thought about the past eighteen years. He had learned much during His visit to the Temple when He was twelve. He always knew that God was His Father. He learned more of what that meant as He observed the Passover festival. By remembering the prophecies of the Messiah and observing the sacrifices, Jesus learned that He came to die. "And he shall confirm the covenant with many for one week: and in the midst of the week he shall cause the sacrifice and the oblation to cease" (Dan. 9:27). "But when the fulness of the time was come, God sent forth His Son, made of a woman, made under the law" (Gal. 4:4). He remembered Daniel 9:27. He could not get that verse out of His mind. That time had to be now! That prophetic "week" had started. We can imagine the scene at the carpenter's shop.

Brother James came bustling in. "Have you got that chair finished yet, Jesus?"

"I'm almost finished, James. I just need to sand down a few rough spots. This is for Julius, the centurion, and you know how picky he is."

"Good job, Jesus." James inspected Jesus' work. "Everyone has heard about John, your cousin. He is preaching down at the Jordan. I hear he does not mince words when he talks about sin. Even priests, rabbis, and Roman soldiers are going out to hear him. He baptizes those who believe, as a sign of their beginning a new life."

They worked in silence for some time. The carpenter shop had provided a decent income for the family. Since their father Joseph had died, the sons—Jesus, James, and Joseph—had continued the family business. The people in Nazareth had come to expect quality workmanship from them.

James took a short break and then spoke what was running through his mind. "The people believe John might be the Messiah himself, or maybe Elijah or the prophet who is to come. John denies it but says he is a voice crying in the wilderness to prepare the way for the Lord and to make his paths straight.[1]

Brother Joseph frowned and kept on working. His younger brothers did entirely too much talking.

Jesus turned and faced His brothers, "Joseph and James, I must speak. The time has come, and I must be about my Father's business. I am going to the Jordan to see John."

"You've finished that chair, so go ahead and take a break. But, why are you so serious today? You are coming back, right? We have more work than we can handle, and we get a decent living for this work. You won't find a better job anywhere else."

Jesus said no more as He quietly hung up His carpenter's apron and walked out the door.

Baptism at the Jordan

Jesus traveled for two days. It was hot and dusty, and it was refreshing to see the Jordan valley with the river, the trees, and the green fields nearby. In the distance, He could see a crowd and a rustically dressed man speaking to them. The man's voice carried well, and Jesus could hear him clearly. The crowd listened attentively.

As Jesus came closer, He could hear him say, "…but one mightier than I cometh, the latchet of whose shoes I am not worthy to unloose: he shall baptize you with the Holy Ghost and with fire" (Luke 3:16).

As Jesus reached the edge of the river, John suddenly looked up and, with a loud voice, said, "Behold the Lamb of God, which taketh away the sin of the world" (John 1:29). Everyone turned and stared. All they saw was an ordinary man, tired and dusty from His travel. He was nothing much to look at, like a root pulled up out of the ground (Isa. 53:2).

Jesus returned the next day. "Then cometh Jesus from Galilee to Jordan unto John, to be baptized of him" (Matt. 3:13). As they stood by the water's edge, John shook his head. "I have need to be baptized of thee, and comest thou to me?" (Matt. 3:14). Jesus quietly said, "Let it be so now; it is proper for us to do this to fulfill all righteousness." John consented (Matt. 3:15, NIV).

> And Jesus, when he was baptized, went up straightway out of the water: and, lo, the
> heavens were opened unto him, and he saw the Spirit of God descending like a dove,

and lighting upon him: and lo a voice from heaven, saying, This is my beloved Son, in whom I am well pleased. (Matt. 3:16, 17)

When all the people were being baptized, Jesus was baptized too. And as he was praying, heaven was opened and the Holy Spirit descended on him in bodily form like a dove. And a voice came from heaven: "You are my Son, whom I love; with you I am well pleased." (Luke 3:21, 22, NIV)

This anointing of the Holy Spirit (Isa. 61:1; Luke 4:18, 19) marked the beginning of Jesus' ministry and the beginning of the week of years prophesied in Daniel 9:27. In the midst of that week, Jesus would take the sins of the world on Himself, becoming sin for humankind. His baptism symbolized the death of the "man of sin" and would serve as an example to His followers throughout history. Jesus also received the testimony of John the Baptist and the testimony of His heavenly Father. The next day two men joined Him as His first disciples (John 1:35–37). Jesus needed this confirmation, for His faith would soon be tested.

Jesus and John conversed as they had time. It was a pleasant visit between cousins who had much in common. John said, "Jesus, you are the Messiah, the hope of Israel. Why do you not work with me here? Together, we could do much more than either of us alone."

"Thank you John, I know you are asking that out of love. Yet, I cannot stay. I must seek the Father to realize His will." With that, Jesus took leave of John and of His two new disciples and walked to the nearby wilderness.

Forty Days in the Wilderness

"Then was Jesus led up of the Spirit into the wilderness to be tempted of the devil" (Matt. 4:1). When Satan tempted Jesus in the wilderness, the temptations were the same as those that confronted Adam and Eve in Eden. Jesus met the devil at every turn while on earth, but He never sought him out. Matthew 4:1 describes what happened not Jesus' purpose in going into the wilderness.

Moses was in the mount with God forty days and forty nights with neither food nor water when God gave Moses the law written on tables of stone (Exod. 34:28). Jesus also fasted forty days in the wilderness. Moses led Israel at the beginning of their formation as a nation. Jesus now came to lead Israel in completing the holy work He gave them to do. Jesus came to establish the kingdom of grace and confirm the covenant with many, and He came to bring "an end of sins," "to make reconciliation for iniquity and to bring in everlasting righteousness," the object of an everlasting covenant (Dan. 9:24).

Jesus fasted forty days praying and communing with the Father. During His ministry, Jesus was active in His prayer life (Luke 6:12). He went often to pray in the mountain. Sometimes He would spend the night there in prayer.

How can a person pray for forty days, or even all night? Most of us have a hard time praying for ten minutes. Jesus was not new to prayer. He had been praying all His life. A large part of His prayers consisted of praise for what God had done. He also spent time in prayer meditating and listening for the still small voice of His Father. Jesus' life was so focused on the will of His Father and their purposes so closely intertwined that they needed this time of fellowship together. Jesus' prayers refreshed and strengthened Him for whatever might occur during the day. As a prophet, He received practical information from the Father for His ministry.

Jesus is the Christian's example. We may not be called to fast and pray for forty days, but can we not spend an hour a day in prayer? What would this do for you, for the church, for the world? We now draw the curtain over this precious time Jesus spent with the Father. After forty days in the wilderness, it was time for Jesus to begin His work. It was time that He confront the enemy.

Confrontation in the Wilderness

After forty days, Jesus felt dry and weak. He looked around. There was no food in the wilderness. As He sat there thinking, an angel appeared. The angel's face was cunning and loveless. "God sent me to help you. Your fast is at an end." His eyes shifting from one rock to another, never looking Jesus full in the face, the angel said, "If you are the son of God, command that these stones be made bread."

Jesus was appalled. How could an angel, so quickly forget God's confirming words, "This is my beloved son, in whom I am well pleased" (Matt. 3:17)? Had the Holy Spirit not given witness to His identity, resting on Jesus in the form of dove? Had this angel not witnessed this sign when even non-angels had recognized His mission? John and His two new disciples recognized His divinity. Jesus thought to Himself, *This can be none other than a fallen angel, or the devil himself.*

Jesus' answer was terse, "It is written, Man shall not live by bread alone, but by every word that proceedeth out of the mouth of God." Jesus refused to perform a miracle to satisfy His own hunger or to prove His divinity to a doubter. He came to earth as a human, and as a human He must live.

The "angel" took Him to a pinnacle of the Temple. Now exposed for who he was, the devil said, "You are wise. You must do the will of God. Your ministry is just beginning. The people must know who you are. If you are the Son of God, cast yourself down: for it is written, 'He shall give his angels charge concerning thee: and in their hands they shall bear thee up, lest at any time thou dash thy foot against a stone' (Matt. 4:6; cf. Ps. 91:11, 12)." He continued, "The people seek a sign. This miracle would show them that you are the Messiah, and many people will believe!"

Satan had used Jesus' method in quoting Scripture, but he left out the part of the verse that says "to keep thee in all thy ways." God had already testified that Jesus was His beloved Son. If Jesus asked for another proof, He would be denying what God had already said. Jesus refused to force God to come to His rescue. Instead, He responded, "It is written again, Thou shalt not tempt the Lord thy God."

The devil was not through. Taking Him up into a high mountain, he made the kingdoms of the earth pass before Him in review. He represented the best the world had to offer and said:

> All this power will I give thee, and the glory of them: for that is delivered unto me;
> and to whomsoever I will I give it. If thou therefore wilt worship me, all shall be thine.

And Jesus answered and said unto him, Get thee behind me, Satan: for it is written, Thou shalt worship the Lord thy God, and him only shalt thou serve. (Luke 4:6–8)

Satan was offering Him an easy way to obtain power and glory. The easy way would not eradicate sin from people's lives or restore the image of God in them. Rather, sin would become a permanent blot on the perfection of God's creation. Jesus knew that His mission could be fulfilled only through suffering. Before Him lay a life of sorrow, hardship, and conflict. He would die a sacrifice on the cross, bearing the sins of the whole world. Jesus turned the devil's offer down flat. "Get thee behind me, Satan," He declared, "for it is written, Thou shalt worship the Lord thy God, and him only shalt thou serve" (Luke 4:8).

This was Jesus' first substantial victory over Satan.

Triggers of Temptation

Jesus lived on this earth as a human being, and He had the same appetites as all human beings. It is through these normal human drives that Satan tempts people to sin. When Jesus lived on earth, He laid aside His divine prerogatives and lived as a human (Phil. 2:5–8), depending wholly on God, the Father, for His work (John 5:30; 8:28; 14:10). The life He lived is an example to us of what we can do, through grace.

Jesus had reason to be tempted on appetite while Eve did not. Satan tempted Him to begin His ministry by a spectacular sign of divine power. It would make Him "look good." Finally, Satan offered to make things easy, he would give Jesus all the kingdoms of this world if only Jesus would worship him. In these three temptations, Jesus "was in all points tempted like as we are, yet without sin" (Heb. 4:15).

For all that is in the world, the lust of the flesh [craving for sensual gratification], and the lust of the eyes [greedy longings of the mind] and the pride of life [assurance in one's own resources *or* in the stability of earthly things]—these do not come from the Father but are from the world [itself]. (1 John 2:16, AMP)

Jesus refused to doubt the testimony of the Father. When Satan said, "If," Jesus knew it was not an angel of God but was Satan himself. When he offered the kingdoms of the world, Jesus knew that Satan was a deceiver and a usurper. He had gained rulership of the earth through intrigue. Jesus came to reclaim those kingdoms, but not the easy way. The time would come when even the devil would bow the knee and confess that Jesus is Lord![2]

Jesus answered each temptation with a firm statement from Scripture—"It is written." He climaxed the third temptation by a direct command, which He forced Satan to obey, "Get thee behind me, Satan." Jesus faced the devil precisely where Adam and Eve had failed. He won a crucial victory for humankind, under the most difficult of circumstances. Ahead of Him were His life and ministry and His sacrifice on the cross. Scripture says that temptations can be broken down into three classes, as the comparison below reveals:

Temptations	Eden (Gen. 3:6)	Wilderness (Matt 4:2–11)	1 John 2:16
Appetite	Good for food	Make these stones to be bread	Lust of the flesh
Greed	Pleasant to the eyes	Cast thyself down	Lust of the eyes
Power	Wisdom without effort	The world on a silver platter	Pride of life

One can understand the temptation on appetite. The Amplified Bible describes this as "the lust of the flesh [craving for sensual gratification]." Appetite is a general term for the normal desires of the body. Only when a person wrongly yields to appetite is it sin.

To see sin in the temptation from its appearance is not easy. It requires discrimination and the guidance of the Holy Spirit. The Amplified Bible presents this as "the lust of the eyes [greedy longings of the mind]." With Jesus in the wilderness, Satan tempted Jesus to demonstrate His divinity to announce His ministry. By a miracle, Satan was saying, He could gain the attention of the people. Yet, Jesus came to live as a human being. He never performed a miracle to satisfy curiosity, to prove His divinity, or to protect Himself. Jesus' miracles were always practical and for others.

Satan offered Jesus the power and glory of this world if Jesus would worship him. It was an easy way out. Satan promises wisdom without effort and fame without substance—all for the very low payment of worshipping a false god instead of the true. To yield to this temptation would be to abandon the human race to sin, slavery, and the oppression of Satan and to leave a permanent blot on the universe of God. Jesus came to this world, not for riches or military honor, but to change people's lives. He came to restore in human beings the image of God. The only wisdom that Jesus accepted was wisdom from the Word of God. He answered every temptation with, "It is written."

Endnotes

1. Texts on the voice of one crying in the wilderness are Isaiah 40:3–5; Matthew 3:3; and John 1:23.
2. Texts on every knee bowing before Jesus are Isaiah 45:23; Matthew 28:18; Romans 14:11; Philippians 2:9–11; and Revelation 5:13.

Chapter 25
Jesus' Mission

For the Son of man is come to seek and to save that which was lost.
Luke 19:10

Jesus confirmed the everlasting covenant of God by His sacrifice on the cross. His sacrifice was the realization of the pledge of the animal sacrifices of Old Testament times. It was His sacrifice that made possible His blessings to the human family. Calvary was *not* the end of an old covenant or the beginning of a new covenant. It was the confirmation of the everlasting covenant of God, given to Adam and Eve and to all His people through history. As Psalm 136 emphasizes, the covenant of God is more than a promise, it is God's commitment to humankind through what Jesus did on the cross.

Beginning with the Sermon on the Mount, Jesus emphasized heart religion. His actions and words spoke strongly against mechanical observance of the law, the sacrifices, and the Temple rituals when love for God and humankind was missing. Through His sacrifice on the cross, Jesus gave human beings grace and power to keep the law with love. He came to establish the kingdom of grace, to prepare the way for the kingdom of glory!

Who Was Jesus Christ?

Jesus Christ came as a man, a human being in every respect. Yet, He was also God, though He laid aside the prerogatives of His divinity to live as a human being (Phil. 2:5–8). The exact nature of His being will always remain a mystery. As God, in His perfect divinity, He is our Redeemer and our substitute in the judgment. As a human being, He lived as all human beings must live (Rom. 8:3; Phil. 2:7; Heb. 2:16). In His perfect, sinless life, depending on the Father, He is our example.

Covenant language was common and emphasized in the Old Testament, but less common in the New Testament. The words "faith" and "grace" are covenant terms emphasized in the New Testament. Paul's primary goal was that people accept Jesus for who He is and that they center their hope for salvation on the person of Christ. Paul also emphasized doctrinal beliefs, but always accompanied by a heart changed by grace.

Could People Recognize Jesus for Who He Was?

John the Baptist was born into a priestly family and grew up to be a man of God. The families of John the Baptist and Jesus were among those few families committed to God and knowledgeable in the Scriptures. Thus, John the Baptist knew that Jesus was the Lamb of God who would die for the sins of the world. He knew the prophecies (Isa. 53; Dan. 9:24–27). He recognized Jesus, not just from his study, but also by the Spirit's revelation, as Peter had done, when Jesus said, "Flesh and blood hath not revealed it unto thee, but my Father which is in heaven" (Matt. 16:17). Saving truth comes to the heart by the Spirit of God.[1]

Jesus came into a family carefully chosen by God. Mary and Joseph were both willing to listen to what the angel had to say. When guided by the Holy Spirit, they obeyed promptly. Mary and Joseph knew that Jesus was unique. They knew that He was the Messiah, even though their concept of the Messiah, like the Jews, was faulty. They raised Jesus to the best of their ability in the truths of the "law and the prophets."

How did Jesus know that He was to suffer and die for the sins of humankind? Did He retain His divine consciousness so that He knew already? No, He did not! This would make Him more than human and not subject to the human experience. We do know that Jesus studied the prophecies enough to ask, as a child, hard questions of the learned doctors in the Temple (Luke 2:46, 47).

The Jews believed that the Messiah would take the throne of David and restore Israel to her former glory. There are also prophecies in the Old Testament that the kingdom of Christ should last forever. Thus, the Jews could not comprehend why Jesus would say that He would die (John 12:32–34).

Many of the Jewish leaders did not believe that the Messiah would die. To believe that the Messiah came to die for them and become the substitute for their guilt and condemnation was a new concept for them. They trusted for their salvation in their lineage from Abraham and in their scrupulous observance of the laws of Moses. John the Baptist's call for repentance from sin was also new. They looked for salvation from observance of the law, from living a moral life, and from sacrifices and performance of ceremonies.

Watching the Lamb

Jesus' family went to the Passover in Jerusalem every year. When Jesus was about twelve, He accompanied them there. New thoughts came into His mind while watching the ceremonies and sacrifices. He thought about the sacrifice of the Passover lamb, the blood sprinkled on the doorposts, and the salvation of the firstborn as the destroying angel passed over the houses marked by the blood of the lamb. He began to comprehend what His mission was. *The Lamb of God came to die!* He did not flinch, but determined to do the will of His Father.

After the services, He lingered to talk to the learned doctors of the law. Jesus had resolutely refused to attend the schools of the rabbis. Yet, He had knowledge that far surpassed theirs. "And the Jews marvelled, saying, How knoweth this man letters, having never learned" (John 7:15)? Meanwhile, His parents, not finding Jesus in the crowd of people returning to Galilee, rushed back to Jerusalem. After three days, finally they found Him, sitting among the doctors of the law in the Temple, asking questions:

> And it came to pass, that after three days, they found him in the temple, sitting in the midst of the doctors, both hearing them and asking them questions. And all

that heard him were astonished at His understanding and answers. And when they saw him, they were amazed: and his mother said unto him, Son, why hast thou thus dealt with us? behold, thy father and I have sought thee sorrowing. And he said unto them, How is it that ye sought me? wist ye not that I must be about my Father's business. (Luke 2:46–49)

How much information did God the Father tell Him directly? The Father gave Jesus strength, wisdom, and information during His many seasons of prayer. Jesus faced difficult situations every day. He could rely on information from the Father and support from the Holy Spirit. Today, we need to experience and know what God will do for us in answer to prayer (James 1:5; 5:15). We must learn to pray and listen as Jesus did.

Recognizing Jesus for Who He Was

The circumstances and timing of His birth, His patience under duress, and the works He did were all signs of who He was. The common people saw this clearly. However, the leading Jews could not put aside their preconceived opinions and recognize what was taking place before their eyes.

Jesus lived a sinless life even as a child. Because of His kindness, His willingness to stand for what was right, and His desire to study the Bible and nature, He was different from His childhood companions. Children do not understand when other children are so different. Jesus early learned to face opposition and ridicule. "The world cannot hate you, but me it hateth, because I testify of it that the works thereof are evil" (John 7:7).

Jesus was selfless in His ministry, working with the multitudes, teaching, healing and comforting. People loved to be in His presence, even the little children. On occasion, He hardly had time to eat. In all this, there was the constant presence of the Pharisees, closely following everything He said or did to find occasion against Him.

By His sinless life and His sacrificial death, Jesus confirmed the covenant and brought to fruition the promise of all the sacrifices of centuries past (Heb. 9:15). He was the real Lamb of God. This was a new idea for the Jews of that day. They were diligent in doing sacrifices and ceremonies, but had lost sight of the Redeemer typified in the sacrifices.

When people demanded a sign (Matt. 12:38; 16:1; Luke 11:29; John 6:30), why did Jesus not comply? He knew that a sign would intensify their opinion of Him as just a miracle worker. He was quite willing to invoke the power of God to help and to heal, but never just to satisfy curiosity.

They often asked Him if He were the Messiah. Jesus knew this question was a trap, and He always responded that His works testified to who He was (John 5:36). In the course of His ministry, He raised to life the daughter of Jairus and the son of the widow of Nain. Jesus raised these two in small towns a distance from Jerusalem. Then the day came when He raised Lazarus, who lived in Bethany, near Jerusalem. Many of the leading Jews witnessed this miracle. Now they had their sign!

Rapid Events Before Passover

As Jesus' ministry neared its climax, momentous events came in rapid succession. He raised Lazarus from the dead—four days after he died! Lazarus was undeniably dead![2] Yet, instead of believing, the Pharisees and the chief priests united to plot Jesus' death—and Lazarus' death as well (John 11:47–53; 12:10). What more could God do to reach them?

Simon the Pharisee made a feast for Jesus and the disciples. At that feast, Mary anointed Jesus' feet with spikenard, extravagant in quantity and cost! Judas objected at the extravagance, whispering to the others that she should have given the money to the poor. But Jesus commended Mary: "Then said Jesus, Let her alone: against the day of my burying hath she kept this. For the poor always ye have with you, but me, ye have not always" (John 12:7, 8).

Judas took offense at Jesus' rebuke (Matt. 26:14, 15). He went to the Jewish leaders and arranged a secret betrayal for thirty pieces of silver. The Jewish leaders were afraid to arrest Jesus openly because of the people. They needed what Judas would provide.

Five days before Passover, Jesus made a triumphal entry into Jerusalem. He cleansed the Temple but did not leave immediately as He had the first time. He continued to teach "daily" in the court (Luke 19:45–47). He stood vigilant, not allowing any activity that was not in accordance with Mosaic law and the dignity of His Father's house (Mark 11:16, 17).

For several days, He held control of the Temple. The Jewish leaders expected Him to take the throne of David, but Jesus had other plans. Finally, the time came when Jesus, "the light of the world" would leave the Temple in darkness! "Behold, your house is left unto you desolate" (Luke 13:35), He said.

Endnotes

1. We must be willing to believe in order for the Holy Spirit to reveal truth to us (Matt. 16:16, 17; John 14:26; 1 Cor. 2:12–14).
2. Jesus raised three people to life: the son of the widow of Nain (Luke 7:11–14), Jairus' daughter (Luke 8:54, 55), and Lazarus, after Lazarus had been dead four days (John 11:39–44, 53). The resurrection of Lazarus was a public event. Many people were witnesses to it. The Jewish leaders had asked for a sign that they might believe (John 6:30). With Lazarus' resurrection, they had their sign. However, instead of believing on Jesus, they intensified their plans to put Him to death—as well as Lazarus (John 12:9, 10).

Chapter 26
Gethsemane

And when he was at the place, he said unto them, Pray that ye enter not into
temptation. And he was withdrawn from them about a stone's cast, and kneeled
down, and prayed, Saying, Father, if thou be willing, remove this
cup from me: nevertheless not my will, but thine, be done.
Luke 22:40–42

Three times the Father, the Son, and the Holy Ghost confronted the implications of the everlasting covenant, the plan of salvation, with a decision. Before the foundation of the world, it was a plan, audacious in its detail and operation, but still future.

Father, Son, and Holy Spirit had to decide to implement the plan to meet the emergency occasioned by Adam and Eve's sin. Each step in the plan must now be taken in real time. Again the heavenly host mourned at the prophesied death of the Son of God, yet rejoiced that God had provided a way for humanity to be redeemed.

Jesus faced the third decision in implementing the plan in Gethsemane. Knowing that sin cannot exist in the presence of the Father and that human beings could be saved only if He took their sins on Himself, Jesus, as a human being, could not then know whether the plan would be successful or whether He would be brought forth from the grave a victor. But He chose to go ahead.

The Hour Has Come

Momentum toward the supreme event in His ministry, Jesus' sacrifice on the cross, was increasing in intensity. On four occasions during His ministry, Jesus had said, "Mine hour is not yet come."[1] He was acutely conscious of the importance of fulfilling prophecy. Knowing the prophecies, He actively worked to fulfill each one. He avoided all situations that might impair that purpose, even when forced into one confrontation after another with the Pharisees and others. His responses were always measured and careful. He never got into a fight. In achieving His goal, timing was essential, and He was well aware of the proper time each event was to occur.

When the time of His crucifixion arrived, He unapologetically repeated, "My time is at hand."[2] His goal was to be the sacrifice. Just before His death on the cross, He declared in triumph, "It is finished!" Satan had failed to make Him sin even once (John 14:30). Jesus had paid the penalty, redeemed humankind, upheld the law of God, and assured for eternity the future of humankind and the security of the throne of God.

The seventy-week (or 490-year) prophecy of Daniel 9:24 was about to close. In the middle of its last week (a seven-year period), the Messiah would die on the cross, "confirm the covenant," and bring to a close the "sacrifice and the oblation." The 490-year prophecy began when King Artaxerxes gave the third decree, in 457 BC, to restore Jerusalem and Israel's national identity. With this decree, the people rebuilt Jerusalem, restored the Temple services, and established local government (Dan. 9:24–27; Ezra. 7).

> And he shall confirm the covenant with many for one week: and in the midst of the week he shall cause the sacrifice and the oblation to cease, and for the overspreading of abominations he shall make it desolate, even until the consummation, and that determined shall be poured upon the desolate. (Dan. 9:27)

Daniel gave the exact time the Messiah would begin His ministry and the exact time He would die a willing sacrifice on the cross (Dan. 9:26, 27). The nature of His death had been foretold (Isa. 53; Ps. 22).

The Last Supper

Jesus and His disciples had a quiet, memorable Passover supper (Matt. 26:17–29). The atmosphere was heavy. The disciples were aware of the evil designs of the chief priests.

> Then saith Jesus unto them, all ye shall be offended because of me this night: for it is written, I will smite the shepherd, and the sheep of the flock shall be scattered abroad. But after I am risen again, I will go before you into Galilee. (Matt. 26:31, 32)

Jesus spoke with the disciples at length (John 13 and 16). He washed their feet, and they partook of the food. Then He prayed His memorable prayer for unity (John 17) and announced that He would be betrayed by one of their number. It was a time of sorrow and foreboding. As they ate, Jesus invested the supper with new meaning. This was to be the *new* Passover, a memorial of Jesus' death and a promise of reunion in the hereafter.

> And when he had given thanks, he brake it, and said, Take, eat: this is my body, which is broken for you: this do in remembrance of me. After the same manner also he took the cup, when he had supped, saying, This cup is the new testament in my blood: this do ye, as oft as ye drink it, in remembrance of me. For as often as ye eat this bread, and drink this cup, ye do show the Lord's death till he comes. (1 Cor. 11:24–26)

In this simple ceremony, Jesus showed a side that all need to see. Jesus was human. He did not just want to be messiah, teacher, and healer. In His humanity, He wanted to be loved as their friend (John 15:13–15). Jesus deeply appreciated Mary's love when she broke the box of costly ointment and anointed His feet. It helped sustain Him in the ordeal of the cross. Christians now show their love for Jesus every time they take part in the communion service.

New Testament in My Blood

"This cup is the new testament in my blood" (1 Cor. 11:25). These few words invest the new covenant—the everlasting covenant—with deep meaning. This was the basis for the everlasting gospel, which would be preached in all the world (Matt. 24:14). All this and much more was only possible because Jesus went to the cross for us! The cross was the central point in human history, where heaven and earth met for the redemption of humankind! "For this is my blood of the new testament ['new covenant'], which is shed for many for the remission of sins" (Matt. 26:28).

For three and a half years, Jesus had confronted the old covenant thinking of the Jewish people and leaders. The everlasting covenant, God's "My covenant" and the new covenant given to Abraham, was now to be confirmed by His sacrifice on the cross. The wine represented the blood of Jesus that confirmed the new covenant of grace—God's everlasting covenant.

By the power of the cross, Jesus gives salvation to both the living (the church) and to the dead (Old Testament Israel). "For to this end Christ both died, and rose, and revived, that he might be Lord both of the dead and living" (Rom. 14:9). Paul wrote Hebrews to show Jewish Christians that Jesus was the fulfillment of the sacrifices and rituals. Christians must now look in faith to Jesus' true sacrifice for sin. The Old Testament sacrifices were merely a shadow of the true!

> For this reason Christ is the mediator of a new covenant, that those who are called may receive the promised eternal inheritance—now that he has died as a ransom to set them free from the sins committed under the first covenant.... When Moses had proclaimed every commandment of the law to all the people, he took the blood of calves, together with water, scarlet wool and branches of hyssop, and sprinkled the scroll and all the people.... It was necessary, then, for the copies of the heavenly things to be purified with these sacrifices, but the heavenly things themselves with better sacrifices than these. For Christ did not enter a man-made sanctuary that was only a copy of the true one; he entered heaven itself, now to appear for us in God's presence. (Heb. 9:15, 19, 23, 24, NIV).

Jesus ratified the new covenant, the everlasting covenant, by His sacrifice on the cross. This gave power to the covenant promises, made the covenant effective for every human being (Heb. 9:15), and brought to an end the sacrifices and rituals (Dan. 9:27). His death insured, ratified, and made possible the fulfillment of the promises of God, reaching all the way back to Eden.

Jesus' sacrifice on the cross is the one effective sacrifice. It brings meaning to the animal sacrifices of the past. Christ's high priestly ministry in heaven could not begin until He had given Himself as a sacrifice on the cross, fulfilling the types of the earthly sanctuary. Hebrews 9:11–14 contrasts the ceremonial law and the new covenant. The rituals and the blood of animals could not cleanse the soul. Only the sacrifice of Jesus Christ is effective.

Only now that Christ ministers as High Priest in the heavenly tabernacle can souls, in Old as well as New Testament times, be redeemed. Jesus is the only One who lived, died, and came to life again that we might live. His is the only name "whereby we must be saved" (Acts 4:12).

Example and Command

Jesus formally established the Lord's Supper at this time. Christians "shew the Lord's death" whenever they take part in the Lord's Supper. He also gave baptism by immersion to remind us of His death and resurrection. "Therefore we are buried with him by baptism into death: that like as Christ was raised up from the dead by the glory of the Father, even so we also should walk in newness of life" (Rom. 6:4).

The ceremonies of the Lord's Supper and baptism were significant enough that Jesus established each by His example and command. Did Jesus change anything else?[3] Did He change the fourth commandment or the day of worship before ratifying the covenant? The Jews kept the seventh-day as the Sabbath. Had Jesus changed this law or the day of worship, He would have given us His example and command, just as He did with the Lord's Supper and baptism.

The original purpose for the seventh-day Sabbath was as a memorial to creation. To change the day would destroy this meaning. We are His—both by creation and by redemption. The story of the fall of our first parents and our need of a Redeemer rest upon the truth of the creation.

Jesus' resurrection gave meaning to the Passover and power to the crucifixion. Without His resurrection, faith is vain. Yet, He said and did nothing about making the first day of the week a memorial, nor did He change the Sabbath from the seventh day to the first. He made no mention of the "Lord's day" being a first-day "Sabbath" or Sunday.

The term the "Lord's day" comes from the words of Jesus: "And he said unto them, The sabbath was made for man, and not man for the sabbath: Therefore the Son of man is Lord also of the sabbath" (Mark 2:27, 28). The setting for Jesus' statement was Jesus' reply to the Pharisees' accusation of the disciples eating grain on the Sabbath—the Jewish seventh-day Sabbath. Jesus, here, emphasizes that He is Lord of the Sabbath.

After the supper, Jesus and the disciples sang a hymn and went out to the Mount of Olives and the Garden of Gethsemane.

Dark Gethsemane

The crucial event in Gethsemane was the struggle that Jesus endured in accepting all that bearing the sins of humankind entailed. He knew that the offense of sin would separate Him from the Father. Isaiah said, "Your iniquities have separated between you and your God, and your sins have hid his face from you, that he will not hear." (Isa. 59:2). Habakkuk said of God's attitude toward iniquity, "Thou art of purer eyes than to behold evil, and canst not look on iniquity: wherefore lookest thou upon them that deal treacherously, and holdest thy tongue when the wicked devoureth the man that is more righteous than he?" (Hab. 1:13)

Jesus came to this earth to live as a human being. His ministry and His miracles were all performed through faith in the power of God the Father. Now the time had come to "bear the iniquity of us all." As a human being, Jesus did not know whether sin was not so offensive to God that it would cause eternal separation from the Father. His bearing the sins of humanity and suffering separation from the Father was His heaviest trial of all.

> Jesus … fell prostrate, overcome by the horror of a great darkness [Gen. 15:12]. The humanity of the Son of God trembled in that trying hour. … The awful moment had come—that moment which was to decide the destiny of the world. … Christ might even now refuse to drink the cup apportioned to guilty man.… The words fall tremblingly from the pale lips of Jesus, "O My Father, if this cup may not pass away from me, except I drink it, Thy will be done."
>
> Three times has He uttered that prayer. Three times humanity shrunk from the last, crowning sacrifice.… He sees that the transgressors of the law, if left to themselves, must perish. He sees the helplessness of man. He sees the power of sin.… And His decision is made. He will save man at any cost to Himself.… And He will not turn from His mission.… "If this cup may not pass away from Me, except I drink it, Thy will be done."
>
> Having made the decision, He fell dying to the ground from which He had partially risen.… But God suffered with His Son. Angels … saw their Lord enclosed by legions of satanic forces, His nature weighed down with a shuddering, mysterious dread. There was silence in heaven. No harp was touched.… The angelic host … watched the Father separating His beams of light, love, and glory from His beloved Son … how offensive in His sight is sin.
>
> The powers of good and evil waited to see what answer would come to Christ's thrice-repeated prayer.…In this awful crisis … the mighty angel who stands in God's presence, occupying the position from which Satan fell, came to the side of Christ. The angel came not to take the cup from Christ's hand, but to strengthen Him to drink it, with the assurance of the Father's love. He came to give power to the divine-human suppliant.…
>
> Christ's agony did not cease, but His depression and discouragement left Him.… The storm had in nowise abated, but He who was its object was strengthened to meet its fury. He came forth calm and serene. A heavenly peace rested upon His blood-stained face. He had borne that which no human being could ever bear; for He had tasted the sufferings of death for every man.[4]

Jesus knew the promises of the covenant. He knew the plan and purposes of God. He remembered the divine affirmations He received as "My beloved Son," the refreshment of hours spent in prayer, and the prophecies that the Redeemer would be victorious over evil. After a terrible struggle, faith won the battle and He accepted the will of the Father.

This is the faith of Jesus, a faith that holds onto God even when everything is black and the outcome is unsure. Jesus showed us that, in the plan of God, we should not wait until we know for certain. Jesus' victory is ours. Strengthened by the angel, Jesus went forth to meet the mob.

Endnotes

1. Jesus repeated statements similar to "Mine hour is not yet come" several times (John 2:4; 7:6, 8, 30; 8:20).
2. Nine times Jesus announced that the time of His death was at hand (Matt. 26:18, 45; Mark 14:35, 41; Luke 9:51; John 12:23, 27; 13:1; 17:1).
3. Hebrews describes the changing of the law concerning the priesthood. "For the priesthood being changed, there is made of necessity a change also of the law" (Heb. 7:12). If it were not changed, then Jesus could not have been a priest, for He was not of the tribe of Levi. He was from Judah, the royal tribe, and His priesthood is after the order of Melchizedek. This enables Him to be both priest and king.
4. Ellen G. White, *The Desire of Ages* (Mountain View, CA: Pacific Press Publishing Association, 1940), pp. 690, 693, 694.

Chapter 27
The Trial

I adjure thee by the living God, that thou tell us whether thou be the Christ, the
Son of God. Jesus saith unto him, Thou hast said: nevertheless I say unto you,
Hereafter shall ye see the Son of man sitting on the right
hand of power, and coming in the clouds of heaven.
Matthew 26:63, 64

In the events that led up to and included Christ's crucifixion and resurrection, we reach the high point of the everlasting covenant. These events express the deep truths underlying the legal foundations of Israel and the Church. These truths are easily understood, yet their meaning challenges the greatest minds.

Through these events the fiercest battle of the "great controversy between Christ and Satan" were fought. The purpose of the everlasting covenant would be accomplished. Christ, the victim, would arise from the grave, the victor and the champion for all creation and for all time.

Willingly Arrested!

Jesus came to pay the penalty of the broken law that human beings might live. In doing so, He would establish the government of God upon love, mercy, justice, and free will. Freedom and happiness would be forever restored.

There are clues in the trials themselves that reveal Jesus' purpose. In Gethsemane, when accosted by the mob, Jesus identified Himself. "As soon then as he had said unto them, I am he; they went backward and fell to the ground" (John 18:6). This demonstrates that Jesus could have walked away, but He chose not to.

When it appeared that Jesus would not defend Himself, "Simon Peter having a sword drew it, and smote the high priest's servant, and cut off his right ear" (John 18:10). Jesus immediately stopped Peter and healed Malchus' ear. Jesus knew that His hour had come, and He determined to meet it with no unforeseen delays.

A Preliminary Night Trial in Annas' Court

At midnight, Jesus had a hearing before the court of Annas. Annas tried to establish a charge of sedition as he questioned Jesus directly. Even though a prisoner was not to be convicted on his own testimony, Annas pursued this end.[1] Aghast at this illegality, Jesus said:

> I spake openly to the world; I ever taught in the synagogue, and in the temple, whith-
> er the Jews always resort; and in secret have I said nothing. Why askest thou me? ask
> them which heard me, what I have said unto them: behold, they know what I said.
> (John 18:20, 21)

Spies had continually followed Jesus. Why not call them to testify? Jesus denied saying anything in secret. This silenced Annas, embarrassed the court, and almost stopped the proceedings. Jesus knew that His hour had come. Many times in His ministry, He had met these men and exposed their ignorance, hypocrisy, and criminal intent. Now He could not delay what must be done. He remembered the prophecy, "As a sheep before her shearers is dumb, so he openeth not his mouth" (Isa. 53:7). From this point on, He was careful not to defend Himself. There were at least 300 prophecies regarding the coming Messiah. Eighteen verses in Matthew show fulfillment of prophecy. In eleven of these, the fulfillment can be attributed to the foreknowledge of God. In the other seven, Jesus took direct action to fulfill prophecy.[2]

With Caiaphas and the Sanhedrin

Caiaphas next examined Jesus in the presence of the Sanhedrin, though he had not notified Nicodemus and Joseph of Arimathea. The Sanhedrin were not all against Jesus. Those who did not oppose Him would need to be persuaded, and Caiaphas had a hard time doing so. Both Annas and Caiaphas failed to obtain a conviction from the vague and contradictory witnesses who testified (Matt. 26:59–61). The evidence they offered was not sufficient to obtain a sentence of death either by Romans or Jewish standards! Caiaphas was getting desperate.

Caiaphas decided to question Jesus Himself. "I adjure thee by the living God, that thou tell us whether thou be the Christ, the Son of God" (Matt. 26:63). Caiaphas issued this charge with an oath. Jesus knew that His answer would condemn Him to death, but He also knew that millions throughout the coming ages would hear it. Through it, many would come to believe on Him. "Jesus saith unto him, Thou hast said: nevertheless I say unto you, Hereafter shall ye see the Son of man sitting on the right hand of power, and coming in the clouds of heaven" (Matt. 26:64).

Caiaphas suddenly saw himself confronted with his own judgment and with Jesus as His judge. He paled in terror at the thought. With malignant hatred, Caiaphas tore his robe, which was forbidden for priests to tear (Lev. 10:6; 21:10). He declared, "What further need have we of witnesses?" (Matt. 26:65). Upon Jesus' own testimony, the Sanhedrin issued a hasty determination of blasphemy, a sin worthy of death. Jewish law required two witnesses to convict a person. In convicting Jesus, the ruling members of the Sanhedrin violated Scriptural juridical principles.

The flawed character of Judas, Annas, Caiaphas, and Pilate were pitiful to behold. Jesus did not ignore them. In each of His responses was an appeal for His judge to believe in Him for salvation. People build character by exercising faith in the day-to-day temptations of life. They build character as they consent to the work of grace in their life. Their response in the crisis displays their true character.

Cocksure Peter

During this time, Peter and John managed to gain entrance to the court. John did not attempt to hide his identity while Peter tried unsuccessfully to mingle with the crowd. Three times, bystanders asked Peter if he were a believer. The third time, Peter answered with cursing and swearing, "I know not the man." Immediately, the cock crowed (Matt. 26:74). "And the Lord turned, and looked upon Peter," and "Peter went out and wept bitterly" (John 22:61, 62). Jesus' loving look broke Peter's heart, and forever after he willingly and enthusiastically confessed Jesus as his Lord![3]

All during this tragic affair, there only One who was calm and serene, only One who knew where He was going and who was in control. Jesus came to this world to give His life a ransom for many. Throughout each trial, He held His peace and did not defend Himself, allowing the Father to direct affairs. Yet, there was one thing He could do, and this He did do. He gave evidence to all participants that He was the Son of God, and He appealed to their souls.

Did Jesus' sacrifice need the help of human beings? Was not Jesus' death prophesied? Was not His death necessary in the plan of salvation, chartered "from the foundation of the world"? The Bible tells us that God Himself will see to the outworking of His covenant and that His plans are best. Human devising was not necessary. God did not need human beings to ensure that Jesus' sacrifice would take place.[4] "The Son of man goeth as it is written of him: but woe unto that man by whom the Son of man is betrayed! it had been good for that man if he had not been born" (Matt. 26:24).

Pilate Plays to the Crowd

Pilate quickly noted that Jesus was no ordinary prisoner; He took Jesus' case very seriously. Yet, he was at a disadvantage. Worldly people just cannot understand the issues of the church, and it is not fair to embarrass them by asking them to resolve the church's affairs. However, in this situation, Pilate not only assessed Jesus correctly, but he also knew the Jews. He quickly concluded that Jesus was innocent and unworthy of punishment of any kind, much less death. Pilate tried repeatedly—almost desperately—to save Jesus.

In Pilate's hearing, Jesus explained the nature of His kingdom. Jesus was not interested in worldly affairs. The charge of sedition was bogus. Pilate believed Jesus and tried to save Him. However, he lacked courage and was unwilling to sacrifice his position for truth. God sent a dream to Pilate's wife, who attempted to warn her husband, "Have thou nothing to do with that just man" (Matt. 27:19). Pilate attempted to reason with the unreasonable mob, but to no avail. He washed his hands, as if so doing would lessen his guilt. He declared Jesus innocent, yet he had Him scourged and given over to the mob for crucifixion. One can only pity Pilate's weakness under pressure.[5]

As Pilate declared Jesus' innocence, the mob, led by the high priest Caiaphas, roared back, "His blood be on us, and on our children" (Matt. 27:25).[6] They could not know then how prophetic were their words. As soldiers led Jesus out for the crucifixion, He was unable to bear the cross. Soldiers forced Simon of Cyrene to carry His cross. It is said that this act of kindness changed Simon's life. Ever after, he considered it a blessing to have carried Jesus' cross.

Nailed to the cross and hanging between two thieves, Jesus recognized the faith of one who appealed to Him to be remembered in His kingdom. He gave him mercy and the assurance of paradise (Luke 23:42, 43). As Jesus died, the rough centurion confessed, "Truly this was the Son of God" (Matt. 27:54).

In all this, Jesus' love showed through as He gave person after person the opportunity to confess Him and be saved. Pilate, especially, had an incredible opportunity to confess Jesus, but he did not have the strength required to stand up for what he knew to be right.

Herod, Curious But Unmoved

When Pilate found that Jesus was from Galilee, he sent Him to Herod, the governor over Galilee who happened to be visiting during the Passover. Herod was glad to see Jesus. He had heard of Him, and he wanted to see Him perform a miracle. When Jesus arrived, Herod questioned Him at length. All the while, the chief priests and scribes assailed Jesus, and the soldiers of Herod insulted Jesus and made Him an object of sport. But Jesus did not respond; he did not attempt to even speak to Herod.

Why was this? Did not Herod have a soul, at least as valuable as that of Caiaphas or Pilate? Why did not Jesus reach for Herod's soul as He did for the other inquisitors? The answer is that it would do no good. This was the Herod who had beheaded John the Baptist and murdered members of his own family. Friends warned Jesus, on His last trip to Jerusalem, that Herod wanted to kill Him. Jesus' metaphor for the ruler is telling. He said, "Go ye, and tell that fox …" (Luke 13:32). Jesus was rarely this blatant in describing others. However, the time came when He called the scribes and Pharisees "hypocrites" ("actors" or "pretenders") and "a generation of vipers" (Matt. 12:34; 23:33). When Herod beheaded John the Baptist, he cut off his last avenue to Heaven. He had closed his own probation, and God could no longer reach him. Knowing this, Jesus "answered him nothing" (Luke 23:9).

A few who were present as participants or onlookers during Jesus' trial and crucifixion, such as Peter, Simon of Cyrene, the thief on the cross, and perhaps the centurion, gave their hearts to God. The vast majority, such as the chief priests and scribes, increased in obstinate rebellion. For many this was the close of their probation and the loss of salvation. Pitiful weak and fearful Pilate simply failed to do the right thing. When God speaks to the heart, one must promptly do the right thing, regardless of the circumstances.

Endnotes

1. The Sanhedrin violated Scriptural juridical principles (Deut. 17:6; 19:15–19; Prov. 18:13; Matt. 26:59–61, John 7:51).

2. Eighteen verses in Matthew show fulfillment of prophecy. Eleven are attributed to the foreknowledge of God (Matt. 1:22; 2:15, 17, 23; 4:14; 5:17, 18; 21:4; 24:34; 27:9, 35). In seven, Jesus purposely acted to fulfill prophecy (Matt. 3:15; 8:17; 12:17; 13:13, 14, 35; 26:54–56).

3. Peter denied His Lord (Matt. 26:69–75; Mark 14:66–72; Luke 22:54–62; John 18:15–18, 25–27).

4. Human agents were not required for Jesus' crucifixion (Matt. 26:24; cf. Luke 17:1; 22:22).

5. After his first examination, Pilate asked Jesus, "Art thou the king of the Jews?" (Matt. 27:11; Mark 15:2; Luke 23:3;

John 18:33). Jesus answered, "Sayest thou this thing of thyself, or did others tell it thee of me?" (John 8:34) Pilate deflected any personal interest and asked, "What hast thou done?" Jesus responded, "My kingdom is not of this world: if my kingdom were of this world, then would my servants fight, that I should not be delivered to the Jews: but now is my kingdom not from hence" (John 18:36).

Pilate responded, "Art thou a king then?" Jesus said, "Thou sayest, that I am a king. To this end was I born, and for this cause came I into the world, that I should bear witness unto the truth. Every one that is of the truth heareth my voice" (John 18:37). Pilate responded, "What is truth?" Then he walked out to the crowd and said, "… I find in Him no fault at all," and then attempted to release Jesus instead of Barabbas (Matt. 27:17, 18; Luke 23:4; John 18:38–40). When the people said they preferred Barabbas over Jesus, Pilate asked, "What evil hath he done?" (Matt. 27:21–23). Then Pilate tried to pass the responsibility off to another, sending Jesus to Herod. When Herod tried Jesus and found no cause of death in Him, he returned Him to Pilate.

Finally, Pilate said, "I have found no cause of death in him: I will therefore chastise him, and let him go" (Luke 23:20–22). Pilate's soldiers scourged Jesus, gave Him a crown of thorns, and then Pilate brought him out, saying "I find no fault in him. … Behold the man!… Take ye him, and crucify him: for I find no fault in him" (John 19:4–6). The Jews cry out, "He made himself the Son of God." Recognizing that there was more than humanity in Jesus, "Pilate sought to release him" (John 19:7, 12). Pilate tried to release him one more time, saying: "Behold your King! … Shall I crucify your King?" The Jewish rulers retorted, "We have no king but Caesar" (John 19:14, 15).

The sign Pilate had the soldiers install over the cross was his response to their duplicity: "JESUS OF NAZARETH THE KING OF THE JEWS" (John 19:19). It was a statement of Jesus' crime that Pilate would not change.

6.   "When Pilate declared himself innocent of the blood of Christ, Caiaphas answered defiantly, 'His blood be on us, and on our children.' The awful words were taken up by the priests and rulers, and echoed by the crowd in an inhuman roar of voices. The whole multitude answered and said, 'His blood be on us, and on our children.'" (Ellen G. White, *The Desire of Ages*, p. 738).

Chapter 28
Crucifixion

And when they were come to the place, which is called Calvary, there they crucified
him, and the malefactors, one on the right hand, and the other on the left.
Luke 23:33

The purpose and focus of the everlasting covenant of God is the trial, crucifixion, and resurrection of Jesus. God had prepared for these events before the creation of the world. After Adam and Eve sinned, the plan moved to the second stage of implementation, when God presented His covenant to the human family. In the third stage, Jesus' lived a sinless life as a human being on earth, took the sins of humankind on Himself, and paid the penalty through His willing sacrifice on the cross. He is now completing the purpose of the covenant by His priestly intercession in the heavenly sanctuary.

The resurrection proved the victory of Jesus Christ in the great controversy between Him and Satan. This was a victory gained in many small steps and in many daily victories in Jesus' confrontations with Satan. The victory over Satan in Jesus' life, death, and resurrection is the pledge to humanity of eternal life, and the pledge of the restoration of all that was lost in Eden.

There is deep pathos in Jesus' gift to humanity. There is a challenge to human beings to have faith in Jesus and to consent to the work of grace in their life. This brings joy everlasting, praise to God, and a deep love for God forever and ever.

He Took Our Sins

It was in Gethsemane that Christ took the sins of the world upon Himself. It was there that He challenged the powers of darkness and chose to endure humiliation and torture. It was there that His disciples forsook Him, and that His Father apparently abandoned Him, turning His face away (Matt. 27:46; Mark 15:34; Ps. 22:1). It was there that He looked into "an horror of great darkness," as if He were looking into eternity without God and without life.

While making the final decision that He would do the will of the Father, He sweat "great drops of blood" (Luke 22:44) and fell dying to the ground. The mighty angel, who stands where Satan stood in the presence of God, came to Jesus' side. He did not come to take away the cup of sorrow, but to strengthen Jesus to drink it. Christ's agony did not cease, but His depression lifted, and He came forth calm and serene. He had tasted the sufferings of "death for every man" (Heb. 2:9; cf. Gen. 15:12).[1] Heavenly peace was now His throughout His several trials and crucifixion.

Jesus' sacrifice on the cross was a ministry of the first apartment of the heavenly sanctuary. He continued His first apartment ministry when He ascended to heaven to be our High Priest. In 1844, the antitypical Day of Atonement and the cleansing of the sanctuary began.[2] This was the beginning of Christ's second apartment ministry. The completeness of the atonement made at the cross also included the application of His blood in the heavenly sanctuary.

The time will come when Christ will have finished His intercession in heaven, and there will be no more sins presented for forgiveness.[3] This closes the period of probation.[4] At that time, He will throw down His priestly censer, change into His kingly robes, and come to deliver His people.

A Willing Sacrifice

Some believed that the trial and crucifixion of Jesus represented the failure of Jesus' ministry. Others have accused the Jews of being "Christ killers," ignoring the fact that the early Christian church was a Jewish church.[5] Jesus Himself gives His defense:

> Therefore doth my Father love me, because I lay down my life, that I might take it again. No man taketh it from me, but I lay it down of myself. I have power to lay it down, and I have power to take it again. This commandment have I received of my Father. (John 10:17, 18)

How do we know that Jesus willingly made the sacrifice on the cross? How do we know that this was the culmination of His mission, His victory over Satan, and the proven success of the purpose of God?

John declared Jesus to be the "Lamb slain from the foundation of the world" (Rev. 13:8; cf. John 1:29, 36). The Father, Son, and Holy Spirit, in council, laid out the plan of salvation. It was an audacious plan, difficult even in the making. It became urgently more difficult when Adam and Eve sinned, and the plan, of necessity, was put into effect. In Gethsemane, it was a crisis when Jesus, as a human being, faced the powers of darkness alone.[6]

God knew that people would choose to do wrong. However, the Father, Son, and Holy Spirit covenanted to support their creation and win it back again through God's loving nature. Intelligent beings would not be forced to obey but would be persuaded by truth and love. God would show that He founded His government on mercy and justice.

When the Father Turned His Face Away

During the trial, Jesus was careful to not defend Himself. He suffered in silence the illegality of the night trials, the contradictions of the witnesses, and the high priest's dependence on Jesus' testimony to arrive at a verdict. In spite of the illegality, the Sanhedrin declared Him guilty—guilty of blasphemy. The Jewish leaders manipulated Pilate through his fears of losing his position. "And from thenceforth Pilate sought to release him: but the Jews cried out, saying, If thou let this man go, thou art not Caesar's friend: whosoever maketh himself a king speaketh against Caesar" (John 19:12). The Jews falsely accused Jesus of sedition. It was only under this pressure that Pilate consented to His crucifixion.

The crucifixion took place about the third hour (9:00 a.m.). At the sixth hour, darkness fell over the land. At the ninth hour (3:00 p.m.), Jesus "cried with a loud voice, … My God, my God, why hast thou forsaken me" (Matt. 27:46)?

Did God forsake Him? Does God ever abandon those who are His? Would God forsake a faithful believer at the time of death? No, He would not! Why then did Jesus say, "Why hast thou forsaken me?" Remember the struggle Jesus faced in Gethsemane. In those dark hours, Jesus took the sins of the whole world upon His shoulders. He knew that sin is offensive to God. He felt the separation from God that the lost sinner will feel in the judgment. Would the sins of the world, taken vicariously by Jesus, separate Him from the Father?

The gross unfairness and the vicious abuse He suffered during the trial accentuated His burden. The surging, angry, abusive crowds at the crucifixion made His suffering worse. There were only glimmers of hope, only glimmers of the good in humanity: the thief on the cross, His mother Mary and His disciple John grief-stricken near the cross, the thoughtful soldier who offering Him something to drink. These gave Him a shred of courage. Still, He went to the cross as a human being. He could not see through His approaching death, and could not know but that His burial would be permanent.

He had only His faith and the memory of His Father's words—"This is my beloved Son in whom I am well pleased" (Matt. 3:17; 17:5). God reassured Him with these words at His baptism and again at the transfiguration. He remembered the hours of prayer and fellowship with the Father. He remembered the throngs of people, not those who were now abusive, but those who so much needed and appreciated Him. This memory bolstered His faith.

Did Jesus Die the Second Death?

Some say that Jesus died for sinners the "second death," mentioned in Revelation 2:11; 20:5, 14; 21:8. Every human being who dies, sleeps the sleep of death until Jesus comes again. "And as it is appointed unto men once to die, but after this the judgment" (Heb. 9:27). It would not be sufficient for Jesus to simply "sleep." When He died on the cross, He saved us from the second death, and only by dying the second death could the atonement be made. The problem is that Jesus' resurrection on the third day was a resurrection that is not possible from the second death.

A great metaphor of Jesus' experience occurred in God's covenant ceremony, when "a deep sleep fell upon Abram; and, lo, an horror of great darkness fell upon him" (Gen. 15:12). Nothing more is said to explain this phenomena, but in a "great darkness" Abram felt that which Christ would suffer during the crucifixion, when Jesus would look into an eternity without life and without God.

There is no explicit statement in the Bible that Jesus died the second death. However, the Bible does depict His beginning to feel the weight of sin in Gethsemane and His suffering the sting of rejection and the pain of abuse during His trials and crucifixion. Knowing that sin is offensive to the Father, Jesus felt the "horror of great darkness"; He bore that which no human being could ever bear, for He was to taste death for every human being (Heb. 2:9). There is no pain in death itself. Pain comes only in the approach to death.

In His humanity, Jesus could not see beyond the tomb. He shrank from the separation from the Father that His becoming sin for us would cause. In the horror of the cross, He cried out, "My God, My

God, why hast thou forsaken Me?" (Matt. 27:46).

Then His faith revived. He remembered His Father's words, "This is my beloved Son, in whom I am well pleased" (Matt. 3:17; 17:5). These words had sustained Jesus in the forty days in the wilderness, and they strengthened Him again now. The "faith of Jesus" is to hold onto God's promises when there seems no reason to hope. Just before Jesus bowed His head in death, He cried out to the Father, "Into thy hands, I commend my spirit." His victory of faith on the cross is for each one of us.

What Was Finished?

> When Jesus, therefore, had received the vinegar, he said, It is finished: and he bowed his head, and gave up the ghost. (John 19:30)

> And the sun was darkened, and the veil of the temple was rent in the midst. And when Jesus had cried with a loud voice, he said, Father, into thy hands I commend my spirit: and having said thus; he gave up the ghost. Now when the centurion saw what was done, he glorified God, saying, Certainly this was a righteous man. (Luke 23:45–47; see also Matt. 27:54)

God is the Creator and the source and sustainer of all life. "For in Him we live and move and have our being" (Acts 17:28). God is not contained within His creation; rather, He works through His creation on a continual basis. Without His sustaining power, life would cease. Thus, God could say, "In the day that thou eatest thereof thou shalt surely die" (Gen. 2:17).

God delighted in the gifts He gave the human family. He loved His new creation. He would support His creation without using force or acting arbitrarily. Otherwise, He would violate the principles on which He bases His government. He had to show mercy and justice, and act with love and persuasion.

To refuse God, to rebel against Him, is to cut off the source of life. The Redeemer Himself paid the price and held in check this result of the sin of humanity. Only the Lawgiver can pay the cost of breaking the law and live beyond it. God conceived this plan before the foundation of the world. Jesus offered Himself, the Father offered His only begotten Son, and the Holy Spirit sustained Him on this earth.

Jesus, the second person of the Godhead, became a human being. He lived in every way as humans do. Yet, He lived a sinless life under severe provocation. This life He gave freely to pay for our sins. The trial and crucifixion of Jesus was much worse than what even Jesus expected. Yet, He did not flinch. He followed the will of the Father even unto death.

Satan failed to induce Jesus, even by a thought, to sin. Jesus' sinless life He willingly offered for us as He "became sin for us" with its burden of disapproval from the Father. Because of His sinless life, He also came forth a victor on the third day. The reign of sin would now end. Jesus accomplished the work He came to do. He atoned for the sins of humankind and confirmed the covenant of redemption. His sacrifice on the cross confirmed the faith of sinners who, during Old Testament times, sacrificed animals for their sins (Heb. 9:15), and faith in Jesus' shed blood has continued to provide grace to overcome sin in the succeeding centuries.

> Jesus, when he had cried again with a loud voice, yielded up the ghost. And, behold, the veil of the temple was rent in twain from the top to the bottom; and the earth did quake, and the rocks rent; and the graves were opened; and many bodies of the saints which slept arose, and came out of the graves after his resurrection; and went into the holy city, and appeared unto many. Now when the centurion, and they that were with him, watching Jesus saw the earthquake, and those things that were done they feared greatly, saying, Truly this was the Son of God. (Matt. 27:50–54)

"It is finished," Jesus declared. What was finished? He had made a complete atonement. The covenant was now confirmed and ratified. In His sacrifice on the cross, He took the penalty for our sin. The centuries of animal sacrifices were now made effective in the offering of the real sacrifice, Jesus Christ (Heb. 9:15). The sacrifices and rituals pointing forward to His death were fulfilled, and their significance had come to an end.

The sacrifices for sin and trespass describe the sinner as confessing his sin on the head of the sacrificial animal. The priest then took the blood into the sanctuary or placed it on the horns of the altar to "make an atonement for him … and it shall be forgiven him" (Lev. 4:26; see also Lev. 4:31, 35; 5:5, 10, 16, 18). The action of the priest was a necessary part of the sacrifice, which involved the shedding of blood and the application of the blood. Jesus, our High Priest, is now applying His blood in the heavenly sanctuary to pardon the sins of His people. Another necessary step is described in Leviticus 16 where sins were removed from the sanctuary and the sanctuary was cleansed.

Endnotes

1. Ellen G. White, *The Desire of Ages* (Mountain View, CA: Pacific Press Publishing Association, 1940), pp. 693, 694.
2. Some complain that the sanctuary in heaven does not need cleansing or purifying. However, Scripture declares that it does. "It was therefore necessary that the patterns of things in the heavens should be *purified* with these; but the heavenly things themselves with better sacrifices than these" (Heb. 9:23, emphasis supplied). While it is true that this is describing the inauguration of the heavenly sanctuary at Jesus' ascension, it sets up the expectation that the heavenly sanctuary should follow the pattern of the earthly one in a final cleansing.
3. "So Christ was once offered to bear the sins of many; and unto them that look for him shall he appear the second time *without sin* unto salvation" (Heb. 9:28, emphasis supplied).
4. "He that is unjust, let him be unjust still: and he which is filthy, let him be filthy still: and he that is righteous, let him be righteous still: and he that is holy, let him be holy still. And, behold, I come quickly; and my reward is with me, to give every man according as his work shall be" (Rev. 22:11, 12).
5. For more on the influence of the Jerusalem church in the church of the east, see Benjamin George Wilkinson, PhD, *Truth Triumphant* (Ringgold, GA: TEACH Services, Inc., 2005) pp. 21–26, 34–44.
6. See chapter 26, "Gethsemane."

Chapter 29

Atonement

And he shall lay his hand upon the head of the sin offering, and slay the sin
offering in the place of the burnt offering. And the priest shall take of the blood
thereof with his finger, and put it upon the horns of the altar of burnt offering,
and shall pour out all the blood thereof at the bottom of the altar. … and the
priest shall make an atonement for him, and it shall be forgiven him.
Leviticus 4:29–31

"My covenant," the covenant made *by* God *for* human beings, has given human beings assurance and security all through history. In the fullness of time, Jesus confirmed this covenant by His sacrifice on the cross. People often ask, "What did Jesus do for humanity on the cross?" The answer is:

1. He demonstrated true humility. Fully divine, He became fully human, giving up His glory to come to earth as a common man, as a servant (Col 2:9; John 1:1–4; Isa. 53:2; Phil. 2:7, 8).
2. He revealed the Father to human beings, reestablishing face-to-face communication (Exod. 34:6, 7; John 1:18; 14:9).
3. He gave His presence to human beings as our redeemer and friend (Luke 12:4; John 15:15).
4. He provided grace to change people's lives (Heb. 4:16; 2 Peter 3:18).
5. He prepared His disciples to become apostles and to form His church once He ascended (Matt. 10:1–14).
6. He opened the way to "the throne of grace" where people can "find grace to help in time of need" (Heb. 4:16; 10:20).
7. He took upon Himself our sin and our punishment for sin.

In a few words, through Jesus' sacrifice on the cross, we are ransomed, redeemed, and reconciled to God.

Leviticus 4

The sacrifices for sin in the Old Testament were symbolic of the true sacrifice of Jesus on the cross. The sinner brought a kid of the goats or a lamb to a place near the altar of burnt offering. He transferred his sin to the animal when "he shall lay his hand upon the head of the sin offering, and slay the sin offering" (Lev. 4:29). "And the priest shall take of the blood thereof with his finger, and put it upon the horns of the altar of burnt offering, and shall pour out all the blood thereof at the bottom of the altar. … and the priest shall make an atonement for him, and it shall be forgiven him" (Lev. 4:30, 31). By laying his hand on the head of the animal, and slaying it, the sinner confesses his sin. In a distinct and separate action, the priest ministers the blood to "make an atonement for him, and it shall be forgiven him." A crucial point is that the sin offering is a single ceremony, in two distinct steps.

There are some who believe that all aspects of the atonement were completed at the cross. To believe this is to create problems regarding pardon for sins after Calvary and the need for a judgment. To believe the Bible teaching that Jesus mediates His blood for sinners in the heavenly sanctuary solves many of these problems.

Theories of the Atonement

Through the everlasting covenant, God reconciles sinful humanity to Himself. With this as a background, there are a number of theories of the atonement, each with variations. In studying these theories, one can see that there are Bible verses that can be applied to nearly every one. Yet, to discover truth, one must put the whole picture together, allowing all aspects of truth to fit naturally. A key issue is whether Jesus' atonement at the cross is complete or whether there is a further step to atonement in Christ's heavenly ministry.

Ransom Theory

This view of atonement teaches that when Adam and Eve sinned, they sold humanity to the devil; thus, justice required that the devil be paid a ransom to purchase humankind's freedom and release us from enslavement. The Bible does use the term "ransom" (Mark 10:45; 1 Tim. 2:5, 6), and it describes redemption as our being "bought with a price" (1 Cor. 6:20). People generally think of ransom as a price that a person pays to secure the release of a loved one when kidnapped.

However, there is no scriptural support for the idea that either God or human beings owe anything to Satan. (On the contrary, throughout Scripture, we see that God is the One who required a payment for sin.) True, the sinner is a slave to sin, but this is only because of his choice. God put enmity between the seed of the woman and Satan, giving the sinner a new probation and freedom to choose to serve Him. Satan does not "own" humanity or any part of God's creation. Paying the devil off would not release human beings from his control. Satan's power over the sinner can exist only through the sinner's own choice; when the sinner submits to God, the devil must flee (James 4:7).

Origen, an Alexandrian scholar, was an early proponent of the ransom theory of atonement. He taught that Adam and Eve sold humanity to the devil. Justice required that grace pay a ransom, with Jesus taking humanity's place. God tricked Satan in that Christ could not be held by death. With this, is the concept of the redemption, or "buying back," of humanity. The church taught this for 1,000 years. Since then, the theory has had few supporters.

Moral Influence Theory

The moral influence theory of the atonement teaches that the purpose and work of Jesus Christ was to promote positive moral change for humanity. It teaches that atonement demonstrates God's love, bringing people to love and repentance. This moral change came through the teachings and example of

Jesus, the Christian movement He founded, and the inspiring effect of His crucifixion and resurrection. According to this theory, human beings are spiritually sick and in need of help but capable of accepting God's forgiveness when they see His love for humankind poured out through Jesus' giving Himself on the cross (Gal. 1:4; 2:20; Eph. 5:25; 1 Tim. 2:6; Titus 2:14). This theory denies that Christ died to satisfy divine justice, but teaches rather that He died to inspire humankind with a sense of God's love, softening their hearts and leading them to repentance. It ignores the true spiritual condition of human beings, dead in transgressions and sins (Eph. 2:1), and it denies that sin is a debt requiring payment (Matt. 6:12). Thus, the Atonement does not focus on God, with the purpose of maintaining His justice, but on humankind with the purpose of persuading human beings to right action.[1] *Moral Influence* is a subjective, personal, and localized view. It says nothing about God's dealing with sin on a cosmic level (1 Cor. 4:9; 1 Peter 1:12). It says nothing about God's initiative in the work of grace and leaves humans to form their own character, which leads to legalism.

Satisfaction Theory: Christ Took the Sins of Humanity

In the view of Anselm of Canterbury, the first two theories were inadequate. He suggested that human beings owed God a debt of honor. This debt creates an imbalance in the moral universe, which could not be satisfied by God's simply ignoring it. In Anselm's view, the only possible way of repaying the debt was for a divine being to act as a human being on behalf of human beings and repay the debt of honor owed to God. Therefore, when Jesus died, He did not pay a debt to Satan but to God the Father.

Penal substitution is a variation of this theory. It portrays the atonement of Christ as a vicarious, substitutionary sacrifice that satisfied the demands of God's justice for sin. Thus, Christ died on the cross, taking the penalty for sin (the penal part) in the sinner's place (the substitution part), thereby satisfying the demands of justice so God can justly forgive sins. Penal substitution states that God gave himself in the person of His Son, Jesus Christ, to suffer the death, punishment and curse due to fallen humanity as the penalty for humankind's sin.

The doctrine of the Trinity is essential in this view. It stipulates that God took the punishment upon Himself rather than putting it on someone else. The doctrine of union with Christ affirms that by taking the punishment upon Himself, Jesus fulfills the demands of justice. His resurrection completes this process and is the basis for the renewal and restoration of righteousness.[2]

Those who hold this view believe that every aspect of human beings—mind, will, and emotions— has been corrupted by sin and that we are totally depraved and spiritually dead. Thus, Christ's death paid the penalty for sin, and through faith, human beings can accept Christ's substitution as payment for sin. This view of the atonement aligns most accurately with Scripture in its view of sin, human nature, and the results of the death of Christ on the cross. Its weakness is that it sees sin only in legal terms, when sin is more than a violation of law.[3]

God so Loved the World

Jesus is the Lamb "slain from the foundation of the world." This is the essence of the plan of salvation and the everlasting covenant, which God made before the creation of this world and which became effective after sin. Through His sacrifice on the cross, Jesus exercised His authority and ownership over all creation. He permitted Satan to demonstrate to the universe that, in sin, there is slavery and death. Contrarily, in the law of God, there is freedom, creativity, love and eternal life (James 1:25; 2:12). Through the atonement He will restore all that Adam lost by sin.

> To wit, that God was in Christ, reconciling the world unto himself, not imputing their trespasses unto them; and hath committed unto us the word of reconciliation. (2 Cor. 5:19)

> For God so loved the world, that he gave his only begotten Son, that whosoever believeth in him should not perish, but have everlasting life. (John 3:16)

> Therefore doth my Father love me, because I lay down my life, that I might take it again. No man taketh it from me, but I lay it down of myself. I have power to lay it down, and I have power to take it again. This commandment have I received of my Father. (John 10:17, 18)

Why would God love this world? A master craftsman, who has put heart and soul into a project and brought it to completion, will love what he has made. By nature a woman will love her child no matter what it is like simply because it is her child. When God looked at what He had made—what He had given "birth"—in creating this world, He saw "it was very good" (Gen. 1:31). When sin entered the world, God would not give it up. He created this earth to last into eternity, and He was prepared to do whatever necessary to make it a success.

In the everlasting covenant, the Creator of this earth, the only begotten Son of the Father, came to earth. He gave up the beauty and the position He enjoyed in heaven, the power that He held, and the praise of millions of created beings. He would become a human being that He might live as a servant. He would even accept death. Jesus did this so "whosoever believeth in him should not perish, but have everlasting life."

Jesus died for the sins of every human being. He died for you and for me!

Jesus Loves Even Me

Jesus "had compassion" on the people (Matt. 20:34). He suffered with them in their sickness and pain. Both occasions that He cleansed the Temple, He flared in anger at evil men desecrating the house of God. When Mary washed Jesus' feet with perfume, He deeply appreciated her action. This memory was an encouragement to Him on the cross.

At the last supper, Jesus appointed the bread and juice as symbols of His crucifixion and as a memorial to Him. When Peter denied Him during the trial, one look from the Saviour conveyed His disappointment and pain, such that Peter rushed out weeping bitterly. At the seaside after the resurrection,

Jesus significantly asked Peter three times if He loved Him. He did this so Peter would know that Jesus had forgiven him for thrice denying Him and had reinstated him.

The actions and attitudes of God's people still affect Jesus Christ today. In the new earth, we will learn more of what redemption cost Jesus. His sacrifice on the cross will reach deep into the soul of each person, providing an emotional bond with the Savior that will provide a barrier against sin that will never be crossed again.

Restoring the Bond of Faith

A Christian must understand that his relation with God is paramount. "Without faith it is impossible to please Him" (Heb. 11:6). Faith is commonly defined as belief and trust in God. In addition there must be an emotional commitment or love for God and His truth. The faith relationship can be broken only by sin. In fact, "whatsoever is not of faith is sin" (Rom. 14:23). The nature of a human being is described by the statement from Genesis: "The Lord God formed man of the dust of the ground, and breathed into his nostrils the breath of life; and man became a living soul" (Gen. 2:7). The breath of life is part of his being. In sin and separation from God, there is nothing but death.

Jesus gave Nicodemus a beautiful expression of the everlasting covenant: "For God so loved the world, that he gave his only begotten Son, that whosoever believeth in him should not perish, but have everlasting life" (John 3:16). God gave His only begotten Son to die for the sins of men. However, Jesus also came and *lived* among humans for thirty-three years. He gave them His presence, His example, and His love. He became a friend to the human family.

When humans sin and break the bond of faith, pardon for sin requires renewed faith and love for God and our fellow human beings. When Jesus came and died for us, He won a victory for us over sin and Satan (1 Cor. 15:57; 1 John 5:4).

Does love demand that someone must be punished to forgive someone else? No! It does not! This is a classic wrong question! God will not and Satan cannot punish Jesus. Rather, Jesus willingly paid a debt caused by sin. Sin causes death. One small sin opened the gate to all the sin, disease, and death that we have today. Every sin separates from God, and only the death of the sinner or the Lawgiver as a substitute can meet the penalty, but only the death of the Lawgiver can reopen the way to eternal life.

Why does God demand that someone has to die because of a broken law? This question ignores the holiness of God and assumes that the law of God is no more important than human laws and that sin is trivial. However, sin shows separation from God, and it brings death (Rom. 6:23; Isa. 59:2). Even in what one might consider to be small sins, there is pride, rebellion, disobedience, and selfishness, which are evidences of the sinful nature. It is only by God's grace that a person can be changed and receive eternal life.

The sacrifice of Jesus on the cross offers complete atonement for all who believe (Lev. 4). This atonement must be completed by Christ's priestly ministry in the heavenly sanctuary.[4] Neither step alone is complete and effectual.

Sinners are guilty, condemned to die (Rom. 5:12), and slaves to the sinful nature. Jesus came to release the bonds of sin (Isa. 61:1). By grace and with the sinners' consent, sinners partake of the divine nature and overcome the sinful nature (2 Peter 1:4–8). In Christ, sinners are free and do not need to sin![5] In short, sinners do not pay a ransom to Satan. Through the cross of Calvary, Jesus removes the condemnation and reconciles sinners to God (Rom. 8:1; Heb. 4:16; 2 Cor. 5:18).

Since God is all-knowing and all-powerful, why does He not just deal with sin directly and forgive all sinners without Christ's having to be crucified? For God to do this would trivialize sin. A person who understands the holiness of God will quickly see that there is no small sin. Sin—no matter how big or small—is a blot on the perfection of God's creation and cannot be permitted. To trivialize sin is to bring disorder into the government of God and open the way for the recurrence of sin.

While the old serpent has "bruised the heel" of the Redeemer in Jesus' suffering on the cross, the Redeemer will ultimately bruise the serpent's head (Gen. 3:15). Both sin and Satan will be destroyed (Rev. 20:10, 14, 15). In the new earth, cleansed and purified of sin, Jesus will live forever among the redeemed.

Endnotes

1. Peter Abelard (1079–1142) promoted the moral influence theory in reaction to Anselm's satisfaction theory. The sixteenth century Socinians held to a version of the moral influence theory. Versions of it can be found later in Friedrich Schleiermacher (1768–1834) and Horace Bushnell (1802–1876). Liberal Christian circles tend to hold this view today (http://www.theopedia.com/Moral_Influence_theory_of_atonement, accessed 8/4/12; see also Richard Fredericks, "The moral influence theory: its attraction and inadequacy," available at http://www.ministrymagazine.org/archive/1992/March/the-moral-influence-theory, accessed 8/4/12). Some historians claim that the moral influence theory was one of the earliest theories of the atonement and that it was popular in the early church. See http://en.wikipedia.org/wiki/Moral_influence_theory_of_atonement, accessed 8/4/12.

2. Jesus died for humankind's sin, supporting the concept of penal substitution, also called Vicarious Atonement (Isa. 53:4–6, 10, 11; Matt. 26:28; Rom. 3:23–26; 1 Cor. 15:3; 2 Cor. 5:21; Gal. 1:4; 3:10, 13; Eph. 1:7; 5:2; Heb. 10:12; 1 Peter 2:24; 3:18; 1 John 2:2). His death on the cross also supports the concept of the power of the cross (Matt. 28:18; John 17:2; Rom. 14:9; Rev. 5:9).

3. Besides these, scholars have put forward various other views of the atonement. Because the Bible reveals many truths about Christ's atonement, it is difficult to find any single theory that fully explains the richness of the atonement. In the atonement, we find many interrelated truths concerning the redemption that Christ has accomplished. Much of what we can learn about the atonement needs to be understood from the perspective of God's people under the sacrificial system of the old covenant. The following are summaries of these additional views of the atonement:

    Recapitulation theory pictures the atonement as reversing the course of humankind from disobedience to obedience. It theorizes that Christ's life recapitulated all stages of human life, reversing the course of disobedience initiated by Adam. This theory is not scriptural. The view originated with Irenaeus (AD 125–202), who saw Christ as the new Adam, systematically undoing what the first Adam had done.

    Dramatic theory (*Christus Victor*) pictures Christ as securing the victory in a conflict between good and evil and as winning humankind's release from bondage to Satan. The purpose of Christ's death was to ensure God's victory over Satan and provide a way to redeem the world out of its bondage to evil.

    Example theory sees the atonement as providing an example of faith and obedience to inspire people to be obedient to God. Adherents of this view hold that humans are spiritually alive and that Christ's life and atonement were simply an example to inspire human beings to live a similar life of faith and obedience. This theory and the moral influence theory both deny that God's justice requires payment for sin in Christ's death on the cross. *Example theory* fails to recognize every human's true spiritual condition and that God's justice requires payment for sin beyond the capability of each.

Commercial theory conceives of atonement as that which brings infinite honor to God. It portrays God's giving Christ a reward that He did not need so that Christ could pass that reward on to humankind. Adherents believe that, because humanity's spiritual condition dishonors God, Christ's death, which brought infinite honor to God, can be applied to sinners for salvation. This theory denies the true spiritual state of unregenerate sinners and their need of an entirely new nature, available only in Christ (2 Cor. 5:17).

Governmental theory emphasizes God's high regard for His law and His attitude toward sin. Adherents evaluate humanity's spiritual condition in having broken the law of God. Christ's death allows God to forgive the sins of those who repent and accept Christ's substitutionary death, but the theory is not clear about Christ's death paying the penalty for sin. Hugo Grotius developed this theory in response to the Socinians, who held to a moral influence theory. For more on the subject, see Paul Enns, *The Moody Handbook of Theology*, available at http://www.gotquestions.org/atonement-theories.html, accessed 8/4/12.

4. Hebrews 4:15; 5:6, 9; 9:28; 10:12–14; 12:24 describe Christ's priestly ministry in the heavenly sanctuary.

5. 1 John 2:1; 3:5–9, 24; 2 Peter 1:4–8; and Romans 8:1, 2. Texts about freedom from sin are John 8:32, 33, 36 and Romans 6:7, 18, 22 support the idea that Christians do not need to sin.

Chapter 30
The Resurrection

*For I delivered unto you first of all that which I also received, how that Christ
died for our sins according to the scriptures; And that he was buried,
and that he rose again the third day according to the scriptures:*
1 Corinthians 15:3, 4

At the cross, Jesus not only paid the penalty for the sins of humanity, but He conquered death and hell (Rev. 1:18). Jesus' death on the cross overwhelmed the disciples. They had questions for which they had no answers. To the disciples, it was the failure of all their hopes and aspirations.

To Jesus, it was a glorious victory. He confirmed the everlasting covenant of God, which passed from anticipation to fact. He confirmed the efficacy of the many animals sacrificed for sin. He confirmed converted sinners in their assurance of salvation. During His life on earth, He met Satan repeatedly in confrontations with wicked men, many of whom were intent on putting Him to death. In healing the sick, casting out devils, and teaching the people, Jesus showed His kindness and commitment to restore all that was lost in Eden. This was climaxed in four trials and the horror of crucifixion, which He bore without complaint.

Satan claimed a victory, but he failed to understand the nature of Jesus as Messiah, and he failed to reckon with the power of God. God sent one angel to roll the stone away and to call Jesus to come forth. The unnumbered millions of fallen angels could not stop that one angel, nor could they hold Jesus in the grave.

After the resurrection, there was joy, power, and glorious praise, and there were no more questions. The resurrection gave power to the gospel. In Jesus' resurrection, God promises that He will also resurrect His people to live with Christ forevermore.

Supernatural Events During the Crucifixion

During Jesus' life, He did many miracles of healing, casting out demons, and even raising the dead—all in the power of the Father. Supernatural events also occurred at the time of Jesus' trial, crucifixion, and resurrection. These were a powerful witness of who He was. Had those who were against Him been open to the truth, they could have turned from their evil path.

When arrested and questioned, Jesus answered, "I AM He." As He said, "I AM"—the name of God—there was a brilliant flash of light as an angel stood before Jesus and the crowd fell backwards to the ground. The mob ignored this sign of divinity, for they got up and began to bind Jesus. In a brief scuffle, Peter cut off Malchus' ear. Jesus immediately healed the ear and let the mob bind Him without resistance and take Him to trial.

Pilate's wife dreamed of Jesus' innocence, advising Pilate, "Have nothing to do with that just man." At the time of the crucifixion, Jesus cried out, "Father, forgive them; for they know not what they do" (Luke 23:34). At noon, supernatural darkness, lasting three hours, hid the countryside. When Jesus died, an unseen hand tore the veil of the Temple from top to bottom, a visual representation that animal sacrifices were no longer needed, as Jesus became the true sacrifice on the cross. An earthquake tore the rocks and opened the graves of many sleeping saints, who arose and came out of their graves after Jesus' resurrection and went into the city and appeared to many people" (Matt. 27:52, 53).

"Thy Father Calls Thee"

Jesus lay in the tomb for three days. Pilate and the chief priests, still unbelieving, thought that they could hold Him in the tomb. They ordered the tomb sealed and a guard placed to watch over the tomb. They did not realize that the guards' testimony would serve as witness to the stupendous event of Jesus' coming forth alive from the tomb.

Was it not the purpose of God that the disciples also be witnesses? Had not Jesus told them that He would rise again? They should have taken comfort, but, instead, they were utterly discouraged and were hiding from the authorities. What about us today? Could God be giving us prophecies that would open our eyes and give us courage? If He is, and we fail to listen, then we too could be taken by surprise.

> Before anyone had reached the sepulcher, there was a great earthquake. The mightiest angel from heaven, he who held the position from which Satan fell, received his commission from the Father, and clothed with the panoply of heaven, he parted the darkness from his track. His face was like lightning, and his garments white as snow. As soon as his feet touched the ground it quaked beneath his tread. The Roman guards were keeping their weary watch when this wonderful scene took place. God enabled them to endure the sight, for they had a message to bear as witnesses of the resurrection of Christ. The angel approached the grave, rolled the stone away as though it had been a pebble, and sat upon it. The light of heaven encircled the tomb, and the glory of the angels brightened the whole heaven. Then he spoke, "Thy Father calls Thee; come forth."[1]

> If the soldiers at the sepulcher were so filled with terror at the appearance of one angel clothed with heavenly light and strength, that they fell as dead men to the ground, how will His enemies stand before the Son of God, when He comes in power and great glory, accompanied by ten thousand times ten thousand and thousands of thousands of angels from the courts of heaven?[2]

The Witness of the Roman Soldiers

The chief priests and Pharisees realized that they made a mistake in crucifying Jesus. They remembered Jesus' words, "after three days I will rise again." The day following "the preparation" they had gone to talk to Pilate (Matt. 27:62, 63). At their insistence, Pilate posted a guard about the tomb and set a seal upon the stone covering the entrance. Their nighttime watch began that night.

After the spectacular events that occurred in the early morning hours of the first day of the week, the Roman soldiers abandoned their post and entered the city. The chief priests and elders met the soldiers. The events of the pre-dawn hours had terrified the soldiers, and they were unable to deny *who* Jesus was. The chief priests and elders, adding determined rebellion to their unbelief, bribed the soldiers to lie about what they had seen. "Say ye, His disciples came by night, and stole him away while we slept" (Matt. 28:13). Their explanation made no sense. How could twelve disciples get past one hundred soldiers to silently steal their Master's body?

The truth could not be hidden, and others soon learned that Jesus was alive. Evidence for the truth of the resurrection can be seen in the transformation in the perspective of the disciples and in the explosion of growth in the early church. The death of Jesus terrified the disciples, but the resurrection made them joyful and bold to tell the "good news" of salvation. The resurrection served to make effective the sacrifice of Jesus on the cross, and it energized the disciples in their mission. For the chief priests and elders, it only deepened their hatred of Christ and fixed them in rebellion. This shows that the closer people come to God, they will either love Him more or they will hate Him more. The disciples now better understood Jesus' mission.

Satan's Greatest Failure

When Jesus came to this earth, Satan tried desperately to overcome Him. Did Satan assign this task to an "associate demon?" No, he took charge of it himself. The crucifixion was Satan's last chance and his greatest failure.

- He failed to kill Jesus as a baby.
- He failed to tempt Jesus in His youth to sin or to turn from His God-appointed task.
- He failed to tempt Jesus in the wilderness to doubt God or to take the easy way.
- During the next three and one half years, he failed to make Jesus sin in any way.
- He failed to make Jesus turn away at Gethsemane, when everything looked dark.
- He failed to overcome Jesus at the crucifixion by insult, pain, or desertion.
- He failed to prevent the resurrection.

What else could Satan do? He could no longer reach Jesus personally. However, he could reach His "body," the church, and he has viciously assailed the church from that time forward. Satan has tried to prove that grace was not sufficient to save! He began immediately to tempt the new converts to the church (Heb. 6:6; *The Great Controversy*, p. 489). It rests with Christ's followers today to consent to the work of grace that God may change their lives, proving that grace is sufficient to save.

While Satan had failed, Jesus had gained a glorious victory. What did Jesus accomplish by His death on the cross?

- He met the demands of the broken law of God.
- He demonstrated that God is a God of justice and mercy and unfathomable love.
- He wrested from Satan the lost dominion.
- He reconciles human beings to fellowship with God.
- He restores in humanity the image of God.
- He gives human beings eternal life (see John 3:15, 16).

Other Theories of Resurrection

There are many articles on the Internet describing alternate theories for what happened after Jesus died. The theory that the disciples stole the body comes from the Gospel account itself (Matt. 28:12–14). It is the most common rationale for the resurrection story being false. The stolen body theory provides a convenient excuse to those who do not want to believe, but they are ignoring the facts.[3]

- Besides the Roman guards at the site of the tomb, there was a giant stone covering the tomb, which would have taken several people to move. The guards could not have overlooked its being moved from its place.
- Were it not for the Roman officials' collaboration with the chief priests and elders—and a substantial bribe—the soldiers' false testimony, in perpetuating the lie to cover the resurrection, would have brought them certain death for abandoning their post of duty and allowing the body to be taken (Matt. 28:12–14).
- Had the body been stolen by His followers, all that would be needed to disprove the disciples' claim would be to produce the body. Yet, the body has never been produced.
- Historically, the early followers of Jesus suffered persecution for their belief. National leaders gave them the ultimatum to either renounce their belief in the resurrection or die. It seems unlikely that, were the disciples to have stolen the body that they would have been ready to die rather than confess their misdeed.

It is true that people often die for beliefs that are not true, but in such cases, they do not know that they are untrue. How often do people die for what they know to be a fabrication? (It would only make sense if they were spies or were dying to cover family shame.) Whatever else can be said about the original followers of Jesus, they certainly believed that Jesus rose from the dead, and they could not have stolen the body.

In 1929, *The Saturday Evening Post* interviewed Albert Einstein about a number of subjects, one of which was whether he believed that Jesus was a real person. He responded:

> Unquestionably! No one can read the Gospels without feeling the actual presence of Jesus. His personality pulsates in every word. No myth is filled with such life.[4]

A Jew and British author of the last century who knew about the life-changing experience of the resurrection was Alfred Edersheim. He published his scholarly book, *The Life and Times of*

Jesus the Messiah, in the 1880s. It is still one of the most authoritative sources on the subject. In it he wrote:

> The importance of all this cannot be adequately expressed in words. A dead Christ might have been a Teacher and Wonder-worker, and remembered and loved as such. But only a Risen and Living Christ could be the Saviour, the Life, and the Life-Giver—and as such preached to all men. And of this most blessed truth, we have the fullest and most unquestionable evidence.[5]

Endnotes

1. Ellen G. White, Ms. 115, 1897, in *Christ Triumphant* (Hagerstown, MD: Review and Herald Publishing Association, 1999), p. 283, and in Francis D. Nichol, *Seventh-day Adventist Bible Commentary* (Washington, D.C.: Review and Herald Publishing Association, 1956), vol. 5, p. 1110.

2. Ellen G. White, *Signs of the Times*, April 22, 1913, in Francis D. Nichol, *Seventh-day Adventist Bible Commentary* (Washington, D.C.: Review and Herald Publishing Association, 1956), vol. 5, p. 1110.

3. David Mishkin, "Did He or Didn't He? Jewish Views of the Resurrection of Jesus," *Issues: A Messianic Jewish Perspective*, vol. 11, no. 6, pp. 1–6, available at http://www.jewsforjesus.org/files/pdf/issues/issues-11-06.pdf, accessed 2/28/13.

4. Interview, Albert Einstein, "What Life Means to Einstein: An Interview by George Sylvester Viereck," *The Saturday Evening Post*, October 26, 1929, p. 117, available at http://www.saturdayeveningpost.com/wp-content/uploads/sateve-post/einstein.pdf, accessed 2/28/13.

5. Alfred Edersheim, *The Life and Times of Jesus the Messiah* (Grand Rapids, MI: Eerdmans Publishing Company, 1971), vol. 2, p. 629.

Chapter 31

The Walk to Emmaus

---

*And he said unto them, What manner of communications are these that ye have
one to another, as ye walk, and are sad? And the one of them, whose name was
Cleopas, answering said unto him, Art thou only a stranger in Jerusalem, and
hast not known the things which are come to pass there in these days?*

Luke 24:17, 18

Jesus confirmed the everlasting covenant. The redemption of humankind was an accomplished
fact. Jesus had finished the work He came to do. The sacrifice on the cross established for eternity the
government of the universe upon love, persuasion, and freedom. Eden would be restored. The image of
God would be placed again in people's heart, and sin and sinners would be no more. All would see that
God is "just, and the justifier of him which believeth in Jesus" (Rom. 3:26).

In the meantime, Jesus must build and encourage His church. Yet, His disciples were crestfallen
and in hiding.

The Walk to Emmaus

It had been two days since the crucifixion, and two friends stood talking together. "Shall we go,
Cleopas? It is not safe for us to be in Jerusalem. Come with me to my village."

"Yes, Jonas, you are right. Who knows what that serpent, Caiaphas, will do next!"

With these words, the two men, silent and sad, walked rapidly away from the city, taking the
northwest road. The crucifixion had shattered their lives. It seemed now that nothing mattered. They
had seen their beloved Master crucified just two days before, and, with Him, all their hopes and aspirations had died. Many people crowded the road, as it was the Passover. But the two men kept their
heads down, avoided eye-contact in the crowd, and spoke quietly to one another when by themselves.

"Cleopas, it was time for the Messiah. He came just at the time prophesied by Daniel the prophet."

"That's right, Jonas, and He came from Bethlehem just as Micah had prophesied."

"All Israel loved Him, except those wicked men who call themselves our leaders."

"Jonas, I have no love for the Romans, but Pilate tried to save Him. If only he had more backbone!
And even that centurion, he confessed that Jesus was the Son of God."

"Right, and He was a friend of publicans and sinners. That gave me hope too."

"It is all over now. May God bring justice to those who did this evil deed."

As they continued walking, a Fellow Traveler caught up beside them. He seemed pleasant and
earnest. "What are you talking about, and why are you so sad?"

Jonas turned his shoulder, looked at Cleopas, and kept walking. The Stranger failed to take the hint and continued walking beside them. Finally, Jonas turned to Him and, with a little irritation, said, "Were you not here for the Passover? Have you not heard about the crucifixion?"

The Stranger rejoined with, "What are you talking about?"

They said, "About Jesus of Nazareth. He was a prophet who said and did many powerful things before God and all the people. Our leaders and the leading priests handed Him over to be sentenced to death, and they crucified Him. We were hoping that He would free Israel. Besides that, today is now the third day since these things happened" (Luke 24:19–21). Even worse, the grave is empty. Next thing you know, they will send soldiers for us, His disciples."

The Stranger looked thoughtful, then said with some authority, "How slow you are to believe what the prophets predicted. They prophesied that the Messiah would need to suffer these things before He is taken into glory" (Luke 24:25–27). Then Jesus showed them from the books of Moses and the prophets what had been predicted about Him.

What the Stranger Said

Do not you remember that, after Adam and Eve sinned, God did not abandon them? He was still their God. He put within every human being a desire to do right, an enmity against sin, a conscience. Humans are not to be helpless before the evil one. God paid the price for this Himself. Through His suffering, He will destroy sin and evil and reconcile His people to Him. In His own words, He said, "And I will put enmity between thee and the woman, and between thy seed and her seed; it shall bruise thy head, and thou shalt bruise his heel" (Gen. 3:15).

Then "by faith Abel offered unto God a more excellent sacrifice than Cain" (Heb. 11:4). How was the sacrifice of Abel "more excellent"? From Genesis 3:15 we know that the promised Redeemer would have to suffer. The sacrifice shows that He would give His life, for "without shedding of blood is no remission" (Heb. 9:22).

Later, God called Abraham to sacrifice Isaac, his only son. On the surface, this demand made impossible God's promise in the covenant of making Abraham a great nation through Isaac—unless God performed a miracle and raised Isaac from the dead. Abraham wrestled with God and his own thoughts for hours over this matter. However, he had learned to trust God, and, in the end, he knew that blessing comes only by implicit obedience to God.

> By faith Abraham, when he was tried, offered up Isaac: and he that had received the promises offered up his only begotten son, of whom it was said, That in Isaac shall thy seed be called: accounting that God was able to raise him up, even from the dead; from whence also he received him in a figure. (Heb. 11:17–19)

To Isaac's question about where the sacrifice was, Abraham responded with this truth, "God will provide himself a lamb for a burnt offering" (Gen. 22:8). Not knowing that God had a different plan in mind than he was thinking, Abraham proceeded with the sacrifice. By faith, Isaac willingly cooperated. At the last moment, the "angel of the Lord" stopped the proceeding. Abraham and Isaac found a ram caught in a thicket and offered a sacrifice. In the first part of this dramatized parable, Isaac represented Jesus, the Lamb of God. In the second part, God showed in a beautiful way that He would provide the sacrifice. Isaac was "a figure" of Jesus—the only begotten Son who became the sacrifice for every child of God.

In the Passover, each family was to slay a lamb and sprinkle its blood on the doorposts and the lintel. It was the blood of the lamb that saved the firstborn from death. Why did a lamb have to die? A lamb cannot save a person from the consequences of sin. Yet, its death must still mean something. It pointed forward to a Redeemer who would suffer and die for the sins of humankind.

Isaiah 53 showed what the death of the lamb accomplished. The Redeemer would not just die, but He would experience physical suffering, opposition, and rejection.

> He was oppressed, and he was afflicted, yet he opened not his mouth: he is brought as a lamb to the slaughter, and as a sheep before her shearers is dumb, so he openeth not his mouth.… He shall see the travail of his soul, and shall be satisfied: by his knowledge shall my righteous servant justify many; for he shall bear their iniquities. (Isa. 53:7, 11)

"Though he were a Son, yet learned he obedience by the things which he suffered" (Heb. 5:8). Through His suffering, He learned what it is to obey to the greatest degree. Through His suffering, He paid the price for the sins of humankind. His sacrifice qualifies Him to intercede with the Father for all people (Heb. 4:15, 16).

Daniel prophesied the exact time He would come (Dan. 9:24–27). He came and died as prophesied to the day! The sacrifice and oblation had now met their fulfillment. Making this sacrifice was the will of God and the purpose of His life.

God told Joseph, husband of Mary, to "call his name JESUS, for he shall save his people from their sins" (Matt. 1:21). He was not just to teach nor just to forgive, He was to save His people from their sins.

Returning to the Story

By now, the three had walked the five miles and arrived at Jonas' house. "Come in and have some refreshment," Jonas invited. "I have learned much from your words, and I would like to hear more."

"Thanks, but I need to be moving on."

"Sir, please, if you do not need to come in for your own sake, please do so for ours. Please come in!" By this time, Cleopas and Jonas had each taken one arm of their new friend and nudged Him to the door. He willingly went with them.

Jonas hurried to get cold water and some bread. As he placed these on the table, the Stranger "took bread, blessed it, and brake, and gave to them" (Luke 24:30).

"Jonas, it is He!"

"My Lord and my God!"

They both jumped up and ran to bow at His feet. But He had vanished. With great excitement, they forgot the cold water and uneaten bread. They even forgot the soldiers swarming Jerusalem as they ran out the door and hurried back down the road to Jerusalem. Panting as he spoke, Cleopas said, "Did not our heart burn within us, while he talked with us by the way, and while he opened to us the scriptures" (Luke 24:32)?

Now their eyes were bright with hope. There was no more sadness as they talked rapidly to each other as they stumbled excitedly on their way. They repeated the words over and over again, "He's alive!" Travelers on the road looked on and wondered. Their Unseen Companion smiled as the two men quickly found their way to the disciples and gave them the news.

Over the course of several days and weeks, Jesus made His presence known to the disciples, proving to all that He had indeed conquered death. Then they watched Him return in the clouds to His Father, with the hope of His soon return.

A New Message

The resurrection made effective all that had gone before: Jesus' sinless life, His sacrificial death on the cross, and the promise of His coming again. For the first time, the disciples began to see the purpose of Jesus' coming. Their new understanding energized them with a new message. In emphasizing the commandments, Jesus had emphasized the *agape* love that was to motivate all that they did and taught. "Jesus Christ and Him crucified" was the message to go to the world. People's lives and the direction of nations would now be changed. Jesus Christ was alive and in heaven, ministering the blood of the covenant and preparing to return again soon!

Was this message new? Moses gave a message of love in Deuteronomy. David wrote of the love of God in the Psalms. Love is a frequent subject in the Bible (Deut. 6:5; 7:8, 10; 10:19; Lev. 19:18; Isa. 43:4; 63:9; Jer. 31:3; Hosea 14:4; Matt. 19:19). However, the Jews forgot these things in the stresses of time, war, and the cares of this life. Rather than submitting to the sweet influences of a God of love, they chose the "easy way" and tried to earn their way to salvation. It became a heavy burden.

Christians put all these things aside for the love of Him who died for us. Religion became something for everybody and every nation, not for just one people or one nation. All were welcome, and people from all backgrounds began to join the new church. The grace of God began to conquer the world!

Emmanuel: God With Us

Christians must learn that prophecies are not always clear ahead of time. Yet, the prophecies always contain details that make it possible to recognize their fulfillment and strengthen the believer's faith when they are fulfilled. Jesus said, "And now I have told you before it come to pass, that, when it is come to pass, ye might believe" (John 14:29).

When Jesus gave Himself to join the human race, He did not take the gift back. He is still a human being and will continue to be for all eternity. In doing this, He laid aside some of the attributes of divinity. He is even now physically limited to one place at a time. He is in heaven, but He is coming back again! The angels told the disciples, as they strained their eyes to catch one more glimpse of the Master:

> Ye men of Galilee, why stand ye gazing up into heaven? this same Jesus, which is taken up from you into heaven, shall so come in like manner as ye have seen him go into heaven. (Acts 1:11).

Yet, His humanity is glorified as ours shall be.

> Beloved, now are we the sons of God, and it doth not yet appear what we shall be: but we know that, when he shall appear, we shall be like him; for we shall see him as he is. (1 John 3:2)

The scars in His hands are an eternal reminder of the cost of redemption.

> His splendor was like the sunrise; rays flashed from his hand, where his power was hidden. (Hab. 3:4, NIV)

> And one shall say unto him, What are these wounds in thine hands? Then he shall answer, Those with which I was wounded in the house of my friends. (Zech. 13:6)

"This same Jesus" is human, eternally human. "We shall be like Him," who is eternally a member of the human race. His commitment to us is: "I will be to them a God, and they shall be to me a people" (Heb. 8:10). The everlasting covenant is now eternal—God is one with the human family. We have His promise: "And I heard a great voice out of heaven saying, Behold, the tabernacle of God is with men, and he will dwell with them, and they shall be his people, and God himself shall be with them, and be their God" (Rev. 21:3).

The Jewish Basis for Salvation

The Jews did not recognize personal sin in their lives. Most based their assurance of salvation on their lineage from Abraham and their meticulous observance of the ceremonies and sacrifices written in the book of Moses (Deut. 31:24–26). It was a new experience for the Jews to be called to repentance as John the Baptist was doing. Jesus' forgiveness of sins when He healed the sick was likewise new. In the Sermon on the Mount, Jesus called for a change of heart, not a mere repetition of forms and ceremonies. Even a strict keeping of the moral law falls short if a person does not have a change of heart. The kingdom of grace must be established before the kingdom of glory can come.

Before the crucifixion, not even the disciples understood that Jesus came, not only to live among humans but also to die for them. After Peter's confession, "thou art the Christ, the Son of the living God," in recognition of who Jesus was, Peter still misunderstood Jesus' mission:

> From that time forth began Jesus to show unto his disciples, how that he must go unto Jerusalem, and suffer many things of the elders and chief priests and scribes, and be killed, and be raised again the third day. Then Peter took him, and began to rebuke him, saying, Be it far from thee, Lord: this shall not be unto thee. But he turned, and said unto Peter, Get thee behind me, Satan: thou art an offence unto me: for thou savourest not the things that be of God, but those that be of men. (Matt. 16:21–23)

The misunderstanding was also reflected in the competition among the disciples for the highest place in the kingdom that they expected Jesus to establish. They were expecting the restoration of the throne of David and the past glories of Israel. "And there was also a strife among them, which of them should be accounted the greatest" (Luke 22:24).

The story of the walk to Emmaus illustrates the feelings of the disciples immediately after the crucifixion. Jesus' crucifixion had devastated the disciples and had destroyed their expectations of a glorious earthly kingdom. The disciples felt that they had lost everything and that Jesus had failed as the Messiah. The two walking to Emmaus said:

"But we trusted that it had been he which should have redeemed Israel: and beside all this, to day is the third day since these things were done" (Luke 24:21). On that famous walk, Jesus explained these things to the grieving disciples.

For forty days, Jesus appeared to the disciples before He ascended to heaven. It was only after another ten days of intense and united prayer, followed by the outpouring of the Holy Spirit at Pentecost, that the disciples finally began to understand the purpose of Jesus' life on earth. The culmination and purpose of the entire sacrificial system was Jesus' sacrifice on the cross. Jesus' power to heal and His grace to forgive were dependent upon His death and resurrection. The crucifixion was not a failure; rather, it was Jesus the Messiah's supreme victory over Satan. In statements on Pentecost and shortly thereafter, Peter demonstrated that he understood that the suffering and crucifixion of Jesus Christ fulfilled prophecy.

> But those things, which God before had showed by the mouth of all his prophets, that Christ should suffer, he hath so fulfilled. (Acts 3:18)

> Yea, and all the prophets from Samuel and those that follow after, as many as have spoken, have likewise foretold of these days. (Acts 3:24)

> For of a truth against thy holy child Jesus, whom thou hast anointed, both Herod, and Pontius Pilate, with the Gentiles, and the people of Israel, were gathered together, For

to do whatsoever thy hand and thy counsel determined before to be done. (Acts 4:27, 28)

Stephen, in his last sermon before the Sanhedrin, began to touch on the fact that the ceremonial system and even the Temple itself were a type and not the reality. The Sanhedrin cut his sermon short when he quoted Isaiah 66:1, 2: "Heaven is my throne, and earth is my footstool: what house will ye build me? saith the Lord: or what is the place of my rest? Hath not my hand made all these things" (Acts 7:49, 50)?

Why did it take so long for the disciples to understand? Why did Jesus not tell them these things before they happened? The truth is, Jesus did tell them of His impending death at least four times before it happened. They simply could not grasp what He was saying. Until they believed that He came to die, they would not have understood if He tried to tell them why it needed to occur. In speaking of the gift of the Holy Spirit, Jesus said, "I have yet many things to say unto you, but ye cannot bear them now" (John 16:12).

Chapter 32
Why Was Jesus Rejected?

The Jews answered him, We have a law, and by our law
he ought to die, because he made himself the Son of God.
John 19:7

The covenant gives people faith through His presence, hope through His promise, and love through His death. Why would people ever turn against a covenant that gives faith, hope, and love? Is it not because God also asks for a response, a commitment of faith?

It is difficult to determine what the Jews in the time of Christ believed about the Messiah. The wars with Rome (AD 70 and 132) destroyed records and required that Jewish thinking be reconstituted from memory, from records in the Diaspora, or assumed from later writings of the rabbinic Jews. The New Testament writings are valuable, but they express the Christian viewpoint. However, much can be inferred about the general views of other sects of Judaism. Loss of the Temple led to the development of rabbinic Judaism. However, the Jewish views of Jesus as Messiah persist in rabbinic Judaism. Even now, Jews oppose belief in Jesus as the Messiah. This chapter is to examine some of those beliefs.

Why Jews Do Not Accept Jesus as the Messiah

The reasons Jews do not accept Jesus as Messiah include differences in prophetic interpretation and theology and other historical factors. Different writers will list different reasons. The four reasons presented below are commonly cited, but the list is not exhaustive.

1. Jesus did not fulfill the messianic prophecies.

Jesus fulfilled some 300 Old Testament prophecies. These depict the Messiah in two seemingly contradictory ways: some, as a conquering king and others, as a suffering servant. To the Old Testament scholar in the time of Christ, the Messiah was a conquering king who would never die and who would rule on the throne of David forever. Texts from the Dead Sea Scrolls depict the Messiah as being divine.[1]

When Jesus came as a humble servant (Phil. 2:5–8), the leaders of the nation did not recognize Him. As Jesus' popularity increased, the leaders could not ignore Him, and they feared that He might take the throne of David. (Should they not expect that if He were a conquering king?) When Jesus refused to be a conquering king and accepted death on the cross, they rejected Him. (Actually, they rejected Him long before He was crucified, as He preached a spiritual kingdom of God.) With this as their litmus test, it is easy to understand how they believed that Jesus did not fulfill the following expectations for the Messiah:

- Building the third temple (Ezek. 37:26–28)
- Gathering all Jews back to the land of Israel (Isa. 43:5, 6)
- Bringing in a reign of righteousness to the world (Isa. 2:4)
- Advancing the knowledge of God (Isa. 11:9)
- Uniting all humanity as one (Zech. 14:9)[2]

Many Jews held a corrupted view of Jesus' mission. They were not all wrong in their expectations; mostly they were just impatient. It was not reasonable that all these expectations should be fulfilled at one time. Isaiah, Ezekiel, and Old Testament authors suggest that it was God's purpose to institute a reign of righteousness on the earth through the Messiah.

Daniel 9:24 outlines the mandate to Israel for their 490-year probation. The people and the "holy city" were to complete their God-given mission during this time. John the Baptist came as "the voice of one crying in the wilderness," a last call to the nation to fulfill their mission. Because of the error and corruption of Israel at the time, Jesus faced rejection and opposition from the very first.

Building on the message of John the Baptist, Jesus preached repentance from sin and obedience from the heart. He came to establish the kingdom of grace. Human lives had to be changed before Israel could give a message to the world. In attempting to circumvent the kingdom of grace, the Jews rejected their Messiah. This postponed the kingdom of glory until Christ's second coming.

2. Jesus did not embody the personal qualifications of the Messiah.

The Messiah was to be a prophet. The leaders did not accept Jesus as a prophet, but the people whom He helped immediately called Him a prophet. Many felt that the canon of prophecy closed with the book of Malachi. However, Jesus was a prophet in His own right, as He expounded upon the prophecies about Himself and gave the prophecies of Matthew 24. John the Baptist was also a prophet.[3] Besides these two being prophets, there were a number of later New Testament prophets, and the gift of prophecy is one of the spiritual gifts the Holy Spirit gave the church.[4]

Some have thought that Israel should be inhabited by the majority of the Jews in the world in order for prophecy to be fulfilled. Yet, this is an odd proposition since the majority of the Jews in the world have not lived in Israel since the Babylonian captivity. Even since the restoration, only a fraction of the Jews of the world have lived in Palestine. With Israel being a small nation, hemmed in by hostile neighbors, a majority of the Jews in the world will never live there.

Messiah was to be of the tribe of Judah and descend from David. Some argue that it must be on His father's side, but Genesis 49:10 and Isaiah 11:1 indicate a general descent only. However, the standard today for being a Jew is that one's mother is a Jew! The genealogies support these variations (Matt. 1:1–17; Luke 3:23–38). Joseph and his sons accepted Jesus as part of their family.[5] To deny the virgin birth raises questions about the genealogy, while belief in the virgin birth requires only that the person understand the prophecies and the omnipotence of God.

Jesus came to this world to fulfill the Ten Commandments by living a sinless life. He also came to fulfill the symbols of the ceremonial law through His true sacrifice for sin on the cross. Jesus supported the true meaning of all the laws of Moses. The Jews accused Him of breaking the Sabbath by healing sufferers on Sabbath (John 9:16). In truth, He always kept the Sabbath; He just did not keep all the thirty-nine categories and hundreds of ordinances added to the Sabbath. At His trial, no one charged Him with Sabbath breaking!

Jesus spoke strongly against any change in the Torah (Matt. 5:16, 17). In the Sermon on the Mount, He emphasized that the law must be kept from the heart and that love is to be our motive (Matt. 5–7; cf. Jer. 31:31–34). He declared that a superficial keeping of the letter of the law is not pleasing to God (Matt. 5:20).

3. Bible verses referring to the prophecies fulfilled by Jesus are mistranslations.

The Christian idea of a virgin birth comes from Isaiah 7:14, which describes an *alma* giving birth. The Hebrew word *alma* has always meant a young woman. It does not distinguish whether she is a virgin or not. However, the Greek equivalent for *alma* in this passage in the Septuagint is *parthenos*, which does mean "virgin." That is why Matthew 1:23 could legitimately quote Isaiah as, "Behold, a virgin shall conceive and bear a son ..."

Some critics claim that the idea of a virgin giving birth came from the first century pagan idea of the gods fathering children by humans and that it was worked into the story by later Christian theologians. However, the stories from paganism have maidens consorting with the gods, and Luke merely states that Mary conceived by the "power" of the Holy Spirit, while Matthew recorded the fact of the virgin birth (Matt. 1:18–25; cf. Luke 1:26–38). This was long before Christian theologians arrived on the scene. The story of Jesus' birth in the Gospels is clear. The "pagan idea of gods impregnating mortals" raises the question of which came first, the "pagan belief," in anticipation of Jesus' birth (Satan also is a student of the Scriptures), or the actual birth of Jesus as recorded in the Gospels. The evidence supports the gospel story.

Some argue that Isaiah 53 refers to a description of the exile and redemption of the Jewish people. The description of the suffering servant begins in Isaiah 52:13–15. Verse 14 says "his visage was so marred more than any man," which can only refer to Jesus' mistreatment at His trials and crucifixion. It cannot refer to the nation of Israel. There are other verses in Isaiah 53 that refer to Jesus' being a sin bearer and to His being buried with the rich. Jesus fulfilled these prophecies, and they cannot refer to the exile and redemption of the Jewish people.

4. National revelation is the basis for Jewish belief.

Of all the religions in human history, only Judaism bases its belief on God's speaking to the entire nation and not on claims of miracles. Jews accept that God will sometimes give the power of "miracles" to charlatans for the testing of Jewish loyalty to the Torah (Deut. 13:4). Maimonides stated in *Foundations of Torah*, chapter 8:

> The Jews did not believe in Moses, our teacher, because of the miracles he performed. Whenever anyone's belief is based on seeing miracles, he has lingering doubts,

because it is possible the miracles were performed through magic or sorcery. All of the miracles performed by Moses in the desert were done because they were needed, and not as proof of his prophecy.

> What then was the basis of [Jewish] belief? The Revelation at Mount Sinai, which we saw with our own eyes and heard with our own ears, not dependent on the testimony of others … as it says, "Face to face, God spoke with you …" The Torah also states: "God did not make this covenant with our fathers, but with us—who are all here alive today" (Deut. 5:3).

It is impossible to expect that national revelation has been the sole basis for Jewish beliefs. Many Jewish beliefs have come through individual patriarchs and prophets. Moreover, the Jews believe the revelations given individually to Abraham. At Sinai, after their first exposure to God, the Jews refused to hear Him further, and asked Moses to intercede for them and repeat all the messages of God to them. "And they said unto Moses, Speak thou with us, and we will hear: but let not God speak with us, lest we die" (Exod. 20:19). Throughout their history, God spoke through prophets and their writings, rather than to the nation as a whole, as at Sinai. The only significant belief given in the ears of the whole nation was when God spoke the Ten Commandments from Sinai.

What about miracles? A number of miracles accompanied the exodus of Israel through the desert, all of which served as teaching devices. Specifically, the daily manna and the water from the rock showed God's provision for His people. The pillar of cloud and of fire showed God's daily leading of the nation. The serpent on a pole demonstrated healing through faith in God. Korah, Dathan, and Abiram's falling into a crevice opened by an earthquake demonstrated judgment on the wicked. We could cite other examples.

Christianity Contradicts Jewish Theology

The real conflict between Judaism and Christianity is that Christians believe in God as the Father, the Son and the Holy Ghost (Matt. 28:19). Contrast this with the *Shema*, the heart of Jewish belief: "Hear O Israel, the Lord our God, the Lord is *one*" (Deut. 6:4, emphasis supplied). Jews declare the *Shema* every day. The *Shema* is often the first words a Jew learns to speak and the last words he or she utters before death. Christians do not deny the *Shema*. God is indeed one. Yet, we recognize from the testimony of the Old and New Testaments that three Persons make up the unity of God. It is a mystery that we cannot explain.

In Jewish law, worship of a three-part God is idolatry. In the wisdom of God, He did not emphasize the concept of a God who is "Three in One." However, this concept became prominent in the New Testament in explaining the Messiah, God's Son, who lived as a human being and died that human beings might live, and in explaining the work of the Holy Spirit in making effective the work of grace. The Son often prayed to the Father, and the Holy Spirit continued the work of Christ after His ascension to heaven. We see God as being three personalities perfectly united in essence and purpose.

The Jewish critics of the Trinity, fail to recognize that there are several references to the Son and to the Spirit in the Old Testament (though more is said about the plurality of God in the New Testament) and that *Elohim,* the masculine plural, refers to the Creator God and allows for a plurality within the Godhead.[6] "Let *us* make man in *our* image," *Elohim* said in Genesis 1:26.

Endnotes

1.   "I note that recent texts from Qumran indicate that the concept of a divine son was part of the messianic expectations of some sections of pre-Christian Judaism. Texts from the Dead Sea Scrolls attest that some Jews believed that the Messiah would possess divine qualities. For example, he will be "begotten of God" (1Qsa); he will be called "Son of God" and "Son of the Most High" (4Q246); heaven and earth will obey him; he will heal the sick and raise the dead (4Q521); and, he will be as Melchizedek and the very things said of God should be said of him (1Q13)" (Dean L. Overman, *A Case for the Divinity of Jesus: Examining the Earliest Evidence* [Lanham, MD: Rowman & Littlefield Publishers, Inc., 2010], p. 70).

   The *Aramaic Apocalypse* (4Q246) says: "**9** [… Gr]eat will he be called and he will be designated by his name, **ii 1** He will be called son of God, and they will call him son of the Most High. Like the sparks **2** of the vision, so will their kingdom be. They will rule (several) years over **3** the earth and crush everything. People will crush another people and city another city. **4** *vacat* Until the people of God arise and make everyone rest from the sword. **5** His kingdom will be an eternal kingdom and all his paths in truth. He will judge **6** the earth in truth and all will make peace. The sword will cease in the earth **7** and all the cities will pay him homage. The great God is his strength, **8** he will make war with them. He will place peoples in his hand and **9** cast them all away before him. His kingdom will be an eternal kingdom and all the abysses …" (Géza G. Xeravits, *Kings, Priest, Prophet: Positive Eschatological Protagonists of the Qumran Library* [Leiden, The Netherlands, Koninklijke Brill, 2003], vol. 47, pp. 83, 84).

2.   Shraga Simmons (born July 1, 1961), an Orthodox Jewish rabbi involved in Orthodox Jewish outreach, gives his own list of reasons that Jews reject Jesus as the Messiah at "Why Jews do not Believe in Jesus," available at http://www.aish.com/jw/s/48892792.html, accessed 8/6/12.

3.   Jesus and John the Baptist were called prophets (Matt. 21:11, 26; Luke 1:76; 7:16, 26).

4.   Prophecy is a gift of the Spirit in the New Testament (Rom. 12:6; 1 Cor. 12:10; and Eph. 4:11). The New Testament lists other prophets besides Jesus and John the Baptist (Acts 2:17, 18; 11:27; 13:1; 15:32; 21:9, 10).

5.   Jesus was considered "the carpenter's son" or the son of Joseph (Matt. 13:55, 56; Luke 3:23; 4:22; John 1:45; 6:42). He was also called the son of Mary and accepted into a family with brothers and sisters (Mark 6:3; Matt. 12:46). This shows that Jesus was adopted by Joseph and his family on a practical basis and probably on an official one as well.

6.   Rich Deem, "The Triunity (Trinity) of God in the Old Testament," available at http://www.godandscience.org/apologetics/triunity.html, accessed 8/6/12.

Chapter 33
Symbolism of Sacrifice

And he made his grave with the wicked, and with the rich in his death; because
he had done no violence, neither was any deceit in his mouth. Yet it pleased the
LORD to bruise him; he hath put him to grief: when thou shalt make his soul an
offering for sin, he shall see his seed, he shall prolong his days, and the pleasure
of the LORD shall prosper in his hand. He shall see of the travail of his soul, and
shall be satisfied: by his knowledge shall my righteous servant
justify many; for he shall bear their iniquities.
Isaiah 53:9–11

After Adam and Eve sinned, God gave them the covenant of redemption. A Redeemer would come and die to take Adam's sin. As an illustration and a reminder of this plan, an animal must die in place of the sinner—to represent the Redeemer who would come. Shortly after God barred Adam and Eve from Eden and the tree of life, humans began offering sacrifices.

In time, the heathen, who "worshiped and served created things instead of the Creator," "in the futility of their thinking" (Rom. 1:25; Eph. 4:17, NIV), corrupted the concept of sacrifice. To them, sacrifice became a method to appease an angry god. In some heathen societies, ritual prostitution became part of cultic services; parents gave their children to "pass through the fire" to Molech, the god of the Ammonites (Lev. 18:27–30; 2 Kings 23:10; Jer. 32:35); and other heathen societies allowed human sacrifice. (In some cases, even people in Israel did these things.)

Among God's people, many forgot the Redeemer to whom the sacrifices pointed. They adopted the heathen view that sacrifices and temple services had intrinsic value, furnishing pardon for sin and assurance of salvation. Thankfully, there was always a believing remnant who looked for the Redeemer in the sacrifices.

Slaves to Sin

At creation, Adam and Eve naturally bonded to their Creator, as God was the first one they saw when they opened their eyes (Gen. 2:7, 22). God created them in His image, integrating His eternal law into their personalities (Gen. 1:26, 27). This included free will with freely chosen obedience, creativity, and love.

When they sinned, they lost all this, became slaves to sin, and their natures became sinful.[1] It became natural for people to do evil (Rom. 7:15–23; Jer. 13:23), and they loved neither God nor their fellow human beings. Under condemnation and death, humankind became weak and resisted coming to God.

Yet, God was still Owner and Creator of this world. Before the sun set that day, God announced the everlasting covenant. Exercising His authority as Owner and Creator of this world, He put within humanity enmity against evil (Gen. 3:15); He gave them a conscience with the desire to do what is right. He also took upon Himself the sins of the human family and committed Himself to die in their place. This gave the human race a new probation and freedom to choose again to serve God (Acts 13:39). By God's initiative, before humans exercised faith, He bought the human race "with a price" (1 Cor. 6:20) and opened the way to grace (Heb. 4:16; 10:20).

Sacrifices in Ancient Times

At first, God instructed His people through the *Masorah,* or oral tradition, which worked well when people had excellent memories and lived long lives. The symbolic meaning of sacrifice was probably well known in early centuries through individuals who listened to God, as God has always revealed important things through His prophets (Amos 3:7). It was during the exodus that details of the performance and meaning of sacrifices became part of the written record.

How much did people before the time of Moses know about the sacrifices? Most of the early sacrifices were burnt offerings. The first presentation of the covenant (Gen. 3:15) revealed that the Messiah would destroy sin and Satan, at the cost of His own suffering. When God commanded Abraham to sacrifice "thine only son Isaac, whom thou lovest" (Gen. 22:2), this symbolized another Father, giving His only begotten Son that people might have eternal life (John 3:16). God did not allow Isaac to be sacrificed, but completed the illustration of His gift of His only Son with a representation of substitution, when He provided the sacrifice—a ram caught in a thicket.

The Passover

In Egypt, on the night of the exodus, the people sprinkled the blood of a lamb on the lintel and doorposts to protect the firstborn from death. This illustrated how all their sacrifices served to protect the sinner from judgment.[2] The Passover stood as a major reminder of the power and purpose of God to save human beings.

Even with these demonstrations, what did the people know about the prophesied Messiah, or the meaning of sacrifice? In the Old Testament, the people learned from the prophets, the priests, the princes, and the Levites.[3] The sanctuary and its services were also an illustration of the plan of salvation. This knowledge was available to Israel of old and it was believed by many. Apparently John the Baptist understood, for, when he saw Jesus beside the Jordan River, he cried out, "Behold the Lamb of God, which taketh away the sin of the world" (John 1:29).

Rabbinic Support for Substitution

Famous rabbis from the past support the meaning of the sacrifice as a substitute for the sinner. Yet, they saw the sacrificed animal itself as providing pardon and atonement. In Hebrews 9:10, this corrupted view of sacrifice contrasts with the true and effective sacrifice of Jesus on the cross.

Rashi, a.k.a Shlomo Yitzhaki (February 22, 1040–July 13, 1105), was a medieval French rabbi, famed for authoring a comprehensive commentary on the Talmud and the Tanakh (Hebrew Bible). He commented on Lev. 17:11: "The soul of every creature is given it to atone for the soul of man—one soul should come and atone for the other." God had said, "For the life of the flesh is in the blood: and I have given it to you upon the altar to make an atonement for your souls: for it is the blood that maketh an atonement for the soul" (Lev. 17:11).[4]

Aben Ezra, a.k.a Rabbi Abraham ben Meir Ibn Ezra (1089–1164), was a Jewish scholar and writer of the Middle Ages. Ibn Ezra excelled in philosophy, astronomy/astrology, mathematics, poetry, linguistics, and exegesis. He wrote, "One soul is a substitute for the other."[5]

Moshe ben Nachmann, a.k.a Rabbi Moses ben Nahman Girondi, Bonastruc ça Porta (Girona, 1194–Land of Israel, 1270), was a leading medieval Jewish scholar, Catalan rabbi, philosopher, physician, cabbalist, and biblical commentator. He commented, "I gave the soul for you on the altar, that the soul of the animal should be an atonement for the soul of the man."[6]

R. Bechai summarized the concept: "Properly speaking, the blood of the sinner should have been shed, and his body burned, as those of the sacrifices. But the Holy One—blessed be He!—accepted our sacrifice from us as redemption and atonement. Behold, the full grace, which Jehovah has shown to man! In His compassion, and in the fullness of His grace, He accepted the soul of the animal instead of his soul, that, through it, there might be an atonement."[7]

By contrast, Maimonides, the noted Talmudist, denied the existence of Christ or any purpose for the sacrifices in Israel![8] The corruption of the priesthood was very deep in Jesus' time. From the above quotations one must see that rabbinic Judaism understood animal sacrifices to directly provide pardon and atonement with no reference to a prophesied Redeemer. The high priests were Sadducees, and they did not believe in a resurrection. One must consider that this corrupted view of sacrifice was quite general.[9]

A Prophetic "Promissory Note"

To the believing Israelite the sacrifice was a symbol, pointing to a future reality, which in *prolepsis* gave immediate blessing—the forgiveness of sin.[10] The sacrifice removed sin from the penitent ones; the blood of the sacrificed lamb brought sin into the sanctuary or put it on the horns of the altar, giving them pardon and atonement. The true sacrifice of Christ on the cross made good all the sacrifices for the forgiveness of sins in the Old Testament. Now, since New Testament times, we look back by faith to the reality of Jesus' sacrifice on the cross.

The question arises: Was forgiveness of sin in the Old Testament conditional? From the human standpoint, it might seem so. However, the purposes of God know no failure, and forgiveness through the sacrifices was sure. Like a "promissory note," the sacrifices served as legal tender for the forgiveness of sin based on future payment in Jesus' death on the cross.

The sacrificed animal symbolically took the place of the sinner, and its blood paid for the sin of the sinner. This illustrated what Jesus did for us on the cross. Substitution is the central concept of sacrifice in the Old Testament and the basis for other larger concepts, such as redemption, vicarious punishment, forgiveness, and atonement. The sacrifice of an animal had no real effect on sin or guilt (Heb. 9:9; 10:4). However, in anticipation of Jesus' true sacrifice on the cross, God pardoned sins at the time of sacrifice (Heb. 9:15; 10:1).

In redemption, Jesus' sacrifice on the cross bought the human race from slavery under sin to freedom in Jesus Christ.[11] Jesus Christ, the second person of the Godhead, took the guilt of our sins and paid the penalty of death on the cross of Calvary. In taking sin and guilt from the human race, the sins of humans were forgiven and their atonement was fulfilled.

The human priesthood of Israel ended at Calvary, though priesthood was continued under the true and effective priesthood of Jesus in the heavenly sanctuary. In heaven, Jesus applies His own blood before the judgment seat of God to complete the atonement for each person, wiping clean the record of sins. "Blessed is he, whose transgression is forgiven, whose sin is covered, ... unto whom the Lord imputeth not iniquity" (Ps. 32:1, 2).[12]

Another question arises: Are there two atonements—one atonement at Calvary when Jesus died and another in the heavenly sanctuary when Jesus pleads His blood for the sins of humankind? A review of the sin offerings in Leviticus shows that the sacrifice and the priestly atonement in the sanctuary were a single procedure (Lev. 4:28-31), albeit with different components. The atonement of Jesus at Calvary must also include the heavenly component of His pleading His blood on the sinner's behalf.

Corrupted View of Sacrifice

The term "old covenant" is used more broadly than Israel's reaction at Sinai and is applied to a corrupted view of sacrifice at other times. At Sinai, God offered the Abrahamic covenant with divine blessings, including His law and His grace to make obedience possible. However, the people promised to obey in their own strength, thereby ratifying, in effect, not God's covenant, but their own. This was the *historical* old covenant, which lasted just forty-six days.

In Genesis, Cain had rejected Jesus' offering of redemption, and, by offering his own sacrifice, expected to gain salvation by his own works. This was an example of old covenant action.

The unbelieving majority in Israel, influenced by the heathen sacrifices in Egypt and by their neighbors in Canaan (Eph. 4:17, 18, NCV), looked increasingly to the performance of sacrifices as a means of gaining divine favor. They forgot the promised Redeemer to whom the sacrifices pointed.

During the captivity, the Jews finally learned their lesson about idol worship and never again fell into that trap. In captivity they became educated and prosperous and were exposed to the sophisticated heathen societies of the Babylonians and Greeks. When the Medo-Persian rulers gave permission to go back to their land and rebuild Jerusalem (457 BC), only a remnant chose to return. To maintain their belief in God, they built synagogues and established schools to study the Torah and made a serious effort to worship the true God in their villages and towns.

Before long, the people again viewed the performance of sacrifices and temple services as the means of salvation. Again they lost track of what the sacrifices and rituals meant. In the Jewish leaders' confrontations with Jesus, they repeatedly spoke of keeping the laws of Moses as their hope for salvation. Even today, modern Jews look to ethical living, observing God's law, prayers, and fasting, as their hope for the world to come. It is a corruption of the ceremonial law and a denial of God's "My covenant."

The people forgot their need for grace—grace that is available only through the sacrifice of the Messiah at Calvary. Oppressed by the Romans, they expected the Messiah to be a conquering king who would remove foreign influence and lead the people to the glories of David and Solomon. They rejected a Messiah like Jesus, who refused the military option and came instead to change people's lives and forgive their sins.

After Jesus' return to heaven, when Gentiles began to come into the church, it was hard for many Jewish converts to Christianity to give up the sacrifices and ceremonies. How could people worship God if they did not engage in ceremonies? It was difficult for them to comprehend that Jesus' objective was to write the law in their hearts and minds. The sacrifices and ceremonies were not the covenant. They were merely an illustration or a parable of the covenant, pointing forward to the Redeemer who would save them from their sins.

Hebrews 8 uses the terms "first," not "faultless," "continued not in," "waxeth old," and "decayeth" in discussing the covenant and the people's relation to it.[13] The animal sacrifices, festivals, rituals, circumcision, human priesthood, and the Temple made up their concept of the covenant. They added to this their own meticulous observance of the Ten Commandments, the other 603 *mitzvot* (regulations in the law of Moses), and the voluminous Talmudic expansions, as well as their lineage from Abraham. Law keeping had become a burden, and they forgot the Messiah-Redeemer who would come, die for their sins, and bring salvation.

People became satisfied with doing works as a means of appeasing God because it allowed them to continue with their old sinful way of life. To deny self and submit to the lordship of Jesus Christ is not natural to the sinful human heart. It is only by faith in the life and death of Jesus that the heart can be melted and that human beings will consent to the work of grace.

Refreshing the Illustration

Ancient Israel saw little meaning in sacrifices except to accommodate the general heathen environment of the day. Even when instructed, the people did not understand sin, repentance, and their need of a Redeemer or the Redeemer's taking the penalty for their sins. However, Jesus was always clear about His mission. At the Last Supper, He said, "Drink ye all of it; For this is my blood of the new testament, which is shed for many for the remission of sins" (Matt. 26:27, 28; Mark 14:24). (Here the King James translates "covenant" (Greek *diathēkē*) as "testament.") Thus, the grape juice symbolized the blood of the new covenant, shed for the forgiveness of sins.

The new covenant is the covenant of grace mediated through the sacrifice of Jesus on the cross. God gave this covenant to Adam and Eve, Abraham, and Israel at Sinai. He ratified or confirmed this covenant at the cross. The ceremonial law was never said to be a covenant. It was rather an illustration of the covenant of Abraham. The Ten Commandments, by which Israel would become "an holy nation," were the basis and reality of "the covenant."[14]

In time, people forgot that forgiveness of sin came through the true and effective sacrifice of the Messiah. They did not understand the need and power of grace, and there was no change in their life (Isa. 1:11–20; Micah 6:6–8). The New Testament spoke of sacrifices, offered in outward compliance without real repentance (Rom. 2:28, 29; Heb. 9; 2 Cor. 3:6), as the "righteousness of the scribes and Pharisees" which "shall in no case enter into the kingdom of heaven" (Matt. 5:20).

It was a regression to the old covenant mindset. Some Jewish converts to Christianity, even though they did not sacrifice, could not entirely let go of the ceremonial law.[15] They expected Gentile converts to become Jews in order to be saved (Acts 15:5; Gal. 5:2, 3; Exod. 12:48). This was why the Jerusalem Council met and discussed the issue. In his epistles, the apostle Paul emphasized the effectiveness of Jesus' sacrifice, with no further need of animal sacrifice.

Endnotes

1. References for the slavery of sin are John 8:34; Romans 6:16; and 2 Peter 2:19.

2. Alfred Edersheim, "Sacrifices: Their Order and Their Meaning" *The Temple: Its Ministry and Service* (London: Religious Tract Society, 1874), pp. 79–95, available at http://books.google.com/books?id=LHT6a0E909QC, accessed 3/7/13.

3. Animal sacrifices symbolized the Redeemer (Gen. 3:15; 22:1, 8; Exod. 12:12, 13; Lev. 17:11). Messianic passages about the suffering Messiah are Psalm 22 and Isaiah 52:13–53:12. Christ is our substitute (Matt. 20:28; Rom. 5:8–10, 16–18; 1 Cor. 15:3; Eph. 5:2; Heb. 9:12–15; 10:14). He is "our Passover" (Exod. 12:12–14; 1 Cor. 5:7). He is our Redeemer (Job.19:25; Ps. 19:14; 78:35; Prov. 23:11; Isa. 41:14; 43:14; 44:6, 24; 47:4; 48:17; 49:7, 26; 54:5, 8; 59:20).

4. Prophets, priests, princes, and Levites taught the people (Lev. 10:11; Deut. 33:10; 2 Chron.17:7–9; 35:3; 30:22; Mal. 2:7).

5. Hebrew translated from August Wünsche, *Die Leiden des Messias in ihrer Uebereinstimmung mit der Lehre des Alten Testaments und den Aussprüchen der Rabbinen in den Talmuden, Midraschim und andern alten rabbinischen Schriften*, p. 7, available at http://books.google.com/books?id=S6dAAAAAcAAJ, accessed 3/18/13, by Alfred Edersheim, *The Temple* (1874), p. 92, available at http://books.google.com/books?id=LHT6a0E909QC, accessed 3/18/13.

6. Hebrew translated from Wünsche, p. 7, by Alfred Edersheim, *The Temple* (1874), p. 92.

7. Hebrew translated from Wünsche, pp. 7, 8, by Alfred Edersheim, *The Temple* (1874), p. 93.

8. Hebrew translated from Wünsche, p. 12, by Alfred Edersheim, *The Temple* (1874), p. 93.

9. See http://www.mhcny.org/pdf/MN/Maimonides%20on%20Sacrifices.pdf.

    "Were sacrifices a symbol of the savior to come? Not according to Judaism. Quite the contrary, some would say that the original institution of sacrifice had more to do with the Judaism's past than with its future. Rambam suggested that entire sacrificial cult in Judaism was ordained as an accommodation of man's primitive desires.

    "Sacrifice is an ancient and universal human expression of religion. Greeks and Romans and Canaanites and Egyptians all offered sacrifices to their gods. Sacrifice existed among the Hebrews long before the giving of the Torah. Cain and Abel offered sacrifices; Noah and his sons offered sacrifices, and so forth. When the laws of sacrifice were given to the Children of Israel in the Torah, the pre-existence of a system of sacrificial offerings was understood, and sacrificial terminology was used without any explanation. The Torah, rather than creating the institution of sacrifice, carefully limited the practice, permitting it only in certain places, at certain times, in certain manners, by certain people, and for certain purposes. Rambam suggests that God designed these limitations to wean a primitive people away from the debased rites of their idolatrous neighbors" (Tracey R. Rich, "Qorbanot: Sacrifices and Offerings" available at http://www.jewfaq.org/qorbanot.htm, accessed 3/1/13).

Contrary to the popular Jewish view, God ordained sacrifices at the beginning of human history to illustrate His covenant. Heathen sacrifices were a corruption of God-ordained sacrifice and served a different purpose. Modern Judaism replaces the sacrifices by fellowship meals, prayers, giving to the poor, fasting, and the reading of Torah.

The following links resulted from a search in May 2012 on "Jewish views on substitutionary sacrifices."

- http://en.wikipedia.org/wiki/Abraham_ibn_Ezra,
- http://en.wikipedia.org/wiki/Rashi,
- http://www.jewishvirtuallibrary.org/jsource/biography/rashi.html,
- http://www.chabad.org/library/bible_cdo/aid/63255/jewish/The-Bible-with-Rashi.htm,
- http://tenminasministries.blogspot.com/2007/06/modern-day-jewish-atonement.html,
- http://theologyconversation.blogspot.com/2010/07/substitutionary-atonement-and-sacrifice.html.

10. All blessings flow from the cross of Christ. In the Old Testament, God gave forgiveness of sins and His other blessings in *prolepsis*, which means to act as if a future event (that is, Jesus' sacrifice for sin) had already taken place.

    Yahweh is a God of mercy (Exod. 20:6; 34:6, 7; Deut. 5:10) and a covenant keeper (Deut. 7:9; Ps. 89:28, 34). He accomplishes what He has purposed (Job 23:13; Ps. 135:6; Dan. 4:35; Isa. 14:24; 46:10, 11; Acts 4:28; 5:39; Eph. 1:9–11; 3:11). His counsel will stand (Prov. 19:21; Ps. 33:11), and His word will stand forever (Isa. 40:8, 22, 26). He keeps His promise to bless (Num. 23:19, 20). His "servant," the Messiah, would not fail nor be discouraged (Isa. 42:1–4).

11. We can be free only as servants of Christ (John 8:36; 1 Cor. 7:22, 23; Rom. 6:16).

12. The lid of the ark of the covenant, translated "mercy seat" as a result of Luther's *Gnadenstuhl*, is in Hebrew *kapporet* (Exod. 25:17), which literally means "covering."

13. See chapter 15, "The Historical Old Covenant."

14. The Ten Commandments are the covenant. They are also known as "the testimony" (Exod. 32:15; 34:28; Deut. 9:9, 11, 15; Heb. 9:4).

15. Evidence of Christian Jews who could not let go of the ceremonial law is found in Acts 15; Romans 2:21–29; 2 Corinthians 3; Galatians 3, 4; Ephesians 2; and Hebrews 8–10.

Chapter 34
Probation Closed for Israel as a Nation

When Pilate saw that he could prevail nothing, but that rather a tumult was made, he took water, and washed his hands before the multitude, saying, I am innocent of the blood of this just person: see ye to it. Then answered all the people, and said, His blood be on us, and on our children.
Matthew 27:24, 25

The Father, Son, and Holy Spirit originated the everlasting covenant of God before the creation of this world. The covenant existed in the mind of God from times eternal. God announced the covenant to Adam and Eve after they sinned. From the beginning of history, the covenant has formed the basis for God's interaction with human beings and His promises to them.

Jesus Christ confirmed the covenant on the cross that people might receive eternal life by faith. It reaches its completion with the close of probation and a series of climactic events. These will conclude with an end-time judgment and the descent of the New Jerusalem to the new earth, cleansed of the last vestiges of sin.

Throughout history, a crucial issue has always been whether human beings would consent to the work of grace in their life and whether they would accept the gift of the new covenant law written in their heart. When people receive God's pardon and salvation, God has His angel write their names in the Lamb's book of life. There is no further probation after a person dies. Just before Jesus returns, probation will close for all living human beings, whether righteous or rebellious.

The Chosen People

One can see the "remnant" of God's chosen people from the beginning of human history. From the time that Cain killed Abel, the distinction between the people of God and the people of the world has been manifest. The people of God came through the lineage of Seth and Noah. As the population sank into apostasy after the flood, God found Abram, a man whom He could bless because He saw him as a man who would "command his children and his household after him" (Gen. 18:19). Abram obeyed God in faith, influencing his descendants for many generations.

God called Abram to leave Ur and go to Canaan. Genesis describes his departure from Ur to Haran with his father Terah, his nephew Lot (son of Haran who had died in Ur), and his wife Sarai (Gen. 11:31). They remained in Haran until Terah died. Then Abram and his company continued on to Canaan. God presented His covenant—the everlasting covenant—to Abraham seven times. That covenant promised redemption from sin, eternal life, and restoration of all that was lost at Eden. It is through the covenant that people's lives are changed and that they are made fit for eternity. Additionally, God promised Abraham the land of Canaan, a multitude of descendants, and His personal presence with Abraham and with his descendants in perpetuity (Gen. 17:7). His descendents included Isaac, Jacob, Moses (Exod. 3:16, 17), and the nation of Israel. When God gave the covenant at Sinai, He promised to make of Israel a "peculiar treasure, … a kingdom of priests, and an holy nation" (Exod. 19:5, 6).[1]

That the nation of Israel became God's chosen or covenant people has been a focal point in Jewish thinking for centuries. The Bible emphasizes this concept frequently—in positive terms when the people are obedient and in negative terms when they are disobedient.[2]

Israel's Special Talents and Blessings

Because of His plan for Israel as a nation, God gave them unique gifts. One of these was that He entrusted them with the "oracles of God" (Rom. 3:2; Heb. 5:12). His making Israel a "kingdom of priests" was a mandate to represent God to other people and to evangelize the world (Exod. 19:6; Ps. 102:15; Isa. 43:10–12; Ezek. 36:23). Israel was to represent to the world God's excellence in every aspect of life (Deut. 28:13). This explains why Jesus would say, "… salvation is of the Jews" (John 4:22). The Jews were not the originators or source of salvation; they were merely the conduit through whom the knowledge of salvation would flow.

God gave the covenant in terms of enduring promises. The will and purposes of God cannot be broken, but they can be modified and delayed by people's decisions. To emphasize this point, God called forth from Mt. Gerizim the blessings they would receive if they obeyed and kept the covenant, and He called forth from Mt. Ebal the curses they would receive if they should rebel or fall into idolatry.[3]

The covenants that God gave to Phinehas (Num. 25:7–13), David (2 Sam. 23:1), and Solomon (2 Sam. 7:11–16; 1 Kings 9:4–7; 11:11), He announced in positive terms. God also promised them blessings or curses, dependent on their obedience to His will. These conditions played out in subsequent history when repeated apostasy resulted in Israel's and then Judah's captivity.

Jesus' Rejection

When Jesus came to this earth, He came on time and to the right place (Gal. 4:4; Matt. 2:5). At the very time prophesied (Dan. 9:25–27), John the Baptist baptized Jesus in the Jordan. As Jesus came up out of the water, His heavenly Father acclaimed Him "My beloved Son, in whom I am well pleased" (Matt. 3:17), and the Holy Spirit descended upon Him as a dove, anointing Him as the Messiah (Acts 10:38).

During Jesus' ministry, the Jewish leaders asked Him for a sign. Jesus told them to look at His works of healing and His casting out of devils. Despite this miraculous evidence of who He was, they refused to believe Him. Many witnessed or heard how that Jesus raised Lazarus from the dead after Lazarus had been in the grave four days. Yet, despite this public display of miraculous power, the Jewish leaders still refused to believe and actively sought Jesus' arrest and execution.

The time came when Jesus entered Jerusalem in triumph. As He looked over the city, knowing that Jerusalem would be destroyed, He wept and declared:

> For the days shall come upon thee, that thine enemies shall cast a trench about thee, and compass thee round, and keep thee in on every side, And shall lay thee even with the ground, and thy children within thee; and they shall not leave in thee one stone upon another; because thou knewest not the time of thy visitation. (Luke 19:43, 44)

Jesus warned the Jewish leaders about the results of what they were doing. He told them a parable about a householder who planted a vineyard and rented it out to husbandmen. When the householder sent servants to collect the rent, the husbandmen beat up and killed the servants and eventually even killed the owner's son. When Jesus asked His hearers what the householder would do to these husbandmen, they responded, "He will miserably destroy those wicked men, and will let out his vineyard unto other husbandmen, which shall render him the fruits in their seasons." Jesus answered, "The kingdom of God shall be taken from you, and given to a nation bringing forth the fruits thereof" (Matt. 21:41, 43).

Jesus exposed the hypocrisy of the Pharisees and pronounced woes upon them. With tears, He addressed the city, "O Jerusalem, Jerusalem, thou that killest the prophets, and stonest them which are sent unto thee, how often would I have gathered thy children together, even as a hen gathereth her chickens under her wings, and ye would not! Behold, your house is left unto you desolate" (Matt. 23:37, 38).

Jesus, in unequivocal language, warned the Jewish leaders that they would be rejected. Nonetheless, the early Christian church was largely Jewish. It was Jews who believed on Jesus by the thousands and strongly supported the church. These were the "remnant of Israel" of that day. On the other hand, the chosen leaders of Israel, as well as the Jews who rejected Jesus, opposed Jesus and His followers at every turn. An understanding of these two classes is essential in order to avoid making false interpretations in theology.

Replacement Theology and Israel's Close of Probation

Replacement theology refers to a close of probation for the Jewish nation. The term covers a number of different views that range from outright anti-Semitism from non-Jews to the bitter opposition of non-believing Jews. Between these extremes are moderate views in which well-meaning, Bible-believing people attempt to understand the truth as revealed in the Bible. Here is a general definition of Replacement theology:

> Replacement theology is the teaching that the Christian church has replaced national Israel regarding the plan, purpose, and promises of God. Therefore, many of the promises that God made to Israel must be spiritualized. For example, when it speaks of Israel being restored to the land, this really means that the Christian church will

be blessed. Also, covenants made with Israel are fulfilled in the Christian church so, for example,

1. The Jewish people are no longer God's chosen people. Instead, the Christian church now makes up God's chosen people.
2. In the New Testament after Pentecost, the term "Israel" refers to the church.
3. The Mosaic covenant (Exod. 20) is replaced by the new covenant (Luke 22:20).
4. Actual circumcision is replaced by a circumcision of the heart (Rom. 2:29).[4]

It is difficult to see replacement theology as a theology at all, for it is a reaction to the persistent actions and attitudes of the Jewish leaders . Whereas the core of the new Christian church, the remnant, were believing sons and daughters of Israel. The work of God has always been to support and encourage His true believing remnant. In the history of Israel, it was always the faithful remnant who worshiped God in truth.

Where was the remnant when the Jews brought Jesus to trial and conviction? Most of the disciples had fled and were in hiding. Yet, John and several of the women, including Jesus' mother, stayed by the cross, sorrowing. Simon of Cyrene was drafted by the Romans to carry Jesus' cross, though he would not become a believer until after the event. Nicodemus and Joseph of Arimathea, at some personal risk, petitioned Pilate for the body of Jesus, to give Him a decent burial. Many of the common people, who were friends of Jesus, were at the Temple, looking for Him and asking embarrassing questions. Thus, the remnant were scattered and perplexed on that preparation day, but relief would come on "the third day"!

Fifty days after the Passover, on Pentecost, the Holy Spirit filled the praying disciples with power to witness, and the church grew explosively. The early church quickly reached an estimated 20,000 believers, yet they were still a small, persecuted remnant in Jerusalem. Who, now, were the true Israel? Who were the people specially loved and cared for by God? They were the disciples of Jesus and the new converts. These were the true Israel of God.

Who are True "Jews" Today?

Paul's statements in Romans 2 help answer the question of who is a true Jew: "For he is not a Jew, which is one outwardly; neither is that circumcision, which is outward in the flesh: but he is a Jew, which is one inwardly; and circumcision is that of the heart, in the spirit, and not in the letter; whose praise is not of men, but of God" (Rom. 2:28, 29).

The Jewish leaders, as representatives of the nation, had rejected their Messiah. Time would show that the unthinking, unbelieving majority of the people supported these leaders. Their 490-year probation would end, and the covenant would pass to a believing remnant.

Remarkably, the believing remnant were, at first, all Jews! In replacing literal Israel, the covenant did not pass over to the Gentiles, but to believing Jews! Read carefully Romans chapters 9 to 11. Paul speaks of "a remnant according to the election of grace," declaring that "the election hath obtained" what Israel looked for—salvation (Rom. 11:5, 7). It is true that the unbelief of the nation broke Jewish branches off the olive tree, allowing for the "wild branches" of the Gentiles to be grafted into the trunk (Rom. 11:17). Yet, the trunk of the tree is still Israel—the chosen covenant people of God.

Paul's statement in Galatians makes the point clearer, "Know ye therefore that they which are of faith, the same are the children of Abraham.... If ye be Christ's, then are ye Abraham's seed, and heirs according to the promise" (Gal. 3:7, 29). People of all nations, who believe in Christ, are now under the covenant of Abraham! Jesus came to break down all the walls of separation. Christ's church, based on the true message of God to Israel, is Christ's bride. Christ welcomes into the church all races, including the Jews. Yet, God still has a special regard for the people whom He first called (Rom. 11:25).

The Chosen Nation Rejected

God gave Israel 490 years after the restoration from captivity to fulfill their divine purpose (Dan. 9:24). During this time, they were to put away sin and prepare to receive their Messiah. The Jews had learned to avoid worship of images, but their concept of the covenant was not much better than idolatry. They forgot their Messiah and looked to the keeping of the law, the performance of rituals and sacrifices, and their relation to Abraham as the basis for their assurance of salvation.

Throughout Jesus' mission to planet earth, He was met with opposition at every step. It began when the leaders in Jerusalem ignored the news of His birth. During His popular ministry, spies followed Him constantly, seeking to find something for which they could indict Him. The Sanhedrin, the ruling body of the nation rejected Him, put Him on trial, and had Him crucified. Yet, Jesus rose again on the third day and gave the church a commission to go into all the world and make disciples.

For three and a half years after His death and resurrection, the disciples preached, healed, and taught in Jerusalem. When one of these, Stephen, gained an audience with the Sanhedrin and presented the Christ of prophecy, they became enraged, dragged him out of the city, and stoned him to death. This event marked the exact ending point of the 490-year probation. The Jewish nation had finally and irrevocably rejected their Messiah, who was their only hope.

The Rise of the Remnant

God's people have been separate from the world ever since Eden. Very quickly, God's people became a minority, described as a "remnant." Even within Israel and Judah, this was true. What a tragedy! At Sinai, after Moses interrupted the heathen festival at the base of the mountain, he asked, "Who is on the Lord's side?" Immediately all the sons of Levi stood by him, but they were just one tribe out of twelve!

When twelve spies searched out the land, only Caleb and Joshua urged the people to have faith in God and proceed to take the land—only two out of the twelve—and the people almost stoned them to death (Num. 14:10)! When Gideon called for volunteers from Israel to fight the enemy, only 300 showed courage and determination to drive out the Midianites. Each of these groups were the "remnant" in their day.

Other examples could be listed. Sometimes the remnant was just one person, as with Samson,

David, and others. On Mt. Carmel, Elijah discredited the prophets of Baal and then slew them all. When Jezebel threatened him, he fled to Mt. Horeb, complaining that he was the only one who still believed in the Lord. God responded that He had 7,000 who had not bowed the knee to Baal (1 Kings 19:8, 9, 18). Elijah was not alone, but visible people of faith have a big influence.

The history of Judah is instructive. Under good kings, the people rallied to true worship. When a good king was followed by a bad one, there was almost universal apostasy into idolatry, showing where the people's true interest was. Yet, the story of Daniel and his three companions reveals the existence of a small, believing remnant even in those desperate times.

When Jesus came to this earth, there was a believing remnant who quickly followed Him and believed in Him. These formed the core of the Christian church after Jesus' resurrection. Among these were the shepherds, Simeon and Anna in the Temple, Zacharias and his family, Jesus' immediate family and relatives, the chosen twelve disciples minus one, the pious women who supported Him, and at least 500 others.

Revelation speaks of an end-time remnant church, which will again be a small group compared to world population (Rev. 12:17).

Endnotes

1. God gave the Abrahamic covenant to Moses and to Israel just before the exodus was to begin (Exod. 2:24; 3:6, 15, 16; 4:5, 30, 31; 6:3, 6–8), and then He affirmed it once they were free (Exod. 19:4–6).
2. The concept of a chosen people of God is found in the following passages: God chose Abraham to be the father of the covenant people (Gen. 17). God said: "And I will take you to me for a people, and I will be to you a God" (Exod. 6:7). Balaam said: "The people shall dwell alone, and shall not be reckoned among the nations" (Num. 23:9). Moses said: "The LORD thy God hath chosen thee to be a special people unto himself" (Deut. 7:6); "He chose their seed after them [the fathers], even you above all people" (Deut. 10:15); "You are a holy people to the Lord your God Out of all the people on the face of the earth, the Lord has chosen you to be his treasured possession" (Deut. 14:2, NIV). David said: "For the Lord hath chosen Jacob unto himself, and Israel for his peculiar treasure" (Ps. 135:4).
3. The blessings for obedience are enumerated in Deuteronomy 7:1–26; 8:1–10; 11:10–15; and 28:1–14. The curses for apostasy are enumerated in Deuteronomy 27:15–26; 28:15–68; and 29:18–29.
4. Matt Slick, "What is replacement theology?" available at http://carm.org/questions-replacement-theology, accessed 3/7/13.

Chapter 35

The Vision of Stephen

But he, being full of the Holy Ghost, looked up stedfastly into heaven, and saw
the glory of God, and Jesus standing on the right hand of God, And said, Behold,
I see the heavens opened, and the Son of man standing on the right hand of God.

Acts 7:55, 56

The stoning of Stephen marked a significant change in direction for the covenant. The leaders of the nation of Israel, supported by the majority of the people, had finally and irrevocably rejected their Messiah. From this point forward, the church accepted the responsibility of the covenant and began to move away from Judaism.

Jesus had gloriously fulfilled the covenant in redeeming humankind at Calvary. Believers could now look by faith to His finished work at Calvary. Thousands joined the new church. There was a love and fellowship that was unique. Many priests joined the movement. There were wealthy people who willingly sacrificed to support the new church, and people of power and intellect joined the church and proclaimed the risen Christ with the power of the Spirit. Among these capable ones was Stephen, whose appointment as a deacon became a door open for ministry, which he joyfully entered.

Daniel 9:24: A Determined People

God's word through Daniel, "Seventy weeks are determined (*hatak*, lit. "cut off") upon thy people and upon thy holy city" (Dan. 9:24), describes the probation granted Israel to fulfill God's purpose for them as a nation. If they should fail again, all Jewish privileges as the covenant people would be given to another people (Deut. 32:21; 1 Peter 2:10; Jer. 18:6–10; Matt. 21:41). The last week of the seventy-week prophecy began with Jesus' anointing at His baptism. In the midst of that final week, sacrifice and oblation ceased with Jesus' death on the cross. The end of the week and the end of the seventy-week prophecy of Daniel 9:24 came with the official and final rejection of the Messiah, marked by the stoning of Stephen in AD 34.[1]

Within the next year or so, Saul was converted by Jesus' personal appearance, which blinded him on the road to Damascus. At the same time, Jesus also appeared to Ananias in a vision, telling him that Saul was "a chosen vessel unto me, to bear my name before the Gentiles and kings and the children of Israel" (Acts 9:15). Ananias sought out Saul and prayed for him, and God healed him of his blindness. Saul also received the Holy Ghost and was baptized. Immediately, Saul began to preach Christ in the synagogue. When Saul and Barnabas went on their first missionary journey to Cyprus, Saul was called "Paul" from that time on (Acts 13:9). For several years, Paul preached the gospel largely to the Jews.[2]

The gospel to the Gentiles began with preaching to the Samaritans (Acts 8:5–17, 25), the baptism of the Ethiopian eunuch about AD 34 (Acts 8:27–39), and Peter's visit to the house of Cornelius about AD 41 (Acts 10). However, taking the gospel to the Gentiles did not take root until the missionary journeys of Paul and Barnabas about AD 45.

To Seal Up "Vision and Prophet"

> Seventy weeks are determined upon thy people and upon thy holy city, to finish the transgression, and to make an end of sins, and to make reconciliation for iniquity, and to bring in everlasting righteousness, and to seal up the vision and prophecy, and to anoint the most Holy. (Dan. 9:24)

"What was so significant about the stoning of Stephen? Why was his martyrdom more" influential "than that suffered by others at that time?" According to William H. Shea, who examined these questions, "the verb 'to seal up' (hatam) may be understood" in this instance "as either to validate or authenticate, to close up (until a later opening), or to bring to an end."[3] The two objects to be sealed were the "vision" (hazōn) and the "prophet" (nabi).

Shea prefers the third interpretation, "to bring to an end," and explains why. First, without the article, "prophet" suggests a collective meaning, and "bringing to an end" makes "sense if referred to prophets as persons instead of to their words. Second, the verb hatam also occurs three phrases earlier in this same verse with the clear idea of bringing to an end ("to put an end to sin"). Third, this interpretation fits the immediate context better because the text says that seventy weeks were decreed for Daniel's people and his holy city." Thus, Shea concludes, "vision" and "prophet" were to come to an end for the nation of Israel "by the time this prophetic period closes."[4]

There were several New Testament prophets (Acts 11:27, 28; 13:1; 15:32; 21:10) who spoke for the church, but none who spoke for Israel as a nation. Saul himself had a vision on the road to Damascus (Acts 9). There were a number of New Testament prophets who spoke early in the history of the church. The apostle John wrote the book of Revelation written around AD 100![5]

This contradiction increases interest in the second interpretation, "to close up (until a later opening)," which fits the context of the vision of Daniel 8, which was sealed. See also, "for the words are closed up and sealed [hatam] till the time of the end" (Dan. 12:9; cf. Dan. 8:26). This view hinges on whether or not Israel would accept their Messiah and fulfill the other mandates of Daniel 9:24.

One could also make a case for the first interpretation, which interprets the 490-year fulfillment of Daniel 9:24 as authenticating or validating the larger prophecy in Daniel 8 by providing details that can be aligned with known historical dates.

Early Christian Witness

Members of the early Christian church willingly sold what they had and pooled their resources, supporting those who were poor and needy in their midst (Acts 4:32–37). Contention developed over the distribution of food being given to the "Grecians" (or Hellenists) in Jerusalem (Acts 6:1) These were Jewish widows "who had been born in Greco-Roman lands, had moved to Jerusalem, and then become Christians."[6] Stephen was also a Hellenist. By contrast, "the 'Hebrews' … were Aramaic-speaking Palestinian Jews who formed the original nucleus of the Christian community in Jerusalem. The Twelve belonged to this group (6:2)."[7]

There were other issues that separated the two groups. The Greek-speaking Christians probably had separate worship services, as did the Jews in their synagogues (Acts 6:9). Within Judaism, those from Greco-Roman lands were considered religiously liberal and probably lax in their observance of the law (1 Maccabees 1:10–15; 2 Maccabees 4:7–20).[8] The Hellenists had no roots in the Palestinian Hebrew traditions. Most of them were not able to read the Hebrew Scriptures, and they did not attend the Hebrew synagogues. Proselytes naturally would associate more with the Hellenists.

When serving tables got to be a burden, the twelve apostles called a meeting and appointed "seven men of honest report, full of the Holy Ghost and wisdom" (Acts 6:3) to take on that responsibility. "The election of the Seven … and the persecution that came thereafter probably … indicate that theological differences played" a prominent "role in that dissension and that the Hellenists' complaint … was only the symptom of a deeper problem."[9]

Stephen was an enthusiastic Christian, naturally brilliant and probably educated. His ordination as a deacon was an open door to ministry. Stephen and the ministers selected with him "are never referred to as 'deacons' (diakonoi) in the book of Acts."[10] Their calling was as much to preach the word of God as to serve tables. Stephen was truly gifted, as Luke described in Acts:

> And Stephen, full of faith and power, did great wonders and miracles among the people. Then there arose certain of the synagogue, which is called the synagogue of the Libertines, and Cyrenians and Alexandrians, and of them of Cilicia and Asia, disputing with Stephen. And they were not able to resist the wisdom and the spirit by which he spake. (Acts 6:8–10)

Stephen's preaching was powerful, for "the only biblical reference that there were many conversions, even among the priests, appears in the context of Stephen's preaching (cf. 6:7)."[11] His preaching also called forth strong opposition from the Jews (Acts 6:9–12). The Sanhedrin arrested Stephen, and, through false witnesses, accused him of blasphemy. The high priest asked him one question, "Are these things so?" Stephen immediately began his defense as a sermon to the Sanhedrin.

Stephen's Trial and Defense

False witnesses were induced to say: "This man incessantly speaks against this holy place and the Law; for we have heard him say that this Nazarene, Jesus, will destroy this place and alter the customs which Moses handed down to us" (Acts 6:13, 14, NASB). Stephen's statement, "the Most High does not dwell in houses made by human hands" (Acts 7:48, NASB), "could be interpreted not only as a protest against the idolatrous relationship that Israel maintained with the Temple but also as a statement of the definitive end of the entire ceremonial system, for the Temple was never intended to become a permanent institution," except as a location for praise to God (see Isa. 2:1–4).[12]

"From the time of the Maccabees," the Jews "regarded any attack on Torah and temple as sacrilege. Stephen, however, as well [as] the other Hellenistic Christians, may have quickly understood that the mission of Christ involved the abrogation of the whole temple order and its being superseded" by the sanctuary in heaven (Heb. 8:1, 2, 7, 13; 9:24; 10:1, 2), and a superior temple "not made with hands."[13]

They listened willingly until Stephen pointed out that the Temple on earth is merely a copy of the temple in heaven. This enraged the Sanhedrin. Stephen abruptly terminated the historical narrative and confronted them.

> Ye stiffnecked and uncircumcised in heart and ears, ye do always resist the Holy Ghost: as your fathers did, so do ye. Which of the prophets have not your fathers persecuted? and they have slain them which showed before of the coming of the Just One; of whom ye have been now the betrayers and murderers: who have received the law by the disposition of angels, and have not kept it. (Acts 7:51–53)

The Sanhedrin immediately dragged Stephen out of the city and stoned him to death. This was the culminating event of rejection by the official governing body of the nation of Israel. From this point on, the Jewish leadership intensified their persecution of believers in Christ, scattering them and causing them to go "every where preaching the word" (Acts 8:4). This was also the exact date of the end of the 490-year prophecy. Probation for Israel as a nation, as the chosen people of God, had ended. The promises and responsibilities of the everlasting covenant passed to another people.

Michael Stands Up

At the time of Stephen's death, the martyr saw a vision of deep significance. It was of Jesus standing (Greek *histēmi* "to establish, to set, to stand") on the right hand of God.

> But he, being full of the Holy Ghost, looked up stedfastly into heaven, and saw the glory of God, and Jesus standing on the right hand of God, and said, Behold, I see the heavens opened, and the Son of man standing on the right hand of God. (Acts 7:55, 56)

We have always taken this vision as an encouragement to Stephen in his martyrdom and a confirmation to the Christian church for their message, and that it was. There is, however, a deeper significance to Jesus' standing, which Luke mentions twice for emphasis.

The close of probation for the Jewish nation can be compared to the close of probation for the world at the end of time. Daniel 7:9, 10 describes a scene of judgment, in which "thrones were cast down, and the Ancient of days did sit … the judgment was set, and the books were opened." During any judgment, God sits on His throne. What will happen when Jesus finishes His mediation in heaven? He will stand up (Dan. 12:1, Hebrew *awmad*' "stand or stood"), as a sign that judgment is completed![14]

Opportunity Rejected

The stoning of Stephen ended the probation for the Jewish nation as the chosen people of God. Jesus' priestly ministry for the Jews as a nation closed, and Jesus stood up beside the throne of God. He was now ready to work with a people who would bring forth the fruits of righteousness (Matt. 21:41–43; 2 Cor. 9:10; Phil. 1:11; Heb. 12:11; James 3:18).

However, God did not wholly cast the Jews away. There were many common people and members of the council, such as Nicodemus and Joseph of Arimathea, who heard Jesus gladly (Mark 6:20; 12:37; John 19:38, 39; Mark 15:43). People in the professions, including scribes, lawyers, and wealthy publicans, such as Matthew and Zacchaeus, also heard Jesus and followed Him (Luke 5:27; 19:8). On the day of Pentecost, "a great company of the priests were obedient to the faith" (Acts 6:7). Thus, many active, intelligent people joined the church. Even unlearned fishermen became educated in the presence of Jesus. The chief priests in council "took knowledge of them that they had been with Jesus" (Acts 4:13).

There was a spirit and a power in the early church that could not be resisted except by force and persecution. The early church was a Jewish church, made up of people who heard the gospel message and responded in faith.

On the other hand, the Jewish nation, particularly its leadership, rejected Jesus right from the beginning. During the three and a half years of His ministry, they repeatedly tried to trap Him, arrest Him, and stop Him in any way possible. They finally arrested Him at night, condemned Him in an illegal trial, and influenced Roman officials to have Him crucified. There is no question but that the vast majority of the Jewish leadership rejected Jesus, the Messiah.

Yet, Jesus is long-suffering and not willing that any should perish (2 Peter 3:9). The Jewish nation's opportunity did not end with Jesus' death. For another three and a half years, the leaders and people could observe the effect of His ministry on the lives of His apostles and the new converts coming into the church. The brilliant and persuasive Stephen brought the message directly to the Sanhedrin. However, the Sanhedrin rejected Stephen's message and stoned him to death.

This act marked the final rejection of Jesus by the Jewish nation. The 490-year prophecy came to an end, closing their probation. At this time, God rejected the Jewish nation as the chosen people of God and passed the privileges and responsibilities of the covenant to the church.[15] God received those Jews who made up the early church. It was the official leaders and the Sanhedrin, representing the nation, whom He rejected.

When Jesus ascended to the Father, He "sat down on the right hand of the Majesty on high" (Heb. 1:3). Stephen in his dying vision saw "Jesus standing on the right hand of God" (Acts 7:55). As has been mentioned, this showed that Jesus' mediation and judgment had finished, and He now stood to begin the final phase of judgment.[16]

In the persecution that followed, "only the Hellenistic Christians were scattered from Jerusalem.... The apostles were able to stay there (cf. Acts 8:1, 14), as were the other Hebrew Christians (cf. 11:1, 18, 22).... 'Those who had been scattered went about preaching the word' (Acts 8:4; cf. 8:5–8; 11:19–21). The Hellenists, therefore, 'became the real founders of the mission to the Gentiles, in which circumcision and observation of the ritual law were no longer required.' "[17]

Endnotes

1. Wilson Paroschi, Seventh-day Adventist Theological Seminary, Andrews University, *Journal of the Adventist Theological Society*, 9/1-2 (1998), pp. 343–361.

2. When the Jews refused Paul's message, he turned to the Gentiles (Acts 13:46–48; 18:6; 28:28, 29).

3. Paroschi, p. 345.

4. William H. Shea, "Daniel and the Judgment," a manuscript on the sanctuary and the judgment doctrine, Andrews University, July 1980, p. 366. Shea's thesis was finally published in "The Prophecy of Dan. 9:24–27," in *The Seventy Weeks, Leviticus, and the Nature of Prophecy*, Daniel & Revelation Committee Series, vol. 3, Frank B. Holbrook, ed. (Washington, D.C.: Biblical Research Institute, 1986), pp. 75–118.

5. The gift of prophecy was an essential part of the New Testament church (1 Cor. 12:28, 29; Eph. 4:11).

6. Paroschi, p. 347.

7. Paroschi, p. 347.

8. Evidence for their laxness is found in First Maccabees. "From them came forth a sinful root, Antiochus Epiphanes, son of Antiochus the king; he had been a hostage in Rome. He began to reign in the one hundred and thirty-seventh year of the kingdom of the Greeks. In those days lawless men came forth from Israel, and misled many, saying, 'Let us go and make a covenant with the Gentiles round about us, for since we separated from them many evils have come upon us.' This proposal pleased them, and some of the people eagerly went to the king. He authorized them to observe the ordinances of the Gentiles. So they built a gymnasium in Jerusalem, according to Gentile custom, and removed the marks of circumcision, and abandoned the holy covenant. They joined with the Gentiles and sold themselves to do evil" (1 Mac. 1:10–15, RSV).

9. Paroschi, p. 348

10. Paroschi, p. 348.

11. Paroschi, p. 349.

12. Paroschi, p. 349.

13. Paroschi, p. 350.

14. Scripture indicates that judgment proceeds from the "judgment seat." (Mt. 27:19; Jn. 19:13; Acts 18:12, 16, 17; 25:6, 10, 17; Ro. 14:12; 2 Cor. 5:10). When the judgment is finished probation is closed and Jesus, the judge stands. The final (executive) phase of judgment is about to begin. (cf. Job 19:25: Isa. 3:13; Dan. 12:1). See chapter 48, "The Close of Probation."

15. The church, at this time did not yet bear the name "Christian," for they did not receive that designation until the headquarters of the church moved to Antioch of Syria (Acts 11:26). Before this, they were designated "the way" or "Nazarenes" (Acts 24:5). In the second century, they were called by the Jews, *minim*, "a term used in the Talmud and Midrash for a Jewish heretic or sectarian" (http://www.jewishencyclopedia.com/articles/10846-min, accessed 3/18/13).

16. *New International Commentary on the New Testament* (Grand Rapids, MI: Eerdmans, 1993), p. 587; Darrell L. Bock, "Luke," *Baker Exegetical Commentary on the New Testament* (Grand Rapids, MI: Baker, 1996), vol. 2, p. 1800.

17. Martin Hengel, *Between Jesus and Paul: Studies in the Earliest History of Christianity* (Philadelphia, PA: Fortress Press, 1983), p. 13, quoted in Peroschi, p. 350.

Chapter 36
Grace and the Ceremonial Law

For the law was given by Moses, but grace and truth came by Jesus Christ.
John 1:17

The apostle Paul was well educated, a deep thinker, and probably had more contact with Greek thought than the other apostles. He studied under the brilliant Gamaliel.[1]

Because of his education, he may have been a more astute theologian and may have been the first to identify problems when they arose. Possibly because of his familiarity with Greek thought, he wrote much more about abstract concepts than did the other New Testament writers. This was significant because Greek thought has influenced western civilization to this day. It is Paul's insight that we need to comprehend the relation of grace, covenant, and the ceremonial law.

Jewish Christians at that time had difficulty letting go of their worship traditions. Paul wrote about this in his epistles. The issue faded away as the church became predominantly Gentile.

Saul Becomes an Apostle

Saul was a Jew, a Pharisee of the Pharisees, and a student of the famous rabbi Gamaliel. He came from Tarsus, in Asia Minor (Acts 22:3; 23:6; 26:5; Phil. 3:5). How long he lived in Jerusalem we do not know. He was present when Stephen gave his sermon to the Sanhedrin. He observed the godly demeanor of Stephen and the vicious fury of his compatriots. Coming from a leading member of the Sanhedrin, Saul's consent was a significant influence in the stoning of Stephen (Acts 7:58).

Following this, Saul zealously persecuted the Christians, hauling them off to prison (Acts 8:3). On the road to Damascus, Jesus Christ came to Saul in a vision and changed him from a zealous persecutor of Christians to an even-more-committed Christian preacher and missionary. It was a major upheaval in his life. After his conversion, he was blind and had to be led by the hand. God called Ananias, a believer in Christ, who looked for Saul and then baptized him, after God restored Saul's sight in response to Ananias' prayer.

Saul then preached to the Jews in Damascus, meeting all their objections, until he had to flee Damascus to save his life. He went into Arabia for three years, where in solitude, he had time for self-examination, confession of sin, and blessed pardon. Jesus Christ spoke to him, established him in the faith, and taught him more of his mission.

Saul returned to Damascus and again preached to the Jews. Once again, he was met with hatred and plans to take his life. An angel warned him to leave the city, but his enemies guarded the gates. Saul escaped as fellow believers let him down over the wall in a basket.

Saul traveled to Jerusalem, and Barnabas introduced him to the brethren. Again, he preached to the Jews until hostility and hatred threatened his life. Warned by an angel, the brethren took Saul to Caesarea and from there to Tarsus. It was in Tarsus that Barnabas eventually found him, and together they began their missionary journeys (Acts 9:27; Gal. 1:17, 18; 2:1; 1 Cor. 9:6; 15:3, 4, 8; Acts 22:17–21).

When Paul returned to Jerusalem, he was prepared to speak *for* Christ, not against Him as he had done before. The issue of grace became the main focus of his preaching. He determined "… not to know any thing among you, save Jesus Christ, and him crucified" (1 Cor. 2:2).

Missionary Journeys

The church in Antioch ordained Saul and Barnabas and sent them on their missionary journeys (Acts 13:2). In each new city, they attended the synagogue on Sabbath where Paul spoke to the Jews. Then they might be asked to speak to the Gentiles (Acts 13:42). The issue for the Jews was that the Messiah, prophesied since Eden, had come, and His name was Jesus of Nazareth. He had now come to earth, lived a sinless life, died on the cross as a willing sacrifice for the sins of humankind, and came back to life. He was now with the Father in heaven. (Saul's preaching to the Gentiles seems to be a transition point in the story, for he is now called "Paul" from this point on in Luke's narrative.)[2] Paul preached in Antioch of Pisidia, giving the message of Christ crucified (Acts 13:14–43). Christ had vanquished Satan. He had paid the penalty for the sins of humankind, and the door was now open for human beings to come to the throne of God for help in time of need (Heb. 4:15, 16).

Many Jews of the Diaspora believed, and increasing numbers of the Gentiles believed and joined the church.

Messianic Mosaic Mayhem

After Jesus' death on the cross and His resurrection, He ascended to heaven to begin His heavenly priesthood. In sanctuary terminology, He had made the true sacrifice on the cross for humanity's sins. He took the sacrificial blood into the heavenly sanctuary where He continued, through that blood, to give pardon and to make atonement for sin. Sacrificial animals were no longer needed; circumcision was no longer a requirement. Jesus' true sacrifice now provided pardon for sin in the heavenly sanctuary.

God gave the covenant of grace at Sinai (Exod. 19:5, 6; 34:10). At the same time, God gave the ceremonial law, with its symbolic sacrifices and rituals, pointing to the Messiah, the true sacrifice for sin. As time passed, belief in the coming Messiah dimmed, and the people began to look on the sacrifices, ceremonies, traditions, and their descent from Abraham as a means to obtain salvation. Their performance of the "law of Moses" cemented into an old covenant mindset.

In the New Testament church, there was always a tension between the law of Moses and the grace of Christ. Certain Jewish converts to Christianity had a hard time letting go of their dependence on Abraham as their father and their meticulous keeping of the law, the sacrifices, and the ceremonies as a means for obtaining salvation. These were a tradition that had lasted 1500 years, and these externals were how they identified themselves as Jews. They could not understand how anyone could be saved unless he or she kept "the law of Moses."

Circumcision and Ceremonies

Genesis 17 described circumcision as the means by which a person enters the covenant. When Moses proclaimed the tenth plague on the Egyptians, many non-Jews wanted the deliverance promised by the Passover. To attend a Passover required being circumcised (Exod. 12:43, 44, 48). With this history, one cannot blame Jewish Christians for standing for what they felt was a fundamental principle.

As Paul evangelized the Roman world, the Gentiles readily accepted the grace of Christ. This upset certain of the Messianic Jews who felt that Gentile believers must accept circumcision and other ceremonies in order to be saved. Peter had seen the centurion Cornelius receive the Holy Ghost and recognized that God intended to bring the Gentiles into the gospel as well as Jews (Acts 10). This brought tension between groups of Messianic believers who strongly held different opinions.

The church councils in Jerusalem and at Antioch (Acts 15) dealt with these issues. They decided that Gentiles need not follow the ceremonial law except for four issues: (1) Gentile believers did not need to be circumcised; (2) fornication among Gentile believers must be dealt with as a sin; (3) Gentile believers should not eat things offered to idols, and (4) Gentile believers should not eat the meat of strangled animals or blood.

While the leaders agreed on these points, there was still a problem. Certain Jewish converts to Christianity followed Paul to the new churches and taught Jewish customs to the Gentile converts. Several passages in Paul's epistles deal with this problem, including the books of Hebrews, Romans, 1 Corinthians, and Galatians. Paul compared legalistic perceptions of these Jewish Christians with the grace of Christ through the cross of Calvary. To continue to hold onto the ceremonial law was to deny the grace of God and the effectiveness of Jesus' sacrifice on the cross.[3]

Epistles Meet a Crisis

"For I determined not to know anything among you, save Jesus Christ, and him crucified" (1 Cor. 2:2). This verse sums up Paul's message.[4]

Circumcision was the token of the covenant from the time of Abraham (Gen. 17:11). Even in Old Testament times, the man receiving circumcision must be converted, or the ritual itself was meaningless (Rom. 2:25–29). Paul applies this spiritual standard: "But he is a Jew, which is one inwardly; and circumcision is that of the heart, in the spirit, and not in the letter; whose praise is not of men, but of God" (Rom. 2:29). To hold to their descent from Abraham and the laws of Moses was to deny what Jesus had done for them on the cross.

Paul goes on to say, "Therefore no one will be declared righteous in his sight by observing the law … This righteousness from God comes through faith in Jesus Christ …" (Rom. 3:20, 22, NIV). In 2 Corinthians 3, there are several comparisons:

- tables of stone vs. fleshy tables of the heart
- the letter kills vs. the spirit gives life
- the ministration of death vs. the ministration of the Spirit
- the ministration of condemnation vs. the ministration of righteousness
- their minds blinded by a veil vs. the veil removed in Christ

In this chapter, Paul compares what Christ has done for us with a mistaken perception of the law on tables of stone and the law spelled out in writing. The law is holy, just, and good, and a guide to what is sin. The ability to keep that law must be through grace, which is not from the law (Gal. 2:21).

Paul wrote the book of Galatians to correct the damage to the Galatians church by false teachings. For people to depend on their keeping the law to deliver them from sin is a denial of the grace of Christ "who gave himself for our sins, that he might deliver us from this present evil world, according to the will of God and our Father: ... To whom be glory for ever and ever. Amen. I marvel that ye are so soon removed from him that called you into the grace of Christ, unto another gospel" (Gal. 1:4–6).

Further, Paul says, "a man is not justified by the works of the law, but by the faith of Jesus Christ" (Gal. 2:16). In Galatians 3 he directly confronts the problem: "O foolish Galatians, who hath bewitched you, that ye should not obey the truth, before whose eyes Jesus Christ hath been evidently set forth, crucified among you? ... Received ye the Spirit by the works of the law, or by the hearing of faith?" (Gal. 3:1, 2).

Galatians 3:1 to 5:6 is an ardent call to make Christ first and to purge dead works as a means of salvation. In these passages, the word "law" is not an attack on the ten-commandment law. Paul recognized that grace received through faith is what gives the Christian the ability to obey the law (Rom. 3:31). However, keeping the law—either moral or ceremonial—as a means of salvation was and is wrong.

It is necessary for Christians to consent to the work of grace to cleanse the life of sin, which is violation of the law (Rom. 3:20; 1 John 3:4). The sinful nature comes from a lack of love for God, which leads to pride and unbelief, and a lack of love for our fellow human beings, which leads to selfishness. These motives of the heart can be changed only by grace, in the power of the Holy Spirit. Christians cannot change their motives by force of will.

Besides these passages, Paul wrote extensively on faith, grace, and justification, always with an emphasis on the cross of Christ, leading the church away from the deeply ingrained traditions of Jewish thinking.[5]

Lasting Legalistic Legacy

Concerns about the ceremonial law did not end with the early church. Some churches today have a legalistic approach to salvation. Many individuals believe in grace, yet they live an old covenant life. If people can do something to be saved, then they feel at liberty to live as they please. (Others use legal justification to achieve the same end. As long as they have justification, they believe they can live as they please.) Either way, it requires a higher commitment to submit to Christ and consent to the work of grace in the life. Not everyone wants his or her life changed, but Christ has promised His Holy Spirit to give love, joy, peace, longsuffering, gentleness, goodness, and faith. In Him, we have life everlasting (Gal. 5:22).

Many Christians today have swung to the other side. They believe that keeping the law—carefully obeying God's commandments—is legalism. Yet, failure to uphold the law is causing untold misery and evil in society today. It comes back to our obligation to keep the law. How does one keep it? The Christian must make a commitment to obey the law and consent to the work of grace. Once one decides to obey the law and cooperates with the Holy Spirit, then obedience to the law is the gift of God.[6]

Endnotes

1. The term "Diaspora" refers to a scattering or dispersion, for whatever reason, of a people from their ancestral homeland. It generally requires that the dispersed people maintain their ethnic identity. For instance, seventy years after Judah went into captivity to Babylon, a small part of the Jewish nation returned to Judah. The greater population remained in Babylon or scattered to other locations in what would become the Roman Empire. Most of these met together regularly and maintained their Jewish identity.

   Gamaliel the Elder, or Rabban Gamaliel I, was a leading authority in the Sanhedrin, in the mid-first century AD. He was the son of Simeon ben Hillel, and grandson of the greatest Jewish teacher Hillel the Elder. Gamaliel died twenty years before the destruction of the Second Temple in Jerusalem (AD 70). He fathered a son, whom he called Simeon, after his father, and a daughter. The name Gamaliel is the Greek form of the Hebrew name meaning "reward of God." Christians recognize Gamaliel as a Pharisee, doctor of Jewish Law. Acts of the Apostles speak of Gamaliel with consummate respect, a man who spoke in favor of arrested Christian apostles. He taught Jewish Law to Paul the apostle. In the Talmud, Gamaliel is described as the president of the Great Sanhedrin in Jerusalem. Many consider Gamaliel one of the greatest teachers in all the annals of Judaism. Since Rabban Gamaliel, the Elder, died, society has lost purity, piety, and reverence for the law. The teaching of Hillel is presented collectively, making it difficult to identify what is Gamaliel's. See http://en.wikipedia.org/wiki/Gamaliel, accessed 8/15/2012.

2. "Then Saul, (who also is called Paul,) filled with the Holy Ghost, set his eyes on him" (Acts 13:9).

3. Judaism is the religion, philosophy and the way of life of the Jewish people. It is a monotheistic religion, originating in the Hebrew Bible (the Tanakh). Rabbinic Judaism holds that God revealed his laws and commandments to Moses on Mount Sinai in the form of both the written and oral Torah. (Yet, monotheistic religion originated with Adam and Eve, long before the Hebrew Scriptures were written!)

   Jews are an ethno-religious group and include those who were born Jewish and those who converted to Judaism. Jewish religious movements include Orthodox Judaism, which teaches that the Torah and Jewish law are divine in origin, eternal, and unalterable, and that they should be strictly followed. Conservative and Reform Judaism are more liberal, with Conservative Judaism promoting a more "traditional" interpretation of Judaism's requirements than Reform Judaism. A typical Reform position is that Jewish law should be viewed as a set of general guidelines rather than as a set of restrictions and obligations whose observance is required of all Jews.

   According to Jewish Law, a Jew is anyone born of a Jewish mother or converted to Judaism in accordance with Jewish Law. American Reform Judaism and British Liberal Judaism accept the child of one Jewish parent (father or mother) as Jewish if the parents raise the child with a Jewish identity. Traditional Judaism maintains that a Jew, whether by birth or conversion, is a Jew forever. Thus, a Jew who claims to be an atheist or converts to another religion is still considered, by traditional Judaism, to be Jewish. According to some sources, the Reform movement has maintained that a Jew who has converted to another religion is no longer a Jew, and the Israeli Government has also taken that stance after Supreme Court cases and statutes. The Reform movement has indicated that this is not so certain and unchangeable, and different situations call for consideration and differing actions. "A proselyte who has become an apostate remains, nevertheless, a Jew" (Walter Jacob, *Contemporary American Reform Responsa* [Mars, PA: Publishers Choice Book Mfg., 1987], pp. 100–106).

4. Paul strongly believed and taught "Jesus Christ, and Him crucified" (1 Cor. 1:22–24; 2:2). To the unbelieving Jews this has always been offensive, a rock of stumbling. At the same time, Paul had a deep regard for his Jewish brethren (Rom. 1:16; 2:9, 10; chaps. 9–11; Heb. 3:1) and worked for their salvation. Was Paul Anti-Semitic? See http://www.beliefnet.com/Faiths/2004/04/Is-Paul-The-Father-Of-Anti-Semitism.aspx, accessed 8/15/2012.

5. More on this topic will appear in the chapters discussing Hebrews 8–10.

   In some Jewish circles, today, Paul is described as "Romanized" and "anti-Semitic" (Rom. 2:21–29). As Gentile converts flooded into the Christian church, they quickly learned the story of Jesus, His life, trials, crucifixion, and resurrection. This always put the Jews in a bad light, and many Jews accepted a different account of these events, promoted by the Jewish leaders at that time. Consequently, there was strong opposition from many Jews, leading to riots and persecution of those who believed in Jesus, many of whom came from a Jewish background.

6. Can a decision to keep the law, be a "work"? (1 Cor. 9:26, 27; 2 Cor. 3:18; 10:3–5; Gal. 2:20; Eph. 6:10–18; Phil. 3:12–14; 1 Tim. 1:18; 6:12; 2 Tim. 4:7; James 2:17, 18).

Chapter 37

Christ Our Heavenly High Priest

---

*For we have not an high priest which cannot be touched with the feeling of our
infirmities; but was in all points tempted like as we are, yet without sin. Let us
therefore come boldly unto the throne of grace, that we may
obtain mercy, and find grace to help in time of need.*
Hebrews 4:15, 16

The priesthood in ancient Israel provided stability, instruction, and help in their worship services. Through the sacrifice, the sinner received pardon and atonement. The sacrifice and application of blood were part of a single unit by which the sinner obtained pardon and atonement. In the same way, Jesus' sacrifice on the cross and His heavenly priesthood are a unit to give pardon and atonement to sinners today. To believe otherwise is to raise confusing questions about the judgment.

A priest mediates between God and humanity, providing pardon for sin through the sacrifice, an illustration of the covenant of God. A pastor proclaims the gospel, which is the good news about the covenant of God, and cares for his congregation. Each member of his congregation now has direct access to the throne of God for help and pardon for sins (Heb. 4:16). The duties of the priest and pastor often overlap.

The human priesthood was temporary, ending with Jesus' sacrifice on the cross. It was a symbol of Jesus' true priesthood, which He now continues in the heavenly sanctuary. Jesus Christ is now our heavenly High Priest, and by mediating His blood in the heavenly sanctuary, He provides pardon for sin and atonement for all believers.

Jewish Identity in Jesus and Not in the Temple

The Christian church in Jerusalem began as a Jewish church. Their worship—even their teaching—centered largely on the Temple. The first five chapters of Acts make frequent references to the Temple. Surprisingly for some, the Christian church was, at this time, still a part of Judaism! After Pentecost, opposition from Jewish leaders began to grow. After Acts 5, the Bible does not mention the Temple until Paul attempted to fulfill certain vows (Acts 21), causing a riot. The Jews arrested Paul and put him in jail, before sending him to Rome.

Many Jewish Christians continued to keep the feasts and faithfully observed the Jewish ceremonies until the destruction of the Temple in AD 70. When Gentiles began to enter the church, the question arose about circumcision, the law of Moses, and how much of the law Gentiles were expected to fulfill. The church held a council in Jerusalem. After members of the council had adequately discussed the matter, James, presiding at the council, summed up their conclusion:

> Wherefore my sentence is, that we trouble not them, which from among the Gentiles are turned to God: But that we write unto them, that they abstain from pollutions of idols, and from fornication, and from things strangled, and from blood. (Acts 15:19, 20)

A group of men returned with this message to Antioch, where a largely Gentile church gladly accepted the council's decision.

It would be excellent if we could say that this solved the problem. However, it is difficult to stop a centuries-old tradition. Jewish identity was tied to their forms of worship. Many Jewish believers in Jesus could not or would not make the change. They believed that to become a follower of the true God one had to become a Jew (Exod. 12:48, 49; John 4:22). Certain of them began visiting the churches that Paul had raised up, urging a return to the ceremonial law.

The everlasting gospel, that Jesus gave His life a sacrifice to pay for the sins of every human being, was to many a "new truth." They did not yet understand that "sacrifice and oblation," which served only to point to Jesus Christ, had fulfilled their purpose and were no longer needed or in force (Dan. 9:27). Paul, in his epistles and in Hebrews, responded to Jewish Christians who held onto these ceremonies that to continue these services would be to deny the meaning of Jesus' sacrifice. "Christ our passover is sacrificed for us" (1 Cor. 5:7).

It was because of these "Judaizers" that Paul made such a strong emphasis on faith and grace in his epistles.[1] He dealt with the subject extensively in Hebrews. Paul was sympathetic and persuasive. His first priority was to win Jewish Christians to a full and complete commitment to Jesus Christ.

The opening salutation in Hebrews comes in chapter three, "Wherefore, holy brethren, partakers of the heavenly calling, consider the Apostle and High Priest of our profession Christ Jesus" (Heb. 3:1). Who were these "holy brethren"? Who were the partakers of the heavenly calling? They were the Jews, for whom Paul always had a kind regard.

Paul begins immediately to describe the work of Jesus Christ, while the Jews looked back to the words of the prophets. God had now "spoken unto us by his Son" (Heb. 1:2). He is the Creator, above all the angels; yet He became a man, "a little lower than the angels." He even tasted "death for every man … that through death he might destroy him that had the power of death, that is, the devil" (Heb. 2:9, 14).

Christ "was in all points tempted like as we are, yet without sin" (Heb. 4:15). His sinless life He offered at Calvary. He ascended to heaven and sat down in the Father's throne (Heb. 1:3) as a "priest for ever after the order of Melchisedec" (Heb. 5:6). The sacrifice and oblation had met its purpose. The Aaronic priesthood had ended, and Jesus began His heavenly priesthood.

These are the basic principles of Christianity. It was time for these Christians to grow in grace, and deepen their experience in Christ (Heb. 5:12–6:2).

Jesus Christ, Heavenly High Priest

Priests were from the tribe of Levi and specifically from the family of Aaron. The Jews were diligent about maintaining genealogies to qualify any man before he served as a priest (Ezra 7:1–5; 8:18–21).

Jesus' qualification, like those of Melchizedek, was of a different type (Heb. 7:11–17). He was a priest-king without ancestry or descendants (Heb. 7:3) and was directly appointed by God (Ps. 110:4).

A priest mediates between God and humanity. Jesus was a kind and cordial priest. He recognized needs when even the people themselves did not. He was always ready to help. This was the beginning of His priestly ministry. His life demonstrated that God is love. Continuing as our High Priest in heaven, He remains the same (Heb. 13:8).

> For we have not an high priest which cannot be touched with the feeling of our infirmities; but was in all points tempted like as we are, yet without sin. Let us therefore come boldly unto the throne of grace, that we may obtain mercy, and find grace to help in time of need. (Heb. 4:15, 16)

After His ascension, Jesus began His ministry in the first apartment, forgiving the confessed sins of His people (1 John 1:9, 10). Animal sacrifices in the Old Testament could not of themselves forgive sins or change the life. They were effective in anticipation of Jesus' true sacrifice on the cross.

The sanctuary and the ministries on earth were a copy and a symbol of the reality of the sanctuary and ministries in heaven.[2] The "daily," first-apartment ministry had to do with the forgiveness of sin by the blood of the sacrifice and the transfer of sins into the sanctuary. In Jesus' heavenly first-apartment ministry, He mediated His blood, shed at Calvary. Until His sacrifice on Calvary, He could not open His ministry in the heavenly sanctuary (Heb. 10:12).

When Jesus ascended to heaven, the Bible describes Him as being on the "right hand" of the Father.[3] To be on the throne with the Father in the Most Holy Place is the role of a King. To perform His ministry in the Holy Place is the responsibility of a priest. Jesus is our "Priest-King," "after the order of Melchisedec" (Heb. 5:6; Gen. 14:18).

> Now of the things which we have spoken this is the sum: We have such an high priest, who is set on the right hand of the throne of the Majesty in the heavens. Who serve unto the example and shadow of heavenly things, as Moses was admonished of God when he was about to make the tabernacle: for, See, saith he, that thou make all things according to the pattern shewed to thee in the mount. (Heb. 8:1, 5)

Once a year, in ancient Israel, the high priest cleansed the forgiven sins of the past year from the Most Holy Place. The record of forgiven sins was symbolically blotted from the book of record. In the true, heavenly service, as sins were blotted from the record, they were also blotted from memory (Jer. 31:34; Heb. 8:12). It was critical that the people confess and repent of all sins before that day. In preparation for the Day of Atonement, God told the people to afflict their souls as they sought to discover and confess all the sins in their lives (Lev. 23:27, 29).

The Superior Ministry of Jesus

> But now hath he obtained a more excellent ministry, by how much also he is the
> mediator of a better covenant, which was established upon better promises. For if
> that first covenant had been faultless, then should no place have been sought for
> the second. For finding fault with them [with the people, not with the covenant], he
> saith, Behold, the days come, saith the Lord, when I will make a new covenant with
> the house of Israel and with the house of Judah. (Heb. 8:6–8)[4]

The superior ministry of Jesus provides grace and pardon for sins (Exod. 19:4–6; Jer. 31:31–34). The "first" covenant, which was based on human promises, could not provide pardon for sin (Exod. 23:21). God gave the Ten Commandments so the people would know what their promises entailed. Under the old covenant, people promised to do "all that the Lord hath spoken"; under the new covenant, God writes the law on their hearts and by grace gives them the ability to obey the law.[5]

> For by grace are ye saved through faith; and that not of yourselves: it is the gift of
> God: not of works, lest any man should boast. For we are his workmanship, created
> in Christ Jesus unto good works, which God hath before ordained that we should
> walk in them. (Eph. 2:8–10)

In making their own self-confident promises (Exod. 19:8), the people failed to understand the majesty and holiness of God, denied the grace He offered (Exod. 19:4), and attempted to covenant with God as equals! It was an impossible situation and doomed to failure from the start. Within forty-six days, they broke their covenant by a heathen festival at the base of Mt. Sinai. Moses interceded for the people until God renewed the everlasting covenant and promised to go with Israel into the Promised Land.

After Sinai, the people understood that they were to keep the Ten Commandments. Yet, they failed to understand the preamble, "I am the Lord thy God, which have brought thee out of the land of Egypt" (Exod. 20:2), which indicated that God would fulfill the promises of the Ten Commandments in their lives by His grace. Instead, they endeavored to keep the law in their own power. In so doing, they listed an additional 603 regulations/*mitzvoth* (as enumerated by Maimonides) as being on par with the Ten.[6]

As time passed, the people focused on the performance of sacrifices and ceremonies rather than looking by faith to Jesus Christ, the Messiah. They made these rituals the sum and substance of their religion and ignored the Redeemer who was to come.

After Jesus' death and resurrection, it was hard to give up all their sacrifices, ceremonies, and rituals. Did Jesus' sacrifice on Calvary bring to an end the sacrifices and ceremonies of the Temple? How could people worship God if they did not perform ceremonies? It was hard for many Jewish Christians to comprehend God's writing the law on their hearts, or to believe that they did not need to perform sacrifices and ceremonies.

Not all Christians understood that they must be born again and become a new creature in Christ. Life should never be "business as usual" for Christians. Those who hold that the sum and substance of religion is to go to church once a week and put some money into the offering plate are living by the old covenant! Not that these things are bad, for they are not. Yet, God has so much more in mind for His people.[7]

Endnotes

1. Paul writes on the issue of continuing Jewish ceremonies, which have become obsolete, since Jesus' true sacrifice on the cross (Rom. 2:21–29; 9:1–11:36; 2 Cor. 2:14–3:18; Gal. 1–4; Eph. 2, 3; and Heb. 1–3 and 7–10).

2. The term "patterns" (Greek *hupodeigma*), used in Hebrews 9:23 to describe the earthly sanctuary, has also been translated in several versions as "copies." Interestingly, the word means both "patterns" and "copies." Both fit the earthly sanctuary quite well. The earthly sanctuary was a *copy* of the "holy places" in heaven as well as a *pattern* for "heavenly things" that would take place through Jesus.

3. When Jesus ascended to heaven, He sat in the throne at the right hand of the Father (Acts 7:56; Rom. 8:34; Eph. 1:20; Heb. 1:3; 8:1).

4. The weakness in the former covenant was "them." What was their "fault"? God says: "because they continued not in my covenant" (Heb. 8:9).

5. For more on the old covenant, see chapter 15, "The Historical Old Covenant."

6. In the second century, Jewish synagogues ceased to quote the Ten Commandments together with the *Shema* because it appeared to support the contention of the Christians of Jewish and Gentile backgrounds (called *minim* by the non-believing Jews) regarding the uniqueness and continuity of the Ten Commandments. "Removing the Ten Commandments from the public reading of the *Shema* prayer was intended to get away from the claim of the *minim* that they were indeed essential, unlike the other *mitzvot* in the *Torah*, especially those between humankind and God. According to the *minim*, the Destruction of the Temple, which was clearly caused by God as the ruler of history, is in fact evidence that God no longer wants the *mitzvot* in the *Torah* to be observed, for many of them—for example, the sacrifices—could not be carried out with the Temple" (Aharon Oppenheimer, "Removing the Decalogue from the *Shema* and Phylacteries: The Historical Implications," *The Decalogue in Jewish and Christian Tradition* [New York and London: T & T Clark International, 2011], edited by Yair Hoffman and Henning Graf Reventlow, p. 99). "By the *minim* they meant at this time the Jewish-Christian sects, or even Christians themselves" (Oppenheimer, p. 98).

7. The covenant promise is to all God's people (Gen. 17:8; Exod. 6:7; 33:14–17; Lev. 26:12; Deut. 29:13; Jer. 11:4; 24:7; 30:22; 32:38; Ezek. 11:20; 14:11; 36:28; 37:23; Zech. 8:8; 2 Cor. 6:16; Heb. 8:10; Rev. 21:3).

Chapter 38

Distinguishing the
Old Covenant From the New

*In that he saith, A new covenant, he hath made the first old. Now that which
decayeth and waxeth old is ready to vanish away.*
Hebrews 8:13.

The terms "new covenant" and "old covenant" come up frequently in religious discussions. It is not enough just to use the terms; we need to carefully explain what the terms mean and where they are applied.

The *new covenant* is the covenant of grace, which is also known as the *everlasting covenant*, "My Covenant," and the Abrahamic covenant. The new covenant describes the "born-again" experience and being made a "new creature." It represents what God will initiate and perform for His people. Jesus confirmed the new covenant at Calvary and made effectual all the sacrifices in the past.

The old covenant is implied in Jeremiah 31:31–34, where a former, broken covenant is compared with the new covenant. The former covenant is the historical old covenant of human promises (Exod. 19:8; 23:20–23; 24:3–11; Jer. 31:31, 32; and Hebrews 9:18–21). That covenant was broken at Sinai but came back as an idolatrous, corrupted view of the ceremonial law (Heb. 8–10). The old covenant is the effort of humans to do what only God can do.

Review of the Controversy

The place of the ceremonial law and its usage in Christian life produced the most controversial issue in the apostolic church. Jewish Christians felt that Gentile converts needed to become Jews before they could be Christians. After all, "salvation is of the Jews" (John 4:22). The council at Jerusalem freed Gentile Christians from the obligations of the ceremonial law except for four practical recommendations (Acts 15:20), and the report was carried to the church in Antioch.

The many Jewish-Christians were still reluctant to let go of circumcision and certain temple rituals. They failed to realize that, for all people, the ceremonial observances had met their fulfillment in Jesus Christ. This created an unhealthy tension in the church, inasmuch as one large segment followed an elaborate system of religious practices disregarded by the other.

Jewish Christians had only a vague idea of Christ's work in the heavenly sanctuary. They did not realize that their sacrifices were ineffective in view of Jesus' sacrifice on the cross. It was time for the Jewish Christians to learn faith in the heavenly realities and in the Rock, Christ Jesus, on which the church was built.

Comparisons Between the Covenants

The epistle to the Hebrews makes a number of comparisons between old and new. One must understand that there are several different "laws" that make up the ceremonial law. The human performance of many of these laws ended at Calvary, to be replaced by the ministry of Jesus Christ in heaven.

At Sinai, God gave Israel what He called "My covenant," which was a covenant previously established—the *everlasting covenant*, which is also called the Abrahamic covenant and the new covenant. Redemption through Jesus' sacrifice on the cross was the basis for this covenant. The Abrahamic covenant was to continue to all Abraham's descendants and to the Christian church to the end of time (Gal. 3:29).

Moses presented the Sinai covenant to the elders of Israel. They responded with, "All that the Lord hath spoken we will do" (Exod. 19:8). This was a promise of dedication. Their intent was admirable, but they did not know their own weakness (Deut. 5:28, 29) or the holiness of God. They had bypassed the promise of grace (Exod. 19:4) and offered to "obey [His] voice and keep [His] covenant" by their own strength![1]

Three Ratifications

God promised Abram that he would have descendants in number as the stars of heaven. "He believed in the Lord; and he counted it to him for righteousness" (Gen. 15:6). God then promised him the land of Canaan. Abram must have thought it too much to believe since he asked, "Whereby shall I know that I shall inherit it?" (Gen. 15:8).

In His mercy, God carried out a ratification ceremony, according to the custom of the time (Gen. 15:9–17), to reassure Abram of His promise of land. By contrast, the everlasting covenant of God could be ratified only by Jesus' sacrifice on the cross.

At Sinai, God offered Israel unique blessings with the covenant He called "My covenant"—they would be the exclusive treasure of God, a kingdom of priests, and a holy nation. They were to obey God's voice and keep His covenant by the power that God had shown in their deliverance from Egypt.

The people promised to obey, but they failed to recognize the holiness of God and forgot God's promise of grace. Their presumptuous human promises were a separate covenant from what God had offered, one that required a separate ratification ceremony! It was a covenant doomed to fail from the start. This was the *historical* old covenant. Within forty-six days, they broke their promises by a rebellious, heathen festival at the base of Sinai.

The focus and center of the everlasting covenant of God is Jesus Christ and His sinless life on earth, His death on the cross for our sins, His resurrection, and His high priestly intercession for us in the heavenly sanctuary. All that human beings can do in response to the covenant of God is to bow in reverent awe and accept it by faith. It is the covenant of redemption, which Jesus ratified or confirmed at Calvary.

Jesus' power and authority are based on His sacrifice. It is through the cross that Jesus breached the walls of evil and blessed His people. The prayers of the saints give Jesus "permission" to act.

The New and the Old

We discuss the new covenant often in other chapters of this book. The new covenant is the covenant of redemption and grace, and it is the same as the everlasting covenant or "My covenant." God gave it to Adam and Eve, Noah, Abraham, Isaac, Jacob, Moses, and Israel, and He finally passed it on to the Christian church. It is the covenant that Jesus confirmed at Calvary and that He now mediates in heaven.[2]

Israel ratified the *historical* old covenant at Sinai. This separated it from the covenant of God, which Jesus ratified at Calvary. It was temporary, dependent on the weak promises of the people, and it lasted just forty-six days.

The old covenant is the covenant of works, whereby humans try to do the work of God in their own strength, bypassing grace. The old covenant is also seen as a corrupted view of the ceremonial law. That corrupted view of the ceremonial law has taken different forms, and it was dominant when Jesus was here on earth. For the first time in Scripture, Paul discussed the concept of the old covenant in Hebrews, chapter 9.

A common belief is that the old covenant was the ceremonial law and that the ceremonial law was "nailed to the cross" and brought to an end (Col. 2:14). The problem with this proposition is that large parts of the ceremonial law, such as the human priesthood, changed. The Levitical priesthood of the Old Testament ended at Calvary, while the priesthood continued with Jesus' ministry for us in the heavenly temple. Nowhere does the Bible say that the sacrifices or sanctuary services were the old covenant.

Further, Exodus 23:21 asserts that there was no pardon for transgressions in the proposed covenant of human promises (the *historical* old covenant).[3] Since the ceremonial law specifically provided for pardon for sins, one must place it as an illustration of the everlasting covenant, also known as Abrahamic covenant or the new covenant.

Corrupted View of the Sacrifices

By the time of Jesus, the people had come to believe that salvation came through the mere performance of the sacrifices and sanctuary services. Many took this one step further in that they looked to the death of the animal itself as making atonement for their sins. They had largely overlooked the Redeemer to whom it pointed. Their false assurance also rested on faith in their descent from Abraham and in their rigorous observance of the law.

Many observant Jews today believe that salvation comes through keeping the law and living a clean, ethical life. What is lacking here is the need for a change of heart, which comes only through the grace and power of God.[4]

Hebrews 9 described this corrupted view of the ceremonial law, calling it that which was old and about to vanish and comparing it with the true and effective sacrifice of Jesus on the cross and His effective priestly ministry in the heavenly temple.

Because the Jews looked for a Messiah who would take the throne of David, drive out the Romans, and restore the former glory of Israel, they did not identify a Messiah who came to bring the kingdom of grace. These beliefs influenced even Jesus' disciples. They did not understand His mission until after the resurrection. Even then, there were among the Christians of Jewish background those who believed that one had to perform sacrifices and rituals and be circumcised to be saved.

Paul wrote many times about this corrupted view of the covenant. An understanding of Paul's writings is essential in grasping the purpose of the old covenant, what Jesus accomplished on the cross, and the differences in the new covenant.

Sacrifices Illustrate the "New Covenant in My Blood"

Hebrews 8 speaks of a covenant that was *first, faulty, not continued in, growing old, decayed,* and *ready to vanish away*.[5] Hebrews 9 goes into more detail in comparing the true and effective sacrifice and priesthood of Jesus Christ, with the symbols and shadows of the animal sacrifices and the human priesthood. Bible writers sometimes used the term "old covenant" to describe this faulty perception of the ceremonial law, which was common at the time of Jesus.[6]

There was no pardon in the covenant of human promises (Exod. 23:20–23).[7] It offered strict accountability and atonement for sins of ignorance. In the new covenant were better promises, forgiveness of sins, and grace to renew the heart.[8] The ceremonial law, which provided pardon for sin, had nothing to do with the *historical* old covenant. It was, instead, an illustration of the new or everlasting covenant. Here are several proposals that support this view:

The sanctuary services were merely symbols to point forward to the realities of the new covenant.[9]

The Bible makes no statement that the sanctuary services were a part of any covenant. Rather, the ten-commandment law is "the covenant." Moses kept the tables of this law inside the ark, and he kept the "book of the law," which was the ceremonial law, in the side of the ark.[10] Further, human beings carried out these ceremonial activities. A man cannot effect his own salvation, even by doing sacrifices. They can serve only as an illustration of the covenant and a sign of personal commitment.

The sanctuary services were a connecting link whereby people in Old Testament times could look forward by faith to the coming of the Messiah, the true sacrifice.

The ceremonial law was never ratified as a covenant.

Even though God gave the ceremonial law, He is displeased with sacrifices if there is no change in the life.[11]

God gave the ceremonial laws, which were an illustration of the plan of salvation, as symbols to point forward to eternal realities. God pardoned sin through faith in the prophesied sacrifice of Jesus. The sacrifices pointed to the new covenant in which Jesus' sacrifice atoned for the sins of mankind (Luke 22:20) and provided grace to remove condemnation and guilt (Rom. 8:1) and write God's laws in the heart (Heb. 8:10; 10:16). Jesus is the Mediator of this new covenant.

What the Jews Should Have Known

God gave Israel many advantages. They had seen the direct intervention of God in the ten plagues against Egypt. God opened the way for them through the Red Sea and then destroyed the Egyptian army that followed them. Every day they witnessed the pillar of cloud and every night the pillar of fire. The people gathered manna on a daily basis, and water came from a rock for their use. God demonstrated His power and majesty on Mt. Sinai when He spoke the ten-commandment law. Prophets, priests, and Levites instructed them in the ways of God. Miraculous victories paved their way into the land of Canaan. Even after 40 years of wandering in the desert, no one got sick, and no one's clothes wore out.

That God is alive, merciful, and able to save should have been abundantly clear. However, people are inclined to take even remarkable things for granted. When the sinful human nature reasserted itself, the people repeatedly fell into idolatry and apostasy. The concept of a Messiah to come, bringing peace, righteousness, and eternal life, would and did appeal to people of a spiritual nature. Unfortunately, these were few in number. When Jesus came, He had to deal with all these unsolved problems.

The question may be raised: Are we better than they are? As we look over the world, we see selfishness in all levels of society; we see crime, violence, broken homes, and willing ignorance of eternal realities. In the churches, it seems that things are not much different.

The first of the Ten Commandments is "Thou shalt have no other gods before me." People break this commandment more than any other. God must be first in a person's life, and that means making Him first in the daily schedule. The Christian must take time daily for family worship and personal time for Bible study and prayer. God must be first in business affairs, in social life, and in helping others.

Endnotes

1. See chapter 15, "The Historical Old Covenant."
2. Jesus is the Mediator of the new covenant (Matt. 26:26–29; Mark 14:24; 1 Cor. 11:23–26; 1 Tim. 2:5; Heb. 7:22; 9:15; 8:6; 12:24).
3. However, it is God's nature to forgive iniquity and transgression and sin (Exod. 34:7; Num. 14:18).
4. People need to have their lives changed (Matt. 5:20; John 3:3; Rom. 2:25–29).
5. See chapter 15, "The Historical Old Covenant."
6. The ministration that was faulty is described in Hebrews as (a) having repetitious animal sacrifices, which cannot take away sins (Heb. 9:9; 10:4); (b) possessing a human priesthood that is mortal and changeable (Heb. 7:8–12); (c) being inferior to the better covenant, to the better promises, and to Jesus, who is separate from sinners (Heb. 7:26; 8:6); (d) having a worldly sanctuary that is only a copy of the true (Heb. 8:5; 9:1, 11); (e) being a shadow of things to come (Heb. 10:1); (f) having come first (Heb. 8:8, 13; 9:1); (g) being faulty because of "them" (Heb. 8:8); (h) being broken by the fathers (Heb. 8:9); and (g) decaying and growing old and being ready to pass away (Heb. 8:13).
7. "Behold, I send an Angel before thee, to keep thee in the way, and to bring thee into the place which I have prepared. Beware of him, and obey his voice, provoke him not; for he will not pardon your transgressions: for my name is in him" (Exod. 23:20, 21). Ellen White commented: "This angel, Christ, gave Moses the ceremonies and ordinances of the Jewish law to be repeated to the people. The rebellion of Israel against the law and authority of God, caused their destruction" (*Advent Review and Sabbath Herald*, April 29, 1875). The Psalmist explains what God meant by not provoking the Angel. "How oft did they provoke him in the wilderness, and grieve him in the desert! Yea, they turned back and tempted God, and limited the Holy One of Israel" (Ps. 78:40, 41). In provoking Him, they grieved Him and caused Him to not pardon their transgressions.
8. "The terms of the 'old covenant' were, Obey and live: 'If a man do, he shall even live in them' (Ezekiel 20:11; Leviticus18:5); but 'cursed be he that confirmeth not all the words of this law to do them.' Deuteronomy 27:26. The 'new covenant' was

established upon 'better promises'--the promise of forgiveness of sins and of the grace of God to renew the heart and bring it into harmony with the principles of God's law. 'This shall be the covenant that I will make with the house of Israel; After those days, saith the Lord, I will put my law in their inward parts, and write it in their hearts.... I will forgive their iniquity, and will remember their sin no more.' Jeremiah 31:33, 34.

"The same law that was engraved upon the tables of stone is written by the Holy Spirit upon the tables of the heart. Instead of going about to establish our own righteousness we accept the righteousness of Christ. His blood atones for our sins. His obedience is accepted for us. Then the heart renewed by the Holy Spirit will bring forth 'the fruits of the Spirit.' Through the grace of Christ we shall live in obedience to the law of God written upon our hearts. Having the Spirit of Christ, we shall walk even as He walked. Through the prophet He declared of Himself, 'I delight to do Thy will, O My God: yea, Thy law is within My heart.' Psalm 40:8. And when among men He said, 'The Father hath not left Me alone; for I do always those things that please Him.' John 8:29" (Ellen G. White, *Patriarchs and Prophets* [Nampa, ID: Pacific Press Publishing Association, 2005], p. 372).

9. The ceremonial law used animal sacrifices, which pointed to the Messiah-Redeemer. It also had a sanctuary ministry and human priesthood that ended and were replaced by the true and effective sacrifice of Jesus and His ministry in the heavenly sanctuary. Rituals for cleansing from defilement and circumcision were temporary. Because the Most Holy Place is the throne of God, the festivals could only continue if they were invested with new emphases and meanings.

10. Moses put the two tablets inside the ark (Exod. 25:16, 21) with the pot of manna (Exod. 16:33, 34), attaching staves to carry the ark (Exod. 40:20). Later, he placed Aaron's rod that budded inside the ark (Num. 17:10). The covenant was written on tables of stone (Deut. 4:13) twice (Deut. 10:2, 5). Later, only the covenant remained (1 Kings 8:9; 2 Chron. 5:10). Hebrews mentions all three items (Heb. 9:4).

   Moses put the book containing the ceremonial and other laws in the side of the ark. "And it came to pass, when Moses had made an end of writing the words of this law in a book, until they were finished, that Moses commanded the Levites, which bare the ark of the covenant of the LORD, saying, Take this book of the law, and put it in the side of the ark of the covenant of the LORD your God, that it may be there for a witness against thee" (Deut. 31:24–26).

11. The Bible speaks of the pleasure that God and the holy angels enjoy over the conversion of a sinner to Christ. In the sacrifices, this is expressed as "an offering made by fire, of a sweet savour unto the Lord." In actual experience, we quickly realize that burnt flesh, fat, and hair are not a pleasant smell. However, as symbols of a dedicated life, they are pleasing to God. Forty-four times the Bible uses the expression "sweet savour(s)" with reference to God's pleasure in such offerings (e.g. Gen. 8:21; Exod. 29:18, 25, 41; Lev. 1:9, 13, 17; 2:2, 9; Ezek. 6:13; 16:19; 2 Cor. 2:15).

Chapter 39

Presenting Jesus Christ to the Hebrews

Wherefore, holy brethren, partakers of the heavenly calling, consider
the Apostle and High Priest of our profession, Christ Jesus.
Hebrews 3:1

Paul wrote the Book of Hebrews for Jewish Christians. When Jesus came to earth, His life, teachings, and healings were a cataclysmic change from what people expected of the Messiah. By His example, teachings, and healings while on earth, Jesus cut across the beliefs, lifestyles, and politics of the nation. In every confrontation with the leaders of the nation, He was able to expose their ignorance, false beliefs, and wishful thinking. Our society today is again ignorant of the teachings of Christ, too willing to believe strange doctrines, and not willing to see or act on the problems we face.

The epistle to the Hebrews describes aspects of the ceremonial law, covenant, and the priesthood of Christ, including practical applications for belief and practice. In this chapter, we will reflect on Jesus as Redeemer and High Priest in heaven.

Hebrew Christians

The Hebrews had centuries of tradition. They also had the writings of the prophets. God demonstrated His presence among them repeatedly and in different ways. The people spent much time studying and discussing the Scriptures. They rested in their beliefs. In spite of this, the leading priests and rabbis, and possibly the majority of the people had false expectations of the Messiah and false concepts of what He was to do. It was the leaders of the people who led the way in rejecting Him, and they were responsible for His eventual crucifixion.

In Hebrew society, there were people who were "in expectation" of the Messiah's soon appearing and who welcomed Him when He came. However, even His disciples, who loved Him, did not fully understand His mission until after the resurrection. Even then, it required the teaching of the Holy Spirit to make the change. For many of the Jewish believers, it was hard to give up centuries of tradition. Paul wrote the epistle to the Hebrews for such people. It is one of the deepest and most carefully written books in the Bible. "Wherefore, holy brethren, partakers of the heavenly calling, consider the Apostle and High Priest of our profession, Christ Jesus" (Heb. 3:1). In this salutation, Paul shows his love for his fellow Israelites.

Jesus Christ, the Son

In Hebrews, Paul pictures Jesus' mediation in heaven. It is a continuation of what He did while on earth. In every possible way, Paul tried to convince his fellow Jews that Jesus is the Messiah and the heavenly High Priest. The purpose of the sacrifices and the ceremonies was only to point to Him, and it is only through Him that we humans are saved.

Chapter 1 begins with a picture of Jesus, the Son. He is Heir of all things and Creator of the worlds. He is the express image and glory of the Father. When He had purged the sins of humanity, He sat down on the right hand of the Father. He is High Priest and King. If the creation of God should become old and worn out and perish, Jesus does not change. He lives forever. As Paul wrote in the final chapter: "Jesus Christ the same yesterday, and to day, and for ever" (Heb. 13:8).

In chapter 2, Jesus becomes human and is "made a little lower than the angels." Angels are holy, just, and intolerant of disobedience. God made human beings a little lower than the angels and gave them dominion over all the creation on this earth. Jesus condescended to come as a man, experiencing temptation, suffering, and even death. Through Jesus, we have mercy and salvation—He is still human as our merciful and faithful High Priest! Considering the wonderful sacrifice of God in Jesus Christ, dare we neglect the mercy and salvation that Jesus gives?

In chapter 3, Paul depicts Moses as faithful in all that he did when Israel left Egypt—as their leader, lawgiver, and mediator with God. While Moses was faithful as a servant, Jesus is faithful as God's Son. Moses had to deal with complaints, rebellion, and insubordination from a stubborn people. Jesus, the Son, suffered even deeper rejection but offered grace and salvation to His people. Paul urges that every one of the children of Israel exhort one another to belief while it is "today" when that rest is available, contrasting it with "the provocation" and "the day of temptation in the wilderness" (Heb. 3:8).

Chapter 4 is an often-misunderstood chapter. God had promised Israel rest after the finished work of God in delivering them from Egypt and giving them the Promised Land. Paul compares this rest with the Sabbath rest. However, God could not give Israel the rest He promised them because of their apostasy and unbelief. Of necessity, He can only give it later. Jesus is patient, touched with human infirmities, tempted as a man as we are. He opened the way to the throne of grace that we may come boldly for help in time of need.

Jesus, High Priest in Heaven

Chapters 5, 6, and 7 of Hebrews discuss the priesthood of Christ after the "order of Melchisedec" (Heb. 5:6, 10; 6:20; 7:11, 17, 21). Melchizedek was a priest of God and the king of Salem (Gen. 14:18).

A man cannot make himself a priest; he must be called by God. Of Christ, the Father said, "Thou art my Son, today have I begotten thee," and, "Thou art a priest for ever after the order of Melchisedec" (Heb. 5:5, 6). As a human being, Jesus has compassion on the sinner because He also suffered temptation with the risk of sinning (Heb. 4:15). Christ "learned ... obedience by the things which he suffered" (Heb. 5:8).

Paul challenges his Jewish brethren to grow in grace, even attaining perfection (Heb. 6:1). They must move on from the basic doctrines of Christ and study the deeper truths of Scripture. They must obtain the faith and endurance of Abraham. Through the cross, Jesus entered within the vail and opened the way to the throne of grace, through which we may go on to perfection!

Melchizedek was a priest "without father, without mother, without descent, having neither beginning of days, nor end of life; but made like unto the Son of God; abideth a priest continually" (Heb. 7:3). Melchizedek, a priest and king, foreshadowed the priesthood of Christ. Had God not called Jesus to be a priest after the order of Melchizedek, He would not have otherwise had the genealogy to be a priest, being from the tribe of Judah.

Mediator of a Better Covenant

As we get into chapter 9, we find Jesus' ministry compared, not with the covenant, but with a corrupted view of the sacrifices and ceremonies of the sanctuary. This was a problem among Jewish Christians. They could not understand that Jesus' sacrifice on the cross wholly replaced the animal sacrifices and ceremonies of the Temple. With the delay in Jesus' return, they were being drawn back to their Jewish roots.

At His ascension, Jesus Christ went directly to the Father, to sit at His right hand. He is a Priest-King after the order of Melchizedek (Heb. 8:6). He had made sacrifice for the sins of humankind. Now as our High Priest, He presents His blood before the Father that all who believe in Him will be cleansed (Heb. 1:3).

Humans cannot fully understand why Jesus, second person of the Godhead, became a human being and lived on the earth (Heb. 2:7, 9, 11). But by doing so, He became "captain of their salvation" (Heb. 2:10; see also Heb. 2:14).

The work of Creation was finished in six days, and God rested on the seventh day. Jesus went to the cross and defeated sin and Satan that all who have faith and believe in His finished work might be saved (Heb. 4). It was the finished work of the covenant, and in this we have assurance and rest.

God gave to Israel, through Moses, the sanctuary patterned after the heavenly sanctuary. It was an earthly tabernacle and an earthly priesthood pointing forward to the prophesied Redeemer. These earthly things, while glorious, were temporary and would pass away when Jesus the Redeemer came.

The people responded with a first covenant (Ex. 19:8; 23:20–23; 24:3–11), which was faulty, based on human promises, and lacking in grace. It was the historical old covenant that was soon broken.

After Moses interceded with God, the people were brought back under the Abrahamic (new) covenant. The sanctuary services and the priesthood were given as an illustration of the covenant, and an easily understood means for sinners to see how the coming Redeemer would take the penalty for sin and provide grace and pardon for humankind.

Before long, most people forgot the promised Redeemer and looked to mere performance of sacrifices and rituals as a means of obtaining pardon for sins, atonement, and salvation. It was the old covenant experience again, depending on human works, and ineffective to offer pardon for sins or salvation. It was a human tendency to "be religious and do religious things" yet to continue to live in sin.

Jesus came and gave a more excellent ministry, a better covenant (the new covenant), true and real promises, and the heavenly priesthood.

In the early Christian church there were Jewish converts who could not give up their dependence on animal sacrifices, rituals, and an earthly temple (Heb. 9). To maintain and depend on these outmoded ceremonies was to deny what Christ had done on the cross. It was Paul's desire to help these Jewish converts to fully understand and believe in what Christ had done for them.

Jesus' willing sacrifice on the cross was the single, effectual sacrifice for sin. It is through His sacrifice that the animal sacrifices of the previous centuries were effective in pardoning sin (Heb. 9:12, 15, 24, 28). In the heavenly sanctuary, Jesus mediates His own blood to pardon sin and change people's lives. He made the sacrifice once, and He now "ever liveth" to make intercession.

The Theme of Living by Faith

Hebrews 10 emphasizes again that animal sacrifices cannot "make" human lives "perfect." Verse 10 says: "He taketh away the first, that he may establish the second." Then verses 16 and 17 of the chapter repeat the new covenant promise. The chapter also introduces the righteous living by faith in the context of continuing in faith until Jesus returns (Heb. 10:37–39).

Hebrews 11 is the well-known faith chapter. Faith is "substance"—something to hold onto to stabilize one's life.[1] It is evidence, based on what a person believes. It is trust in the promises and work of God. It is an emotional commitment and a love for God. "… without faith it is impossible to please him: for he that cometh to God must believe that he is, and that he is a rewarder of them that diligently seek him" (Heb. 11:6).

Why would a chapter on faith be inserted in the epistle to the Hebrews when the emphasis of the epistle has been on Jesus' priesthood, the new covenant of grace, and a discussion of the corrupted view of the ceremonial law held by the Jews? It is because some Jewish Christians could not let go of the tradition of sacrifices, ceremonies, meticulous observance of the law, and belief in their lineage from Abraham. These activities were all works-oriented and a source of personal pride for what an observant Jew could accomplish.

When God presented the covenant to Abraham, he "believed God" and he "fell on his face," having faith that God would do all that He said (Gen. 15:6; 17:3). His was a response of faith. The New Testament contains much about faith, and faith is what God has always looked for in His people and what He desires in His people awaiting Jesus' return.

What some Jewish Christians were lacking was faith. These were the Judaizers.[2] They needed faith based on what Jesus Christ had done on the cross, a trust in grace to make a person a new creature, and a love for Christ that empowers one's commitment to Him. Hebrews chapter 11 is a collection of stories of outstanding heroes of faith and an appeal for all Christians to live by faith.

In Hebrews 12, faith is compared to a race. An effective faith requires practice and endurance. The Bible speaks of the "faith of Jesus," a faith which holds on even when there seems to be no hope. Christians must develop a faith that will endure weariness, delay, and hunger. Jesus gives every person a spark of faith (John 1:9), and He strengthens that faith until it can stand testing and trouble.

Each Christian must "make straight paths for his [or her] feet" (Heb. 12:13) and must believe and follow Christ in all things. He or she will stumble into "besetting, impulsive sins," but Jesus is our advocate to pardon sin. For continued, conscious, rebellious sin, there is no sacrifice (Heb. 6:4–6). In the fully committed life, there is peace and holiness. These are attitudes that prepare one to see the Lord.

A Faith That Works by Love

Hebrews 13 turns to routine aspects of church life. It lists five essential Christian qualities we need:

1. **Brotherly love.** One of the most difficult things to do is to love and appreciate those with whom we deal most closely. It may be easier to love someone who lives in another country. However, we cannot be Christians without loving the "brethren."

2. **Hospitality to strangers.** God's people sometimes need to travel in their work, and it is a blessing if they can stay in a home and sit at a table.

3. **Ministry to those in prison.** In some countries, prisoners need help from those who are on the "outside," even food at times. They always need visits and encouragement. This is not an easy task. Prisoners need to be sought out. Non-family visitors may need qualifications. Though it may be difficult, the qualifications are obtainable.

4. **Purity.** In ancient Greek society, sexual promiscuity was the norm. Even in western societies, it is becoming more common. Christians are to be different—especially in this regard.

5. **Contentment with what a person has.** Materialism and money are the new idolatry. The Bible says, "The love of money is the root of all evil" (1 Tim. 6:10). Materialism can cause disorder and complication in one's life. If people buy a boat, they soon find that they do not own the boat; the boat owns them!

The final chapter of Hebrews deals with other aspects of the Christian life. Christians must be loyal to their faith and to the leadership of the church because God uses church leaders to bring blessings to the church members. To find fault with the pastor may cut off an avenue for God to use in giving someone guidance.

Besides loyalty, Christians must show "holy boldness." It takes courage to stand for one's faith, yet this is what God wants each person to do. God calls Christians to have faith and boldness and to be willing to give up everything for Christ, who gave up all for us.

God's people also need to be worshipful. Others can see and feel a worshipful attitude, which is a witness for God.

In the final verses, Paul asks that others pray for him as he works with different people. Through the resurrected Christ, we have peace and blessing. Christians are never alone when doing God's will.

The epistle to the Hebrews presents Jesus Christ crucified and risen again. He is the heavenly High Priest, the Advocate, and the Judge for His people. Hebrews emphasizes the meaning of the new covenant and appeals to God's people to believe in what Jesus has done and consent to the grace that prepares us to meet Jesus when He comes again.

Endnotes

1. The word "substance" comes from the Greek *hupostasis*, which G. Harder renders "confident assurance" (*The New International Dictionary of New Testament Theology* [Grand Rapids, MI: Zondervan Publishing House, 1975, 1986], vol. 1, p. 713).

2. The term "Judaizers" is not used in the Bible. Writers use this term to describe Jewish Christians, who could not let go of circumcision, Jewish traditions, and the ceremonial law. As a matter of principle, they felt that the new Gentile converts needed to observe these Jewish customs and, in effect, become Jews before they could be saved. Later, in a time of apostasy, the popular Christian church changed the day of worship from the seventh day to Sunday, the first day. Many opposed this change, and the ecclesiastical hierarchy termed those who continued to worship on the seventh-day "Judaizers." For more information about the Judaizers, see the following websites: http://www.newadvent.org/cathen/08537a.htm, which is an excellent discussion from the *Catholic Encyclopedia*, and http://www.deusvitae.com/faith/denominations/judaizers.html, which emphasizes the reaction of Paul in his epistles to the Judaizers.

Chapter 40
Letter and Spirit

Forasmuch as ye are manifestly declared to be the epistle of Christ ministered
by us, written not with ink, but with the Spirit of the living God; not in tables of
stone, but in fleshy tables of the heart. And such trust have we through Christ
to God-ward: Not that we are sufficient of ourselves to think any thing as of
ourselves; but our sufficiency is of God; who also hath made us able
ministers of the new testament; not of the letter, but of the spirit:
for the letter killeth, but the spirit giveth life.
2 Corinthians 3:3–6

Moses has always been closely connected with the divine covenant given to Israel. The ten-commandment law of God was the basis for the covenant. The ceremonial law illustrated the covenant. The rainbow was the symbol of God's continued support for His creation. Circumcision was the symbol of adoption, of becoming a member of God's family. The Sabbath is the memorial of God's Creatorship and of His power and grace to change our lives. The focus for the everlasting covenant was the death of the Redeemer to pay for man's sins.

At the time of Jesus and Paul, the "ministry of Moses" had become sterile and corrupt, and the prophesied Messiah had been reduced to a military general. The Jews looked for redemption in meticulous observance of the law of Moses, including the ceremonial law, the moral law, and the many ordinances added to the law by the rabbis. Their descent from Abraham added to their assurance of salvation. It was a pointless, loveless religion (Matt. 5:20).[1]

What was lacking was grace. Grace is the supernatural power of God given to change the lives of men. It is the creative power of God to recreate humans as a "new creature" (2 Cor. 5:17). After Jesus' resurrection from the grave, the apostles understood that Jesus' mission was to establish the kingdom of grace and to change human hearts, saving "his people from their sins" (Matt. 1:21). The messages of the twelve apostles and Paul focused on Jesus' life, death, and resurrection (1 Cor. 15:3, 4). It was only through the power of the cross and the resurrection that human beings could be saved.

God Takes the Initiative

Jeremiah was first to use the term "new covenant" (Jer. 31:31–34).[2] The fundamental principle of the new covenant is that God takes the initiative. By grace, He writes the ten-commandment law in the heart and mind of each believer. "He will so blend our hearts and minds into conformity to His will, that when obeying Him, we shall be but carrying out our own impulses."[3] This principle can be found in the new covenant given to Adam and Eve (Gen. 3:15), given to Abraham (Gen. 17), and given to Israel at Sinai (Exod. 19:4–6; 20:1–17).

After Adam and Eve sinned, God took the initiative and "put enmity between" the serpent and "the woman." This was an act of grace and the first application of the new covenant. Later, God promised Abraham that he would be "a father of many nations" and "all the nations of the earth" would be blessed in his "seed" (Gen. 17:3, 4; 22:18). It was only through grace that God fulfilled these promises.

At Sinai, the preamble of grace came before the terms of the covenant and before the ten-commandment law (Exod. 19:4; 20:2). It was through the power of God to deliver His people from Egypt that they received grace to obey the law, keep God's (My) covenant, and consent to the promises inherent in the Ten Commandments.

Even in the Old Testament, the people lived by faith in the grace of God. The people were to take by faith God's promise to "fight for" them in taking the land (Deut. 1:30). God showed His power in battle by defeating Sihon, king of the Amorites, and Og, king of Bashan. The people had to show faith in His promises (Deut. 2:30; 3:4). They were to seek God, and, in turn, He would not forget the covenant nor forsake them (Deut. 5:29–31). The people were to know that there is one God and were to love Him above all else (Deut. 6:4, 5). God chose them for Himself and gave them memorable blessings (Deut. 7:6, 14). These verses are only a partial listing in just one book, Deuteronomy, demonstrating that the people were to exercise faith and receive grace from God in the Old Testament.[4] To focus on mechanical observance of God's commands corrupts His purpose for those commands, and it is the substance of keeping "the letter of the law"—attempting to obey without God's grace![5]

Grace and Truth Came by Jesus Christ

"For the law was given by Moses, but grace and truth came by Jesus Christ" (John 1:17). Now that Jesus had become our sacrifice, risen from the dead, and ascended to heaven, the mystery of Godliness became clear. Paul taught the people to have faith in Jesus and His sacrifice on the cross. Lacking faith and strictly adhering to the letter of the law was to follow the old covenant. While the letter of the law is "holy, just and good" (Rom. 7:12), it can only show a person where he has sinned and bring condemnation and death (Rom. 3:20; 7:5; 1 Cor. 15:56). The law *cannot* save. It is only by the power of God through the Holy Spirit that a person becomes alive to Christ and can obey the law from the heart.[6]

> Indeed, in view of this fact, what once had splendor [the glory of the Law in the face of Moses] has come to have no splendor at all, because of [compared to] the overwhelming glory that exceeds *and* excels it [the glory of the Gospel in the face of Jesus Christ]. (2 Cor. 3:10, AMP).

It is God's plan to write the law in the heart of the sinner, changing him by grace. The Spirit gives life (2 Cor. 3:6; Rom. 8:1–4).

The letter of the law "was glorious" (2 Cor. 3:7, 11). As a sacred document, the Ten Commandments give a picture of the holy life when motivated by love. It was God who gave the Ten Commandments, the civil law, and even the sacrifices and ceremonies. The ten-commandment law—the moral law—reveals sin. The civil law keeps order in society. The sacrifices and ceremonies pointed forward to the promised Messiah.

Yet, none of these laws can save (2 Cor. 3:7–11). They can only lead a person to Christ to receive salvation, grace, and mercy in time of need (Heb. 4:15).

Ministries of Moses and Paul Compared

Paul's exposition on this topic in his second letter to the Corinthians begins with chapter 2, verse 14 and runs through to chapter 4, verse 6. Chapter 3 contains the main points. The table below, which compares Moses' ministry with that of Paul, gives needed background. Take enough time to digest what the comparison is saying.

The Old Covenant Represented by Moses' Ministry	The New Covenant Represented by Paul's Ministry
"Written … with ink" (2 Cor. 3:3)	"Written … with the Spirit of the living God" (2 Cor. 3:3)
"On tablets of stone," "in letters on stone" (2 Cor. 3:3, 7, NIV)	"On tablets of human hearts" (2 Cor. 3:3, NIV)
"The letter kills" (2 Cor. 3:6, NIV)	"The Spirit gives life" and "freedom" (2 Cor. 3:6, 17)
"The ministration of death," "the ministration of condemnation" (2 Cor. 3:7, 9)	"The ministration of righteousness" (2 Cor. 3:9)
A "glory" that "was fading away" (2 Cor. 3:11, NIV)	"Ever-increasing glory" "that which remains" (2 Cor. 3:18, 10, NIV)
"A veil that covers their hearts" (2 Cor. 3:15, NIV)	"The veil is taken away" (2 Cor. 3:17, NIV)

The comparison is explained in a selection from Skip MacCarty's book, *In Granite or Ingrained?*

Many interpreters view this passage from a dispensational, historical perspective, understanding the characteristics in the left column as representative of the teaching of the Old Testament, and more specifically of God's covenant with Israel at Sinai. These same interpreters understand the characteristics in the right column to refer to the full gospel teaching of the New Testament which was lacking in the Old. But such a strictly historical interpretation would leave all Old Testament people without hope of salvation.

In reality the left-column characteristics describe a lost condition, not a partially enlightened salvation. They describe stone cold hearts that resist the appeal of God's covenant. And the right-column characteristics describe the results of the Holy Spirit's work in the life of "anyone [who] turns to the Lord" (3:16) and is "being transformed into his likeness" (3:18). This describes a saving condition fully experienced by all believers in both Old and New Testament eras.

In other words, Paul employed these terms primarily to describe experiential, not historical, conditions which apply to all believers (right column) and unbelievers (left column) of all time. Thus, the characteristics in these two columns represent experientially-based, timeless, and eternal truths describing responses to the gospel by believers and unbelievers, rather than different gospels (or even differing levels of understanding of the one true gospel) ordained by God for separate historical eras.[7]

Moses had a strong faith relationship with God. He talked to God "face to face." He obeyed God even in fulfilling His most difficult requirement, which was to leave the quiet life of herding sheep and take up the immensely difficult task of leading Israel out of Egypt. He was meek and humble, always willing to listen to people. He selflessly refused God's proposal to make of him a strong nation. The real Moses was quite different from the notion that later grew in the minds of the Jews. In Moses' last message to Israel, he reaffirmed the close relationship between love for God and keeping the Ten Commandments.[8]

The Veil Taken Away in Christ

After Moses had dashed the tables of the law upon the rocks because the people had broken their covenant (Exod. 32:19), he interceded for the people and brought them to repentance. God again called Moses up into the mountain and instructed him to bring two tables of stone that Moses had hewn from the rock. Afterward, God put Moses into a cleft in the rock, and Moses saw God's back as He passed. Then God renewed the new or Abrahamic covenant with Israel (Exod. 34:9–11). Moses presented the people with the tables of stone on which God had again written the Ten Commandments with His finger.

When Moses returned to camp, his face still shone with the glory of God (Exod. 34:29–33). He had to wear a veil to obscure the brightness while he talked with the priests and elders. Paul used this veiling to illustrate the unbelief of the Jews in his day. Lifting the veil meant understanding the purpose of the sanctuary sacrifices and priesthood. It also meant grasping the effectiveness of Jesus' true sacrifice and His heavenly priesthood.

In Paul's day the Jews followed the letter of the law and meticulously performed the sacrifices and rituals for pardon from sin. In addition, they looked to their descent from Abraham and added hundreds of detailed ordinances to the law to assure them of salvation. Their obedience to law, ritual, and the ceremonies was formal and external. This was old covenant living at its worst, which was to bypass grace and attempt to obey the law without a change in their motives. Only God can reach the heart and write His law there. Only by grace can a person truly keep the law from the heart. Truth must be daily applied to the problems of life to be a living, active force.

When the Jews spoke of following "Moses," they referred to the moral, civil, and ceremonial law in Moses' writings, including the sacrifices, rituals, and feasts (Luke 16:29). Paul compared the veil that obscured Moses' face to the difficulty of ancient Israel to find Christ through the sanctuary services. They had perverted the gospel into a system of righteousness by works (Rom. 9:31–33).

> But their minds were blinded: for until this day remaineth the same veil untaken away in the reading of the old testament; which veil is done away in Christ. But even unto this day, when Moses is read, the veil is upon their heart. (2 Cor. 3:14, 15)

Sacrifice and temple ritual were intended to illustrate the work of the coming Sin Bearer. As with any illustration, it was limited—as if looking through a veil at best. Even more, the unbelief of the majority of the people in the redemptive work of Christ obscured the meaning of the sacrifices and temple services. Unbelief led people to go through round after round of sacrifices and temple services, expecting that these exercises, in themselves, would provide pardon for sin and salvation.[9]

For some Jewish Christians, continued dependence on temple ritual became a veil obscuring the redemptive work of Christ on the cross. Christ had already fulfilled the purpose of the sacrifices and ceremonies, which were now no longer needed. Jesus Christ is the glorious reality and the full revelation of the love of God.

> In fact, their minds were grown hard *and* calloused [they had become dull and had lost the power of understanding]; for until this present day, when the Old Testament [the old covenant] is being read, that same veil still lies [on their hearts], not being lifted [to reveal] that in Christ it is made void *and* done away. (2 Cor. 3:14, AMP)

Two phrases in the statement, "when the Old Testament [old covenant] is being read, that same veil still lies [on their hearts]," need to be explained. First, what is meant by the old covenant? For the answer to that question, see chapter 15, "The Historical Old Covenant." Second, Hebrews 8–10 describes the Jewish perception of the earthly sacrificial system and priesthood as the "covenant," which was faulty, decayed, and about to vanish. It was the ceremonial law that was composed of ordinances of divine service and an earthly sanctuary with holy furniture and the ark of the covenant. Nowhere in Scripture is the idea that the sacrificial system and priesthood are the covenant.[10]

Hebrews 8–10 describes the Jews dependence on temple rituals and sacrifices for their salvation. Associated with this was circumcision, meticulous keeping of the "law of Moses," and their lineage from Abraham. Paul describes this as the "old covenant." While all these things pointed to the true sacrifice of Jesus on Calvary for pardon and salvation, many Jews forgot their Redeemer. Continual dependence on these things was to deny what Christ had done on Calvary and to fall into "temple idolatry" and lose salvation.

The earthly sacrificial system is compared to the true sacrifice of Christ, and the earthly priesthood is compared to Christ's heavenly priesthood and mediation of the new covenant. The veil of unbelief hid the true meaning of the sacrifices, which was to illustrate the true sacrifice of Jesus on the cross, paying the penalty for our sins.

Sacrifices Illustrate the Covenant

The sacrifices and the ceremonies were to illustrate the mission of the coming Sin Bearer. The glory of the Mosaic dispensation in sacrifices and rituals was only the reflected glory of Christ, which was not fully revealed until Christ came to earth. The reflected glory of Christ is also the veil through which people looked to see the coming Redeemer. To continue looking through the veil of the sacrifices and ceremonies after Christ had come was to deny the full disclosure of His glory. Even worse, the unbelieving majority had neglected the Messiah, to whom the sacrifices pointed. Forgetting the Messiah in the Old Testament writings was what prepared them to reject Jesus as the Messiah.

At the time of Paul, some Jewish Christians continued to "look through the veil" of the ceremonial law. The ceremonial law, splendid as it was, obscured the glorious truth of Jesus Christ and the full revelation of the love of God. Christ removed the veil and fulfilled the sacrifices and ceremonies. They are no longer needed. "Even to this day when Moses is read, a veil covers their hearts. But whenever anyone turns to the Lord, the veil is taken away" (2 Cor. 3:15, 16, NIV).

Now that Jesus has come, there is freedom from the burden of ritual and ceremony. The sinner can now see Jesus directly by faith and can more fully understand the character of God. Beholding Him changes the sinner.

> But we all, with open face [unveiled vision] beholding as in a glass the glory of the Lord, are changed into the same image from glory to glory, even as by the Spirit of the Lord. (2 Cor. 3:18)

When Jews, led by the Spirit, believed on Christ, they could then understand the true significance of the Jewish economy and realize that Christ, in His own person and work, constituted the essence of the sacrificial system and the entire law of Moses.

Obedience Through God's Grace and Love

As part of His answer to an inquiring scribe about "the first commandment of all," Jesus said:

> … thou shalt love the Lord thy God with all thy heart, and with all thy soul, and with all thy mind, and with all thy strength: this is the first commandment. And the second is like, namely this, Thou shalt love thy neighbour as thyself. There is none other commandment greater than these. (Mark 12:30, 31)

The essence of the ten-commandment law is that we love God and then love our neighbor as ourselves. Actually, loving like that may be more difficult than keeping the Ten Commandments. Let us take this a step further: If a person does not love God, he is proud and unbelieving. If he does not love his fellow man, he is selfish. Pride, unbelief, and selfishness make up the sinful nature. Such a person cannot do merciful things except by his own sinful motives. It is only by the grace and power of God that a person can be lifted out of his pride, unbelief, and selfishness. It is only through grace that a person can truly observe the law of God.

Faith does not eliminate the ten-commandment law. Hear what Paul says: "Do we make void the law through faith? God forbid: yea, we establish the law" (Rom. 3:31).

The gospel of Jesus Christ is a living principle, not a dead system of rules. Through faith in God and our consent to the work of grace, people can obey the law, making the law even more splendid. The sacrifices and ceremonies were superb, even if temporary. That which is lasting and real—the sacrifice of Jesus and His resurrection—is even more majestic. Through Jesus, the law becomes a reality in the life. The true sacrifice of Christ provides pardon for sin and salvation for humankind. Our victory is available only through the grace and power of Jesus Christ.[11]

Endnotes

1. Before meeting Christ, Paul measured himself by Jewish qualifications. The list he gives illustrates what Jews trusted in. "Though I might also have confidence in the flesh. If any other man thinketh that he hath whereof he might trust in the flesh, I more: circumcised the eighth day, of the stock of Israel, of the tribe of Benjamin, an Hebrew of the Hebrews; as touching the law, a Pharisee; concerning zeal, persecuting the church; touching the righteousness which is in the law, blameless" (Philippians 3:4–6).

2. Jeremiah's contemporary, Ezekiel, describes the New Covenant, including the covenantal promise of the Lord's being their God: "A new heart also will I give you, and a new spirit will I put within you: and I will take away the stony heart out of your flesh, and I will give you an heart of flesh. And I will put my spirit within you, and cause you to walk in my statutes, and ye shall keep my judgments, and do them. And ye shall dwell in the land that I gave to your fathers; and ye shall be my people, and I will be your God" (Ezek. 36:26–38).

3. Ellen G. White, *The Desire of Ages* (Nampa, ID: Pacific Press Publishing Association, 1898), p. 668.

4. In Israel's trek through the Sinai desert, God was dealing with an uneducated group of people who had lived alongside opulence and idolatry for 215 years. The people of Israel were decidedly concrete in their way of thinking. They could understand the visible presence of God and His power in giving them victory over their enemies. They could understand the requirement to obey the Ten Commandments and avoid idolatry. They had difficulty with abstractions. The abstract term "faith" occurs just twice in the Old Testament ("no faith," in Deut. 32:20, and the "just shall live by his faith," in Hab. 2:4) By contrast, it occurs 229 times in the New Testament!

5. Paul also used "letter" and "spirit" in Romans 2: "Therefore if the uncircumcision keep the righteousness of the law, shall not his uncircumcision be counted for circumcision? And shall not uncircumcision which is by nature, if it fulfil the law, judge thee, who by the letter and circumcision dost transgress the law? For he is not a Jew, which is one outwardly; neither is that circumcision, which is outward in the flesh: But he is a Jew, which is one inwardly; and circumcision is that of the heart, in the spirit, and not in the letter; whose praise is not of men, but of God" (Rom. 2:26–29).

6. The law cannot provide salvation. "By the law, is the knowledge of sin" (Rom. 3:20). Salvation is given only through the sacrifice of Jesus on Calvary (Rom. 3–5, Heb. 9:26–28, John 3:16). It is by grace, mediated by the Holy Spirit, that lives are changed.

Neither can people change their motives of themselves. Should people attempt to change their life and be saved—even by engaging in religious activities—they will only be acting out the faulty and ineffective old covenant. Jesus is the mediator of the new covenant. If people consent to the work of grace, God will write His laws in their heart and change their motives.

The law continues to have an essential function. It is the ten commandment laws of God that are written in the heart. The ten commandment laws are the law of love, the law of liberty. "For this is the love of God, that we keep his commandments: and his commandments are not grievous" (1 John 5:3). "But whoso looketh into the perfect law of liberty, and continueth therein, he being not a forgetful hearer, but a doer of the work, this man shall be blessed in his deed" (James 1:25).

7.   Skip MacCarty, *In Granite or Ingrained?* (Berrien Springs, MI: Andrews University Press, 2007), pp. 119, 120.

8.   Love was to be the motive for keeping God's law (Deut. 6:2–5; 11:1, 13, 22; 19:9; 30:6, 16, 20). Jesus cited the "[law of] Moses" regarding offerings after purification (Matt. 8:4; Luke 2:22; 5:14); a woman's rights in divorce (Matt. 19:7, 8; Mark 10:3, 4); the law of the Levirate marriage (Matt. 22:24); the authority of Moses (Matt. 23:2; Mark 7:10; Luke 16:31); prophecies about the Messiah (Luke 24:44); and caring for matters of health on the Sabbath (John 7:23). Paul declared that no one is justified by "the law of Moses" (Acts 13:39). Circumcision was linked at the Jerusalem counsel with keeping "the law of Moses" (Acts 15:5). The Pharisees considered themselves to be "Moses' disciples" while accusing the parents of the man born blind, whom Jesus healed, of being Jesus' disciples (John 9:28). Jesus explained the prophecies in "Moses" concerning Himself (Luke 24:27) and declared that Moses wrote of Him (John 5:46). Philip considered Jesus to be the Messiah, based on the prophecies in "Moses" (John 1:45). "The law was given by Moses, but grace and truth came by Jesus Christ" (John 1:17).

9.   For an explanation of the veil of unbelief and the veil of the ceremonial law, see F. D. Nichol, *The Seventh-day Adventist Bible Commentary* (Hagerstown, MD: Review and Herald Publishing Association, 1980), vol. 6, pp. 842–851; and E. J. Waggoner, *The Everlasting Covenant,* (Berrien Springs, MI: Glad Tidings Publishers, 2002), pp. 237–243.

10.   Yet, it would seem that Paul is describing more than just the ten-commandment law. This is the only place that the exact phrase "old covenant" (Greek *tēs palaias diathēkē*) occurs in the New Testament.

11.   It is a distinct problem when God's people "fall away" (Heb. 6:4–6). One who is born of God—a new creature "in Christ"—overcomes the world through faith, needs not sin, does righteousness, and keeps God's commandments (1 John 5:4, 18; 2:1, 5, 29; 3:6, 9, 24; 1 Peter 1:23; 2 Cor. 5:17).

Chapter 41
Foolish Galatians

O foolish Galatians, who hath bewitched you, that ye should not obey the truth,
before whose eyes Jesus Christ hath been evidently set forth, crucified among you?
This only would I learn of you, Received ye the Spirit by the works of the law,
or by the hearing of faith? Are ye so foolish? having begun
in the Spirit, are ye now made perfect by the flesh?
Galatians 3:1–3

Paul was honest with the Galatians. They had taken actions that denied the covenant and the effectiveness of the sacrifice of Jesus Christ. It was a step back into outmoded Judaism.

Paul pointed out that the function of the ceremonial law was to point to Jesus as the Messiah and that He fulfilled the ceremonial law. Christians are not saved by animal sacrifices or the performance of temple rituals. Salvation was and is only through Jesus Christ.

However, there were certain Jewish Christians who believed that a man must be circumcised and become a Jew before he could be saved. These men began to follow Paul to the churches he had established, preaching that they must be circumcised and perform other temple rituals to be saved. To return to ceremony and tradition was to deny Christ. Paul met this issue in a number of his epistles and the carefully written epistle to the Hebrews.

The Galatians were Celts who settled in the mid-portion of what is now Turkey. Paul wrote his letter to the Galatians early, perhaps the earliest document in the New Testament. Paul made strong comments about the Jewish Christians who tried to recruit new Gentile converts to observe the ceremonial law, in essence, to become Jews. It was a serious issue, which threatened to divide the church.

"What Must I Do to be Saved?"

Paul and the other twelve apostles quickly learned that the one question that people have is, "What must I do to be saved?" (Acts 16:30–34; cf. Acts 2:36–38; 8:36–38). Paul learned in Athens that arguments are not successful in converting people to Jesus. After the experience, he wrote the Corinthians, "I determined not to know anything among you, save Jesus Christ, and Him crucified" (Acts 17:22–34; 1 Cor. 2:2).

As Paul raised churches in one city after another, his apostleship was confirmed as people were converted and received the Holy Ghost. In the new churches, lives changed, new hope emerged, and new believers rejoiced in their first love.

The Jerusalem Council

There was a controversy in Jerusalem. Many Messianic Jews felt that the Gentile converts needed to be circumcised and take part in the Temple services as outlined in the books of Moses for participants in the covenant. Those of this viewpoint were the "Judaizers," a term that was originally used to describe Messianic Jews in the early church who held onto the ceremonial law. Later on, the Catholic Church used it to describe those who continued to keep the seventh-day Sabbath for worship rather than Sunday.

About AD 52, the Jerusalem Council met to discuss what should be expected of Gentile converts. Paul, Barnabas, and Titus attended the Council to reassure the apostles that Paul was preaching the gospel of Christ. Peter, Paul, and Barnabas gave reports of Gentiles receiving the gospel and being given the Holy Spirit (Acts 15:7, 8). When the apostles in Jerusalem heard of the grace given to Paul in his work for the Gentiles they gladly accepted him and the gospel that he preached (Gal. 2:6–9). After discussion, the council reached a conclusion with good will and general agreement. Here is how James worded their conclusion:

> Wherefore my sentence is, that we trouble not them, which from among the Gentiles are turned to God: but that we write unto them, that they abstain from pollutions of idols, and from fornication, and from things strangled, and from blood. For Moses of old time hath in every city them that preach him, being read in the synagogues every Sabbath day. (Acts 15:19–21)[1]

These four items had to do with ritual. Fornication was against one of the Ten Commandments, but it was also a practice in some of the religions of the day. A delegation carried the report to the Gentile church at Antioch. The Antioch church received the decision from Jerusalem, and this became the policy of the church.

Unfortunately, the issue continued to raise controversy in the church. On one occasion in Antioch, Peter and some of the other leaders broke off association with Gentiles because of the influence of certain visitors from James. Peter's shunning of the Gentiles reinforced the traditional exclusiveness of the Jews and precipitated a crisis that could have split the church. Paul acted quickly and "withstood [Peter] to his face" (Gal. 2:11–14). The Holy Spirit prevailed, and Peter accepted the rebuke graciously. Some of the Judaizers followed Paul in his missionary journeys to mislead the new converts. There are passages in Romans, First and Second Corinthians, and other epistles dealing with this issue. Paul wrote the epistle to the Hebrews, especially urging belief in Jesus Christ rather than dependence on the ceremonial law.

Galatians 3

About six years after the Council (AD 58), Paul had to face this controversy in the Galatian churches. He began in chapter 3 with the words, "O foolish Galatians" and followed them with this thought:

> This only would I learn of you, Received ye the Spirit by the works of the law, or by
> the hearing of faith? Are ye so foolish? having begun in the Spirit, are ye now made
> perfect by the flesh? (Gal. 3:2, 3)

Are Christians, he argued, going to revert to a false dependence on the law and tradition, or are they to have faith in Jesus' sacrifice? God accounted Abraham's faith to him for righteousness (Rom. 4:3). He did not earn the promises by keeping the law. The faith that Paul is talking about refers to a personal relationship between God and the children of Abraham (Gal. 3:29). This faith includes the promise of a Messiah to come (Gal. 3:8, 16, 18).

> Even as Abraham believed God, and it was accounted to him for righteousness. Know
> ye therefore that they which are of faith, the same are the children of Abraham. …
> That the blessing of Abraham might come on the Gentiles through Jesus Christ; that
> we might receive the promise of the Spirit through faith. (Gal. 3:6–7, 14)

The Bible describes the covenant given to Abraham as an everlasting covenant (see Gen. 17). Paul also described it as the new covenant with "the house of Israel" (Heb. 8:8, 10; 10:16; cf. Gal. 3:7, 9, 14). The covenant passes through Abraham's seed.

> Now to Abraham and his seed were the promises made. He saith not, And to seeds,
> as of many; but as of one, And to thy seed, which is Christ. And this I say, that the
> covenant, that was confirmed before of God in Christ, the law, which was four hun-
> dred and thirty years after, cannot disannul, that it should make the promise of none
> effect. For if the inheritance be of the law, it is no more of promise: but God gave it
> to Abraham by promise. Wherefore then serveth the law? It was added because of
> transgressions, till the seed should come to whom the promise was made; and it was
> ordained by angels in the hand of a mediator. (Gal. 3:16–19)

The law—either ceremonial or moral—coming 430 years after the covenant with Abraham, cannot disannul the covenant. Keeping the law is not a way to obtain the promises of God and enhance their value, nor to modify the provisions of the covenant in any way. The law was not an alternative means of salvation, neither did it create a system of righteousness by works. The law was added, or appended, because of transgressions "till the seed should come …" The people had been in Egypt for 215 years. They were in bondage, were exposed to paganism and immorality and were insensitive to sin. Only by God's moral law being brought into sharp, objective focus, could the Israelites be made aware that they were sinners in need of salvation.

In this same chapter, Paul speaks of the "works of the law" (verses 2, 5, 10), "made perfect by the flesh" (verse 3), and the "curse of the law" (verse 13) with its impossibilities. As he continued writing, he referred only to the "law" (verses 11, 12, 17–19, 21, 23, 24). The "works of the law" do not bring the Holy Spirit; they do not allow for growth in grace; and they do not bring the perfection that is available only through Christ.

Before Faith Came

The faith that Paul is talking about is not a historical event, a dispensation, or a corporate status. It refers to a personal relationship with God. Thus, today, those who have faith in God are the children of Abraham (Gal. 3:7, 29). But before faith came, we were kept under the law, shut up unto the faith which should afterwards be revealed (Gal. 3:23).

Before a person has come to Christ, the law serves as a guardian, a "schoolmaster" to protect him. A natural question arises: Can a person keeping the law be saved, though not yet having come to Christ? The law is "holy and just and good" (Rom. 7:12). However, the Holy Spirit is working with all people, many of who do not yet know of the law (John 1:9). Under the influence of the Holy Spirit, many are saved who do not yet know Jesus Christ or the law (Rom. 2:14–16) but are following Christ by faith. "And if ye be Christ's, then are ye Abraham's seed, and heirs according to the promise" (Gal. 3:29). This is the main message of this chapter. It is a repetition of verse 7, which says, "Know ye therefore that they which are of faith, the same are the children of Abraham." To believe and follow Jesus Christ gives us all the privileges of the covenant given to Abraham.

Several times in this chapter, I have stated that a person cannot be saved by keeping the law. This is true, but the point needs some additional explanation. It is true that a person cannot be saved by unfeeling, mechanical observance of the commandments. Highly disciplined people can "keep the commandments," or better said, they "can keep from breaking the commandments." Another way to say this is that they keep the commandments well enough to stay out of jail! When life is changed by grace, and the law is written on the heart, people will keep the commandments out of love for God and their fellow human beings.

Rote observance of the commandments is not pleasing to God (Matt. 5:20). Jesus taught that we must keep the commandments from a heart of love. The Ten Commandments define what it means to love God and our fellow man. Many New Testament passages indicate that God expects us to keep His commandments (Rom. 13:9; Eph. 6:2; 1 Cor. 7:19; James 2:11; John 14:15; 1 John 3:4; Rev. 12:17; 14:12; 22:14).[2] In the new covenant, God promised to write the law within the believer's heart, that is, to change the believer's life so he or she keeps the law out of love that God put in his or her heart.

Endnotes

1. Their assessment was in harmony with that which the Holy Ghost revealed through Moses: "For it seemed good to the Holy Ghost, and to us, to lay upon you no greater burden than these necessary things; That ye abstain from meats offered to **idols**, and from **blood**, and from things **strangled**, and from **fornication** [*porneia*]: from which if ye keep yourselves, ye shall do well. Fare ye well" (Acts 15:28, 29).

    Notice the requirements of the Gentile sojourners in Leviticus: "Therefore I said unto the children of Israel, No soul nger that sojourneth among you eat blood" (Lev. 17:12).

died of itself, or that which was torn with beasts, whether it be one of your
ash his clothes, and bathe himself in water, and be unclean until the even:

d my judgments, and shall not commit any of these abominations; neither
at sojourneth among you" (Lev. 18:26).

ourselves molten gods: I am the LORD your God" (Lev. 19:4).

day Adventist Bible Commentary (Hagerstown, MD: Review and Herald
p. 806–810.

versions translate the first part of Revelation 22:14, based on fourth centu-
hose who wash their robes [Greek *plunontes tas stolas autōn*]," the earliest
, translate the first part as: "do His commandments [Greek *poiountes tas*

Tertullian (AD 145–220) wrote: "Thus, too, again 'Blessed they who act according to the precepts, that they may have power over the tree of life and over the gates, for entering into the holy city. Dogs, sorcerers, fornicators, murderers, out!' " (Tertullian, On Modesty, chap. 9, available at http://www.tertullian.org/anf/anf04/anf04-19.htm#P1585_463823, accessed 3/8/13).

Cyprian, Bishop of Carthage (AD 200–258) referenced the verse: "Also in the Apocalypse: 'And I saw a Lamb standing on Mount Sion, and with Him a hundred and forty and four thousand; and they had His name and the name of His Father written on their foreheads.' Also in the same place: 'I am Alpha and Omega, the first and the last, the beginning and the end. Blessed are they that do His commandments, that they may have authority over the tree of life' " (Cyprian, *The Ante-Nicene Fathers* [New York: Charles Scribner's Sons, 1903], vol. 5, p. 525). The first Church Father to quote Rev. 22:14 as "wash their robes" was Athanasius, Bishop of Alexandria in the fourth century (AD 298–373).

Chapter 42

The New Testament Covenant

And for this cause he is the mediator of the new testament, that by means of death, for the redemption of the transgressions that were under the first testament, they which are called might receive the promise of eternal inheritance.
Hebrews 9:15

Most of the discussions of the covenant are in the Old Testament. People of that period usually thought of there being just one covenant. The new covenant prophesied by Jeremiah implied that there was also an old covenant, "which my covenant they brake" (Jer. 31:32), but this concept was little discussed at the time.

In the New Testament, we have the story of Jesus Christ. He is the focus, the fulfillment, and the Mediator of the everlasting covenant, also called the new covenant.

How do we know that there is a New Testament covenant? God gave Abraham the everlasting covenant, which was to extend to his seed after him (Gen. 17:7–10, 19). This included Israel through their entire history and the Christian church. Paul summarized this in one verse: "If ye be Christ's, then are ye Abraham's seed, and heirs according to the promise" (Gal. 3:29).

Paul discusses and compares these concepts in Hebrews, Romans 2, 2 Corinthians 3, Galatians, and Ephesians.

All Families Blessed Through Abraham

God gave a foretaste of the new covenant to Adam and Eve, to Noah, and to Abraham and his descendants. The covenant extended to Jews and Gentiles (Gal. 3:29; 1 Peter 2:9). Jesus is the mediator of the new covenant.

Several events in Abraham's life illustrate events that would occur in Jesus' life. God called Abram out of Haran and promised, "Thou shalt be a blessing: ... and in thee shall all families of the earth be blessed" (Gen. 12:2, 3). The descendants of Abraham received this promise in the years to come.

> Understand, then, that *those who believe* are children of Abraham. The Scripture foresaw that God would justify the Gentiles by faith, and announced the gospel in advance to Abraham: "All nations will be blessed through you."
>
> So *those who have faith* are blessed along with Abraham, the man of faith.... That the blessing of Abraham might come on the Gentiles through Jesus Christ; that we

might receive the promise of the Spirit through faith. Now to Abraham and his seed were the promises made. He saith not, And to seeds, as of many; but as of one, And to thy seed, which is Christ. And this I say, that the covenant, that was confirmed before of God in Christ, the law, which was four hundred and thirty years after, cannot disannul, that it should make the promise of none effect. For if the inheritance be of the law, it is no more of promise: but God gave it to Abraham by promise. (Gal. 3:7–9, 14, 16–18, emphasis supplied)

The blessing to "all families" was the gospel given to Jews and Gentiles through faith. God included a significant phrase when He gave Abraham the covenant in detail. In addition to promising Abraham that he would become "a father of many nations," God promised that His covenant with Abraham would extend to all his descendants. God repeats the phrase "thy seed after thee" five times for emphasis. God certainly did not want the object of His purpose to be missed!

And I will establish my covenant between me and thee and *thy seed after thee* in their generations for an everlasting covenant, to be a God unto thee, and to *thy seed after thee*. And I will give unto thee, and to *thy seed after thee*, the land wherein thou art a stranger, all the land of Canaan, for an everlasting possession; and I will be their God. And God said unto Abraham, Thou shalt keep my covenant therefore, thou, and *thy seed after thee* in their generations. This is my covenant, which ye shall keep, between me and you and *thy seed after thee;* Every man child among you shall be circumcised. (Gen. 17:7–10, emphasis supplied)

Illustrations in the Life of Abraham

Shortly after Abram had rescued Lot from the kings of the east, God again presented His promises to Abram. God would be his shield, and Abram did not need to become a man of war. God would give him a son and heir, and his descendants would become as the stars in the sky for number. "And he believed in the Lord; and he counted it to him for righteousness" (Gen. 15:6).

God followed these promises with the promise of land, which was more than Abram could believe. He asked God, "Whereby shall I know that I shall inherit it?" (Gen. 15:8).

God answered Abram with a covenant ceremony according to the customs of the people at that time. In the course of this covenant, "a deep sleep fell upon Abram; and, lo, an horror of great darkness fell upon him" (Gen. 15:12). To experience "great darkness" is to look into an eternity without life or God. That was Jesus' experience on the cross of Calvary.

When Abraham was 100 years old, and Sarah was ninety, Isaac was born as promised (Gen. 17:19; 21:5). When Isaac was between seventeen and twenty years old, God came to Abraham again.[1] "And he said, Take now thy son, thine only son Isaac, whom thou lovest, and get thee into the land of Moriah;

and offer him there for a burnt offering upon one of the mountains which I will tell thee of" (Gen. 22:2).

One can only imagine the terror and sorrow this command brought to Abraham. Without explanation, Abraham took Isaac and two servants and set out on their journey. In response to Isaac's question, Abraham said, "God will provide himself a lamb for a burnt offering" (Gen. 22:8). When the purpose of the journey became clear, Isaac willingly complied. He already knew and obeyed the voice of God. Providentially, a voice from heaven interrupted the sacrifice at the last minute, and Isaac was freed. A ram, caught in a thicket, took his place as the sacrifice.

Through that event, another Son learned that the sacrifice would be an "only begotten Son."

Momentum of the Abrahamic Covenant of Grace

God presented the covenant to Abraham seven times during his life. Yet, it was a single covenant, presented seven times. God also gave the covenant to Isaac, to Jacob, to Moses at the burning bush, and to the elders of Israel when Moses and Aaron returned to Egypt to confront Pharaoh (Exod. 4:28–31; 6:3–9). At Sinai God gave the people the covenant He called "My covenant," an indication that it was a covenant previously given.

> Ye have seen what I did unto the Egyptians, and how I bare you on eagles' wings, and brought you unto myself. Now therefore, if ye will obey my voice indeed, and keep *my covenant*, then ye shall be a peculiar treasure unto me above all people: for all the earth is mine: And ye shall be unto me a kingdom of priests, and an holy nation. These are the words which thou shalt speak unto the children of Israel. (Exod. 19:4–6).

This was the covenant of grace, promised through the strength of God, which He exhibited in His deliverance of Israel from Egyptian bondage. The people ignored the promise of grace, made their own promises to obey, and conducted their own ratification ceremony—a ceremony that was fundamentally different from the ratification of Christ, which took place at Calvary! Their covenant of human promises was the *historical* old covenant, and it lasted just forty-six days.

The Covenant Renewed

After the people had broken their covenant, Moses interceded with God four times until God accepted Israel into the covenant again.

> Then the Lord said: "I am making a covenant with you. Before all your people I will do wonders never before done in any nation in all the world. The people you live among will see how awesome is the work that I, the Lord, will do for you." (Exod. 34:10, NIV).

Was this a renewal of the *historical* old covenant, which the people broke? No, it was not! It was the renewal of the "Abrahamic covenant" (Exod. 19:4–6). In the new covenant, which is identified as the covenant of God, God takes the initiative to do for humans what they cannot do for themselves. To Adam and Eve after they sinned, God "put enmity between" Satan "and the woman" (Gen. 3:15). God would restore all that was lost, destroy sin and Satan, and save mankind, and He would do this through His own suffering. God also gave the new covenant to Abraham (Gal. 3:7–9, 14, 16–18).

How could God "make" a covenant, when the covenant ceremony would not take place until Jesus' sacrifice at Calvary? The everlasting covenant of God, which He calls "My Covenant" and which Jeremiah called the new covenant, refers to the covenant made by God in eternity before the creation of this earth. We humans had no part in making this covenant, and we cannot break it or modify it. All we can do is humbly bow before Him, trusting in what God will do. This covenant was "announced" to Adam and Eve in Genesis 3:15.

Based on the everlasting covenant, God then made a covenant with humans, which required their response. Abraham believed God (Gen. 15:6) and "fell on his face" (Gen. 17:3), knowing that God would do what He had promised. The Abrahamic covenant was comprised of God's everlasting covenant and Abraham's faith response.

The New Covenant

Ten years into the captivity, God gave the promise of a new covenant. He did this to reassure His people that He would restore them after the completion of the seventy years. It was a prophecy of what God would do, when "the days come." He would put His "law in their inward parts, and write it in their hearts; and ... be their God." (Jer. 31:31–34).[2]

"My covenant," the everlasting covenant of God, or the Abrahamic covenant was confirmed by Jesus' sacrifice at Calvary. The parts of the ceremonial law that pointed forward to Jesus' sacrifice were fulfilled. People no longer looked for a Redeemer through the sacrifices but could now look back by faith to the completed sacrifice of Christ. The Levitical priesthood ended but the priesthood continued in the heavenly Melchizedek priesthood of Jesus Christ.[3]

Jesus now mediates the New Testament—the new covenant—through the blood He shed on the cross (Matt. 26:28; Heb. 9:15; 12:24). Through His blood, symbolically presented in the heavenly sanctuary, He pardons our sins.[4] Using the same words He used at Sinai, God extends the covenant to the New Testament church (Exod. 19:4–6; 1 Peter 2:9):

> But you are a chosen people, a royal priesthood, a holy nation, a people belonging to God, that you may declare the praises of him who called you out of darkness into his wonderful light. (1 Peter 2:9, NIV)

The wording and meaning are the same. Christians are included in what God gave Israel at Sinai. As Paul said, "If ye be Christ's, then are ye Abraham's seed" (Gal. 3:29). There is one parent stock—Israel.

If some of the branches have been broken off, and you, though a wild olive shoot, have been grafted in among the others and now share in the nourishing sap from the olive root do not boast over those branches. If you do, consider this: You do not support the root, but the root supports you.... They were broken off because of unbelief, and you stand by faith. Do not be arrogant, but be afraid. (Rom. 11:17, 18, 20, NIV)

The Christian church is "Abraham's seed" and is grafted into the root of God's chosen people. The church, Jews and Gentiles alike, now must bear the privileges and responsibilities of the covenant. There are other passages in the New Testament on the covenant in the writings of Paul.[5]

Endnotes

1. At the time of the test, Isaac was described as being a "lad" (Heb. *na'ar*) able to carry wood (Gen. 22:5, 6, 12). Joseph was described as being a *na'ar* at age 17 and was still a *na'ar* at age 30 (Gen. 37:2; 41:12, 46).

2. Both the Septuagint of Jeremiah 31:33 and the Greek of Hebrews 8:10; 10:16 use the plural "laws" (Greek *nomous*). This eliminates the generic sense of "law" that some expositors attempt to superimpose upon the promise.

3. Jesus is the Mediator of the new covenant (Dan. 9:27; Mark 14:22–24; 1 Cor. 11:23–26; Heb. 9:15).

4. In the symbolism of the Old Testament, the blood of the sacrificial animal was brought into the sanctuary (Lev 4). It was the blood, which was sprinkled before the presence of God in the sanctuary, that brought reconciliation between God and man. The blood still reconciles, and it still cleanses us from sin. As the apostle John said: "... the blood of Jesus Christ his Son cleanseth us from all sin" (1 John 1:7). He says this in the context of God's forgiveness (1 John 1:9, 10) and Jesus' acting as our Advocate (1 John 2:1).

5. More New Testament discussions of the covenant are in Romans 2:21–29 (consistency); 2 Corinthians 3:1–18 (the new covenant being "of the spirit"); Galatians 3 and 4 (contrast between "the works of the law" and "the hearing of faith"); Ephesians 2:19–22; 3:6 (a single household of faith in the church); and Hebrews 8–10 (Jesus' "better covenant").

Chapter 43
The Early Christian Church

But this spake he of the Spirit, which they that believe on him should receive: for the Holy Ghost was not yet given; because that Jesus was not yet glorified.

John 7:39

Jesus won the crucial covenant victory at Calvary. Satan lost all further credibility with the angelic host in heaven. Furthermore, sin, sinners, and Satan and his evil angels were to be destroyed. If this is true, why then did Jesus not return immediately to earth and fulfill the promise of restoration, beginning His reign of righteousness in an earth made new?

One must remember that God can save sinners for eternity only by love and persuasion. God must demonstrate that grace alone is sufficient to save. Under the outpouring of the Holy Spirit, the early church made an excellent beginning. The church was glorious in its first love. After the outpouring of the Holy Spirit on Pentecost, three thousand souls joined the church on that one day, and then "the Lord added to the church daily such as should be saved" (Acts 2:47). This was the beginning of the Christian church. It would quickly showcase the people's love and the Holy Spirit's grace and power as the church spread throughout the Roman Empire. This was the period when the power of Christ crucified and risen again appealed to many.

The Covenant Confirmed

Jesus' willing sacrifice on the cross was the foremost victory for Christ in the great controversy between Christ and Satan. If Christ won that victory, then why has He not come before now? Why has there been such a long delay?

It is easy for humans to think this way. We are impatient. We want to see suffering brought to an end. Yet, one must consider the circumstances as God sees them—

1. Is the church ready? Are the people ready for Jesus to come? God is patient and is willing to wait that more people might be saved (2 Peter 3:9; cf. Gen. 15:16).
2. Satan showed his cruelty, deception, and murderous design at Calvary. The power of grace to change people's lives was yet to be shown (2 Cor. 5:17; 1 Peter 1:22, 23).
3. As the early church fell into division and heresies, the church was "in the wilderness" for 1260 years. God is now working to restore truth and power within the church before Jesus returns.
4. In the far-reaching plans of God, He must be shown to the entire human race and to angels as who He is: righteous, merciful, and just and true in all His dealings (Ps. 85:9, 10; Rom. 3:4; 14:11; Rev. 15:3).

The Gospel to the World

At Calvary, the plan of salvation, initially believed in prolepsis (in anticipation), was now a fact. Jesus confirmed the pardon for sins anticipated in the animal sacrifices and justified human beings by His true and effective sacrifice. He fulfills His promise of salvation in the covenant (Heb. 9:15). Jesus' ministry was in Palestine, a relatively small country. The gospel of pardon and salvation must be taken into all the world.

While on earth, Jesus laid plans to build His church. He trained twelve men as His disciples. They knew what Jesus taught and became like Him in attitude and zeal. They formed the core of the new church. Jesus had definite requirements for His followers, and He took the time to teach these to His disciples.

At Sinai, God gave to Israel the Ten Commandments as a guide to make of them a holy nation. Animal sacrifices illustrated forgiveness through the coming Messiah. People knew the ten-commandment law before Jesus came to this earth. Now He taught that every person must, by God's grace, love God and love his or her neighbor, obeying God's commandments from the heart. Only thus could a person please God and become part of "an holy nation." Simply put, Jesus' requirements are: *Take up your cross daily and follow Me.*

To follow Jesus required commitment. He said, "If any man will come after me, let him deny himself, and take up his cross, and follow me" (Matt. 16:24; Luke 9:23 adds "daily"). To follow Jesus means—

- trusting Him, having faith in Him, following His example, and keeping close to Him
- giving up one's personal plans and doing the will of God[1]
- being willing to take on an unpopular cause and face hostility, opposition, and even death itself
- accepting poverty like Jesus, who had "not where to lay his head"[2]
- Moses gave us an example, "choosing rather to suffer affliction with the people of God, than to enjoy the pleasures of sin for a season" (Heb. 11:25). Christians today must still follow in the footsteps of Jesus, who "endured the cross, despising the shame" (Heb. 12:2) so He could do God's will. It was a call to join the army of God and accept His discipline.

Suffering, Persecution, Even Death

Even as Jesus faced persecution and opposition, those who followed Him would face the same.[3] This is a planet in rebellion. The war that began in heaven continues on this earth. The devil, "as a roaring lion, walketh about, seeking whom he may devour" (1 Peter 5:8). Even John the Baptist, cousin and forerunner of Jesus, suffered persecution, imprisonment, and death. The fellowship of suffering is a gift.

> That I may know him, and the power of his resurrection, and the fellowship of his sufferings, being made conformable unto his death. (Phil. 3:10)

Jesus knew that the church faced long years of opposition, persecution, and death. Why would an all-powerful God permit His people to suffer and die? Here, are some thoughts:

1.   We live in a world temporarily ruled by Satan.
2.   Sin-depraved human nature, and even the righteous acts that humans do, are for selfish reasons.
3.   The fires of affliction can reveal the true beauty in human character.

It required courage to be a Christian in the first century. It still requires courage. Knowing there would be hardships, Jesus' promised His presence, "Lo, I am with you alway, even unto the end of the world" (Matt. 28:20).

Lay Up Treasure in Heaven

A person must deny self to follow Jesus. He said to the rich young ruler to "go and sell that thou hast, and give to the poor, and thou shalt have treasure in heaven: and come and follow me" (Matt. 19:21). To follow Jesus means to put Him above all material considerations. Jesus asks that we commit even our goals and purposes to Him, "So likewise, whosoever he be of you that forsaketh not all that he hath, he cannot be my disciple" (Luke 14:33).

While a man must be attentive to and support his family, he must not let his family come between himself and Jesus (Luke 14:26). If a man loves God first, he will love his family more. A man's example of faithfulness to God, even under opposition, will be a help to his family, too.

New Birth, New Creature, New Nature

When Nicodemus came at night, "Jesus answered and said, … Except a man be born again, he cannot see the kingdom of God" (John 3:3). Paul also said, "If any man be in Christ, he is a new creature" (2 Cor. 5:17). To be a Christian means living an entirely new life. Following this change, there must be growth in grace. Peter wrote, "Whereby are given unto us exceeding great and precious promises: that, by these, ye might be partakers of the divine nature" (2 Peter 1:4). To live as a Christian is not a passive experience.

To keep the Ten Commandments, we must love God and love our neighbor as ourselves.[4] Keeping the commandments reveals the love of God in our heart (John 14:15; John 15:10). In the Sermon on the Mount, Jesus said, "Till heaven and earth pass, one jot or one tittle shall in no wise pass from the law, till all be fulfilled" (Matt. 5:18). Love and freedom can exist only within the boundaries of God's law. Laws guide every aspect of biological life on the planet. Why should we think that human behavior should be any different?

What Is Love?

Love arises from the deep emotions of the heart. It is the positive, attractive aspect of the emotions. Rightly understood, love is the underlying focus of all righteous Christian actions. Godly Christian love is a primary motive. Those possessing such love will love the unlovely. They will take in the unpleasant, ungrateful, and the wicked. They will even take in their enemies. True Christian love is not a soft sentimentality, for it may require applying discipline or a firm response. Love always requires doing what is best for all involved at all times.

The Old Testament teaches love, though the New Testament emphasizes love even more. This is probably because the increased emphasis was needed to unite people through love in a society that was divided into many disparate groups. Because of this increased emphasis, some have placed love in opposition to law, discipline, obedience, doctrine, and "works" of all types. They frequently ask: *Does love not accept everyone? Does it not care for everyone? Does it not help everyone to be happy? Does it not avoid offending anyone?* The answer to these questions is "yes, yes, yes, yes" and "no, no, no, no." We accept all people for who they are, but we do not accept the sins that they may still commit. We care for the needy whenever we can, but we also expect the needy to work and help themselves wherever they can. We want everyone to be happy and joyful in the Lord, yet we must mourn for the sins they commit. A Christian will never purposely offend anyone, but he may need to help a brother see his wrongdoing to save his soul.

Jesus taught that love must support the keeping of His commandments—"If ye love me, keep my commandments" (John 14:15). Love is central to Christianity, and it must be strong. The faith and love of the early church led believers to face persecution and death, preach the Word everywhere, and sell all that they had to help support and establish the church. Does God expect less of us today?

Jesus' Presence Through the Spirit

The requirements of Jesus listed above are all done through the power of the Holy Spirit. Jesus sent the Holy Spirit, and the church "went forth conquering, and to conquer" (Rev. 6:2). Within a generation, the church had spread throughout the Roman Empire. Less known is the spread of the gospel to India, central Asia, and even to China and Japan through the Church of the East.[5]

The fundamental promise of the everlasting covenant is: "I will be to them a God, and they shall be to me a people" (Heb. 8:10). Before Jesus ascended, He met with the disciples in Galilee. There He gave them the Great Commission to spread the gospel to the world and concluded with the promise, "Lo, I am with you alway, even unto the end of the world" (Matt. 28:20). This was a covenant promise; God's people would yet become a "kingdom of priests."

In His promise to be with His church "unto the end of the world," Jesus made a personal commitment. He ascended to heaven in the human nature that He will retain for eternity![6] Because of this, He cannot be in all places at one time. However, the Holy Spirit, who does not have the limitations of humanity, now represents Jesus over all the earth. The power of grace, the direct influence on human hearts, comes through the Holy Spirit. The Spirit converts the heart and helps a person partake of the divine nature.[7]

Why is the Holy Spirit needed? There were many things that Jesus did not tell the disciples, and they needed further instruction through the Holy Spirit. Even after three and one half years, they still did not fully understand His mission. Some of the things the disciples could not understand are—

- The disciples could not believe what Jesus plainly told them about His being rejected, suffering, and dying.
- They did not understand that the Jewish nation would be rejected as the chosen people of God.
- They did not know that the restoration of the throne of David was a future event (and would ask about it just before the Ascension, Acts 1:6).
- It was difficult for some to put the sacrifices and ceremonies aside as no longer needed.
- They did not see the gospel going to the Gentiles.

These were all things that were needed for the salvation of humankind. The Holy Spirit was more than a subjective, emotional experience. The gifts of the Spirit are varied and practical (1 Cor. 12; Eph. 4:11–13). The Holy Spirit came as a teacher, to bring the disciples into the full light of truth (see John 14:26; 16:1–16). The apostles needed time to integrate the teachings of Jesus into their thinking and to understand and believe all that He taught, testing them by experience and making them a part of their lives. The Holy Spirit guided them in this process. Believers from a Jewish background needed to recognize that Jesus fulfilled the purpose of the sanctuary services and that the believer's faith was to be in Him, not in ceremony and ritual.

Endnotes

1. Christ is our example. Thus, Jesus' disciples must be willing to follow Him (Matt. 4:19; 9:9; 16:24; John 13:15; Phil. 2:5; 1 Peter 2:21; 1 John 2:6) and accept poverty as He did (Matt. 19:21; 8:20). They were to be holy because He is holy (1 Peter 1:15, 16), not living according to the flesh (1 Peter 4:1). The prophets are also a worthy example (James 5:10).

2. Jesus says: "Follow Me" (Matt. 4:19, 21, 22; 8:22; 9:9; 16:24; 19:21; Mark 2:14; 8:34; 10:21; Luke 5:10, 11, 27, 28; 9:23, 59; 18:22; John 1:43; 10:27; 12:26; 21:19).

3. Christians should expect opposition and persecution (Matt. 5:10, 11; 10:18; Mark 13:9; Acts 5:41; 9:15, 16; Rom. 8:17; 1 Cor. 4:9; 2 Cor.1:7; Phil. 1:29; 3:10; 2 Tim. 3:12; 1 Peter 3:14; 4:13).

4. Jesus' commandments are fulfilled through love to others (Matt. 5:44; Luke 10:27; John 13:34; 2 John 1:5).

5. The gospel spread to eastern nations through the Church of the East, headquartered in Antioch of Syria (B. G. Wilkinson, *Truth Triumphant* [Ringgold, GA, TEACH Services, Inc., 2005], pp. 21–26, 34–44, 331–364). See also http://en.wikipedia.org/wiki/Church_of_the_East.

6. Jesus will have the marks of the crucifixion throughout eternity (Hab. 3:4, NIV; Zech. 13:6). When Jesus comes again, He will have the glorified humanity that the redeemed will enjoy (1 Cor. 15:49; Phil. 3:21; 1 John 3:2).

7. See John 14–16 for more on the person and work of the Holy Spirit.

Chapter 44
The New Testament Law

This is the covenant that I will make with them after those days, saith the Lord,
I will put my laws into their hearts, and in their minds will I write them;
and their sins and iniquities will I remember no more.
Hebrews 10:16, 17

God spoke the Ten Commandments from Sinai. He also wrote the Ten Commandments—His "fiery law"—in stone by His own finger, to emphasize its permanence.[1] Moses put the stone tablets in the ark of the covenant, under the mercy seat. This was a beautiful illustration of mercy, which modifies every application of the law. God called the Ten Commandments "the covenant."[2]

Within the history of the Christian church, a number of the popular Reformation churches began to replace the law of God, given at Sinai, with vague expressions such as the "law of love" and the "law of Christ." This opened the door to permissiveness in lifestyle. The popular churches also denigrated the Old Testament, in the name of upholding the New. Grace and a new covenant without God's laws became their new focus, with little understanding of grace or the new covenant.

Law in Ancient Israel

Back during the time that Jesus walked the dusty roads of Palestine with His disciples, Israel was a land of law. The Jews were zealous and meticulous in keeping the law. As a nation, they had suffered oppression, invasions, and captivity for their past apostasy and idolatry. Now, 490 years after the restoration, they had rebuilt the nation. Society became much more sophisticated and educated. In the days of Manasseh's long and wicked reign, the people had misplaced the scroll of the Torah. During Josiah's reign the Torah was found again, and the Jews again discussed the Torah regularly in their synagogues.

To educate the people and prevent a recurrence of idolatry and apostasy, the religious leaders of the nation erected safeguards. On top of the Ten Commandments, they added numerous ordinances to "protect the law." They strongly emphasized Sabbath observance, creating thirty-nine categories of law to protect the Sabbath, with hundreds of sub-categories of ordinances. Observant Jews carefully followed all aspects of the sacrifices and sanctuary services. They also established rabbinic schools for their young people.

Still, there were problems. The high priests were unbelievers. The Pharisees followed a carefully crafted life of law, but in their zeal, true love was lacking. Temple sacrifices and services had become a means for the high priests to amass wealth. Now, the Romans occupied the country with cruelty, oppression, and sometimes brutality. The Jews had a king who carried the name of Herod. He was an Idumean who ruled only by permission of the Romans. The believing remnant was a small minority.

Jesus and the Law

When Jesus of Nazareth began His ministry, He healed diseases, cast out demons, and even raised the dead. The people followed Jesus by the thousands and acclaimed Him as the prophesied Messiah! The leaders feared that Jesus would take the throne of David. The irony in this fear is that they ostensibly hoped that the Messiah would do exactly that!

Jesus exposed the emptiness of their futile, mechanical observance of the law. This caused Jewish leaders to hate Him. The Sanhedrin arrested Him and put Him on trial, during which He remained strangely silent. Despairing of gaining a conviction, Caiaphas demanded of Jesus under oath: "Tell us whether thou be the Christ, the Son of God" (Matt. 27:63). On Jesus' affirmation (Matt. 27:64), the Sanhedrin convicted Him of blasphemy upon His own testimony! Pilate crucified Him for an unproven charge of sedition. At no point was Jesus charged with breaking the law!

The Romans crucified Jesus under the instigation of the Jewish leaders. On the third day after His burial, He rose from the tomb. The terrified Roman guards received money to tell Pilate that His disciples had stolen the body and otherwise keep the matter quiet, which was an impossibility. The news of Jesus' resurrection was soon widely known.

Pentecost marked the birth of the church. Thousands quickly joined, affirming their faith in the crucified and risen Messiah. As time went by, there were problems, divisions, heresies, and persecutions. In a society where printed material was not yet available, this seemed inevitable. Yet, by the end of the third century, the gospel had spread throughout the Roman Empire and far into the east.

Jesus emphasized from the first that true religion was, not just performing sacrifices and ceremonies, but practical acts based on love to God and one's fellow man. At the same time, Jesus kept the law in every detail. In some ways, He was liberal in His application of the law, but no one could ever charge Him with breaking it.

The Reformation: One Step Forward

During the Reformation, a number of reformers arose, seeking to correct the errors of the established church. It was a slow process. As the Reformers died, each denomination stagnated and failed to advance beyond its founder's beliefs. When people recognized a problem or error, a new church would form and take a step forward. As the incoming tide reaches higher and higher on the beach, so did the Reformation churches came closer and closer to true biblical doctrine.

In meeting the problems in the early church, the apostle Paul emphasized Jesus Christ and Him crucified. Paul taught much about faith and grace as the work of the Holy Spirit to change lives. The Reformation churches strongly opposed legalism.

While this was good, it was in some ways misguided. One of the first errors of the established church was to change the day of worship from the seventh day to the first. Certain Bible-oriented groups did not accept this change, including the Celtic church, the church of the east, and certain other groups that arose from time to time. The established church strongly opposed and even persecuted any group who kept the seventh-day Sabbath or refused her authority.

The Reformation, starting in the sixteenth century, recognized and taught righteousness by faith and the authority of the Bible and the Bible alone. It was a significant step forward, but only a first step. The Reformers recognized other errors but did not act on them all, because they knew that people could accept only a limited amount of change at a time.

Recent Rationales

The Reformation churches claimed that doctrines must be based entirely on the Bible. That they could not explain their keeping of the first day of the week as a quasi-sabbath was a constant embarrassment to them.[3] The established church claimed that their success in changing worship to the first day of the week was a sign or a mark of their authority.[4]

The Reformation churches attempted to find a biblical basis for Sunday observance. These included the following claims:

1. The Ten Commandments were just for the Jews, not for non-Jews. However, God had established the seventh-day Sabbath in Eden before there were any Jews. People accept nine commandments as binding; why not the fourth? There is no Bible command to separate the Sabbath commandment from the other nine.

2. People felt that if the majority of Christians kept the first day for worship, it must be right. This overlooks the fact that the people of God are often a small minority and that keeping the law of God has never been a popularity contest!

3. While Jesus kept the Sabbath, He did not command His disciples to do so. In Jewish society and the early church, whether or not to keep the Sabbath was never at issue. However, Jesus' example is strong evidence of what His will should be in the believer's life.[5]

4. Some note that certain texts seem to downgrade days or emphasize "another day" (Col. 2:16, 17; Rom. 14:5, 6; Heb. 4).[6] However, Colossians 2:16, 17 refers to the ceremonial law, the "shadow of things to come," not to the eternal law of God (see Heb. 8:5; 10:1, which verses also refer to "shadows"). The weekly Sabbath is a memorial of creation (Gen. 2:1–3; Exod. 20:8–11; Exod. 31:17; Rev. 14:6, 7) and not a "shadow" of anything to come. The "rest" in Hebrews 4 refers to the rest of trusting God and entering Canaan, not the Sabbath "rest" after six days of work.[7]

5. Many insist that the Sabbath belonged to the old covenant and that the new covenant does not have to do with the Ten Commandments. However, the first stipulation of the new covenant is God's writing His law(s)—the Ten Commandments—in the heart of the believer. The new covenant was to provide grace and power to keep His law, which includes the seventh-day Sabbath!

Furthermore, nowhere in the New Testament is there a text that commands Christians to change the day of worship. When Jesus began His ministry, He instituted the rite of baptism. On His last night before His arrest, trial, and crucifixion, He instituted the Lord's Supper. By His example and command, He gave these rites to the church. He said nothing about changing the day of worship.

In an attempt to support the first day of the week as a sabbath, some today would eliminate the law and assert the total discontinuity of the Old and New Testaments. These often say—

1. *Jesus is my Sabbath.* However, Jesus never said that He is our Sabbath![8]
2. *Now we keep the "law of love."* The law of love is the Ten Commandments.[9]
3. *The New Testament did away with the Ten Commandments.* There is no evidence for this. Rather, Paul, Jesus, and James cited specific examples of commandments from God's law that they expected believers to keep.[10] The Bible contains a strong and repeated emphasis on keeping the law of God, the Ten Commandments (Matt. 5:16, 17; 1 Cor. 7:19; Rev. 12:17; 14:12; 22:14).

Jesus carefully kept the law of God. During His trial, the Sanhedrin did not accuse Him of breaking any of the commandments. In the three synoptic Gospels, Jesus identified the commandments to be kept as the Ten Commandments, which believers are empowered to keep through love for God and for their fellow human beings (Matt. 19:16–21; Mark 10:17–22; Luke 18:18–23). He also affirmed that love is the basis for obedience (Matt. 22:36–40; Mark 12:28–34; John 14:15). There are some in the present day who say the law is not binding. When questioned further, they will admit that nine commandments are still binding, but that the fourth commandment is not. There is no statement in the New Testament that separates the Sabbath commandment from the rest of God's Law.

Throughout Israel's history, the Tanakh emphasized the Sabbath commandment in various contexts. More than any other commandment, the Sabbath commandment strengthens the relationship between God and man. Evangelical Christians counter that Jesus did not command observance of the fourth commandment. Yet, by His example, He always kept the Sabbath, and He declared that the Sabbath was made for man.[11] Did Jesus change the day of worship from the seventh to the first day of the week? Nowhere in the New Testament is there any such command—either by Jesus, by Paul, or by any other writer. The ten-commandment law is indispensable to the end of time.[12] It is essential that love be the basis of the law, of obedience, and of all religion. God is love, and He bases His law on love.

Endnotes

1. "And God spake all these words, saying (Exod. 20:1). "And he said, The LORD came from Sinai, and rose up from Seir unto them; he shined forth from mount Paran, and he came with ten thousands of saints: from his right hand went a fiery law for them" (Deut. 33:2). "And he gave unto Moses, when he had made an end of communing with him upon mount Sinai, two tables of testimony, tables of stone, written with the finger of God" (Exod. 31:18).

2. Fulfilling the law does not mean destroying it; the ten commandment law is permanent (Matt. 5:17–19).
   The terms "covenant," "testimony," and "tables" refer to the Ten Commandments (Exod. 31:18; 32:15; 34:28; Deut. 4:13; 9:9, 11, 15). The tables of stone were kept inside the ark (Exod. 25:16, 21; 40:20; Num. 17:10; Deut. 10:2, 5; 1 Kings 8:9; 2 Chron. 5:10; Heb. 9:4).

3. The Lutheran *Augsburg Confession* argues: "For those who judge that by the authority of the Church the observance of the Lord's Day instead of the Sabbath-day was ordained as a thing necessary, do greatly err. Scripture has abrogated the Sabbath-day; for it teaches that, since the Gospel has been revealed, all the ceremonies of Moses can be omitted. And yet, because it was necessary to appoint *a certain day, that the people might know when they ought to come together*, it appears

that *the Church designated the Lord's Day* for this purpose; and this day seems to have been chosen all the more for this additional reason, that men might have an example of Christian liberty, and might know that the keeping neither of the Sabbath nor of any other day is necessary" ("Of Ecclesiastical Power," *The Augsburg Confession*, art. 28, available at http://www.iclnet.org/pub/resources/text/wittenberg/concord/web/augs-028.html, accessed 3/29/13 emphasis supplied).

4. "They [the Catholics] allege the change of the Sabbath into the Lord's day, contrary, as it seemeth, to the Decalogue; and they have no example more in their mouths than the change of the Sabbath. They will needs have the Church's power to be very great, because it hath dispensed with a precept of the Decalogue" ("Of Ecclesiastical Power," *The Augsburg Confession*, art. 28).

5. That Paul continued observing the Sabbath and seeking out those who gathered "where prayer was wont to be made" (Acts 16:13) indicates that Sabbath observance was not an issue for him. Paul insists, "Circumcision is nothing, and uncircumcision is nothing, but the keeping of the commandments of God" (1 Cor. 7:19).

6. The *Augsburg Confession* uses Acts 15:10; 2 Cor. 13:10; Col. 2:16 –23; and Titus 1:14 to argue against Catholic traditions that would make "matters of sin in foods, in days, and like things, and burden the Church with bondage of the law, as if there ought to be among Christians" ("Of Ecclesiastical Power," *The Augsburg Confession*, art. 28).

7. The "another day" of Hebrews 4:8, which is described as "to day" (Heb. 3:7, 13, 15; 4:7), is in contrast to "the provocation" and "the day of temptation" (Heb. 3:8, 15; cf. Ps. 95:8).

8. Rest and peace come in Jesus Christ (Rom. 1:7; Gal. 1:3; Phil. 4:7; Col. 3:15). Hebrews has many *betters* that are contrasted with the shadows of the old covenant: "better than the angels" (1:4), "better things" (6:9), "better hope" (7:19), "better testament" (7:22), "better covenant" (8:6), "better sacrifices" (9:23), "better substance" (10:34), "better [country]" (11:16), "better resurrection" (11:35), and "better thing(s)" (11:40; 12:24), but nowhere does it have a "better Sabbath," and nowhere does the New Testament call Jesus "our Sabbath." Paul does say "Christ our passover," but never does he say *Christ our Sabbath*.

9. Love upholds God's commandments (John 14:15, 21–23; 15:10; 1 John 2:3–10; 5:2, 3).

10. Jesus commanded His followers to keep His commandments (Matt. 5:16, 17; 19:17; 22:36–40; Luke 10:26–28; John 14:15, 21–23; 15:10–14; 1 Cor. 7:19; 1 John 2:3–10; 3:23, 24; 5:3).

   Another name for the Decalogue is the "law of liberty" (James 1:25; 2:12); it is holy (Rom. 7:12); it is the "law of Christ" (Gal. 6:2). Not merely hearers but "doers of the law shall be justified" (Rom. 2:13). By the law is the "knowledge of sin" (Rom. 3:20); sin is imputed when there is a law (Rom. 5:13). Salvation is not by the works of the law (Gal. 2:16; 3:10–13). Paul contrasts circumcision with "keeping the commandments of God" (1 Cor. 7:19).

11. See Mark 2:27. This is the same "man" (Greek *anthropos*) that he used in talking about a "man" leaving father and mother and cleaving to His wife (Mark 10:2–9). In both instances He was answering a question about the commandments. If Christians understand the sweeping nature of the statement about marriage, why is it so hard to understand the sweeping nature about the Sabbath?

12. The Ten Commandments are essential to the end of time (Ps. 112:1; 119:1–6; Isa. 56:2; Matt. 5:17–19; 15:3–6; 19:17; 22:36–40; Mark 12:28–31; John 14:15; Rom. 3:31; 7:12; 13:9; 1 John 2:3, 4; 3:23, 24; 5:2, 3; Rev. 12:17; 14:12; 22:14).

Chapter 45
The Later Christian Church

*Take heed therefore unto yourselves, and to all the flock, over the which the
Holy Ghost hath made you overseers, to feed the church of God, which he hath
purchased with his own blood. For I know this, that after my departing shall
grievous wolves enter in among you, not sparing the flock. Also of your own selves
shall men arise, speaking perverse things, to draw away disciples after them.*
Acts 20:28–30

Once Jesus Christ had ascended to heaven, Satan could no longer reach Him. However, Satan viciously attacked the church, bringing in dissension and persecution. When God's people sinned, Satan taunted Christ and the holy angels, claiming that Jesus died in vain and that grace had no power to save.

As the church increased in popularity, it also became more formal. Heathen philosophy brought heresies into the church. As popularity further increased, spirituality decreased until the church became the state religion. It was not long before the church assumed the characteristics of the paganism it replaced. Yet, it was still God's church, and God still had a people.

The Great Commission

For the three and a half years of Jesus' earthly ministry, the disciples had followed their Master as He preached, taught, and healed the people. They had some intimation of what their future work would be through the missionary journeys on which He had sent them. After the crucifixion, the disciples were frightened and confused. They lost all hope of being a part of the restored kingdom of glory.[1]

After Jesus' resurrection, everything changed for the disciples. Their master and friend was alive! They soon learned that He would return to His Father in heaven but would always be with them, even to the end of the world. Furthermore, He had given them a work to do to prepare the world for His return. They would receive the Holy Spirit, and, with His power, they would take the message to the far corners of the world. The disciples had become apostles (meaning, those who are sent out).

And Jesus came and spake unto them, saying, All power is given unto me in heaven and in earth. Go ye therefore, and teach all nations, baptizing them in the name of the Father, and of the Son, and of the Holy Ghost: Teaching them to observe all things whatsoever I have commanded you: and, lo, I am with you alway, even unto the end of the world. Amen. (Matt. 28:18–20)

Shortly before His ascension, He told His followers, "But ye shall receive power, after that the Holy Ghost is come upon you: and ye shall be witnesses unto me both in Jerusalem, and in all Judaea, and in Samaria, and unto the uttermost part of the earth" (Acts 1:8).

What Jesus told them is what they did. Braving discomfort, hunger, persecution, and opposition, they carried the gospel message, wanting so much for Him to return soon!

Exponential Church Growth

The church was first twelve, then one hundred and twenty, then five hundred, then 3,000, then another 5,000! "The Lord added to the church daily such as should be saved" (Acts 2:47). Jesus was the Head of the church. After Jesus ascended to heaven, under the Holy Spirit the apostles took over the daily operation of the church. They cast aside their striving to be the greatest.

For those who knew Christ on earth, their love for Christ was a burning zeal. Empowered by the Holy Spirit, these men "turned the world upside down" (Acts 16:20; 17:6), carrying the gospel to the entire then known world. An illustration may help understand how the disciples might have felt.

At the Houston airport, a tough-looking soldier was waiting for a flight transfer. He was going to see his wife and child after a tour of military duty. Sitting on the edge of his seat in anticipation, he could *hardly wait* to get on that plane and go the rest of the way home! That is how the disciples felt; they were driven by intense expectation of Jesus' soon return. That is how Jesus anticipates bringing us home. That is how we also should feel!

As the original apostles died, the church slowly changed. Love waned; divisions, persecutions, human failures, and heresies began to appear. Jesus commended the churches for their strengths but rebuked them for their failures. Always He urged His people to overcome sin and receive His promises. He was still guiding the church. (See Rev. 2 and 3.)

Why Does God Permit Persecution?

In the Old Testament God blessed His people Israel. He prospered them and intended to make them "the head and not the tail" in all human endeavors (Deut. 28:13). The actual history of ancient Israel was one of prosperity when they obeyed God, and famine, drought, and oppression by foreigners when they forsook Him.

In the Christian church, we find just the opposite. Often there is persecution, oppression, and sometimes death when the church is faithful, and peace when the church has compromised. Why is this? We do not have all the answers. We might ask: Is the church today living up to the light it has been given? Often, it seems, prosperity leads to apathy. This may be why God is sparing in those He prospers. Most of us learn obedience better through suffering (Heb. 2:10). We are left with the following thoughtful questions:

1. Why would God permit His church, the bride of Christ, to be torn by dissension and apostasy?
2. Why would a sovereign God not defend His loyal followers from persecution?
3. Why does a sovereign God allow suffering, disease, war, and death?

These are difficult questions. Here are a few answers to consider, but even these seem inadequate.

1. This is a world of sin. The war that began in heaven continues now on earth. Satan delights to cause trouble of all kinds. Death is the common lot of all mankind. Even when being careful, one can prolong life only a short time.

2. We bring much of our troubles on ourselves.

3. "All that will live godly in Christ Jesus shall suffer persecution" (2 Tim. 3:12).

4. The honor of God is the central issue in the great controversy between Christ and Satan. God, who knows the end from the beginning, will sometimes protect and will sometimes allow trouble to reveal His grace, power, and love.

5. Those who lived through World War II and the years since have observed that Christianity often shines brightest under adversity.

Once, when the sons of God met at the gates of heaven, Satan came and claimed to rule this earth (Job 1:6–11). God challenged him by referring to His servant Job. Satan replied that God had put a hedge about him and that Job served God out of self-interest. The book of Job disputes Satan's claim and shows that Job was a righteous man who truly loved God, even in suffering.

John the Baptist, forerunner of the Messiah, called the people to repentance. He was not afraid to tell people that they were sinners, including Herod himself. Herod put him in prison (see Matt. 3:1–10; Luke 3:1–20). Jesus did nothing to release John from prison, and Herod soon beheaded him. John was the first martyr among Jesus' followers. Jesus spoke highly of him, calling him "more than a prophet" and saying, "Among them that are born of women there hath not risen a greater than John the Baptist" (Matt. 11:7, 11).

If Jesus had performed a miracle to release John, He would have given support to Satan's charge against God about Job, and future believers would have expected the same, causing a difficulty when God wanted to demonstrate that His grace is sufficient to deal with any problem (2 Cor. 12:9).

> Then Satan answered the Lord, and said, Doth Job fear God for nought? Hast not thou made an hedge about him, and about his house, and about all that he hath on every side? thou hast blessed the work of his hands, and his substance is increased in the land. But put forth thine hand now, and touch all that he hath, and he will curse thee to thy face. (Job 1:9–11)

Even when Jesus' followers suffer persecution, He promises, "Lo, I am with you always, even unto the end of the world" (Matt. 28:20).

The Fellowship of Suffering

Jesus suffered persecution all through His life on earth. He accepted His lot of toil and hardship without complaint. He faced the charge of being illegitimate when He confronted the Jewish leaders about how their plans to kill Him were not what Abraham would have done. "Ye do the deeds of your father," He said. Their response had a barb, "We be not born of fornication; we have one Father, even God" (John 8:41).

In the Sermon on the Mount, Jesus spoke about persecution being a blessing.

> Blessed are they which are persecuted for righteousness' sake: for theirs is the kingdom of heaven. Blessed are ye, when men shall revile you, and persecute you, and shall say all manner of evil against you falsely, for my sake. Rejoice, and be exceeding glad: for great is your reward in heaven: for so persecuted they the prophets which were before you. (Matt. 5:10–12)

Persecution for Jesus' sake is evidence that a person is living right! Paul repeated the teaching: "Yea, and all that will live godly in Christ Jesus shall suffer persecution" (2 Tim. 3:12).

When Jesus worked miracles, the people loved Him. However, they did not understand the real purpose of His mission until after the resurrection. Even His disciples could not understand that He came to die for their sins. The ultimate persecution that He experienced was being rejected by the Jews, being tried and crucified, and then feeling abandoned as His disciples ran away. It seemed that even His heavenly Father forsook Him. Yet, Jesus had a faith that did not fail (Isa. 42:4). Before He died He said, "Father, into thy hands I commend my spirit" (Luke 23:46). Christians need that kind of faith today!

If the world hated Jesus, it will also hate those who love Jesus (John 15:20). We are offered fellowship with Jesus in suffering. Is the gospel of Jesus a pearl of great price, or is it something we are willing to receive only if it is convenient? Jesus has shown that only a total commitment is acceptable to Him. His reward is for those who demonstrate their commitment to Him. He told the church at Smyrna, "Be thou faithful unto death, and I will give you a crown of life" (Rev. 2:10).

New Bad Ideas

Heresies in the church began as intriguing thoughts and whispers in the ear. These thoughts were reinforced by expression in discussions and pride of opinion. Some heresies will cater to the sinful desires of the human heart, and some are brought in as the pre-existing beliefs of new converts. They flourish where Bible study and prayer are neglected. Satan was well aware of what was happening, and he attacked the church as "a roaring lion" (1 Peter 5:8).

The first heresy began as a division between two factions: the Jewish Christians, who were raised in Palestine and had difficulty giving up 1400 years of tradition, and the Greek-speaking Jews and new Gentile converts, who had little or no attachment to the ceremonial law. This issue had far-reaching consequences in Paul's epistles, where the issue is addressed in a number of ways. Initially, this was dealt with in the Councils of Jerusalem and Antioch (Acts 15). While the Jerusalem Council ended well, there was a party of Messianic Jews who continued to follow Paul on his missionary trips and work against him to bring new converts under the ceremonial law (Gal. 1–3).

Most heresies developed because of people's failure to accept and understand Jesus' saving work on the cross. The Jews had their traditions and writings; the Greeks had philosophy. Pagan influences also found their way into the church. The Hellenized school at Alexandria took these ideas and tried to harmonize them with Christianity. Scholars, called "Church Fathers," wrote on these issues, the now popular Church of Rome accepting many of their ideas.

Early Church Heresies

The following are examples of the most predominant heresies in Church history:

- The Ebionites could not accept the triunity of God comprised of Father, Son, and Holy Spirit. They taught that Jesus was a natural son of Joseph and Mary and was endowed with the Holy Spirit at His baptism.
- Docetism (third century) believed in the divinity of Jesus but denied His humanity. This arose from the Greek concept that all matter is evil. They believed His suffering and death on the cross appeared to be real, but were not.
- Monarchians held that God the Father was absolute and transcendent but that the Son had a beginning and was created out of nothing before time began. They believed that He was also God, but not to the degree that the Father is. They were forerunners of the Arians (AD 250–336) in later years.
- Athanasius (AD 296–373) opposed the Monarchians and upheld the unity of the essence of the Father and the Son. The First Council of Nicaea in AD 325 rejected Arianism, though it lived on for several centuries.

During the fourth and fifth centuries, there was a strong debate between the schools of Alexandria and Antioch regarding the nature of Christ and how Jesus could be truly God and at the same time truly man. The Alexandrians focused on the divinity of Jesus and the Word taking on flesh. Those from Antioch stressed Jesus' humanity and that the Word became a human being.

- Apollinaris (AD 310–390) taught that the divine Word took the place of the human mind; he denied the genuine humanity of Christ. This was condemned in the Council of Constantinoplc (AD 381).
- Nestorius (c AD 451) exaggerated the distinctions between the two natures of Christ. He taught Jesus was either two persons or two natures separately existing side by side.
- Eutyches (AD 378–454) contended that, in the incarnate Christ, divinity and humanity coalesced into one, essentially denying the two natures of Christ.

At the Council of Chalcedon (AD 451), the views of both Nestorius and Eutyches were condemned. The council maintained the unity of the person of Jesus as well as the duality of His natures. They taught Christians to confess Christ as fully divine and fully human, to be acknowledged in two natures "without confusion, without change, without division, without separation." This helped to limit confusion, but did not solve all the problems. The controversy continued with the Monophysites, Monothelites, and the Adoptionists. A simple statement regarding the nature of God is that there is *one* God in three persons. Beyond this, "silence is golden."

Later Church Heresies

During the Middle Ages, Augustine and Thomas Aquinas wrote on the person of Christ. They did not add much to what had already been decided, though they brought more attention to the work of Christ.[2] At this time, one would do well to study Luke 1:34, 35; John 1:1–3, 14; and Philippians 2:5–8, and believe what it says.

Anselm of Canterbury (AD 1033–1109) taught that sin, being an infinite offense against God, required a satisfaction equally infinite, one that God alone could provide. Christ took the place of man and, by His death, made complete satisfaction to divine justice. His death was not a ransom paid to Satan, but a debt paid to God.

Peter Abelard (AD 1079–1142) taught that the essence of sin was contempt for God's will. It resided more in peoples' evil intentions than in their actions. This concept trivialized the law of God and the nature of sin. It denied the covenant of God and the substitutionary death of Christ at Calvary. Adherents of this concept taught that Christ's life and death simply aroused in sinners an answering repentance and love, which became their reconciliation and redemption. Christ's death did not pay the penalty for man's sin; it was only a revelation of God's love. This philosophy is called the "moral influence theory."

During the Reformation, there was a dispute between Luther, who believed in the "real presence" of the body and blood of Christ in the bread and wine of the Communion service *(transubstantiation)*, and Zwingli and Calvin, who felt that the body and blood of Christ could be in the bread and wine only symbolically and spiritually.[3]

Through the ferment of these disputes, we can see both the establishment of truth and the adoption of error in the church. This process continues to the present. It is the responsibility of each Christian to test all beliefs by what the Bible teaches.

Endnotes

1. The disciples wanted to be part of a restored Jewish kingdom of glory, based on worldly greatness (Matt. 18:1, 4; 20:20–24; 23:11; Mark 9:34; 10:43; Luke 9:46, 48; 22:24–26; 24:21). The Old Testament prophecies spoke of a restored kingdom (Jer. 23:5, 6; Ezek. 39:24–27; Zeph. 3:15–17). If Israel had fulfilled her mandate before Messiah came, He would have fulfilled these prophecies (Dan. 9:24).

2. Raoul Dederen, "Christ: His Person and Work," *Handbook of Seventh-day Adventist Theology* (Review and Herald Publishing Association, 2000), pp. 190–203.

    See the following websites regarding the Eucharist:

    http://en.wikipedia.org/wiki/Martin_Luther

    http://philofreligion.homestead.com/files/mpaper8.htm

    http://bfhu.wordpress.com/2011/05/13/martin-luther-on-the-real-presence/

Also, search for "Controversy about the Eucharist".

3.   Raoul Dederen, *Handbook of Seventh-Day Adventist Theology.* electronic ed. (Hagerstown, MD: Review and Herald Publishing Association, 2001, p. 880.

Chapter 46
The Remnant Church

And the serpent cast out of his mouth water as a flood after the woman, that
he might cause her to be carried away of the flood. And the earth helped the
woman, and the earth opened her mouth, and swallowed up the flood which the
dragon cast out of his mouth. And the dragon was wroth with the woman,
and went to make war with the remnant of her seed, which keep the
commandments of God, and have the testimony of Jesus Christ.
Revelation 12:15–17

Throughout history, God's people have always been a "remnant." It was always a minority who had faith in God and understood who He was. In the early years of Christianity, many thousands of Jews accepted Christ and joined the church. To be sure, it was a Jewish church, yet it was also a distinct, persecuted minority in Jerusalem. As the Christian church grew and became popular, there was again a minority who had faith in God. When Protestantism took center stage, they were still a "remnant" within the church that truly believed and lived their faith.

The concept of the "remnant church" speaks well of any church. However, it is also a restrictive concept. The end-time remnant church has distinct qualities that are not always popular, though strongly biblical. The clearest designation of the end-time remnant church is that this church will "keep the commandments of God, and have the testimony of Jesus Christ" (Rev. 12:17).

The Hour of His Judgment Has Come

The new world of North America provided a refuge for the persecuted of all lands. Freedom of religion allowed churches to multiply and grow in strength. The growing churches sent missionaries to many countries, supported by generous offerings. A benevolent government "of the people, by the people, and for the people" did not favor any church. This allowed people to follow their conscience without interference.

The result was that the United States of America became the most religious Christian nation on earth. More people willingly attended church in this country than in any other. This was in the providence of God, and now He was ready to act again. The Advent awakening led by William Miller began in 1833 and reached a crescendo in 1844. Miller based his message on Daniel 8:14—"Unto two thousand and three hundred days; then shall the sanctuary be cleansed." He understood the prophecy to signify the cleansing of the earth on October 22, 1844, when Jesus would return to earth to claim the redeemed. Thousands of followers believed that this referred to Jesus' second coming.

The date passed, and Jesus did not come. This was the "Great Disappointment." The Millerites were embarrassed and confused and became the object of ridicule. Reexamination of the calculations only served to confirm the date; the prophesied time did end October 22, 1844. The movement broke up into a number of Adventist bodies who held varying views on the meaning of their experience.

The Remnant Church

One group—one of the smallest—held that William Miller was correct about the date but that he misunderstood the event. The sanctuary to be cleansed was not the earth but rather the heavenly sanctuary. October 22, 1844 marked the beginning of the antitypical Day of Atonement and the Investigative Judgment. The Day of Atonement in ancient Israel (Lev. 16:1–34; 23:27–32) foreshadowed the true antitypical Day of Atonement in the end time (Dan. 7:9–14, 26, 27; 8:13, 14).[1] The antitypical Day of Atonement will end with the close of probation, when the Holy Spirit will have sealed the righteous for eternity. The thousand years of the Millennium and the "executive judgment" will follow, when the lake of fire destroys sin and sinners.

Rachel Oaks Preston, a Seventh Day Baptist, challenged an Adventist pastor named Wheeler about his calling for observance of the Ten Commandments while not keeping the fourth commandment. After studying his Bible, Wheeler became convinced that the seventh day was still the Sabbath of the Lord. Later, Joseph Bates, a retired ship captain, promoted this belief until it became a fundamental doctrine of the church, and the church chose "Seventh-day Adventist" as its name.

At the same time, Ellen Harmon, a frail young girl of fifteen years of age, began to receive visions and messages from God for the church. Her messages were always practical and led to one success after another in the growth of the church. It is significant that the remnant church will "keep the commandments of God" and "have the testimony of Jesus," "for the testimony of Jesus is the spirit of prophecy" (Rev. 12:17; 19:10). Adventists point to the messages of Ellen G. Harmon White as having the inspiration of the Spirit and therefore fulfilling the qualifications of the Biblical "spirit of prophecy."

Other religionists have severely criticized Adventists for their belief that the written ministry of Ellen White qualifies as the spirit of prophecy. Critics claim that the canon of Scripture closed about AD 200 and that there will be no more prophets. However, prophecy is one of the gifts of the Spirit given to the church (1 Cor. 12:8–10; Eph. 4:11; Joel 2:28, 29). Critics assert that Adventists use Ellen White's writings to interpret the Bible. This reveals their lack of awareness of the process by which Adventists came to establish their biblical doctrines. Though, in some cases, Ellen White did play a role in reaching a correct understanding of Scripture, her role never substituted for careful Bible study.[2] Nonetheless, if there ever were a discrepancy between the Bible and her writings, the Bible would have to be accepted as the truth.

Adventists recommend that a person not read Ellen White's writings in isolation from Scripture. Her writings are reasonable, easily understood and useful.[3] In keeping with the "spirit of prophecy," they point to Jesus Christ, our Redeemer and Lord.

Phases of Judgment

Some blame Adventists for teaching a "partial atonement" at the cross because of their belief in the Investigative Judgment. In reply, Adventists ask that a person look at the close connection between the sacrifice and the atonement.[4]

The everlasting covenant of God was not just to provide pardon for sin; it was also to restore the world to the perfection of Eden. Now we are in the "time of the end," a time of judgment before Jesus' return. God conducts this judgment with exceptional care, for all questions must be answered. All the intelligent beings in the universe must understand that God is merciful and just in His judgment, and they must be absolutely convinced that the eternal law of God brings only happiness and freedom.

The first phase of judgment is pardon and atonement. In Israel, the sinner brought a lamb before the door of the tabernacle. He put his hand on the head of the lamb to transfer his sin to the lamb. Then he slew the lamb, and the priest took some of its blood and put it on the horns of the altar. The priest then removed the fat and burned the body of the lamb on the altar. "The priest shall make an atonement for his sin that he hath committed, and it shall be forgiven him" (Lev. 4:35).

Depending on whether the sacrifice was for a common person, for the congregation, for a priest, or for a ruler, different animals would be used and the blood would be put on the horns of the altar of sacrifice or on the horns of the altar of incense, or it would be sprinkled before the veil inside the tabernacle. Confessed sin was symbolically transferred from the sinner into the sanctuary, requiring later removal through the scapegoat. Atonement could be made at the time and place of sacrifice, or inside the tabernacle. The result was the same—the priest made atonement and the sin was forgiven. There was always a direct connection between sacrifice, application of the blood, atonement, and pardon.

When a person chooses to obey God, an angel writes his name in the "Lamb's book of life," with *pardon* written opposite forgiven sins. This is the first phase of judgment.

In ancient Israel, the Day of Atonement came once a year with sacrifices to cleanse the sanctuary from the defilement of forgiven sins. Every member of the congregation was to "afflict his soul" that he might seek and receive pardon for all his sins.[5] Those who did not afflict their soul must be "cut off from among his people" (Lev. 23:29; cf. Lev. 16:1–34; 23:26–32). It was the second phase of judgment.

At Calvary, the first and second phases of judgment moved from earth to heaven under the heavenly priesthood of Christ. It is Jesus Christ who pardons the sins of those written in the Lamb's book of life. At the prophesied time, October 22, 1844 (Dan. 8:14), the antitypical Day of Atonement began in heaven. Forgiven sins are cleansed from the Lamb's book of life, and, where sin is not pardoned, the name is blotted out. This is a serious matter, and it is frightening for some. Please consider how much God gave: "For God so loved the world that he gave his only begotten Son, that whosoever believeth in him should not perish, but have everlasting life" (John 3:16). If God invests this much to save souls, there is no doubt that He will also make every effort to save those who trust in Him. Our assurance is in Jesus Christ.

The third phase of judgment is "executive judgment," when God executes judgment by casting sin and sinners into the lake of fire (Rev. 20:9, 10, 14, 15). At the same time, God welcomes the righteous, the people of God, into the holy city, the New Jerusalem, to be with Christ for eternity in an Eden restored. All phases of judgment and all promises of the everlasting covenant are now accomplished.

God's Last Message

God has a purpose for the remnant church. This is the last church before Jesus comes again (Rev. 3:14–22; 10:1–11; 12:17). This is also the last generation from whom those come who will live to see Jesus return. They will give God's last message to a perishing world. To be alive to see Jesus come again is an exceptional privilege and requires a unique experience.

The end-time message of this church is also the Elijah message:

> Behold, I will send you Elijah the prophet before the coming of the great and dreadful day of the Lord: And he shall turn the heart of the fathers to the children, and the heart of the children to their fathers, lest I come and smite the earth with a curse. (Mal. 4:5, 6)

What was the Elijah message originally? Elijah was the prophet of God in the time of Ahab and Jezebel. The northern kingdom of Israel was in deep apostasy with frank and open idolatry. Elijah confronted Ahab in his court with the judgment of God, "There shall be no dew nor rain these years, but according to my word" (1 Kings 17:1). His message was a call to repentance. This came to a climax on Mount Carmel when God demonstrated His power in answer to prayer. When the people chose to recognize the true God, the rain came and ended the drought.

John the Baptist came as the forerunner of Jesus the Messiah. In the spirit and power of Elijah, he gave his message to an unbelieving nation, "Repent ye: for the kingdom of heaven is at hand" (Matt. 3:2). Jesus confirmed John's mission, "This is Elias, which was for to come" (Matt. 11:14). The end-time "Elijah message"—a message of repentance—will be given again just before Jesus comes the second time (Mal. 4:5, 6).

God's end-time messages are described as the "three angels' messages" (Rev. 14:6–12). The first is an announcement of judgment. In the earthly Day of Atonement, God called for His people to afflict their souls (Lev. 16:29, 30). As then, so now—we must examine our own soul. If there is a sin, we must confess it, ask forgiveness, and receive divine cleansing (1 John 1:9).

The first angel called people everywhere to worship God as the Creator. The original creation week concluded with the establishment of the seventh-day Sabbath rest. God enshrined the Sabbath within the ten-commandment law as a memorial to creation. All aspects of the everlasting covenant and the plan of salvation rest on the foundation of God as Creator.

The second angel's message is a warning to avoid the confusion of the religious world. When churches ask the state for legislation to support their doctrines and money to support their institutions, the bride has sought another lover and is guilty of "fornication."

The third is a warning against the mark of the beast. God judges those who receive the mark of the beast. Opposite those who receive the mark of the beast are the saints who "keep the commandments of God, and the faith of Jesus" (Rev. 14:12).

These three messages are the message of the remnant church and will continue to the end of time. Some have accused the Seventh-day Adventist church of exclusiveness in holding that these messages are God's unique messages for the end time. One must consider, however, that these messages are in the Bible and that the Bible is available to all Christian churches. God will welcome and accept all who preach His message. Jesus said, "Forbid him not: for he that is not against us is for us" (Luke 9:50).

Satan has attacked these messages and those who bear them. He has blunted the effectiveness of these messages so that many have not heard them. Too many have closed their ears to the word of God and have chosen to follow human traditions. However, God is merciful and patient and will save every true child of His. Jesus says, "Other sheep I have, which are not of this fold: them also I must bring" (John 10:16).

Endnotes

1. The "antitypical day of atonement," and the phases of judgment and atonement may be unique doctrines of the Seventh-day Adventist Church. There is not space enough to present these here, but some statements can be made:
   - The Day of Atonement was an important yearly event in Old Testament Israel. At that time, the sanctuary was cleansed of the accumulated sins of the past year, and the sins were completely removed from the camp (Lev. 16:1–34; 23:26–28).
   - This was the symbolic Day of Atonement pointing forward to the real end-time day of atonement and the judgment of the righteous. At that time the book of life will be examined and the forgiven sins of the righteous will be blotted out. Those righteous whose sins are not forgiven will have their names blotted out from the book of life.
   - The typical Day of Atonement foreshadowed the true antitypical day of atonement in the end time (Dan. 7:9–14, 26, 27).
   - The "cleansing of the sanctuary" is prophesied (Dan. 8:14; 9:25).
   - The beginning date is given in Ezra 7:11–26 with the final date given in Daniel 9:25.
   - The wicked are judged by the saints, and all questions will be answered during the thousand years (Rev. 20:4).
2. For a more detailed study of Ellen White's role in the formation of the doctrines of the Seventh-day Adventist Church, see *Messenger to the Remnant*, pp. 34–37, available at http://drc.whiteestate.org/read.php?id=195888, accessed 3/26/13; Paul A. Gordon, "Doctrinal Development, Authority, and Ellen White," pp. 4, 5, available at https://egwwritings.org/?ref=en_DDAEW.6.3, accessed 3/26/13; and Arthur L. White, "Ellen White and Adventist Doctrine: How Basic Doctrines Came to Adventists," *Adventist Review*, July 19, 1984, pp. 4–6, available at http://docs.adventistarchives.org/docs/RH/RH19840719-V161-29__B.pdf?q=docs/RH/RH19840719-V161-29__B.pdf, accessed 3/26/13, and Arthur L. White, "The Certainty of Basic Doctrinal Positions," *Adventist Review*, July 26, 1984, pp. 6–8.
3. Ellen White's writings call attention to biblical teachings that, by and large, have been discovered by others in God's Word apart from her aid. Her own standard is found in *The Great Controversy*, p. 595: "God will have a people upon the earth to maintain the Bible, and the Bible only, as the standard of all doctrines and the basis of all reforms." Notice that she lists two categories of teaching—doctrines and reforms—one must all come from Scripture, the other must be *based* in Scripture.
4. Sacrifice, atonement, and mediation are all one extended event. The sinner brings the sacrificial animal to the door of the tabernacle, places his hands on the head of the animal and confesses his sin. Then he slays the animal. Notice that

the sinner was responsible for killing the sacrifice; the priest gave atonement and mediation. The priest takes the blood and sprinkles it before the veil or places it on the horns of the altar of burnt offering and pours the rest at the base of the altar. The carcass is then burned on the altar of burnt offering. In doing this, "the priest shall make an atonement for him, and it [his sin] shall be forgiven him." (Lev. 4:31). The blood of the sacrifice carries the forgiven sin into the sanctuary. Once a year, the sanctuary must be cleansed, on the Day of Atonement. Forgiven sins are removed from the sanctuary, placed on the head of the scapegoat, and taken to the wilderness by a fit man and lost forever (Lev. 16:1–34; 23:27–32). Atonement, to be complete, requires the total removal of sin from the camp. The "Lord's goat" dies for the sins of the people—Jesus already did that. The goat that is *not* the Lord's (Azazel, the scapegoat) is banished from the camp. In the biblical scenario, the banished goat tries to re-enter the "camp of the saints" at the close of the thousand years. Glory to God—he is not successful.

5. "For on that day shall the priest make an atonement for you, to cleanse [*katharísai*] you, that ye may be clean [*katharisthêsesthe*] *from all your sins* before the LORD.… And he shall make an atonement for the holy sanctuary, and he shall make an atonement for the tabernacle of the congregation, and for the altar, and he shall make an atonement for the priests, and for all the people of the congregation. And this shall be an everlasting statute unto you, to make an atonement for the children of Israel for all their sins once a year. And he did as the LORD commanded Moses" (Lev. 16:30, 33, 34, emphasis supplied). "And he said unto me, Unto two thousand and three hundred days; then shall the sanctuary be cleansed [*katharisthêsetai to hagion*]" (Dan. 8:14). Greek taken from the Septuagint.

Chapter 47
Grace Is Sufficient to Save

For we have not an high priest which cannot be touched with the feeling of our infirmities; but was in all points tempted like as we are, yet without sin. Let us therefore come boldly unto the throne of grace, that we may obtain mercy, and find grace to help in time of need.

Hebrews 4:15, 16

From the first, Satan has attacked the covenant of God. He has declared that the law of God is arbitrary and unnecessary and that it is impossible for created beings to keep the law of God. He claims that God demands worship and obedience only for selfish reasons and will do nothing for mankind if it causes Him discomfort! Satan would have us believe that the Bible and the story of Creation are a myth. Satan claims that the prophecies of the Bible are all wrong in their timing and in the events prophesied. Most of all, he says that Jesus did not need to die and that has His sacrifice did not benefit humanity as claimed.

A Christian knows that there is a God because he talks with Him in prayer and God responds. The Bible is a book that changes the lives of people and nations. Prophecies are fulfilled as predicted. The law of God brings peace, freedom, and order in society. Jesus proved His love by His willingness to live among men and die as a sacrifice on Calvary.

The focus of the covenant of grace is to show God's initiative in saving humankind. Jesus, the Creator God, became a human and lived a sinless life as a human (1 Tim. 3:16; Phil. 2:5–8). This life He gave as a sacrifice on Calvary so that we might live.

Humankind "Bought With a Price"

After Adam and Eve sinned, God came to them in the cool of the evening and announced that He would put "enmity" between Satan and humanity (Gen. 3:15). It was God who took the initiative. He "put" the law back into the heart of mankind. This was a new covenant action.

There were consequences. Adam had "sold" dominion of the earth to Satan. He became a slave to sin and had no power to resist.[1] Christ came, took authority from His anticipated sacrifice on Calvary and purchased man again (1 Cor. 6:20).[2] By this, Christ brought humans back into favor with God so that they could receive pardon for sins. He gave them a new probation to learn about grace and to choose again to serve Him.

It is not easy for people to choose Christ and liberation from sin. Satan uses all methods—fair and foul—to keep mankind enslaved. God, using love and persuasion, gives people freedom in which to again choose to serve Him. At Creation, God gave humans free will. Now they must use that free will and consent to the work of grace in their lives.

Overcoming in Christ

The apostle John received messages for seven churches in Asia Minor while he was on the Isle of Patmos (Rev. 2 and 3). The messages portray the seven epochs of Christianity from that day until now. Following each message is a promise, "To him that overcometh ..." (Rev. 2:7, 11, 17, 26; 3:5, 12, 21). Some claim that once they are "saved," they do not need to keep the law and continue to overcome. When people accept Christ and their life is changed, they receive pardon for sins, salvation, and many spiritual blessings.

The sinful nature is still present, and there are still sins to overcome. Christ stands before the Father for His people. It is only "in Christ" that a person can be perfect in this life. However, by continual consent to the work of grace in the life, those habitual, besetting sins and "blind spots" will be overcome.

As sinners see the perfection and holiness of the Son of God, they can only pray: "God be merciful to me a sinner" (Luke 18:13). The victory they enjoy and the perfection they show are only in Christ. Christ covers their sinful nature with the white robe of His righteousness. It is only when "this corruptible shall have put on incorruption" (1 Cor. 15:53) that Christ removes the sinful nature.

As Jesus looks upon these redeemed ones, "He shall see of the travail of his soul, and shall be satisfied" (Isa. 53:11). Again we read: "Looking unto Jesus the author and finisher of our faith; who for the joy that was set before him endured the cross, despising the shame, and is set down at the right hand of the throne of God" (Heb. 12:2).

The Life of Victory

Satan has been all too successful in deceiving the world into sin. There has always been a faithful remnant—God's unique people. These make God first in their lives and consent to the work of grace that changes their lives. Being human, they still have the sinful nature. Even God's people will sometimes yield to sin. This becomes a peculiar problem to God.

David was a man after God's own heart. He sinned grievously with Bathsheba and in arranging for the death of Uriah the Hittite. When the prophet Nathan pointed out his sin (2 Sam. 12:1–7), David repented deeply and sought the Lord (Ps. 51). Nathan gave David his judgment, with the preface: "Howbeit, because by this deed thou hast given great occasion to the enemies of the Lord to blaspheme" (2 Sam. 12:14).

If one of God's people sins, it is hard to repent, and it is an insult and a disgrace to Jesus.

> If those who hide and excuse their faults could see how Satan exults over them, how
> he taunts Christ and holy angels with their course, they would make haste to confess

their sins and [repent]. Through defects in the character, Satan works to gain control of the whole mind, and he knows that if these defects are cherished, he will succeed. Therefore, he is constantly seeking to deceive the followers of Christ with his fatal sophistry that it is impossible for them to overcome. But Jesus pleads … "My grace is sufficient for thee" (2 Cor. 12:9).… Let none, then, regard their defects as incurable. God will give faith and grace to overcome them.[3]

Satan's claim is that Jesus died in vain and that grace cannot change human lives. This is a lie. Before Christ comes again, He will have a people who gladly show that He has changed their lives.

It is impossible for those who have once been enlightened … who have tasted the goodness of the word of God … If they fall away, to be brought back to repentance, because to their loss they are crucifying the Son of God all over again and subjecting him to public disgrace. (Heb. 6:4–6, NIV)

This verse does not speak of besetting sin, but rather speaks of apostasy and rebellion against Christ. The greatest gift that Christians can give to their Lord, is their own life, changed by grace. We take comfort in this promise, "If any man sin we have an advocate with the Father, Jesus Christ the righteous" (1 John 2:1).

Grace—God's Gift, God's Power

Grace is the supernatural power of God by which He pardons sin and renews the sinner's life in righteousness. The sinner must accept this gift by faith and consent to the work of grace to change the life, choosing to do what is right. It is God's purpose to restore His image in man (2 Peter 1:4–11). The Holy Spirit mediates the power of grace to change lives.

Before His ascension, Jesus spoke to His disciples, "All power is given unto me in heaven and in earth …" (Matt. 28:18). Through the authority of the cross, Jesus sent the Holy Spirit to prepare us for heaven and give us power to witness for Him.

Seeing then that we have a great high priest, that is passed into the heavens, Jesus the Son of God, let us hold fast our profession. For we have not an high priest which cannot be touched with the feeling of our infirmities; but was in all points tempted like as we are, yet without sin. (Heb. 4:14, 15)

Even in their close association, Jesus could not tell His disciples everything they needed to know. There were several reasons for this:

1. There was not time. Jesus was too busy teaching the people and healing.
2. The disciples could not understand theology as could Paul.

3. The disciples did not understand Jesus' mission, even up to the time of His ascension (Acts 1:6).

The Holy Spirit was promised to "teach you all things, and bring all things to your remembrance" (John 14:26). At Pentecost, the Holy Spirit came upon the church with power. He gave the church gifts, by which the gospel went to the then known world.[4] He promised these same gifts in Ezekiel and Jeremiah through the new covenant.[5]

John 6 and 15 emphasize what it means to have "Christ in you, the hope of glory" (Col. 1:25). By this grace, God changes human lives, gives us new birth, and makes of us "a new creature."[6] This process must take place before Christ comes again. The character that is formed is the only thing that a person can take to heaven.

Faith, the Hand That Grasps God's Blessing

While grace is the supernatural power of God to change our lives, faith is another word to describe the experience of the Christian. Faith describes our relationship with God: trust, belief, love, and a willingness to obey Him.

> Now faith is the substance of things hoped for, the evidence of things not seen. Through faith we understand that the worlds were framed by the word of God, so that things which are seen were not made of things which do appear. But without faith, it is impossible to please him: for he that cometh to God must believe that he is, and that he is a rewarder of them that diligently seek him. (Heb. 11:1, 3, 6)

Since Eden, every human being has been given a spark of faith and a desire to avoid evil (Gen. 3:15). John wrote: "That was the true Light, which lighteth every man that cometh into the world" (John 1:9). If you choose to obey, you will be led step by step to Christ. The more you see of the perfection of Christ and the more you see of the cross of Christ, the more you are motivated to follow Him. "So then faith cometh by hearing, and hearing by the word of God" (Rom. 10:17).

Now, while faith is a gift from God, it is also an action that comes from within man. Genuine faith is an active faith (James 2:20–26)! Jesus said much about faith, but He did not use big words. He just said, "Follow me." If a person refused to "follow" Jesus when bidden, he or she was not a Christian—plain and simple (Luke 18:18–24).

Faith is what the believer uses to take hold of grace! To understand faith you must have an intuitive relationship—a commitment—with God. While faith is a gift and an understanding given by God, all must choose to exercise their faith to serve God. "Prayer is the key in the hand of faith to unlock heaven's storehouse, where are treasured the boundless resources of Omnipotence."[7]

The Relationship Between Faith and Works

A crucial question arises: When Jesus died for all people and extended His grace to all, was His grace also effectual for all? By common observation, there are wicked people in this world. Those who have resisted the grace of God and refused Christ will be lost.[8] Is the justification spoken of in Romans 5:16–18 by faith or before faith? Is faith a form of "works?"

"Now faith is being sure of what we hope for and certain of what we do not see…. And without faith it is impossible to please God, because anyone who comes to him must believe that he exists and that he rewards those who earnestly seek him" (Heb. 11:1, 6, NIV). "So then faith cometh by hearing, and hearing by the word of God" (Rom. 10:17).

Faith describes the relationship a person must have with God. It includes trust, belief, and love. In that love, there is an emotional component, a desire for all that God is. Faith is the gift of God, but it must be exercised by human beings. Grace is by the initiative of God and is the supernatural action of the Holy Spirit to change human lives.

With this, one can understand that sinners cannot come to God unless God draws them and opens the way for them. When people are "justified by faith," they take God at His word, believe His promise and His covenant, and accept the grace of God. When Abraham believed God, "It was counted to him for righteousness" (Gen. 15:6).

"Let us therefore come boldly unto the throne of grace, that we may obtain mercy, and find grace to help in time of need" (Heb. 4:16). Yet, we must consent to the work of grace for our life to be changed. This involves our choice, for grace cannot act in a vacuum. Repentant sinners must choose, must make a decision, and must commit themselves to Christ to be saved at last. Is this action a work? Do these things "add something" to the work of grace?

A "work" is usually a ritual, a task, or an act of obedience by which a person hopes to merit salvation. For the person "in Christ," works are the "fruit" of the Spirit—the result of being saved. "… the fruit of the Spirit is love, joy, peace, longsuffering, gentleness, goodness, faith, meekness, temperance: against such there is no law" (Gal. 5:22, 23).

These are actions and attitudes that are quite different from consent, choice, decision, or a commitment to serve Christ. A Christian will be active in his life for Christ. Thus, sinners do not "work" to merit salvation, but rather show works as the fruit of their relationship with Christ.

Endnotes

1.   Sin brings loss of freedom (John 8:34; Rom. 6:12, 16, 17, 19–23; 2 Peter 2:19). It makes people prisoners (Ps. 146:7; Isa. 14:17; 42:7; Zech. 9:12). Paul could speak of being a prisoner of Jesus, because, though kept in chains, he had become Jesus' servant (Greek *doulos* "slave") (Eph. 3:1; 4:1; 2 Tim. 1:8; Philemon 1:1, 9).

2.   Jesus Christ has authority (Greek *exousia*) (Matt. 7:29; 9:6; 28:18; Luke 4:36; 5:24; 9:1; John 5:27; 10:18; 17:2). Before Him, every knee shall bow (Isa. 45:23; Rom. 14:11; Phil. 2:10). Salvation is given through the power of God and Jesus Christ (Exod. 9:16; Deut. 4:37; 9:29; 2 Sam. 22:33; 2 Kings 17:36; Ezra 8:22; Neh. 1:10; Job 26:12, 14; Ps. 62:11; 66:7; 106:8; Isa. 40:26; Jer. 32:17; Nahum 1:3; Hab. 3:7). Jesus possesses power (Greek *dunamis*) that He grants to human beings (Matt. 6:13; 24:30; 26:64; Mark 14:62; Luke 24:49; Rom. 1:4, 16, 20; 1 Cor. 1:24; 4:20; 6:14; 2 Cor. 12:9; Eph. 3:20. Phil. 3:10; Heb. 1:3; 2 Peter 1:16; Rev. 4:11; 7:12).

3.   Ellen G. White, *The Great Controversy* (Nampa, ID: Pacific Press Publishing Association, 1911), p. 489.

For texts on the work of God's grace, see Luke 2:40; John 1:17; Acts 4:33; 11:23; 14:26; 15:40; Romans 1:5; 12:6; 1 Corinthians 3:10; 15:10; Galatians 1:3; Hebrews 4:16. For texts on the work of the Holy Spirit, see Ezekiel 37:11–14; Acts 1:8; Romans 8:11; 1 Corinthians 2:4; 1 Thessalonians 1:5; and Titus 3:5. God's people have His law written in their heart (Jer. 31:33); they are not condemned because they believe in the name of Jesus (John 3:18); they have become a new creature (2 Cor. 5:17); they confess their sins and have them forgiven (1 John 1:9); by abiding in Him they avoid sinning (1 John 3:6–9); by God's love, they keep His commandments and keep from sinning (1 John 5:3, 4, 18); Christ is able to keep us from falling (Jude 1:24). If we do sin, we have an advocate (1 John 2:1). When God's people's "fall away," they crucify Christ afresh (Heb. 6:4–6).

4.   Paul gives three lists of the gifts of the Spirit, with variations in each, though "prophets" or "prophecy" is in each list! (Rom. 12:6–8; 1 Cor. 12:4–11; Eph. 4:11–12). The New Testament describes the spread of the gospel through the Roman Empire. Less known is its spread to eastern nations by the Church of the East.

5.   "But this shall be the covenant that I will make with the house of Israel; After those days, saith the LORD, I will put my law in their inward parts, and write it in their hearts; and will be their God, and they shall be my people. And they shall teach no more every man his neighbour, and every man his brother, saying, Know the LORD: for they shall all know me, from the least of them unto the greatest of them, saith the LORD: for I will forgive their iniquity, and I will remember their sin no more" (Jer. 31:33, 34).

"A new heart also will I give you, and a new spirit will I put within you: and I will take away the stony heart out of your flesh, and I will give you an heart of flesh. And I will put my spirit within you, and cause you to walk in my statutes, and ye shall keep my judgments, and do them. And ye shall dwell in the land that I gave to your fathers; and ye shall be my people, and I will be your God" (Ezek. 36:26–28).

6.   The change that comes by grace is described in Jesus' words, "Ye must be born again" (John 3:7). The change that comes from glory to glory is in Paul's statement about beholding Christ (2 Cor. 3:18). "If any man be in Christ, he is a new creature" (2 Cor. 5:17). It is the will of God that every person be changed by God's grace. To be "in Christ" is to be born again, to become more like Him, to put on the robe of His righteousness, and to overcome sin. Yet, each person still has old habits and the sinful nature to overcome. These are covered by the robe of Christ's righteousness. With our consent and through God's grace, the sinful nature is overcome and new habits are formed. Verses on the new birth and the overcoming of sin include John 3:3, 6; 2 Corinthians 5:17; 1 John 2:1, 2; 3:5–7, 9; 5:18.

7.   Ellen G. White, *Steps to Christ* (Nampa, ID: Pacific Press Publishing Association), pp. 94, 95.

8.   The wicked refuse to believe in Christ and are lost (Philip Schaff and David S. Schaff, *The History of Creeds, The Creeds of Christendom* [Grand Rapids: MI: Baker Books, 1983], vol. 1, 6th edition, p. 518).

Chapter 48
The Close of Probation

The close of probation refers to a time after all the people living have made their decision to accept or not to accept God's covenant offer. It is the momentous climax to earth's history when judgment is complete. At that time, Christ has finished His mediation in heaven for the sins of humanity. Then the seven last plagues are poured out as partial punishment on the wicked.

The righteous are under the stress of the "time of Jacob's trouble" in which they agonize with God over the possibility that all their sins have not been confessed and forgiven. During this time, while the righteous are hated by the world, they are protected from harm and death. After a short time, they are reassured, and soon Jesus comes in the clouds of heaven. The wicked are destroyed by the brightness of His coming. The righteous look up and say, "Lo, this is our God; we have waited for him, and he will save us: this is the Lord; we have waited for him, we will be glad and rejoice in his salvation" (Isa. 25:9).

Now is the time for mankind to prepare, watch, and be ready for Jesus' soon coming.

Probation and Judgment

God gave man a new probation in Eden that will continue to the end of history. It is a time when those who know not God have a chance to learn of Him and seek His grace. Uncommitted "Christians" must examine themselves and repent. Committed Christians must afflict their souls in search of hidden sin that they may take them to God and be forgiven and cleansed (Lev. 23:27, 29; 1 John 1:9).

In all this, Satan is the "accuser of the brethren" (Rev. 12:10; Zech. 3:1–10). He knows every sin a person has committed. He claims that God cannot be just and save people. The person under trial has no answer. Then Jesus steps forward and declares, "Father, My blood! My blood! This person has confessed his sin, has put his trust in Me, and My blood covers his sin." Satan has no answer and retires from the court in shame.

Jesus does not accuse the wicked or those who lived for self. He simply says, "I never knew you" (Matt. 7:21–23).

This is a description of the judgment scene. The book of life has been in preparation since the beginning of the world.[1] It is a record of every person who at any time has confessed Christ. Jesus examines the book of life in the antitypical Day of Atonement. The outcome in each case depends on two things: (1) whether the sinner's name is written in the book of life and (2) whether the sins recorded there have been confessed and covered by Jesus' blood. When this examination is complete, probation closes. Then all who are wicked will remain wicked, and all who are righteous will remain righteous (Rev. 22:11).

Minds Made Up

When Jesus completes His mediation, He has also completed the judgment and has closed probation for all people. The Day of Atonement has come and gone. All those whose names are still written in the book of life receive the gift of God; all those whose names are not written there or that have been blotted out will receive the wages of sin in the lake of fire. "For the wages of sin is death; but the gift of God is eternal life through Jesus Christ our Lord" (Rom. 6:23). "And whosoever was not found written in the book of life was cast into the lake of fire" (Rev. 20:15).

Jeremiah echoes what the lost will feel: "The harvest is past, the summer is ended, and we are not saved" (Jer. 8:20).

Christ calls people today to make a decision for Him. In these times, we have the Bible, churches, preachers, and freedom to speak and hear. Jesus Christ is our High Priest mediating for us at the judgment seat of God. For all people who have confessed their sins, Jesus stands in the judgment, pleading His shed blood "to forgive us our sins, and to cleanse us from all unrighteousness" (1 John 1:9).

Just before the end, there will come a time when the issue is pressed upon all people. Will they choose Christ and receive the seal of God and be saved, or will they choose their own way and receive the mark of the beast and be lost? It will be an issue that all will find easy to understand. When all have made their decision, Jesus will close His ministry in the heavenly sanctuary. He forever seals for salvation those who have chosen Him; those who have rejected Him and received the mark of the beast will be lost.

Jesus is in the business of saving people, and all who desire to be with Him for eternity will know what to do. If there is any advice that needs to be given at this time, it is that *now* is the time to choose Christ and be ready for His soon return.

A One-Day Probation in Eden

Probation has closed several times in history. God gave the first warning of judgment in the Garden of Eden, "But of the tree of the knowledge of good and evil, thou shalt not eat of it: for in the day that thou eatest thereof thou shalt surely die" (Gen. 2:17).

Commonly, a day is twenty-four hours. In a symbolic sense, a "day" can be more than twenty-four hours, as in the "day of judgment." A prophetic day is one year (Num. 14:34; Ezek. 4:6). If Adam and Eve disregarded God's warning in Eden, there were immediate consequences (Gen. 2:17). Since Adam and Eve did not die that day, some interpret the expression, "dying, thou shalt die," as meaning that they began the process of dying.[2] Whatever the meaning, if human beings were to sin, they would lose their relation with God and eventually die the second death (Rev. 2:11; 20:6, 14; 21:8), from which there is no resurrection.

God is merciful, gracious, and longsuffering (Exod. 34:6). When Adam and Eve sinned, their probation of sinless perfection ended immediately. However, before the sun had set, God came to them that same day and gave them the covenant of redemption. "And I will put enmity between thee and the woman, and between thy seed and her seed; it shall bruise thy head, and thou shalt bruise his heel" (Gen. 3:15).

Satan would not have free reign with sinful man. God gave human beings a conscience, which is an inborn enmity against evil. Christ would become humanity's Redeemer and deliver humankind from sin. Through His own suffering, He *bought* all people back and put them under the covenant of grace. God gave Adam and Eve a new probation in which to learn more about God and make an intelligent choice to serve Him. When every human has made a final decision to serve God, or Satan, probation will close.

The Earth Judged and Destroyed by a Flood

Fifteen hundred years after the Creation, evil had increased to a point that God had to act and put a stop to it. Exercising authority as the Creator and owner of this earth and as humanity's Redeemer, God brought the flood on the earth as a judgment against evil. It was a promise, that, in the justice of God, all evil would eventually be destroyed.

> The Lord saw that the wickedness of man was great in the earth, and that every intention of the thoughts of his heart was only evil continually. So the Lord said, "I will blot out man whom I have created from the face of the land, man and animals and creeping things and birds of the heavens, for I am sorry that I have made them." (Gen. 6:5, 7, ESV)

God is patient. He says, "My spirit shall not always strive with man, for that he also is flesh: yet his days shall be an hundred and twenty years" (Gen. 6:3). Noah preached during the 120 years that he was building the ark (2 Peter 2:5). The immense ark was a spectacular achievement and a tourist attraction. Everyone would have known about it and the message that Noah preached. Noah hired helpers, and they got the message too. In the end, only Noah and his family chose to enter the ark and be saved.

As they entered, God Himself shut the door (Gen. 7:16), and no one could enter, and no one could go out. The second probation for the earth had closed, but the people outside the ark did not know it until seven days later, when the waters burst forth and flooded the earth.

The people of that time had passed the bounds of wickedness. God took them away by the flood because they refused to listen or respond to the warning messages that He sent through Noah.

Sodom and Gomorrah's Day of Mercy

About 450 years later, Abraham settled in Canaan, and the wickedness of Sodom came up before God. Even with their wealth, the people of Sodom neglected the poor. Their idleness led them to seek wicked, selfish pleasures such as fornication and perversion.[3] As a warning, God allowed four kings from the east to conquer and put them to tribute. Twelve years later, they lost a second war, and the kings of the east took the wealth of the city as well as Lot and his family. Abraham saved them. However, the sins of Sodom grew worse, and God determined to destroy them. Had there been ten righteous people in the city of Sodom, God would have saved it (Gen. 18:32). However, ten righteous people could not be found.

The people of the cities of the plain had passed beyond the forbearance of God and had failed to heed the warning given them. A third probation had closed. "Then the Lord rained down burning sulfur on Sodom and Gomorrah—from the Lord out of the heavens" (Gen. 19:24, NIV).

When the Cup Is Full, Judgment is Due

Abraham lived among the Amorites for 100 years as an example of the goodness of God. There were an estimated 1,000 souls in Abram's encampment. These lived according to the commands of God (Gen. 18:19).[4] Aner, Eschol, and Mamre were Abram's friends. The Amorites retained knowledge of God, and God continued to be merciful, allowing them time to repent if they would (Gen. 15:13, 16). They did not. God had promised Abram: "In the fourth generation your descendants will come back here, for the sin of the Amorites has not yet reached its full measure" (Gen. 15:16, NIV).

After the prophesied 430 years, the children of Israel were delivered from Egypt and they returned to Canaan. In that land, they found depravity, idolatry and even human sacrifice. The various peoples of the region were determined in their rebellion against God and in their opposition to Israel, God's chosen people. A fourth probation had passed, and the inhabitants of Canaan were due for judgment. Joshua overtook the land in a series of victories. The armies of Israel were an instrument in the hand of God to cleanse the land of idolaters.

Was God being murderous and vindictive to destroy the Canaanites? When the armies of Israel invaded the land, the Canaanites knew how God had delivered Israel from Egypt (Joshua 2:9-11). They could have joined Israel as did Rahab and her family and as did the Gibeonites. Instead, they continued in rebellion and tried to exterminate Israel.

Did Israel commit genocide? They did not, for two reasons: firstly, even with uninterrupted victories under Joshua, Israel did not entirely clear the land of its inhabitants. Secondly, Israel was a theocracy under the direct rule of God, who makes no mistake. It is the prerogative of God and God alone to bring judgment upon an unrepentant people.

Women and children were to be included in this judgment because they were influential in preserving the culture. Their idolatrous practices would have been a continual temptation if they lived side by side with the Israelites. It was necessary to eliminate them too.

Israel was different from any other state in the history of the world—God Himself directed its affairs. The Sinai covenant showed God's purpose for Israel. They were to be "an holy nation" (Exod. 19:5, 6). Isaiah wrote that it was God's purpose to bring a reign of peace upon the earth, even before the final deliverance of His people. This was not possible if idolaters remained.

Israel's Opportunity Lost

After becoming established in Canaan, the next phase of Israel's history was a dreary story of apostasy, idolatry, and oppression by nearby heathen nations. Following each event, a righteous judge arose among them, bringing revival, deliverance, and peace for a period of years. This cycle repeated over and over and continued under the monarchy. Of the twenty-three kings of Judah, only six were God-fearing. The idolatry of the people grew worse, even to the point of passing their children through the fire and performing heathen rites in the court of the Temple (Ezek. 8:5–16). They persecuted, stoned, and killed the prophets. A fifth probation closed, and God allowed the kingdom of Babylon to take them captive for seventy years. "But they mocked the messengers of God, and despised his words, and scoffed at his prophets, until the wrath of Jehovah arose against his people, till there was no remedy" (2 Chron. 36:16, ASV).

Their seventy years in captivity taught them to avoid image worship. God gave them marvelous promises at the restoration of their land, with 490 years' probation to fulfill their purpose as a nation, bringing in righteousness and preparing for the coming Messiah (Dan. 9:24–27).

They started well under Ezra and Nehemiah. In time, their covenant with God became corrupted as they focused, as a means of earning salvation, on the "law of Moses," which included the Ten Commandments, the ceremonial law and the civil law. Then they added hundreds of regulations to ensure that they kept the law. The sacrifices and rituals became a means to earn salvation, and they ignored the Messiah to whom they pointed. Only a few showed love for either God or man.

They developed a rigid concept of the coming Messiah as being one who would expel their enemies and restore the ancient glory of Israel. Jesus' supernatural birth did not interest the national leaders, rather, they turned His single-parent conception into an epithet (John 8:41), rejected Him and crucified Him as a criminal on Calvary. This was an official action by the Sanhedrin, the governing body of the nation.

For another three and a half years, the church spoke to the Jewish nation. Thousands joined the church. The nation as a whole and its leadership in particular rejected their Messiah again through the appeals of Stephen, abruptly ending his life under a heap of stones. This marked the end of their 490-year probation (Acts 6:12, 13; 7:55, 56, 59, 60). In rejecting Christ, Israel rejected the covenant as well as their position as the chosen people of God. The church, made up of Jews and Gentiles, would now be the chosen people.[5]

The Final Sin

We live in an age of enlightenment. However, under the cover of civilization, sin remains in the human heart. As humans become more selfish, cruel, and obsessed with pleasure, there will come a time when God must act, as He did because of the sins of Sodom and Gomorrah. The final sin will be to turn away from the truth of God, doing evil and thinking that they are doing the will of God!

God has shown His love towards the people. He has invited, sought, and wooed sinners to choose Him. Jesus came and died that all might be saved. He sent warnings to all people. In the end time, an issue arises giving every living person an opportunity to make a decision to serve God or choose another master. Then the seventh and final probation will close. Should it be surprising that there is a close of probation? Probation closes every time a man dies. The final close of probation is different only in that it occurs while human beings are still living.

God is a God of love and mercy. He is also a God of justice, which is an expression of His love. He has given every person free will, and He honors the choices that each makes. He does not force anyone to choose Him or to live for eternity where his or her "pleasures" do not exist.

The Christian church has a mandate to preach the gospel to the world before probation closes. After that, Jesus will come to receive His people to be with Him in a world made new. *Now* is the time to get ready. His coming is soon. "And this gospel of the kingdom shall be preached in all the world for a witness unto all nations; and then shall the end come" (Matt. 24:14).

The angels hold the winds of trouble and strife until the gospel reaches the world and God seals His people (Rev. 7:1–4). God's final message will divide those who worship Him from those who persist in rebellion. The issue will be so clear that all will understand it. God is long-suffering. He waits to give everyone opportunity to know Him. After this message reaches all, probation will close.

No Further Appeals

The close of probation marks the completion of the end-time judgment. It is a judgment from which there is no appeal! All have made their decision. There are no more souls to win and no more work for God to do.

> And at that time shall Michael stand up, the great prince which standeth for the children of thy people: and there shall be a time of trouble, such as never was since there was a nation even to that same time: and at that time thy people shall be delivered, every one that shall be found written in the book. And many of them that sleep in the dust of the earth shall awake, some to everlasting life, and some to shame and everlasting contempt. (Dan. 12:1, 2)

There will follow a time of trouble such as never was (Dan. 12:1). The wicked receive the "mark of the beast" (Rev. 13:17; 16:2). The angels pour out the seven last plagues (Rev. 15, 16). Satan and evil human beings are unrestrained, and sin will reach its deepest degradation. The wicked demonstrate the full effect of the reign of sin.

At the same time, there will be an outpouring of the Holy Spirit among God's people, with signs and wonders, that will exceed the outpouring on the early church. His people will shine as stars in the blackest night (Dan. 12:3), showing before the universe the full effect of the love and grace of God. The faithful, believing remnant will recognize the beauty and freedom in God's law and will gladly obey it as the foundation of God's government. Because Jesus died to uphold His law, sin shall not arise again!

Those who choose to serve God will not be alone, for Jesus will be with them even to the end of the world (Matt. 28:20). The Holy Spirit will comfort God's people, and angels who "excel in strength" will guard them (Ps. 103:20; 34:7; 91:10–12). God's people will receive the seal of God (Rev. 7:1–4).

The everlasting covenant of grace is now complete. Jesus is satisfied as the "called, and chosen, and faithful" enter the kingdom with Him (Rev. 17:14). Sin and sinners are no more; purity, love, and harmony permeate an earth made new. "He that is unjust, let him be unjust still: and he which is filthy, let him be filthy still: and he that is righteous, let him be righteous still: and he that is holy, let him be holy still" (Rev. 22:11). "For the Lord shall rise up as in mount Perazim, he shall be wroth as in the valley of Gibeon, that he may do his work, his strange work; and bring to pass his act, his strange act" (Isa. 28:21). "And whosoever was not found written in the book of life was cast into the lake of fire" (Rev. 20:15).

The final warnings above are a call to come to Christ *now*, to receive the hope and blessings He has for you!

Endnotes

1. Is your name written in the Lamb's book of life (Ps. 69:28; Phil. 4:3; Rev. 3:5; 13:8; 17:8; 20:15; 21:27; 22:19)?

2. For more information on the phrase, "thou shalt surely die"/"dying, thou shalt die" (Gen. 2:17, KJV and NASB), see Strong's Greek-Hebrew dictionary. Literally it is "you shall die die" (*mōt* [qal perfect] *tamut* [qal imperfect]). The repetition of the word "die" (Hebrew *mōt*) emphasizes the surety of their death.

3. The sins of Sodom are described in Genesis 13:13; Ezekiel 16:49; and Jude 1:7.

4. "Abraham's household comprised more than a thousand souls. Those who were led by his teachings to worship the one God found a home in his encampment; and here, as in a school, they received such instruction as would prepare them to be representatives of the true faith. Thus a great responsibility rested upon him. He was training heads of families, and his methods of government would be carried out in the households over which they should preside" (Ellen G. White, *Patriarchs and Prophets* [Nampa, ID: Pacific Press Publishing Association, 2005], p. 141).

5. See chapter 34, "Probation Closed for Israel as a Nation."

Chapter 49

The 144,000

And I looked, and, lo, a Lamb stood on the mount Sion, and with him an hundred forty and four thousand, having his Father's name written in their foreheads. And I heard a voice from heaven, as the voice of many waters, and as the voice of a great thunder: and I heard the voice of harpers harping with their harps: And they sung as it were a new song before the throne, and before the four beasts, and the elders: and no man could learn that song but the hundred and forty and four thousand, which were redeemed from the earth. These are they which were not defiled with women; for they are virgins. These are they which follow the Lamb whithersoever he goeth. These were redeemed from among men, being the firstfruits unto God and to the Lamb.
Revelation 14:1–4

In this end time, Satan claims that the covenant was a failure. He claims that Jesus died on Calvary in vain and that grace is not sufficient to save. Professed Christians, he says, while faithfully attending church, are selfish, greedy, pleasure loving, and hypocrites in their claim to love God.

God has always had His faithful, believing remnant. The remnant are vital to God, for even one righteous man challenges Satan's claim to rule this world (Job 1:6–2:10). During the time of Elijah, God claimed that He had "seven thousand" in Israel that had "not bowed the knee to Baal" (1 Kings 19:18). Now in the end time, He will seal 144,000 in their foreheads. There is also a "great multitude, which no man could number" who will stand "before His throne" (Rev. 7:9). God provides the Bible, churches, schools, pastors, and the Holy Spirit to help change the life of each person who consents to the work of grace. He will show that grace has the power to reach and change whosoever will. The 144,000 and the great multitude have been faithful through extreme tribulation!

The Few, the Faithful, the Saved

There are five faculties in the human nature: reason, conscience, and will make up the higher powers; appetites and passions comprise the lower powers. Sinless Adam and Eve possessed these powers in perfect balance. After sin, humanity inherited the fallen nature, which is controlled by unbelief, selfishness, pride, and lack of love for God and man.

Controlled by the sinful nature, humans began to worship self rather than God. They increasingly catered to the desires of the lower powers. The higher powers were weakened and lacked control over appetite and passion.[1]

It is not easy or popular to deny self. Those who choose to serve God have always been few in number. Satan contends that the number is so small that it is insignificant, and many who start well on the path of serving God soon give up (Zech. 3:1–9; Heb. 6:4–6). The sinning of God's people has always been an embarrassment for God's kingdom.[2]

God lays claim to this earth through the presence of even one righteous man (Job 1:8–22). He would have saved Sodom from destruction if even ten righteous people could be found in it (Gen. 18:32). Each of these is only a small remnant. In the flood, God found and saved Noah and his family, a small remnant, out of the entire population of the earth (Gen. 6:9–18).

Grace Is Sufficient to Save

By contrast, there were millions in the Christian era whose commitment to Christ was stronger than death (Rev. 12:11). After the Reformation, many thousands sacrificed money and position to go to foreign lands to carry the gospel.

In this "time of the end," prosperity has brought new temptations, and Satan assails Christianity on all sides. It is the purpose of God to demonstrate that grace is sufficient to save, even in the worst of conditions. He will place the seal of God in the forehead of 144,000 dedicated people. These are they who, consenting to the full work of grace in their lives, survive Satan's unrestrained work of evil in a great time of trouble.

> And after these things I saw four angels standing on the four corners of the earth, holding the four winds of the earth, that the wind should not blow on the earth, nor on the sea, nor on any tree. And I saw another angel ascending from the east, having the seal of the living God: and he cried with a loud voice to the four angels, to whom it was given to hurt the earth and the sea, saying, Hurt not the earth, neither the sea, nor the trees, till we have sealed the servants of our God in their foreheads. And I heard the number of them which were sealed: and there were sealed an hundred and forty and four thousand of all the tribes of the children of Israel. (Rev. 7:1–4)

Four Angels Holding Four Winds

The "four angels … holding the four winds of the earth" is symbolic language. Four winds indicate winds coming from every direction. In Revelation, water is a symbol for peoples and nations, and winds are forces that stir up the waters, symbolic of trouble and war that stir up people and nations.[3] The four angels hold these winds of trouble until God has sealed His servants "in their foreheads" (Rev. 7:3).

God is patient and gives time for all to decide whom they will serve. When this final decision is made by everyone on earth, probation will close; then the winds of trouble will be let loose.

"He that is unjust, let him be unjust still: and he which is filthy, let him be filthy still: and he that is righteous, let him be righteous still: and he that is holy, let him be holy still" (Rev. 22:11).

At the time this becomes reality it will be too late to choose God. The wicked have resisted and grieved the Holy Spirit until the mind is numb; the Holy Spirit can no longer be heard, and they lose salvation. The time to learn faith and accept grace is now. In one's life, every day is a day of probation and a chance to choose Christ. There will come a time when the issue becomes a crisis of whether each person will serve God or not. Every person on earth will understand the issue and make a decision.

Then comes the close of probation. While this can be a terror to the wicked, it is a comfort to the righteous. Christ has sealed the righteous because they have chosen Him. Nothing on earth or below the earth can change their minds.

That decision will soon come. The question is: Are you choosing Christ now?

The 144,000, Living Their Faith

Jesus' sacrifice on Calvary made possible the eventual destruction of sin and Satan—and the restoration of the new earth to the perfection of Eden. The change in people's lives has taken longer. The purpose and power of God is available through grace, but accepting God's grace requires a free-will decision and the consent of each person.

This is the issue in the great controversy between Christ and Satan at that time. Satan says that Jesus died in vain and that grace cannot change people's lives (Zech. 3:1–4; Rev. 12:10). In the time of the end, grace will have transformed the character of the 144,000 (Rev. 14:1, 4). This large group will live their faith in perilous times.

"They that be wise shall shine as the brightness of the firmament; and they that turn many to righteousness as the stars forever and ever" (Dan. 12:3). These are God's unique people at a special time in earth's history, people who are active in witness and evangelism. They "keep the commandments of God and have the testimony of Jesus Christ" (Rev. 12:17) during a terrible time of trouble, but "at that time thy people shall be delivered, every one that shall be found written in the book" (Dan. 12:1; cf. Ps. 91).

The Seal and Character of God

God has a seal. In ancient times, a seal was a lump of clay or wax that was imprinted with the signet ring of the sender to indicate a letter or document's authenticity. Today we use embossed seals and, more often, a witnessed, handwritten signature.

A seal typically stated the name of the person, his authority, and his jurisdiction. God has placed His seal in the middle of the Ten Commandments. In the Sabbath command, He gives His name: "the Lord thy God" and His authority as Creator and His jurisdiction over "heaven and earth, the sea and all that in them is."

But the seventh day is the sabbath of the Lord thy God: in it thou shalt not do any work, thou, nor thy son, nor thy daughter, thy manservant, nor thy maidservant, nor thy cattle, nor thy stranger that is within thy gates: For in six days the Lord made

heaven and earth, the sea, and all that in them is, and rested the seventh day: wherefore the Lord blessed the sabbath day, and hallowed it. (Exod. 20:10, 11)

There are some who will object to this identification of the seal, claiming that we are "sealed with
that Holy Spirit of promise" (Eph. 1:13). While this is undoubtedly true, to be "sealed" by the Holy
Spirit is to use "seal" as a verb, which is an action word. The Holy Spirit is the one who does the sealing.
"Seal" in Revelation is a noun. Identifying the "seal" of God as the Sabbath is to use "seal" as a noun, a
word that names something. When the Holy Spirit seals people, He puts the principle of the Sabbath
("seal" as a noun) into their soul (Exod. 31:13; Ezek. 20:12, 20); He places within them a commitment
and relationship with God, the Creator of heaven and earth.

The Holy Spirit seals them in the forehead because—

1. They are born again.
2. In Christ, they are each one a "new creature."
3. By beholding Christ, they become like Him (John 3:5; 2 Cor. 3:18; 5:17).

Receiving the Sabbath as a seal is to choose to make God first in one's life, choosing His will
above all other influences, even above one's own opinion. This seal is also the sign of sanctification
(Exod. 31:13; Ezek. 20:12, 20). The seal of the 144,000 is a sign of commitment to Christ.[4]

Why keep the seventh-day Sabbath? There are immediate and practical reasons for keeping each
of the other nine commandments. The fourth commandment also has its practical benefits. It provides needed rest, refreshment, and fellowship on a regular basis. Yet, why must this occur on the
seventh-day? There are two reasons: (1) It is a tangible reminder that God is the Creator. (2) We keep
the seventh-day because God made it holy and He said to keep it holy. We show our submission to His
will and our willingness to keep all His commandments, simply because on the basis of His command.

By way of contrast, worship on the first day of the week is entirely of human thinking and authority. A
fallible ecclesiastical system is proud to claim that they transferred the sanctity of the seventh to the first day
in the early history of the Christian church. The change is the sign of their authority. From time to time in
the past, the day one keeps has become a public issue. It will again become an issue at the very end of time.

When the second beast of Revelation 13 creates a copy, or an "image," of the first beast, he will
enforce by law the mark of the first beast on all people (Rev. 13:1–17). When the second beast passes
this law, accepting the mark of the beast in the hand (which signifies outward compliance) or in the
forehead (which signifies inward conviction) is to worship the beast and its image. Thus, to keep the
seventh-day Sabbath becomes the seal of God, and to worship on the first day of the week in response
to the pressure of law becomes the mark of the beast.[5]

Who Are the 144,000?

Revelation 7 gives the number 144,000 in clear, unequivocal terms. Listing 12,000 for each of
the twelve tribes of Israel emphasizes the meaning of 144,000. However, 144,000 is a small number

compared to all the known Christians on earth today. We know that many professed Christians are such in name only and do not have a real faith in Jesus. Does this mean that there are only 144,000 true Christians? No, there are more. Yet, no one knows whether the number 144,000 is a literal grouping of people or if it is merely a symbol. We do know that the 144,000 are a unique group. The wording of Revelation 7 indicates that these individuals are living through the close of probation and the time of trouble. There is evidence that this group lives to see Jesus come, as the following verses would indicate:

> And at that time shall Michael stand up, the great prince which standeth for the children of thy people: and there shall be a time of trouble, such as never was since there was a nation even to that same time: and at that time thy people shall be delivered, every one that shall be found written in the book. And many of them that sleep in the dust of the earth shall awake, some to everlasting life, and some to shame and everlasting contempt. And they that be wise shall shine as the brightness of the firmament; and they that turn many to righteousness as the stars for ever and ever. (Dan. 12:1–3)

Michael stands up when He has completed judgment and closed probation. It is time for Him to return to earth and claim His people. Before He comes, there will be a time of trouble, during which He protects His people who will be living to see Christ come again (Ps. 91). At His coming, He raises the righteous dead to meet Him in the air (1 Thess. 4:16, 17). That is the hope of every Christian.

"They that be wise" are also the 144,000. These are now actively witnessing for Christ, urging people to choose Christ now while they have time. To be a member of the 144,000 is the greatest gift one can give to Jesus. If a person loves Jesus, and he or she wants to honor His name, that person will strive to be one of the 144,000.

Will only the 144,000 be saved? No, in this same chapter in Revelation, there is another group that stands before the throne of God. It is "a great multitude, which no man could number" (Rev. 7:9). This grouping makes room for every person who chooses Christ to be saved. This vast multitude includes the last-day martyrs (Rev. 20:4) and God's people through the ages. They live and reign with Christ for 1,000 years and have a part in the judgment. During this period of time, Jesus answers all questions about His justice and mercy in salvation. To know that God saves a "great multitude" is an encouragement to us all. Yet, who are the 144,000? What is this group?

Are They Jews?

Twelve tribes, named after the sons of Jacob and numbering 12,000 each, make up the 144,000. The tribes listed in Revelation 7 with their meaning are given below. (It should be noted that Revelation does not list either Ephraim, which means "fruitful," nor Dan, which means "judge, plead the cause.")

- Judah – celebrated; praise, give thanks, confess to
- Reuben – see a (first born) son, a proof that his wife will have children

- Gad – to invade, overcome
- Asher – blessed, happy
- Naphtali – my wrestling, struggle
- Manasseh – causing to forget
- Simeon – hearing; hearken, obey
- Levi – attached
- Issachar – he will bring a reward, wages
- Zebulun – habitation; dwell with me
- Joseph – let him add, increase
- Benjamin – son of the right hand.

The numbering of the tribes indicates the significance of the total, 144,000. We do not know now if this number is literal or symbolic. The naming of the tribes, with their varied characteristics, shows that a complete cross-section of humanity with their various characteristics will make up this group.

Are they Jews? They probably are not. At present, the Christian church is largely a Gentile body. However, all Christians are "Abraham's seed." "And if ye be Christ's, then are ye Abraham's seed, and heirs according to the promise" (Gal. 3:29). God gave the covenant to Abraham and to his seed after him.[6] God's people have always been under the covenant of Abraham, including the Christian church today! God grafted the Gentiles into the tree of God's chosen people, and they partake of the covenant of Abraham (Rom. 11:17, 18).

Have the Jews Lost Their Place?

The term "replacement theology" is a sore point with Jews, and they have had untold suffering because of some of the beliefs that fall under this theology. Many evangelical Christians expect the Jews to play a large part in end-time events. Much material on the Internet shows that there is considerable confusion about end-time events. Prophecies of the end times are usually symbolic, allowing room for difference of opinion. The Catholic Council of Trent promoted a futuristic interpretation of Revelation. This built a foundation for the present-day beliefs of the secret rapture, the seven-year tribulation, and various views on the role of the Jews in end-time events. It is beyond the scope of this chapter, or even this book, to discuss these issues.

Suffice it to say that, throughout history, there have always been two classes of people. There is the faithful, believing remnant, and there is the careless, unbelieving majority. Sometimes a clear-cut division exists, but more often there is an overlap between these two groups. Shortly before Jesus comes again, the issue of the seal of God and the mark of the beast will clearly divide all humanity into two distinct groups.

The presence of these two groups in the history of Israel has led to confused viewpoints on the covenant. These two groups were present at the time of Christ. A careful understanding of the faithful, believing remnant (Rom. 11:2–7) will show that there has never been a "replacement" of Israel. The faithful, believing remnant of Israel made up the true Israel of God, and these Jews continued as the early Christian church. Into the trunk of the covenant people of God, God grafted Gentile converts (Rom. 11:17).

Israel, as a nation, lost her place as the covenant people of God, but this was a change that had occurred long before, due to their unbelief. Are the 144,000 made up of ethnic Jews? Many are, but only those in Christ receive the seal of God. To be an ethnic Jew is not enough to be saved. Only in the name of Christ is anyone saved (Rom. 2:25–29; Acts 4:12).

The early church was a Jewish church. Without the Jews, there would be no Christian church. As a nation, they, because of their leaders, turned away from Jesus as their Messiah (Acts 6:12, 13; 7:58–60). At the same time, there were thousands of individuals who chose to accept Him, and they began a strong work of witnessing for Him and spreading the gospel throughout the Roman Empire and beyond.

Will the Jews have a part in hastening the coming of our Lord? Will they be part of the 144,000? Yes, they will! God has not forgotten His people. He is willing to graft back into the tree all who will choose Christ as their Messiah (Rom. 11:23).

Will a large number of Jews be converted and make up the entire number of the 144,000? No, I do not believe that is the case. This is just my belief, but I believe it is risky to think that God is waiting for the return of the Jews as a people. It is risky because we must come to Christ now! Now is the time of salvation. Now is the time to choose Him. Now is the time to develop a faith that will be strong in spite of weariness, hunger, and delay. There is danger in waiting for some event that may never happen.

The significance of the 144,000 is that God will have a distinct, large group of people who have committed their lives 100 percent to Jesus. They will demonstrate to humans and angels that grace is sufficient to save! There is room now to honor Christ in choosing Him. I would be happy to see 144,000 Jews make up this number, but I suspect that most of this number will be Gentiles who have given themselves 100 percent to Jesus.

Endnotes

1. Thomas A. Davis, *Questions That Demand Answers* (Rapidan, VA: Hartland Publications, 1988), pp. 29–31.
2. God's people's sinning creates problems (2 Sam. 12:14; Heb. 6:4–6; 1 John 2:1, 5; 3:5–7, 9, 24).
3. Water is a symbol of people and nations (Jer. 51:13, 55, NIV; Ezek. 26:19; 27:34; Rev. 17:1, 15).
4. God's people receive a new name (Rev. 2:17; 3:12). The seal of God and the name of God are related (Rev. 7:3); Jesus has a new name (Rev. 19:11–13, 15).
5. I must honestly and frankly present what I believe to be the truth about the mark of the beast. I will offend some by what I say, but that does not lessen my responsibility to say what I believe to be the truth and what we need for this time. The topic of the mark of the beast is critically important for each person. It is a matter of eternal life or death. Yet, the mark of the beast is not in effect at the present time. It is only when our nation enforces a false church doctrine by law that she will give the mark of the beast to those who comply. This is just a brief outline; much more could be said.
6. In giving the covenant to Abraham, God gave it to all his descendants (Gen. 17:7–10, 19). Abraham would be the "father of many nations" (Gen. 17:4, 5). Of the seven times that God gave Abraham the covenant, the greatest detail comes in Genesis 17:7–10, 19. The Abrahamic covenant extended to the church (1 Peter 2:9; Gal. 3:29).

Chapter 50

They Follow the Lamb

These are they which were not defiled with women; for they are virgins. These are they which follow the Lamb whithersoever he goeth. These were redeemed from among men, being the firstfruits unto God and to the Lamb.
Revelation 14:4

Has the covenant been successful? Have people's lives been changed? The work of grace was to take people with a sinful nature, often also with sinful habits, and change them into children of God. The happiness and joy found among God's people is in marked contrast to the negative situations and attitudes found among the people of the world. God's people reveal the beauty and happiness there is in living for Christ. They will take to heaven and the new earth a love that will bind together all God's creation for eternity.

A Special People

The 144,000 are essential to God's plan. Revelation 14:1–5 describes this group's character. When Jesus comes again, the 144,000 have the privilege of living to see Him come, and be saved without seeing death. Those in this exceptional group walk with God as did exceptional people in Scripture:

- Adam was created one of the "sons of God" (Gen. 6:2, 4; Job 1:6).
- "Enoch walked with God: and he was not; for God took him" (Gen. 5:24).
- "Noah was a just man and perfect in his generations" (Gen. 6:9).
- "Abraham believed God, … and he was called the Friend of God" (James 2:23).
- "The Lord spake unto Moses face to face, as a man speaketh unto his friend" (Exod. 33:11).
- "David the son of Jesse, [was] a man after [God's] own heart," to fulfill all of God's will (Acts 13:22).
- Daniel was "greatly beloved …" (Dan. 9:23; 10:11, 19).
- "Jesus loved Martha, and her sister [Mary], and Lazarus" (John 11:5).
- John was the disciple "whom Jesus loved" (John 13:23).
- Mary washed Jesus' feet and received His commendation: "against the day of my burying hath she kept this" (John 12:7).

This is a list of ten select people in the Bible, and there are many more. If God is not a respecter of persons, how can he have "select people?" This is not solely because God chose them, but because they responded to God and made Him first in their lives. God responds to love, and that is what made these ten people unique. It is love for God that also makes the 144,000 unique. They have each individually come close to Jesus!

The Lamb Stood on Mount Zion

Jesus is "the Lamb slain from the foundation of the world" (Rev. 13:8). He has paid the penalty of sin for every man.[1] The New Jerusalem has come down from God out of heaven to the Mount of Olives, which has divided into a great plain (Zech. 14:4).

With Jesus on Mt. Zion are the 144,000, a group who are God's elect. They have demonstrated that Jesus' sacrifice on Calvary provided grace that is sufficient to save and sufficient to change the life. The firstfruit of redemption is the 144,000, a gift to Jesus that makes His suffering a success (Isa. 53:11; Heb. 12:2).

They have His Father's name written in their foreheads. A name represents identity and character. God restores His image in the redeemed. They reflect His character fully.

The 144,000 sing a new song—a song that represents a new experience that no one else has ever had.[2] They have lived through a time when Satan is unrestrained in his treachery and cruelty, and they have depended entirely on the grace and power of God for protection and support (Ps. 91; Isa. 33:16). Their main concern is whether there is any unconfessed sin in their life, but they find none. They do not have to consider this long, for Jesus soon comes in the clouds of heaven, raising the righteous dead and delivering the waiting saints! The 144,000 sing their song of experience as they arrive on the sea of glass, before the throne of God. It is a song that no one else can sing (Rev. 4:6; 15:3).

The four "beasts" are present: the lion, the calf, the man, and the eagle, representing the four divisions of the camp of Israel (Rev. 4:7). Twenty-four elders are on thrones about the throne of God. Elders are "old men" of wisdom and responsibility. They may represent the foundation of the living temple of God resting on the prophets and the apostles (Eph. 2:19, 20; 1 Peter 2:5). It is in this setting that we see the portrayal of the 144,000 in heaven.

They Are Virgins

Taken literally, the requirement that they be "virgins" (Rev. 14:4), not having been "defiled with women," would severely limit who would be qualified for this group. However, Revelation is a book of symbols. A woman represents the church, though here the language points to individuals. Being a "virgin" means having purity in life and doctrine and having no other loyalty except to Christ.

Thus, the 144,000 have loyally followed in Jesus' footsteps on this earth. In the new earth, they loyally "follow the Lamb whithersoever He goeth" (Rev. 14:4) The most desirable place in the new earth will be next to Christ. Those who are closest to Christ in heaven are those who have sought to be close to Christ on this earth! Those who are privileged to converse with Christ in heaven are those who have spent time conversing with Him on earth!

The virgins are firstfruits. In an agricultural community, firstfruits are the biggest, the sweetest and the best. These are people who most fully represent the power of grace to change the life and most fully reflect the character of Christ in their lives. For this, Jesus is satisfied.

Without Fault Before the Throne of God

The description of these pure followers of Christ includes the phrase, "In their mouth was found no guile" (Rev. 14:5) This means no deceit, no lying, only the absolute truth. This is a characteristic that all Christians claim. Yet, how often will there be found subtle deceit in one's words and actions? Sometimes telling the truth hurts us (Ps. 15:4). Sometimes it hurts others for us to tell the truth. Shall we then always tell the truth? This is not an easy matter. However, when a Christian always tells the truth, he is putting the results of that action in the hands of God. In saying this, one must also recognize that sometimes there are facts that need *not* be said—ones that will unnecessarily harm another.

It seems that this last characteristic is what it takes to be "without fault before the throne of God." Are we talking about perfection here? Maybe we are! Perfect trust, perfect faith in Christ puts your life in the hands of Christ. He is the Author and Finisher of your faith. He is responsible for your "perfection." Perfection then is in your trust and faith in Christ.

Is such perfection without sin? Here, one must be careful. We will each continue to have a sinful nature and sinful propensities until Jesus comes again, when "this corruptible must put on incorruption" (1 Cor. 15:53). So does the person sin? The Bible says that the person who is in Christ does not sin (1 John 3:5, 6; 5:18). That is reassuring.

How can a person arrive at such a point? Remember that your faith and your perfection are in the hands of Christ. When people contemplate the purity and perfection of Christ, they realize ever more their sin and shortcomings. When people put their life in the hands of Christ, their perfection is by the power of His grace (Gal. 2:20; 1 John 1:6–10).

At conversion, people become a "new creature," and they are given pardon and salvation. However, the sinful nature is still present, which must be covered with the robe of Christ's righteousness until Jesus comes again. Habitual, besetting sins and "blind spots" still remain, which must be overcome by grace. This is the process called "growth in grace." Will a person ever achieve perfection? This is in the hands of Christ, but a person must make his commitment to Christ complete in order to receive the seal of God.[3]

In the beauty of the new earth, we will study the science of salvation. We will learn more—much more—of what it cost for Jesus to come to earth, live a sinless life, and die on the cross that people might be saved. This is a story that will reach deep into the hearts and minds of every person. Since the saved of the earth are the only ones to have this experience, they will travel to other worlds to tell sinless beings the story of salvation.

Jesus came and died to preserve the unique gifts that God gave to humankind. Even in eternity, people will still possess free will and creativity. Knowing the cost for Christ to die for our sins will create a barrier against sin in the minds of each person that no one will ever again cross. "What do ye imagine against the Lord? he will make an utter end: affliction shall not rise up the second time" (Nahum 1:9). The redeemed will focus their activities and lives in such a way as to return to Him the glory that He gave up to save mankind.

The key issue here is that each person's personal probation closes at death. However, there will come a generation that will be alive to see Jesus come. Only the "pure in heart" will see God (Matt. 5:8).

Character must be formed now. Sins must be confessed and forsaken now (Rom. 13:11). When, for any reason, a person refuses Jesus Christ, it becomes more difficult to hear and obey later. A person cannot afford to let salvation pass him or her by.

Endnotes

1. Jesus paid the penalty for sin for every human being (Rev. 13:8; Isa. 53:5, 10, 11; Rom. 5:15–19; 1 Tim. 2:4).

2. There are many passages of Scripture about songs and poetry praising God (Exod. 15:1–21; Deut. 32:1–43; 33:1–29; Joshua 10:12, 13; Judges 5; 1 Sam. 2:1–10; 2 Sam. 1:19–27; 2 Sam. 22; 23:1–7; Psalms; Song of Solomon). There were other songs during these times. Some were recorded in the Bible; many others were not. The figurative language of Revelation contains the songs of the heavenly beings praising God on His throne. "And they sung as it were a new song before the throne, and before the four beasts, and the elders: and no man could learn that song but the hundred and forty and four thousand, which were redeemed from the earth" (Rev. 14:3). There are many songs in heaven, but the song of the 144,000 is unique. These sing about living in the last hours of earth's history and God's deliverance. Satan was unrestrained in his evil designs but could not harm the elect of God. Even in the midst of trouble on all sides, God protected them.

   After the close of probation, Satan is unrestrained in bringing evil on the earth, though the people of God are protected (Ps. 91). Nonetheless, God's people are in agony, knowing that Jesus has finished His mediation in the heavenly sanctuary. Through this time they must live in the presence of a holy God without a Mediator. They do not know, at first, that God has sealed them and that they are safe for eternity. In their agony, they have thrown themselves upon the mercies of Christ. Yet, they cannot find any sin that has not been confessed and forgiven. Then Jesus, who has been with them all the while through His Holy Spirit, appears in the clouds and delivers them.

3. See chapter 47, "Grace Is Sufficient to Save."

Chapter 51

Christ Comes Again

For the Lord himself shall descend from heaven with a shout, with the voice of
the archangel, and with the trump of God: and the dead in Christ shall rise first:
Then we which are alive and remain shall be caught up together with them in the
clouds, to meet the Lord in the air: and so shall we ever be with the Lord.
1 Thessalonians 4:16, 17

It has been 6,000 years since Christ announced the everlasting covenant to Adam and Eve in Eden. For 6,000 years, all creation has waited for the time when sin shall be no more, and the true King—the eternal David—should occupy the throne of His kingdom. Christ has waited 6,000 years to populate the New Jerusalem with the teeming, joyful multitudes He has saved from earth. Now He comes to take them out of this world with Him (John 14:1–3).

The everlasting covenant is a success! Christ has won in every encounter. Satan has built his challenge to the government of God upon deceit, force, slavery, and death. Christ has presented freedom within the bounds of law, a society built on love, persuasion, creativity and joy. Satan's power is at an end. Christ comes to complete His covenant of redemption and restoration. He has received those who have chosen Him, restored in them God's image, and placed them in the earth made new. All heaven rejoices as the redeemed throw off the ravages of sin, and joyfully receive their Savior in the clouds.

Cataclysmic Events

It is an earth-shattering event when God intervenes in the history of mankind. It changes the course of human events for every single person on the planet, for the free and the bond, for the rich and the poor, for every nation and every race. While God uses human beings to effect these changes, it is His will that is behind it. The various covenant events over the centuries have built a scenario that will soon be complete. In this last section of this book, we have outlined cataclysmic final events that will come on this earth in rapid succession.

God has not left humans in the dark. In the words of the prophets, He has outlined the events of the close of history. God has warned and pled with humanity, working through present events to reveal that which is to come. While most people will sleep on as if nothing were happening, those who are wise will prepare for what is soon to happen.

Different Beliefs About Jesus' Second Coming

Christians look forward to Jesus' second coming. While earth's inhabitants have become more involved in the cares of this life and the increasing problems of the day, many are showing increasing interest in Jesus' second coming. However, there are radically different concepts about how Jesus will return to earth.

The most popular belief today is the "secret rapture" of the righteous to heaven before the tribulation takes place. This belief hinges on an interpretation of Matthew 24:40, 41 that flies in the face of the clear teachings of Matthew 24:27, 30, 31, and Revelation 1:7. A complicated theology of end-time events surrounds this belief.[1]

Coupled with the rapture is the belief that people go immediately to heaven when they die. This is a comforting view at a funeral, but knowing the truth of God's plan is always best. If the saints go to heaven at death, then there is no real need for the resurrection or return of Christ.

Another group believes that the 144,000 are the only ones saved and that Christ came in 1914. Lacking objective evidence that this took place, they claim that He came spiritually to set up His kingdom on earth.[2]

Among the Evangelical churches, many discuss whether Jesus will come before or after the millennium, and just what the nature of the judgment will be. In the midst of this welter of ideas, confusion reigns. However, that is not necessary. The Bible is clear on a number of details regarding Jesus' return. Not just Christians, but all people would do well to search God's Word to know for themselves what to expect. Jesus warned four times in Matthew 24 to beware of being deceived.

What Does the Bible Say?

When Jesus comes again, it is in power and resplendent glory. It is a noisy event, for Paul describes the Lord descending with a shout and with the voice of the Archangel—the voice of the Son of God (1 Thess. 4:16; John 5:25), which awakens the dead. Also, angels blow trumpets (Matt. 24:31). A million voices sing (Isa. 26:19). The redeemed of earth come from those who are still living and those of all ages who died trusting in the One who will raise them to life. Jesus changes these in a moment to eternal youth and to a personality recreated in the image of God (1 Cor. 15:52). Jesus points us to five characteristics of His second coming:

1. "Every eye shall see Him" (Rev. 1:7). No one will need to be told or have to see it on television.
2. He will come in the clouds of heaven with myriads of angels (Rev. 1:7; Matt. 25:31; Mark 8:38; Luke 9:26).
3. He will come with power and consummate glory, as the lightning (Matt. 24:30; Luke 21:27; Zech. 9:14; Matt. 24:27; Luke 17:24).
4. He will come audibly, with the voice of the Archangel and the sound of the trumpet (1 Thess. 4:16; 1 Cor. 15:52).
5. All saints who have died will rise from the grave, and those saints still living will rise to meet Him in the air. His feet will not touch the ground (Rev. 20:5b, 6; 1 Cor. 15:55; 1 Thess. 4:17).[3]

Jesus will not permit Satan to copy just how He will come again. God's people, knowing this, will not be deceived. Will any angel want to miss this event? They will not! Every angel will be there! "There was silence in heaven about the space of half an hour" (Rev. 8:1). Considering that this earth is round and that, even where it is without obstruction, the line of sight is limited to about 100 miles on a perfectly clear day, how then can every eye see Him come? God has not revealed this. However, God's people, knowing that nothing is impossible with the Lord, believe that Jesus will have no difficulty finding those who wait for him.

Why Does Jesus Come Again?

Many people may not want Jesus to come back again because much of what they enjoy here will not exist in the new earth. Others can hardly wait for Christ to return, for He will fulfill all the promises of the everlasting covenant. Christ will take His people to the promised land—the earth made new—and there He will dwell among them for eternity!

1. Jesus will come again because he has promised to do so (John 14:1–3). The descriptions of the resurrection and the manner of His coming are also blessed promises of His return!

2. He will come again to complete the plan of salvation, resurrecting the sleeping saints, taking His people to be with Him, and then giving them eternal life on an earth restored to the perfection of Eden (John 5:25–29; Rev. 21:1–5). This will close the history of sin and will mark the transition to eternity.

3. He will bring His reward for the righteous (Rev. 22:12; 1 Thess. 4:15–17) and judge the nations (Rom. 6:23; Isa. 2:4; 1 Peter 4:5).[4]

4. He comes back by His own choice (Isa. 53:11; Eph. 5:25; Heb. 12:2; Dan. 4:35).

Memories of a Loving Friend

The disciples had been with Jesus three and a half years. They had followed Him, eaten with Him, spent days and nights with Him. They had seen His works of mercy, heard His messages of hope, heard Him pray, and seen His strength as He cast out demons and confronted those who opposed Him. They knew Him to be the Messiah and staked their futures on what He would do (Matt. 16:16; John 6:68).

As they ate the Passover with Him in the upper room, there was a foreboding in the atmosphere. They hung on every word, watched for every indication of what was to take place. Jesus spoke to them at length and prayed the prayer of consecration to the Father (John 17).

What they went through next was incomprehensible. They had gone to the Garden of Gethsemane to pray, but He had surrendered willingly to the mob. He had sternly forbidden them to fight for Him; what more could they do but flee?

When they saw Him die, all their hopes came crashing to the ground. Yet, when they saw Jesus alive again after the Resurrection, hope revived! They still had much to learn, but they were His friends. He had loved them as no one had ever loved before.

Greater love hath no man than this, that a man lay down his life for his friends. Ye are my friends, if ye do whatsoever I command you. Henceforth I call you not servants; for the servant knoweth not what his lord doeth: but I have called you friends; for all things that I have heard of my Father I have made known unto you. (John 15:13–15)

He had died for them, and they were now willing to die for Him.

When Jesus had ascended to heaven, the disciples' main question was: When will Jesus return? (Acts 1:7, 8, 11; Luke 21:7). That is the question every Christian still asks today. However, answering the question with a precise date would not help. Referring to date setting among Adventists, Ellen White wrote:

The more frequently a definite time is set for the second advent, and the more widely it is taught, the better it suits the purposes of Satan. After the time has passed, he excites ridicule and contempt of its advocates, and thus casts reproach upon the great Advent movement of 1843 and 1844. Those who persist in this error will at last fix upon a date too far in the future for the coming of Christ. Thus they will be led to rest in a false security, and many will be deceived until it is too late.[5]

Being Ready

It is essential that God's children always remain ready. Jesus said: "Therefore be ye also ready: for in such an hour as ye think not the Son of man cometh" (Matt. 24:44). A person is ready when the life belongs to Jesus and the person lives as in His presence every day.[6] Martin Luther talked about expecting the day of the second coming with joy, and he concluded: "Whoever is not ready and does not desire the day, does not understand the Lord's Prayer nor can he wholeheartedly pray it."[7]

Exodus 19 tells the story of when God came down on the mountain with the loud blast of the trumpet to meet with His people. The demonstration of His power terrified the people. They were afraid and stood afar off. They missed an awe-inspiring opportunity to be with God.

Jesus will come again with power and glory, and with a trumpet sounding loud and long. On that day, God's people will say: "Lo, this is our God; we have waited for him, and he will save us: this is the Lord; we have waited for him, we will be glad and rejoice in his salvation" (Isa. 25:9).

Endnotes

1.   Frank B. Holbrook, "Futurism's Countdown: Fact or Fantasy?" available at
        http://www.adventistbiblicalresearch.org/documents/Futurism%27s%20Countdown.htm, accessed 7/15/2012.
        Ekkehardt Mueller, "Christ's Second Coming," available at http://www.adventistbiblicalresearch.org/Bible%20
     Study/Christ%27s%20second%20coming.pdf, accessed 7/15/2012.
2.   Watch Tower Bible and Tract Society, "When Will God's Kingdom Come?" available at
        http://www.watchtower.org/e/20080101/article_03.htm, accessed July 15, 2012.

3.   How will Christ come again? (Dan. 12:2, 3; Matt. 24:27, 31; 26:64; 1 Cor. 15:51–55; 1 Thess. 4:15–17; Rev. 1:7). The sound of a trumpet far up in the sky may not seem very impressive. Yet, in the Bible, the several times that people heard the voice of God, it sounded like thunder. At Sinai, the trumpet of God "waxed louder and louder." I liken this to a sound I once heard while driving with the family alongside an airport fence. The sound was loud from the start, as it began resonating through the roof of the car. It got louder and louder. My first thought was that it was a missile headed right for us. I thought, *If I drive faster, I will probably drive right under it!* So, I stopped the car, got out, and looked for something to hide behind. Jet fighter maneuvers are common in Grand Junction, Colorado, where I live, so it then occurred to me that they were testing the jet engine of a jet fighter, which is about ten times louder than that of a jet airliner. I believe that is what the "trump of God" will sound like!

4.   Jesus comes to judge the nations (Isa. 2:4; 30:28, NCV; Luke 17:26–30; John 16:8–11; Acts 17:31; 2 Thess. 2:8; Rev. 19:11; 20:10–15).

5.   Ellen G. White, *The Great Controversy* (Nampa, ID: Pacific Press Publishing Association, 1911), p. 457.

6.   There are crucial things that a person can do to keep his relationship with Christ alive:

   a.   **Give God your time.** We often say: "Give your life to God." However, Christians must also give their hours and minutes to God. Why not give God your schedule and then consider interruptions by people as opportunities for witness and service?

   b.   **Have daily worship and Bible study.** Bible study is essential to gain knowledge and receive God's message for each day. Family worship binds the family together.

   c.   **Live all day as in the presence of God.** Pray without ceasing. All day long, everyone carries on a constant conversation in his or her head. Why not let that conversation be a prayer to God?

   d.   **Be active in service and witness.** Find ways to help others.

   e.   **Watch and pray.** Be aware of events around you and their spiritual significance.

   These are things that God's children need to do as we look forward to Jesus' return because only with His coming will salvation be complete, only then—in the fullest sense—will we be His people and will He be our God (Rev. 21:3; 22:20). Are you looking forward to Jesus' return?

7.   Martin Luther, "Christ's Second Coming." available at
   http://www.adventistbiblicalresearch.org/Bible%20Study/Christ%27s%20second%20coming.pdf, p. 2, accessed 7/15/2012.

Chapter 52
It is Done!

When Jesus therefore had received the vinegar, he said, It is finished:
and he bowed his head, and gave up the ghost.
John 19:30

The covenant must finish its work on earth. The time must come when the people of God fully display His love and grace. Those who refuse God's grace and love demonstrate the character of Satan. All people on earth will have made their final decision, and Christ has fought and been victorious in the final battle (Rev. 16:16–21; 19:11–21). His people are ready to be gathered to Him. During this end time, Jesus completes several significant actions.

The Gospel to the World

The church, in its first love, spread the news of Jesus' crucifixion, resurrection (1 Cor. 2:2; 15:3, 4), and His return in glory throughout the Roman Empire and beyond. To His disciples Jesus had become a much-loved friend. They looked for His soon return. Nothing else mattered. They sold their properties to support the new church. They could not stop talking about Him; they talked about Him so much that the people in Antioch began to call them "Christians," a name they gladly accepted!

Jesus commissioned the church to preach the everlasting gospel to the world (Matt. 28:18–20; 24:14); but even better, under the power of the Holy Ghost, they were to be witnesses of what Christ had done (Acts 1:8). They almost reached this goal in the first century.

Their task was not always easy. There was trouble and persecution—from the unbelieving Jews, from the pagans, and then from the apostate Christian church. Not only was there persecution, but there were divisions and heresies that entered the church. Nonetheless, for 1260 years, the church in the wilderness kept the light of truth burning (Rev. 12:14).[1]

As the disciples began to die, they realized that Jesus was not going to return in their lifetime. They were to look first for a "falling away," when pagan philosophies would bring unfortunate changes to the church.[2] In spite of this, there would always be a remnant who would make Jesus first in their lives and follow the true faith as they understood it (Rom. 11:5; Luke 18:8).

A Renewed Commission

As the Middle Ages passed, Christ led His church step-by-step back to the true faith. The churches published the Scriptures and made them widely available. They established missionary societies. The people prospered and supported these activities. God's people learned again about the end-time judgment and Christ's soon return.[3] These doctrines cut across the beliefs of many Christians, causing opposition within the church. Through the prophecies, God commissioned those who believed to bring the truth of the Gospel, true worship, and the judgment before every nation, tribe, tongue, and people before Jesus could come again (Rev. 10:11; 14:6–12; 18:1–4).

This appeared to be an impossible task. The devil opposed Christ at every turn, brought on trouble, and raised prejudice against God's people. He attacked the Bible and the law of God. He claimed that grace is not sufficient to save and that Christians are no better than those who make no profession, while the population of the world was increasing faster than conversions to Christianity.

Christians can only weep that there is truth in some of these claims and pray that God will show Himself strong for His people. However, we look for a time when the honest in heart will renew their consecration and take a new interest in His Word. The Holy Spirit will come in even greater power than at Pentecost.[4] Where human agents cannot penetrate, God will send His angels to bring truth to His people.

The gospel commission was to "teach all nations … to observe all things whatsoever I have commanded you."[5] Not only must the gospel go to all the world, but it must come in full measure to the heart of every one of God's people.[6] The final issue, the seal of God and the mark of the beast, is the dividing line between those who choose to serve God and those who do not. The people of God make their decision by faith, and are finally prepared to see Jesus come again. The 144,000 are sealed as the first fruits, showing the completion of the work of grace in the lives of humanity. The restoration of God's people to the image of God is finished. The people of the world, choosing the easy, popular way or making no decision at all, are given the mark of the beast and are lost.

Trouble, Turmoil, and Plagues

As trouble increases on every hand, we can know "the devil is come down unto you, having great wrath, because he knoweth that he hath but a short time" (Rev. 12:12). God's people will experience the fellowship of suffering for Christ. God's people will be tested by the two phases of a time of trouble. The first is a time of intense activity by the church to carry the gospel to the world, which will lead to persecution and martyrdom (Matt. 24:1–21; Rev. 20:4).

In the time of the end, God's people will be blamed and persecuted for the increased turmoil everywhere. As trouble increases, people will determine to destroy the people of God—choosing a date to accomplish this purpose in one massive effort (Rev. 13:15).

The second phase comes after probation has closed and God has sealed the 144,000. At this time, every person has made his or her decision for or against God, and there is no more evangelism. The wicked will threaten God's people, but holy angels will protect them (Dan. 12:1; Ps. 91). The angels will then pour out the seven last plagues (Rev. 16), but God will protect His people from these, too. Through all this, Jesus has promised, "Lo, I am with you always, even unto the end of the world" (Matt. 28:20).

A Time to Search the Heart

Meanwhile, Jesus continues His daily ministry in the heavenly sanctuary, applying His blood for the forgiveness of sins. In ancient Israel, there was also a Day of Atonement once a year. The sanctuary was cleansed of the sins accumulated during the past year. This pointed forward to divine judgment at the end of earth's history.

The true "Day of Atonement" began in 1844 (Dan. 8:14) and was preached by William Miller in New England from 1831 to 1844. He preached that the sanctuary to be cleansed was this earth and that Jesus would come October 22, 1844. Of course, Jesus did not come. After further study, it was found that the sanctuary to be cleansed was the heavenly sanctuary.

The church was commissioned to "prophesy again" (Rev. 10:11). God's people must learn and accept the true faith and consent to the full work of grace in their lives. The gospel and the judgment-hour message must be given "to every nation, and kindred, and tongue, and people" (Rev. 14:6). The name of every person who has entered into the service of Christ is listed in the Lamb's book of life. In the Day of Atonement, the record of pardoned sins is blotted out, and, where sins are not forgiven, the names are blotted out. It is a time of judgment. In the book of life, the names of God's people show no sins, only an uninterrupted record of victory in Christ.

When Jesus comes, He takes His people to live and reign with Him for "a thousand years" (Rev. 20:4). This is a time for the judgment of the wicked, for when Jesus comes, He brings His reward with Him "to give every man according as his work shall be" (Rev. 22:12). This is the time when God's people have every question answered. As some who were apparently wicked are saved, and some who were apparently righteous are lost, every man and angel must see that God is a God of mercy and justice. It is only when the redeemed are finally brought into the new earth that God wipes away all tears from their eyes and that the reign of sin is forgotten for eternity (Isa. 65:17; 25:8; Rev. 7:17; 21:4).

Armageddon: a Spiritual Battle

Just before the end, the world is divided into just two classes. The Holy Spirit seals the righteous remnant, and they are safe for eternity. The unbelieving, deceived majority, through choice or neglect, receive the mark of the beast. Every person makes his final decision to serve or not to serve God. Then probation closes for all.[7]

The holy angels pour out the seven last plagues as judgments against the wicked (Rev. 15; 16). The plagues are both real and symbolic in some of their details. This is especially true regarding the seventh plague—the Battle of Armageddon. The logistics of gathering the world in the rather small valley of Megiddo are impossible and unnecessary. It will not be a battle with guns and tanks.[8]

The conflict at this time is not with the small nation of ethnic Israel but is rather the final contest between Christ and Satan. The followers of Satan work to destroy the righteous, but God delivers them (Dan. 12:1). The death of God's people after probation has closed would not be a witness to people who have already made their decision not to follow Christ. There will be no more martyrs for there are no more decisions to make!

Christ then comes with power and magnificent glory. It is the glory of "all" the angels (100 million is the largest number Bible writers could conceive of). The glory of Jesus Christ outshines them all. Imagine that! The wicked try to hide themselves in the rocks and the mountains. The righteous gladly welcome their Lord.

Cleansing and Restoration

As Jesus looks at the unnumbered multitudes of the saved, He feels "the joy that was set before him" for which He endured the cross. He is rewarded for the sufferings of His life on earth by "the glory that should follow," and He is satisfied.[9] Jesus welcomes His people.

When Jesus comes the second time, the everlasting covenant has achieved its purpose. Grace has changed the lives of those who have consented to its work. Jesus Christ confirmed the covenant by His sinless life and His sacrifice on Calvary. The gospel in which Jesus has taken our place before the judgment so that we might live has been given to all people. The 144,000, who have made the deepest commitment to Him, are sealed. More than any others, they are like Christ. The work of grace on the hearts of sinful people has been demonstrated to all, as sinful people have been transformed by looking into God's glory. "But we all, with unveiled face beholding as in a mirror the glory of the Lord, are transformed into the same image from glory to glory, even as from the Lord the Spirit" (2 Cor. 3:18, ASV).

After the New Jerusalem comes down to the earth, heaven is where God is. Happiness again reigns in heaven and earth. All creation, in unshadowed beauty and perfect joy, declare that God is love.

> I heard a great voice out of heaven saying, Behold, the tabernacle of God is with men, and he will dwell with them, and they shall be his people, and God himself shall be with them, and be their God. (Rev. 21:3)

Endnotes

1. It was prophesied that there would be a falling away in the church before Christ's second coming. The church was accepted into society, became popular, formal, and increasingly worldly. Pagan doctrines and practices were brought into the church. There was a true, persecuted remnant that kept the light of truth burning for 1260 years until the Reformation dawned and the study of the Bible was revived (2 Thess. 2:3; Dan. 7:25; Rev. 12:13, 14; 13:5).

2. Paul prophesied a falling away in the church before Christ returns (2 Thess. 2:3).

3. Daniel prophesied the end-time judgment (Dan. 7:9–10; 13–14; 26–27; 8:14). Soon Christ will return to earth (Matt. 24:14; 27–31; 1 Cor. 15:51–55; Rev. 1:7; John 14:1–3).

4. God promised that He will pour out His Holy Spirit in the end time to finish the work of proclaiming the everlasting gospel (Joel 2:23, 28–32; Rev. 14:6–12; 18:1–4; Rom. 9:28; Acts 17:31).

5. Jesus said, "And this gospel of the kingdom shall be preached in all the world for a witness unto all nations; and then shall the end come" (Matt. 24:14). The meaning of "preach" is to "proclaim openly" (Strong's). The message of Christ is to be proclaimed throughout the world. The angel told John after the bitter disappointment following the sweet experience of understanding the little book of Daniel, "Thou must prophesy again before many peoples, and nations, and tongues, and

kings" (Rev. 10:11). This occurred after the great Advent awakening of 1840–1844. The message of judgment was given in many places, though not at that time to all peoples. The message was rejected by the popular churches.

"And I saw another angel fly in the midst of heaven, having the everlasting gospel to preach unto them that dwell on the earth, and to every nation, and kindred, and tongue and people, saying with a loud voice, Fear God, and give glory to him; for the hour of his judgment is come: and worship him that made heaven, and earth, and the sea, and the fountains of waters" (Rev. 14:6, 7). The timeframe for Revelation 10:11 and Revelation 14:6 is the same.

6. God's people are changed (2 Cor. 3:18; 5:17; Gal. 5:22; 2 Peter 1:3–8).

7. Following the death decree for those who do not receive the mark of the beast, probation will close for all (Rev. 13:14–17; 14:9–12; 22:11).

8. The battle of Armageddon is described in Revelation 16:13–21. At last, God will say: "It is done" (Rev. 13:17).

9. Jesus endured the cross for the joy that was set before Him (Heb. 12:2; 1 Peter 1:11; Isa. 53:11).

Chapter 53

The Millennium

This is the first resurrection. Blessed and holy is he that hath part in the first resurrection: on such the second death hath no power, but they shall be priests of God and of Christ, and shall reign with him a thousand years.
Revelation 20:5, 6

Why 1,000 years? Satan has had 6,000 years to challenge the law of God. This time has been a frenzy of activity. Now that Jesus has come the wicked are killed by the brightness of His coming, and the righteous will be transported with Christ to heaven. During the millennium only Satan will be alive on this earth. God will set aside 1,000 years for Satan to wander alone over this ravaged earth and contemplate what he has done. At the end of the 1,000 years, Satan will demonstrate that his character has not changed. Satan will marshal evil angels and humans into an army and attempt to take the holy city!

God is careful and orderly in everything He does. Since His character is one of love, freedom, and persuasion, every person and angel in the whole of creation must be convinced that He is merciful and just. Every human being and every angel must understand that God's judgment is fair and that He has done everything possible to save even wicked human beings. Before God brings the New Jerusalem to Earth and imparts His eternal blessings, the angels, the redeemed saints, and Jesus Himself must judge the actions of God for 1,000 years, answering every question.

Mercy and Justice in Jesus

Before the redeemed enter the Holy City and inherit the earth made new, there is one more step to be completed. Christ takes His people to heaven into the very presence of God Himself and places them on thrones of judgment, and "they lived and reigned with Christ for one thousand years" (Rev. 20:4). What judgment do the righteous carry on in heaven?

Often, Christians will look on the plan of salvation as focused primarily on the salvation of the righteous. This is a weighty consideration, but it is not the only consideration and it is not even the most serious one. In the great controversy between Christ and Satan, it is God Himself and His law that Satan has challenged. Is God arbitrary and vengeful, seeking to destroy all those who do not obey Him, as Satan has alleged, or is He a God of love, grace, forgiveness and mercy, seeking to save all that He possibly can? Is the law of God just and reasonable? Is it a help to humans and angels?

If God is just, then how can He also be merciful? If He is merciful, then how can He also be just? In the cross of Calvary, "mercy and truth are met together; righteousness and peace have kissed each other" (Ps. 85:10). All heaven declares Jesus Christ to "be just, and the justifier of him which believeth in Jesus" (Rom. 3:26). Jesus showed His mercy in taking the penalty for the broken law upon Himself and opening the door for humans to be saved and restored to the purity and happiness of Eden. He showed His justice in giving His life to make this possible.

The plan of salvation, as worked out on this earth, is of intense interest to all intelligent beings, "for we are made a spectacle unto the world, and to angels, and to men" (1 Cor. 4:9). The experiences we go through here are "things the angels desire to look into" (1 Peter 1:12).

During this earthly reign of sin and redeeming grace, one makes observations and tentative judgments but does not receive answers to all questions. Jesus saves some known sinners and He condemns some kind and generous people. Why is that? In the eternity of the earth made new, God purposes to have every question answered.

How could angels, who lived in the presence of God, ever sin? How could Lucifer, the highest angel and the closest to God Himself, rebel and sin against God? These questions must be answered. God entrusts to the redeemed of all ages the judgment of not just the unsaved but of the fallen angels (1 Cor. 6:3). Through this judgment, everyone will become perfectly satisfied that God is a God of love. "For it is written, As I live, saith the Lord, every knee shall bow to me, and every tongue shall confess to God" (Rom. 14:11).

A Thousand-Year Cease Fire

"Millennium," the word for one thousand years is not found in the Bible, though John does use the thousand-year period in Revelation 20. Just before this, the earth has received God's judgments. These are the last events on this old earth and include plagues, judgments, and resurrections. Many people have drawn charts attempting to locate each event precisely. This may be impossible. All one can do is have a clear expectation of coming events and then recognize the events as they come. Besides this, one must learn faith and trust in God now. There will not be a "second chance."

A time of trouble will come on the earth. Matthew 24 described it in detail. The Holy Spirit withdraws from the earth, and the wicked are unrestrained in doing evil.[1] This brings on the "time of trouble such as never was" (Dan. 12:1). At the same time, the Holy Spirit is poured out on the righteous with power (Joel 2:23, 28–32).

Probation for mankind closes (Rev. 22:11). This means that all people have made their decisions for good or evil. The Holy Spirit seals the righteous, and the wicked receive the mark of the beast.[2]

During this time, the church gives the three angels' messages (Rev. 14:6–12). These messages urge repentance, warn against living in error, and present the fearful results of failing to choose for God. The loud cry of the fourth angel follows these messages, calling God's people to come out of those churches where truth has given way to confusion (Rev. 18:1–4).

After the close of probation, angels pour out the seven last plagues on the earth (Rev. 15:1; 16:1–21) while angels shield the righteous (Rev. 15:2-4). The battle of Armageddon (the seventh plague) is Satan's last attempt to destroy the people of God. However, God stands up for His people in this battle, destroying Satan's institution of evil (Rev. 16:16–21).

Jesus then comes the second time, accompanied by all the angels of heaven, with a glory never before seen on earth (Heb. 9:28; Matt. 24:27, 30, 31; 25:31). Jesus raises the righteous dead, and with the righteous living, takes them all to heaven. The wicked that are still living are slain by the brightness of His coming.[3]

The one thousand years begin. An angel binds Satan in the bottomless pit, an apt metaphor for an earth when it is in utter destruction with no life on it but Satan's. He has one thousand years to contemplate the results of his rebellion (Rev. 20:1–3). At the same time, the righteous are in heaven, doing a work of judgment. Among the righteous are martyrs from the last climactic time of trouble (Rev. 20:4–6).

At the end of the one thousand years, the holy city, New Jerusalem comes down from God out of heaven (Rev. 21:2). An angel looses Satan, and the wicked are raised to life (Rev. 20:7, 8). In spite of the destruction all about them on the earth and the immensity and strength and beauty of the Holy City, the wicked still listen to Satan. They form an immense army, which surrounds the Holy City (Rev. 20:8, 9).

Their march comes to a sudden halt as the majestic white throne appears above the city, and God opens the books and passes judgment. Each person will see the part he played in disobeying and refusing to believe God (Rev. 20:11–13). Every intelligent being—whether human or angel—will bend the knee and confess that God is merciful and just in His judgments (Rom. 14:11). It is too late for the rebellious to be saved.

The Final Conflagration

God looks on the heart in judgment. It is not just a matter of being "a good fellow." If a person is kind and generous on this earth, he cannot be saved unless he accepts Christ (Acts 4:12). If a person has never heard of Christ and has had no opportunity to learn of Him, God is merciful (Rom. 2:14–16). God determines whether a person still harbors pride and selfishness in his heart. He reads the struggles of difficult and abusive persons. He will be merciful in judgment.

Among the saved in the new earth, Jesus Christ is first in thought, word and action. This must become a habit now. No one will give free reign to habits of anger, domination, profanity, or immoral jesting. If people love brutal sports, alcoholic binges, gambling, drugs, or if they desire to attract attention to themselves, they would be unhappy in the new earth.

God knows these things, and all His decisions are merciful and just. He gives the answer to every question as to why the wicked are lost. Every knee bows to recognize Jesus as Lord—even those of the wicked and Satan himself. After 1,000 years, God brings this stage of judgment to an end.

The Bible is crisp and concise. Satan, his angels, and all the wicked are cast into the lake of fire (Rev. 19:20; 20:10, 13–15).[4] The Bible is also clear at this point: to be cast into the lake of fire is to suffer the second death. It is not an eternity of suffering and anguish. It is a quick and merciful death.[5]

God has not chosen that anyone should die. All people choose their own future by the decisions they make (2 Peter 3:9). The lake of fire is also a purifying fire. Fire cleanses the earth of all sin and sinners. The planet, now cleansed, is ready to be made new to receive the Holy City, New Jerusalem, where the righteous shall dwell forever. Not only the righteous, but God Himself shall dwell with them (Rev. 21:3)!

Endnotes

1. At a certain point, the Holy Spirit withdraws from the earth (Ezek. 9:3; 10:4, 18, 19; 11:23).
2. The righteous receive the seal of God, and the rebellious receive the mark of the beast (Rev. 7:1–8; Isa. 8:16; Ezek. 9; Rev. 13:11–18).
3. Jesus resurrects the righteous and takes them to heaven; the wicked die (1 Cor. 15:51–55; 1 Thess. 4:13–18; Rev. 1:7; 2 Thess. 2:8; Rev. 6:12–17).
4. "And the devil that deceived them was cast into the lake of fire and brimstone, where the beast and the false prophet *are*, and shall be tormented day and night for ever and ever" (Rev. 20:10, original italics retained). The italicized "are" was supplied. The verse does not give a time sequence of when the "beast" power and his agent "the false prophet" (which corresponds to the second beast on the land in Rev. 13) are destroyed. But, even if it did, they are not individuals as the devil and his angels are. Their destruction in symbol is the end of the institutions they represent.
5. The lake of fire consumes the wicked and purifies the earth (Mal. 4:3; Rom. 16:20; Ezek. 28:18, NCV).

Chapter 54

A New Heaven and a New Earth

And I saw a new heaven and a new earth: for the first heaven and
the first earth were passed away; and there was no more sea.
Revelation 21:1

Jesus prepared the holy city.[1] Jesus Christ Himself constructed the spectacular New Jerusalem. Nothing of beauty or usefulness has been left out. After 2,000 years of emptiness and inactivity, the city is about to be filled with the joyous, teeming, human race.

Jesus' sacrifice on Calvary was the watershed event of the everlasting covenant. Anticipation based on the prophecies became a fact to which end-time generations looked in faith. It was the crowning event of the great controversy between Christ and Satan. The Son of God was victorious. He established forever love, persuasion, and freedom as the basis for the government of God. Through art, science, praise, and song, the uncounted multitudes of humans and angels respond to the Redeemer who came, to the Father who gave, and to the Holy Spirit who made effective the grace of God in each life.

The everlasting covenant has achieved its purpose. This is not the end, but rather the beginning—the beginning of a life that has no end, with no separations, and no limit to what God's children can learn and do.

I Have Called You Friends

The disciples had lived for three and half years learning from the master Teacher. His grace, love, and sinless personality drew to Him all who did not resist His drawing. He had become to them a friend, and their attachment to Him was deep.[2] When it became apparent that He would soon leave them, their only question was: When will He come back again?[3]

Jesus spoke of eternal life and other glorious gifts for those who followed Him. In Revelation 21 and 22, the apostle John described the home of the saved in detail, Nonetheless, there were hints of future glory before this.[4]

God So Loved the World

At the creation, "God saw every thing that he had made, and, behold, it was very good. And the evening and the morning were the sixth day" (Gen. 1:31). God was proud of His creation—especially the humans that He made.

"God loved the world so much that he gave his one and only Son so that whoever believes in him may not be lost, but have eternal life" (John 3:16, NCV). Jesus' statement speaks of the plan of salvation laid in the council of the Godhead before the creation.

The perfection of Eden we can only imagine, yet we still see hints of its beauty in this world. Even with our most vivid imagination, we fall short of knowing what God has in store for us, for "No eye has seen, no ear has heard, no mind has conceived what God has prepared for those who love him" (1 Cor. 2:9, NIV).

Reigning With Him

When Jesus comes again, He takes the saints to heaven where "they shall be priests of God and of Christ, and shall reign with him a thousand years" (Rev. 20:6).

While Satan spends a lonely 1,000 years in contemplation of his evil course, the saints are in heaven taking part in a judgment of the wicked. During this time, all questions about the justice and mercy of God are answered. Every person must understand why some people were saved and others lost. Above all, the sorrow of the angels and the pain felt by Jesus in Gethsemane and on the cross will be portrayed. The saints will shed many tears, which will be wiped away in the New Jerusalem. Through this judgment, the saints' love and appreciation for what Christ has done will grow to such dimensions that no one will ever cross into sin. Affliction shall not arise the second time.

It is only after the judgment that Satan and the wicked are brought to life again. It is only at this time that the New Jerusalem descends to this earth, and the saints are permitted to enter. The Bible does not state the exact sequence of events, but it appears that the holy city, new Jerusalem (Rev. 21:2) arrives before God purifies this earth. Satan and the resurrected wicked of all ages encircle "the camp of the saints" (Rev. 20:9) in an attempt to take the city.

It is then that Satan, his angels, and the wicked of all ages are cast into the lake of fire. Sin and sinners are destroyed for all eternity. It is a fire that burns for a short time and then goes out.[5] The saints will then live in a new earth and a New Jerusalem without taint of sin or decay.

The beauty of the new earth cannot be imagined. The redeemed will enjoy perfect health, boundless energy, and expanded powers of the mind. Revelation 21 and 22 describes in more detail the perfection of the new earth. Even more than the beauty of the place is that Jesus is there!

> And I heard a great voice out of heaven saying, Behold, the tabernacle of God is with men, and he will dwell with them, and they shall be his people, and God himself shall be with them, and be their God. (Rev. 21:3)

Jesus, who drew all people and loved them on earth, will draw them even more strongly in the new earth. Jesus has chosen to become a human being for all eternity and live among the human race.[6] What more could one ask? This is a greater gift than the riches and beauty of the new earth.

> His tender compassion fell with a touch of healing upon weary and troubled hearts.
> Even amid the turbulence of angry enemies He was surrounded with an atmosphere
> of peace. The beauty of His countenance, the loveliness of His character, above all,

the love expressed in look and tone, drew to Him all who were not hardened in unbelief. Had it not been for the sweet, sympathetic spirit that shone out in every look and word, He would not have attracted the large congregations that He did. The afflicted ones who came to Him felt that He linked His interest with theirs as a faithful and tender friend, and they desired to know more of the truths He taught. Heaven was brought near. They longed to abide in His presence, that the comfort of His love might be with them continually.[7]

Given to Humanity Forever

When Jesus came to this earth, became human, and lived as a man among men, He gave to humanity a gift that He will not take back. When He ascended to heaven, the angels said, "this same Jesus which is taken up from you into heaven, shall so come in like manner as ye have seen him go into heaven" (Acts 1:11). In the following verses, Scripture more fully describes Jesus' eternal gift of humanity: "Beloved, now are we the sons of God, and it doth not yet appear what we shall be: but we know that, when he shall appear, we shall be like him; for we shall see him as he is" (1 John 3:2). "Even as a human being He will bear the marks of His crucifixion through eternity. His radiance is like the sunlight; He has rays flashing from His hand, and there is the hiding of His power" (Hab. 3:4, NASB). "And one shall say unto him, What are these wounds in thine hands? Then he shall answer, Those with which I was wounded in the house of my friends" (Zech. 13:6). "Beloved, now are we the sons of God, and it doth not yet appear what we shall be: but we know that, when he shall appear, we shall be like him; for we shall see him as he is" (1 John 3:2). "That in the ages to come he might shew the exceeding riches of his grace in his kindness toward us through Christ Jesus" (Eph. 2:7).

> The science of redemption is the science of all sciences; the science that is the study of the angels, and of all the intelligences of the unfallen worlds; the science that engages the attention of our Lord and Saviour; the science that enters into the purpose brooded in the mind of the Infinite—"kept in silence through times eternal"; the science that will be the study of God's redeemed throughout the endless ages.[8] This is the highest study in which it is possible for man to engage. As no other study can, it will quicken the mind, and uplift the soul....

> The themes of redemption will employ the hearts and minds and tongues of the redeemed through the everlasting ages. They will understand the truths which Christ longed to open to His disciples, but which they did not have faith to grasp. Forever and forever new views of the perfection and glory of Christ will appear. Through endless ages the faithful Householder will bring forth from His treasures things new and old.[9]

Affliction Shall Not Rise the Second Time

In the new earth, when God's people understand what their redemption cost, their gratitude and love will deepen, and their praise will be louder. They will dedicate their praise, songs, and creativity to return to Him the glory He gave up to redeem mankind.

Mankind will still have power of choice. If God should take away the human power of choice, then Jesus need not have made His sacrifice on Calvary. We have this promise: "What do ye imagine against the Lord? he will make an utter end: affliction shall not rise up the second time" (Nahum 1:9).

Fellowship with Christ and knowing Him as a friend and the cost of our redemption will raise a barrier against sin in the minds of every intelligent being. Sin shall not rise again!

In this life, even the best of plans can be spoiled by faulty human beings. Will it be different in the new earth? When Jesus comes again, "this corruptible must put on incorruption, and this mortal must put on immortality" (1 Cor. 15:53). The sinful nature we each inherited from Adam, He will cleanse. Pride, selfishness, and unbelief, He will remove. We will forget the sins we have committed. The people who were offended, those who saw the offense, and even God Himself will not remember!

With Christ enthroned in each person's heart, he or she will gladly keep the law of God. Each person will bring forth love, joy, peace, patience, gentleness, goodness, and faith. "They shall not hurt nor destroy in all my holy mountain" (Isa. 11:9; 65:25).

Endnotes

1. "Let not your heart be troubled: ye believe in God, believe also in me. In my Father's house are many mansions: if it were not so, I would have told you. I go to prepare a place for you. And if I go and prepare a place for you, I will come again, and receive you unto myself; that where I am, there ye may be also. (John 14:1–3).
2. Jesus is the believer's friend (Luke 12:4; John 15:13–15).
3. When will Jesus come back? The question and the answer are in John 14:2, 3 and Matthew 24.
4. Hints of the glory to come are in Isaiah 60; 62; 65:17–25; 66; and 1 Corinthians 2:9.
5. The lake of fire burns a short time and then goes out (Rev. 20:10, 13, 14; Rom. 6:23; Mal. 4:1, 3; Isa. 47:14).
6. Jesus will be human for eternity (1 John 3:2; Zech. 13:6; Hab. 3:4).
7. Ellen G. White, *The Desire of Ages* (Nampa, ID: Pacific Press Publishing Association, 1898), p. 254.
8. The science of salvation is a mystery kept in silence through times eternal (Rom. 16:25; 1 Cor. 2:7; Col. 1:26).
9. Ellen G. White, *Maranatha* (Washington, D.C.: Review and Herald Publishing Association, 1976), p. 365.

We invite you to view the complete
selection of titles we publish at:

www.TEACHServices.com

Scan with your mobile
device to go directly
to our website.

Please write or email us your praises, reactions, or
thoughts about this or any other book we publish at:

TEACH Services, Inc.
P U B L I S H I N G
www.TEACHServices.com ● (800) 367-1844

P.O. Box 954
Ringgold, GA 30736

info@TEACHServices.com

TEACH Services, Inc., titles may be purchased in bulk for
educational, business, fund-raising, or sales promotional use.
For information, please e-mail:

BulkSales@TEACHServices.com

Finally, if you are interested in seeing
your own book in print, please contact us at

publishing@TEACHServices.com

We would be happy to review your manuscript for free.

CPSIA information can be obtained at www.ICGtesting.com
Printed in the USA
LVOW05s1149111113

360740LV00002B/5/P